BENCHMARK Series

MICROSOFT®
WORD 2000

CORE CERTIFICATION

NITA RUTKOSKY

Pierce College at Puyallup
Puyallup, Washington

EMCParadigm
PUBLISHING

MICROSOFT® OFFICE SPECIALIST®

Approved
Courseware

Senior Editor	Sonja Brown
Developmental Editor	Mary Verrill
Cover Designer	Chris Vern Johnson
Art Director	Joan D'Onofrio
Text Designer	Jennifer Wreisner
Desktop Production Specialists	Leslie Anderson, Michelle Lewis, Jennifer Wreisner
Tester	Rebecca Pepper
Indexer	Terry Casey

Publishing Team—George Provol, Publisher; Janice Johnson, Director of Product Development; Lori Landwer, Marketing Manager; Shelley Clubb, Electronic Design and Production Manager.

Registered Trademarks—Microsoft, Windows, and the Microsoft Office Logo are trademarks or registered trademarks of Microsoft Corporation in the United States and/or other countries, and the Microsoft Office Specialist Logo is used under license from owner.

EMC/Paradigm Publishing is independent from Microsoft Corporation, and not affiliated with Microsoft in any manner. This textbook may be used in assisting students to prepare for a Microsoft Office Specialist Exam. Neither Microsoft, its designated program administrator or courseware reviewer, nor EMC/Paradigm Publishing warrants that use of this textbook will ensure passing the relevant exam.

Some of the product names and company names included in this book have been used for identification purposes only and may be trademarks or registered trademarks of their respective manufacturers and sellers. The author, editor, and publisher disclaim any affiliation, association, or connection with, or sponsorship or endorsement by, such owners.

Acknowledgments—The author and publisher wish to thank the following reviewers for their technical assistance: Tony D. Gabriel, Computer Learning Center, Glendale, California; Denise Seguin, Fanshawe College, London, Ontario; Janet Sheppard, Collin County Community College, Plano, Texas.

Rutkosky, Nita Hewitt.
      Microsoft Word 2000 : core certification / Nita Rutkosky.
           p.   cm. — (Benchmark series)
      ISBN 0-7638-0339-1 (text). — ISBN 0-7638-0340-5 (text & CD-ROM)
      1. Microsoft Word.   2. Word processing.   I. Title. II. Series :
Benchmark series (Saint Paul, Minn.)
Z52.5.M52R935   1999
652.5'5369—dc21   99-35153
                                                                 CIP

Text + CD package, ISBN 0-7638-0340-5
Order Number 05360

Library of Congress Cataloging-in-Publication Data
© 2000 by Paradigm Publishing Inc.
      Published by **EMC**Paradigm
      875 Montreal Way
      St. Paul, MN 55102
      (800) 535-6865
      E-mail: **educate@emcp.com**
      Web Site: www.emcp.com

10 9 8 7

Contents

Chapter 4

Working with Multiple Documents 149

Chapter 5

Formatting Documents 193

Introduction

Most new personal computers in the marketplace today are preloaded with the Microsoft® Windows® operating system or with Windows-based applications such as Microsoft Word® 2000. The Word 2000 software program is part of Microsoft Office 2000, one of the most popular Windows-based program suites, which includes Word, Excel, Access, PowerPoint, and additional applications in certain editions.

In this textbook, students gain a basic knowledge of Word 2000 and use it to create and process a wide variety of academic and business documents. They learn the beginning and intermediate features of Word, as well as ways in which this program interacts with Windows and the Internet.

Students do not need prior computer experience nor familiarity with using Windows in order to use this textbook. However, knowledge of basic high school freshman mathematics is required.

Approved Courseware for the Microsoft Office Specialist (MOS) Program

The logo on the cover of this text means that Microsoft has approved this text as courseware that teaches all the skills that students need to master to pass the Core Certification exam in Word 2000. These skills and the corresponding page numbers of related instruction in the text are listed on the page that precedes chapter 1. The MOS program is used to test and validate a student's skills and thereby supply objective proof to an employer or prospective employer that the student knows how to use a program efficiently and productively. For more information on the MOS program and where to take the certification exam, visit Microsoft's Web site at *www.microsoft.com* or the specific MOS site at *www.mous.net*.

Focus on Certification

This textbook teaches the skills needed for Word 2000 Core Level MOS certification. Major features covered include creating, printing, and editing Word documents; formatting and using Help; enhancing the visual display and clarity of documents; working with multiple documents; formatting documents; creating and formatting tables; and inserting graphic elements.

Chapter structure—each chapter contains the following sections:

- Performance Objectives that identify the specific learning goals of the chapter.

- Introductory material that provides an overview of new concepts and features.

- Step-by-step exercises at the computer, which allow students to practice using the features(s) presented in the chapter.

- Chapter Summary.

- Commands Review.

- Thinking Offline, a short-answer, knowledge self-check.

- Working Hands-On, skill assessments that require students to complete exercises without step-by-step instructions; this section includes an exercise that requires use of the Help feature as indicated by an icon

Additional simulation exercises called Performance Assessments at the end of each level require students to make decisions about document preparation and formatting. These applied exercises provide ample opportunity to practice new features as well as previously learned features. The Writing Activities offer students the opportunity to write and format business documents. In addition, there is an Internet Activity in which students explore the Internet and use Word to report on the information they discover. In this section, students demonstrate problem-solving, critical-thinking, and creative-thinking abilities as well as hands-on computer skills.

Completing Computer Exercises

Some computer exercises in the chapters require the student to access and use an existing file that is mentioned specifically. Those student exercise files are saved on the CD-ROM that accompanies this textbook. The files for each chapter are saved in individual folders, as indicated by a CD icon with a chapter folder name that appears on the first page of each chapter. Note, however, that some chapters may have no data files to copy.

Chapter 01C

Before beginning a chapter, the student should copy the folder from the CD-ROM to a preformatted data disk. After completing the exercises in a chapter, the student should delete the chapter folder to ensure adequate storage space for the next chapter's files. Students should check with the instructor first, however. The inside back cover provides detailed instructions on how to copy and delete folders.

Industry Standards from the SCANS Commission

This textbook covers the important goals of the Secretary's Commission on Achieving Necessary Skills (SCANS), a joint commission from the Department of Education and Labor. The overall goal of the commission was to establish interdisciplinary standards that should be required for all students. SCANS skill standards emphasize the integration of competencies from the areas of information gathering and research, technology, basic skills, and thinking skills.

In addition, all educators agree that curricula can be strengthened by classroom work that is authentic and relevant to learners, i.e., classroom work that connects context to content. Teaching in context helps students move away from a subject-specific orientation to an integrative learning that includes decision making, problem solving, and critical thinking. The concepts and applications materials in each level of this book are designed to reflect an interdisciplinary emphasis, as well as implement the SCANS standards. SCANS places heavy emphasis on communication skills as well as on activity planning and follow-through, each of which is part of chapter exercises wherever appropriate.

Examples of context-relative and SCANS-related work are found in the chapter skill assessments called Working Hands-On, which reinforce acquired technical skills while providing practice in decision making and problem solving. Other examples, in the Performance Assessments sections, offer simulations that require students to demonstrate their understanding of the major skills and technical features within a framework of critical and creative thinking. The Writing Activities toward the end of each level make it clear that students are not just producers, but editors and writers as well.

Emphasis on Visual Learning

Microsoft Office programs such as Word operate within the Windows operating system, a graphical user interface (GUI) that provides a visually oriented environment by using icons to represent program features. This textbook also emphasizes a graphical environment with icons that represent specific learning components. For example, figures that illustrate numerous steps done at the computer are labeled with callouts that correspond to the steps. The student can easily follow the steps by seeing the exact spot on the computer screen where a certain action is required on their part.

Icons offer additional visual learning cues. A computer icon appears next to Performance Assessments. A hands-on-keyboard icon identifies the Writing Activities at the end of each level. A globe icon displays next to the Internet Activity at the end of each level. Also, the integrated exercises are marked with icons representing the applications used.

Upon completion of the course, students will have mastered the basic-to-intermediate features and/or Core Level MOS skills of Word 2000. They also will have practiced some basic skills in using Windows and acquired a solid foundation in the problem-solving and communication competencies so important in the contemporary workplace.

Learning Components that Accompany This Text

The following products for instructors and students correspond to this text and enhance its teaching possibilities. These products may be ordered by contacting an EMC/Paradigm Publishing Customer Care representative by phone at (800) 535-6865 or via E-mail at *educate@emcp.com* and supplying the appropriate order number:

Textbook Web site at *www.emcp.com*. Watch for updates, tips, and instructional activities for students and instructors at the text's Resource Center link.

Microsoft® Word 2000 Instructor's Guide with CD-ROM, Order Number 41362. The Instructor's Guide contains a suggested course syllabus, grade sheet, and assignment sheet; a comprehensive Word test and its answers to use as final exams; Supplemental Performance Assessments; and a list of PowerPoint slides available on the CD. For each chapter, the Instructor's Guide also provides a summary of chapter contents, Teaching Hints, Thinking Offline answers, and Working Hands-On model answers for all exercises in the text. The Instructor's CD-ROM contains everything found in the print Instructor's Guide plus model answer files for all exercises and PowerPoint slides for classroom use.

Word

CORE LEVEL

MICROSOFT® WORD 2000

CORE LEVEL MOS SKILLS

Standardized Coding No.	SKILL	Page
W2000.1	**Working with text**	
W2000.1.1	Use the Undo, Redo, and Repeat command	25-27, 76-77
W2000.1.2	Apply font formats (Bold, Italic and Underline)	38-39
W2000.1.3	Use the SPELLING feature	128-133
W2000.1.4	Use the THESAURUS feature	139-141
W2000.1.5	Use the GRAMMAR feature	133-136
W2000.1.6	Insert page breaks	113-114
W2000.1.7	Highlight text in document	121-122
W2000.1.8	Insert and move text	160-163
W2000.1.9	Cut, Copy, Paste, and Paste Special using the Office Clipboard	160-166
W2000.1.10	Copy formats using the Format Painter	57-58
W2000.1.11	Select and change font and font size	40-45
W2000.1.12	Find and replace text	205-210
W2000.1.13	Apply character effects (superscript, subscript, strikethrough, small caps and outline)	46-47
W2000.1.14	Insert date and time	119-120
W2000.1.15	Insert symbols	71-74
W2000.1.16	Create and apply frequently used text with AutoCorrect	64-65, 136-139
W2000.2	**Working with paragraphs**	
W2000.2.1	Align text in paragraphs (Center, Left, Right and Justified)	51-56
W2000.2.2	Add bullets and numbering	63-70
W2000.2.3	Set character, line, and paragraph spacing options	48-50, 56-57, 74-76
W2000.2.4	Apply borders and shading to paragraphs	77-82
W2000.2.5	Use indentation options (Left, Right, First Line and Hanging Indent)	58-63
W2000.2.6	Use Tabs command (Center, Decimal, Left and Right)	101-110
W2000.2.7	Create an outline style numbered list	220-221
W2000.2.8	Set tabs with leaders	109-110
W2000.3	**Working with documents**	
W2000.3.1	Print a document	7, 10, 172-174
W2000.3.2	Use print preview	114-116
W2000.3.3	Use Web Page Preview	344
W2000.3.4	Navigate through a document	15-20
W2000.3.5	Insert page numbers	202-205
W2000.3.6	Set page orientation	180-182
W2000.3.7	Set margins	110-113
W2000.3.8	Use Go To to locate specific elements in a document	210-211
W2000.3.9	Create and modify page numbers	202-205
W2000.3.10	Create and modify headers and footers	193-202
W2000.3.11	Align text vertically	116-117
W2000.3.12	Create and use newspaper columns	122-128
W2000.3.13	Revise column structure	127-128
W2000.3.14	Prepare and print envelopes and labels	175-180
W2000.3.15	Apply styles	215-220
W2000.3.16	Create sections with formatting that differs from other sections	123-127, 201-202
W2000.3.17	Use click and type	118-119
W2000.4	**Managing files**	
W2000.4.1	Use save	6-7, 11
W2000.4.2	Locate and open an existing document	12, 159-160
W2000.4.3	Use Save As (different name, location or format)	11, 21-22
W2000.4.4	Create a folder	150-151
W2000.4.5	Create a new document using a Wizard	213-215
W2000.4.6	Save as Web Page	343-345
W2000.4.7	Use templates to create a new document	211-213
W2000.4.8	Create hyperlinks	349-350
W2000.4.9	Use the Office Assistant	82-87
W2000.4.10	Send a Word document via e-mail	182-183
W2000.5	**Using tables**	
W2000.5.1	Create and format tables	235-275
W2000.5.2	Add borders and shading to tables	244-249
W2000.5.3	Revise tables (insert & delete rows and columns, change cell formats)	255-256, 258-261
W2000.5.4	Modify table structure (merge cells, change height and width)	249-254, 261-262
W2000.5.5	Rotate text in a table	265, 269-270
W2000.6	**Working with pictures and charts**	
W2000.6.1	Use the Drawing toolbar	294-299
W2000.6.2	Insert graphics into a document (WordArt, ClipArt, Images)	285-292, 309-318

 **Chapter 01C**

Creating, Printing, and Editing Word Documents

1

PERFORMANCE OBJECTIVES

Upon successful completion of chapter 1, you will be able to:

- Open Microsoft Word.
- Create, save, name, print, open, and close a Word document.
- Exit Word and Windows.
- Edit a document.
- Move the insertion point within a document.
- Scroll within a document.
- Select text in a document.

In this chapter, you will learn to create, save, print, open, close, and edit a Word document. Before continuing in this chapter, make sure you have read the *Getting Started* section presented in the text or at the Benchmark Series Resource Center at www.emcp.com. Choose any Benchmark title, then click Student Resources. This section contains information about computer hardware and software, using the mouse, executing commands, and the Microsoft Office Assistant.

Opening Microsoft Word

Microsoft Office Professional 2000 contains a word processing program, named Word, that you can use to create, save, edit, and print documents. The steps to open Word may vary depending on your system setup. Generally, to open Word, you would complete the following steps:

1. Turn on the monitor and the CPU. (Depending on your system, you may also need to turn on the printer.)
2. After a few moments, the Windows 98 (or Windows 95) screen displays (your screen may vary). At the Windows 98 (or Windows 95) screen, position the arrow pointer on the Start button on the Taskbar (located at the bottom left side of the screen), and then click the left mouse button. This causes a pop-up menu to display.

3. Point to <u>P</u>rograms. (To do this, move the mouse pointer up until <u>P</u>rograms is selected—do not click the mouse button). This causes another menu to display to the right of the first pop-up menu.
4. Move the arrow pointer to *Microsoft Word* and click the left mouse button.

Creating a Word Document

When Microsoft Word is open, a clear document screen displays as shown in figure 1.1. The features of the document screen are described in figure 1.2. (The Standard and Formatting toolbars at your clear document screen may appear on the same line. The two toolbars have been separated for figure 1.1.)

figure

1.1

Clear Document Screen

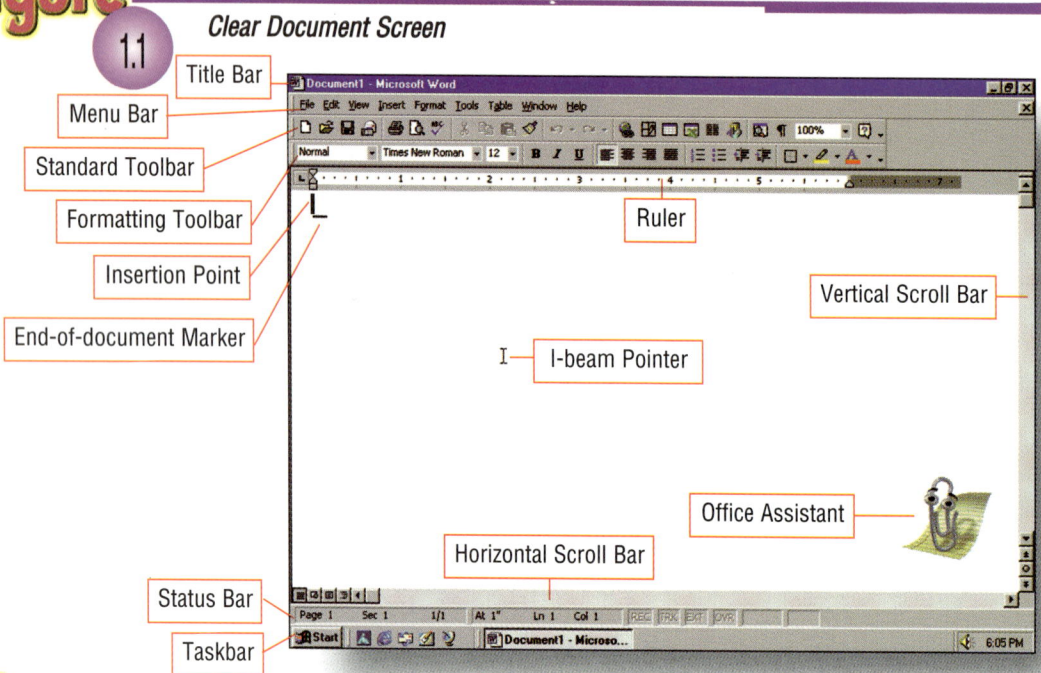

Title Bar
Menu Bar
Standard Toolbar
Formatting Toolbar
Insertion Point
End-of-document Marker
Ruler
Vertical Scroll Bar
I-beam Pointer
Office Assistant
Horizontal Scroll Bar
Status Bar
Taskbar

figure

1.2

Microsoft Word Screen

Feature	Description
Title Bar	The document name displays at the left side of the Title bar followed by the program name (such as *Microsoft Word*).
Menu Bar	The Menu bar contains a list of options to manage and customize documents. Word functions and features are grouped into menu options. For example, functions to save, close, or open a new document are contained in the <u>F</u>ile option on the Menu bar. (Shortcut commands to some common features display at the right side of menus.)
Standard Toolbar	The Standard toolbar contains buttons that are shortcuts for the most popular commands. For example, buttons are available for opening and saving a document. Position the arrow pointer on a button on the Standard toolbar and, after one second, a ScreenTip displays with the name of the button.

Formatting Toolbar	The Formatting toolbar contains buttons that can quickly apply formatting to text in a document such as bold, italics, and underlining. Position the arrow pointer on a button on the Formatting toolbar and, after one second, a ScreenTip displays with the name of the button.
Ruler	Set margins, indents, and tabs with the Ruler.
Insertion Point	The insertion point indicates the location where the next character entered at the keyboard will appear.
End-of-document Marker	The end-of-document marker indicates the end of the document.
Scroll Bars	Use the scroll bars to view various parts of the document.
Status Bar	The Status bar displays information about the text in the document and whether certain working modes are active. The Status bar also displays the current location of the insertion point by page number, section number, line measurement, line count, and column position. At the right side of the Status bar, working modes are displayed. When a working mode is dimmed, it is inactive. When a working mode is active, it displays in black.
Taskbar	The bottom line on the screen is the Taskbar. When a program is open, a program button appears on the Taskbar.
Office Assistant	The Office Assistant is a link to the on-screen Help feature that anticipates the type of help you need and suggests Help topics related to the work you are doing. The Assistant will also point out ways to perform tasks more easily and will provide visual examples and step-by-step instructions for specific tasks.

At a clear document screen, key (type) the information to create a document. A document is any information you choose; for instance, a letter, memo, report, term paper, table, and so on. Some things to consider when keying text are:

- **Word Wrap:** As you key (type) text to create a document, you do not need to press the Enter key at the end of each line because Word wraps text to the next line. A word is wrapped to the next line if it begins before the right margin and continues past the right margin. The only times you need to press Enter are to end a paragraph, create a blank line, or end a short line.

- **AutoCorrect:** Word contains a feature that automatically corrects certain words as they are being keyed (typed). For example, if you key the word *adn* instead of *and*, Word automatically corrects it when you press the space bar after the word.

- **Spell It:** A feature in Word called Spell It automatically inserts a wavy red line below words that are not contained in the Spelling dictionary or are not automatically corrected by AutoCorrect. This group may include misspelled words, proper names, some terminology, and some foreign words. If you key a word not recognized by the Spelling dictionary, Word inserts a red wavy line below the word. If the word is correct, you can leave it as written. If, however, the word is incorrect, you have two choices—you can backspace over the word using the Backspace key and then key it correctly, or you can position the I-beam pointer on the word, click the *right* mouse button, and then click the correct spelling in the pop-up menu.

A book icon displays in the Status bar. A checkmark on the book indicates no spelling errors detected in the document by Spell It, while an X in the book indicates errors. Double-click the book icon to move to the next error.

- **Automatic Grammar Checker:** Word includes an automatic grammar checker. If the grammar checker detects a sentence containing a grammatical error, a green wavy line is inserted below the sentence. At this point, leave the green wavy line. You will learn more about the grammar checker in chapter 3.
- **Spacing Punctuation:** Typically, Word uses Times New Roman as the default typeface. Times New Roman is a proportional typeface. (You will learn more about typefaces in chapter 2.) When keying text in a proportional typeface, space once (rather than twice) after end-of-sentence punctuation such as a period, question mark, or exclamation point, and after a colon. Proportional typefaces are set closer together, and extra white space at the end of a sentence or after a colon is not needed.

Saving a Document

Save

When you have created a document, the information will need to be saved on your disk. A variety of methods can be used to save a document. You can save by clicking the Save button on the Standard toolbar; by clicking <u>F</u>ile and then <u>S</u>ave; or with the shortcut command, Ctrl + S. For many features in this textbook, instructions for using the mouse will be emphasized. (For information on using the keyboard, refer to the *Choosing Commands* section in *Getting Started*.) To save a document with the Save button on the Standard toolbar, you would complete the following steps:

1. Position the arrow pointer on the Save button (the third button from the left) on the Standard toolbar and click the left mouse button.
2. At the Save As dialog box shown in figure 1.3, key the name of the document.
3. Click the <u>S</u>ave button located in the lower right corner of the dialog box.

figure

1.3

Save As Dialog Box

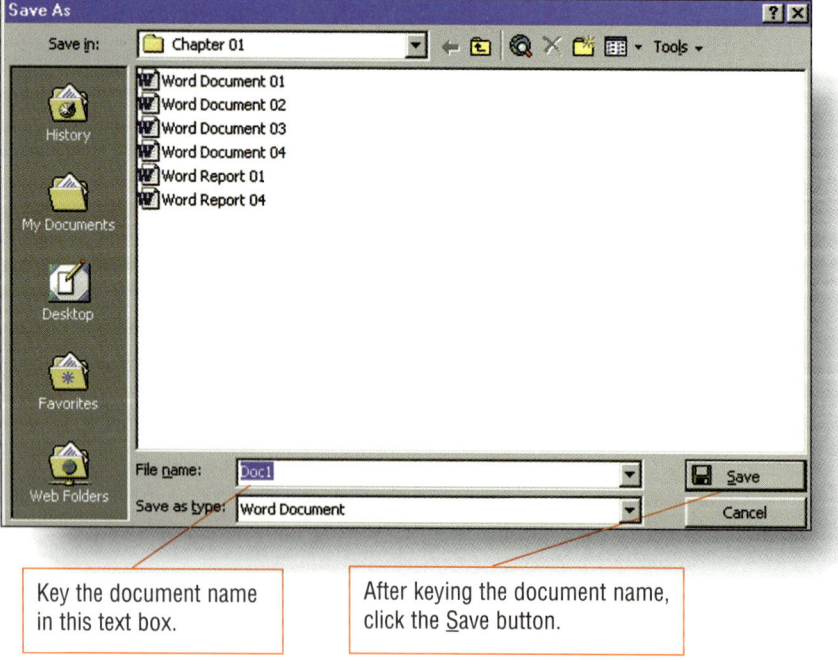

Key the document name in this text box.

After keying the document name, click the <u>S</u>ave button.

You can also display the Save As dialog box by clicking File on the Menu bar and then clicking Save As at the drop-down menu.

Naming a Document

Document names created in Word and other suite applications can be up to 255 characters in length, including the drive letter and any folder names, and may include spaces. File names cannot include any of the following characters:

<table>
<tr><td>forward slash (/)</td><td>question mark (?)</td></tr>
<tr><td>backslash (\)</td><td>quotation mark (")</td></tr>
<tr><td>greater than sign (>)</td><td>colon (:)</td></tr>
<tr><td>less than sign (<)</td><td>semicolon (;)</td></tr>
<tr><td>asterisk (*)</td><td>pipe symbol (|)</td></tr>
</table>

You cannot give a document the same name in first uppercase and then lowercase letters.

Canceling a Command

If a drop-down menu is displayed in the document screen, it can be removed with the mouse by positioning the I-beam pointer in the document screen (outside the drop-down menu), and then clicking the left mouse button. If you are using the keyboard, press the Alt key. You can also press the Esc key twice. The first time you press Esc, the drop-down menu is removed but the menu option on the Menu bar is still selected. The second time you press Esc, the option on the Menu bar is no longer selected.

Several methods can be used to remove a dialog box from the document screen. To remove a dialog box with the mouse, click the Cancel button or Close button. You can also click the Close button located in the upper right corner of the dialog box containing the "X." A dialog box can be removed from the document screen with the keyboard by pressing the Esc key.

Closing a Document

When a document is saved with the Save or Save As options, the document is saved on the disk and remains in the document screen. To remove the document from the screen, click the Close button located at the far right side of the Menu bar (contains the X) or click File and then Close. (If you close a document with the Close button, be sure to use the Close button on the Menu bar, not the Close button on the Title bar. The Close button on the Title bar will close the Word program.) When you close a document, the document is removed and a blank screen is displayed. At this screen, you can open a previously saved document, create a new document, or exit the Word program.

Printing a Document

Many of the computer exercises you will be creating will need to be printed. A printing of a document is referred to as hard copy. (Soft copy is a document displayed in the document screen and hard copy is a document printed on paper.) A document can be sent immediately to the printer by clicking the Print button on the Standard toolbar or through the Print dialog box. Display the Print dialog box by clicking File and then Print. At the Print dialog box, click the OK button.

Print

Exiting Word and Windows

When you are finished working with Word and have saved all necessary information, exit Word by clicking File and then Exit. You can also exit the Word program by clicking the Close button located at the right side of the Title bar. (The Close button contains an X.) After exiting Word, you may also need to exit the Windows 98 (or Windows 95) program. To exit Windows, you would complete the following steps:

1. Click the Start button located at the left side of the Taskbar.
2. At the pop-up menu, click Shut Down.
3. At the Shut Down Windows dialog box, make sure *Shut down* is selected and click Yes.

Completing Computer Exercises

At the end of sections within chapters and at the end of chapters, you will be completing hands-on exercises at the computer. These exercises will provide you with the opportunity to practice the presented functions and commands. The skill assessment exercises at the end of each chapter include general directions. If you do not remember how to perform a particular function, refer to the text in the chapter.

Copying Data Documents

In several exercises in each chapter, you will be opening documents provided with this textbook. Before beginning each chapter, copy the chapter folder from the CD that accompanies this textbook to a floppy disk (or other folder). Detailed steps on how to copy a folder from the CD to your floppy disk are presented in the Getting Started section. Abbreviated steps are printed on the inside back cover of this textbook.

Changing the Default Folder

At the end of this and the remaining chapters in the textbook, you will be saving documents. More than likely, you will want to save documents onto your disk. You will also be opening documents that have been saved on your disk.

To save documents on and open documents from your data disk, you will need to specify the drive where your disk is located as the default folder. Once you specify the drive where your data disk is located, Word uses this as the default folder until you exit the Word program. The next time you open Word, you will again need to specify the drive where your data disk is located. You only need to change the default folder once each time you enter the Word program.

You can change the default folder at the Open dialog box or the Save As dialog box. To change the folder to the *Chapter 01C* folder on the disk in drive A at the Open dialog box, you would complete the following steps (see figure 1.4):

1. Click the Open button on the Standard toolbar (the second button from the left); or click File and Open.
2. At the Open dialog box, click the down-pointing triangle at the right side of the Look in text box.
3. From the drop-down list that displays, click *3½ Floppy (A)*.

4. Double-click *Chapter 01C* that displays in the list box.
5. Click the Cancel button in the lower right corner of the dialog box.

If you want to change the default folder permanently, make the change at the Options dialog box with the File Locations tab selected. To permanently change the default folder to drive A, you would complete these steps:

1. Click Tools and then Options.
2. At the Options dialog box, click the File Locations tab.
3. At the Options dialog box with the File Locations tab selected, make sure *Documents* is selected in the File types list box and click the Modify button.
4. At the Modify Location dialog box, click the down-pointing triangle at the right side of the Look in list box, and click *3½ Floppy (A)*.
5. Click the OK button.

Changing the Default Folder

1.4

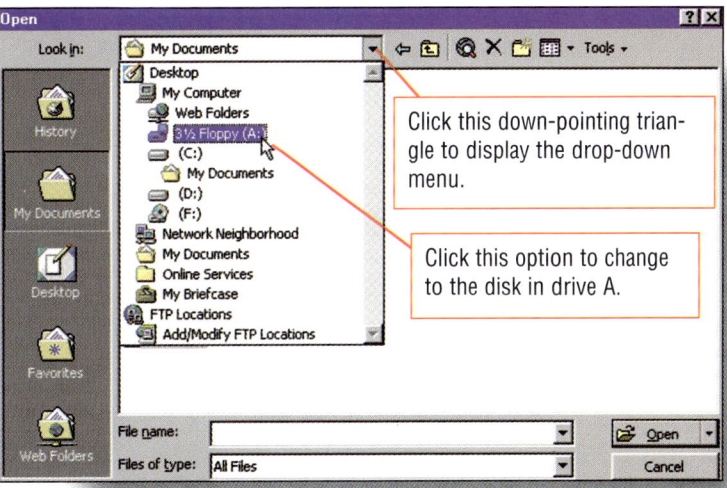

Changing the Default Type Size

Typically, Word uses 10-point Times New Roman as the default font. (You will learn more about fonts in chapter 2.) Exercises in this and other chapters will generally display text in 12-point size. If the system you are operating uses a point size other than 12, you can change the default type size to 12 by completing the following steps (see figure 1.5):

figure

1.5

Changing the Default Font

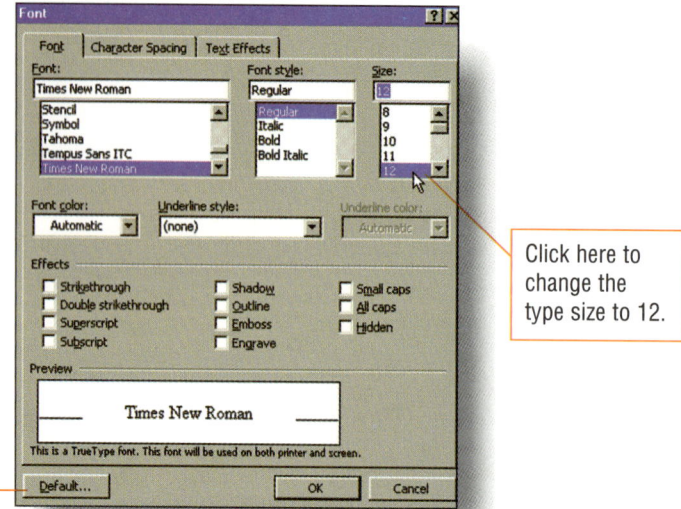

Click here to change the type size to 12.

After clicking the 12 in the Size list box, click the Default button.

1. Click Format and then Font.
2. At the Font dialog box, click *12* in the Size list box.
3. Click the Default command button located in the lower left corner of the dialog box.
4. At the message box asking if you want to change the default font, click Yes.

Once the default type size has been changed in this manner, the new type size will be in effect each time you open the Word program. You need to change the default only once.

(Before completing computer exercises, make sure you have copied the Chapter 01C folder from the CD that accompanies this textbook to a blank, formatted disk.)

exercise

Creating and Printing a Document

1. Follow the instructions in this chapter to open Windows and then Word.
2. At the clear document screen, change to the default folder where your disk is located by completing the following steps: (If the default folder has been changed permanently, these steps are not necessary. Check with your instructor before changing the default folder.)
   a. Click the Open button on the Standard toolbar.

b. At the Open dialog box, click the down-pointing triangle to the right of the Look in option.

c. From the drop-down list that displays, click *3½ Floppy (A:)* (this may vary depending on your system).

d. Double-click the *Chapter 01C* folder.

e. Click the Cancel command button located in the lower right corner of the dialog box.

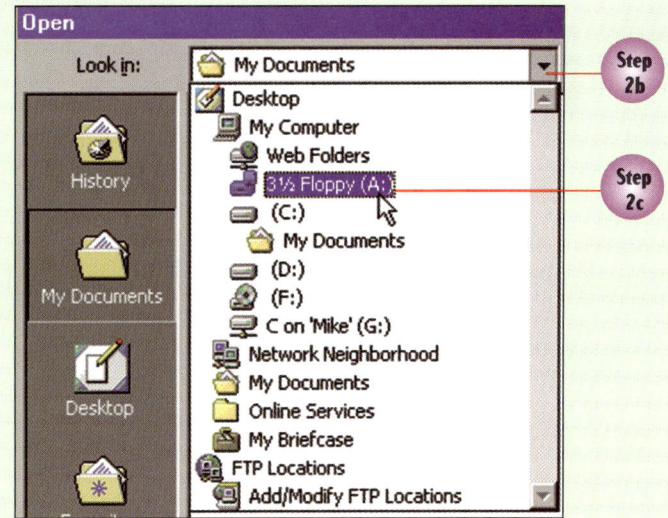

3. At the document screen, make sure that 12-point Times New Roman is the default font. (If not, change the default type size to 12 following the directions listed in the *Changing the Default Type Size* section of this chapter; or, check with your instructor.)

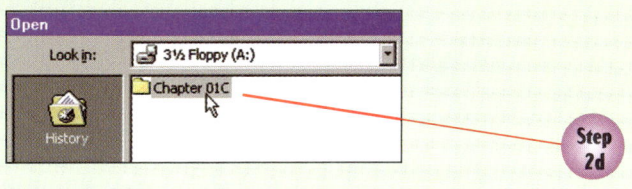

4. Key (type) the text in figure 1.6. If you make a mistake while keying and Spell It inserts a wavy red line, backspace over the incorrect word using the Backspace key, and then rekey the correct word. Ignore any green wavy lines inserted by Word. (Do not worry about doing a lot of correcting—you will learn more about editing a document later in this chapter.) Remember to space only once after end-of-sentence punctuation when keying the text.

5. When you are done keying the text, save the document and name it Word C1, Ex 01 (for Core level chapter 1, Exercise 1) by completing the following steps:

a. Click the Save button on the Standard toolbar.

b. At the Save As dialog box, key **Word C1, Ex 01**. (Key a zero when naming documents, not the letter O. In this textbook, the zero, 0, displays thinner than the letter O. As you key **Word C1, Ex 01**, the selected text in the File name text box is automatically deleted and replaced with the text you key.)

c. Press the Enter key or click the Save button located in the lower right corner of the dialog box.

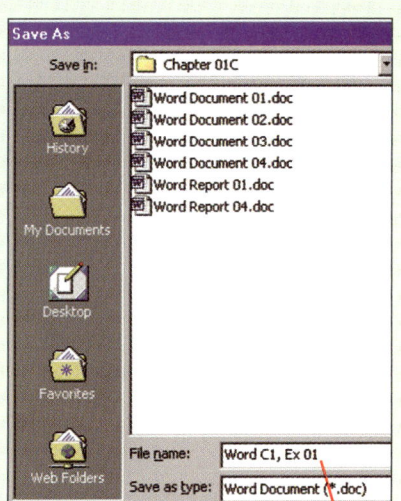

6. Print the document by clicking the Print button on the Standard toolbar.

7. Close Word C1, Ex 01 by clicking File and then Close or by clicking the Close button located at the far right side of the Menu bar. (This displays a blank screen, rather than a clear screen.)

figure 1.6

Exercise 1

A mainframe is a very large computer used, typically, in a large organization to handle high-volume processing. A typical use of a mainframe computer would be to process the financial transactions and maintain the accounts of a large bank.

A keyboard or a keyboard and a display connected to a mainframe or other computer is referred to as a dumb terminal. A dumb terminal is generally used to input raw information and takes its name from the fact that it has no processor of its own. In the early days of computers, the mainframe/dumb terminal configuration was the only one available for computing.

Opening a Document

Open

When a document has been saved and closed, it can be opened at the Open dialog box shown in figure 1.7. To display this dialog box, click the Open button on the Standard toolbar or click File and then Open. At the Open dialog box, double-click the document name.

The names of the most recently opened documents display toward the bottom of the expanded File drop-down menu. To open a document from this drop-down menu, click File, expand the drop-down menu, and then click the desired document.

figure 1.7

Open Dialog Box

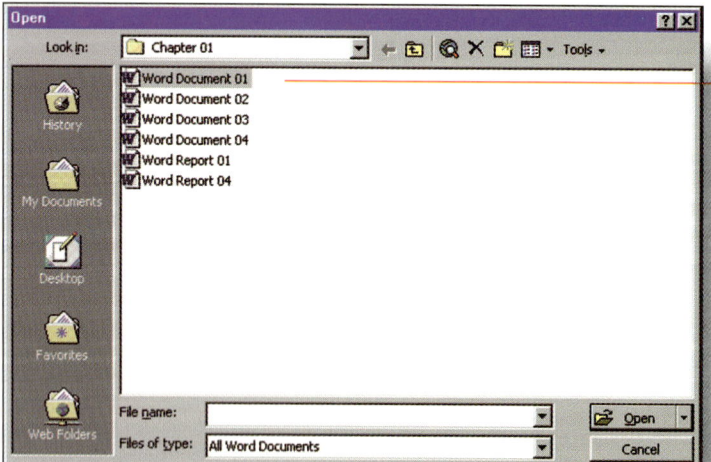

To open a document, double-click the document name.

Creating a New Document

When you close a document, a blank screen is displayed. If you want to create a new document, display a clear document screen. To do this, click the New Blank Document button on the Standard toolbar (the first button).

New Blank
Document

exercise 2

Creating and Printing a New Document

1. At a blank screen, create a new document by clicking the New Blank Document button on the Standard toolbar (the first button from the left).
2. At the clear document screen, key the information shown in figure 1.8. (Correct any errors highlighted by Spell It as they occur and remember to space once after end-of-sentence punctuation. Ignore any wavy green lines inserted by Word.)
3. Save the document and name it Word C1, Ex 02 by completing the following steps:
   a. Click the Save button on the Standard toolbar.
   b. At the Save As dialog box, key **Word C1, Ex 02**.
   c. Click the Save button (or press Enter). 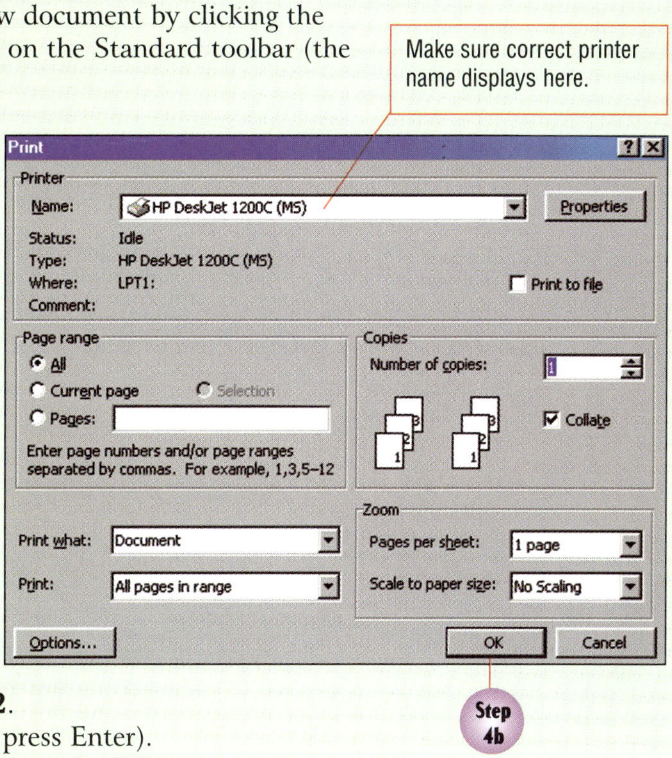
4. Print the document by completing the following steps:
   a. Click File and then Print.
   b. At the Print dialog box, click OK (located in the lower right corner of the dialog box.)
5. Close the document by clicking File and then Close or clicking the Close button located at the right side of the Menu bar.

Make sure correct printer name displays here.

Step 4b

figure

1.8 *Exercise 2*

A workstation is a desktop computer powerful enough to rival the performance of a minicomputer or, in some cases, of a small mainframe. Workstations are used widely for scientific, engineering, and research applications.

A personal computer, or PC, is a desktop computer that is less powerful than a workstation. As personal computers have become more powerful, the distinction between them and workstations has blurred. During the 1980s and early 1990s, networked personal computers took over many of the functions previously performed by mainframes and minis.

Displaying and Moving Toolbars

The Standard and Formatting toolbars display below the Menu bar at the top of the screen. These toolbars may display side by side with only a portion of the buttons visible. To display the hidden buttons, click the More Buttons button (displays with two right-pointing arrows). Clicking the More Buttons button displays a palette of buttons.

The Formatting toolbar in the figures in this textbook displays immediately below the Standard toolbar. At this display, all buttons on the toolbars are visible. To move the Formatting toolbar below the Standard toolbar, complete the following steps:

1. Click <u>T</u>ools, expand the drop-down menu by clicking the down-pointing arrows that display at the bottom of the menu, and then click <u>C</u>ustomize.
2. At the Customize dialog box, click the <u>O</u>ptions tab. (Skip this step if the <u>O</u>ptions tab is already selected.)
3. Click the *Standard and Formatting toolbars <u>s</u>hare one row* check box. (This removes the check mark.)
4. Click the Close button to close the dialog box.

The display of the Standard and Formatting toolbars (as well as other toolbars) can be turned on or off. To do this, position the mouse pointer anywhere on a toolbar, and then click the *right* mouse button. At the drop-down menu that displays, click the toolbar name you want turned on or off. You can also turn on or off the display of a toolbar by clicking <u>V</u>iew on the Menu bar, pointing to <u>T</u>oolbars, and then clicking the toolbar name.

Expanding Drop-Down Menus

Microsoft Word personalizes menus and toolbars as you work. When you click an option on the Menu bar, only the most popular options display (considered first-rank options). This is referred to as an *adaptive menu*. To expand the drop-down menu and display the full set of options (first-rank options as well as second-rank options), click the down-pointing arrows that display at the bottom of the drop-down menu. A drop-down menu will also expand if you click an option on the Menu bar and then pause on the menu for a few seconds. Second-rank options on the expanded drop-down menu display with a lighter gray background. If you choose a second-rank option, it is promoted and becomes a first-rank option the next time the drop-down menu is displayed.

If you want all menu options displayed when you click an option on the Menu bar, turn off the adaptive menu feature. To do this, you would complete the following steps:

1. Click Tools, and then click Customize.
2. At the Customize dialog box, click the Options tab. (Skip this step if the Options tab is already selected.)
3. At the Customize dialog box with the Options tab selected, click in the *Menus show recently used commands first* check box to remove the check mark.
4. Click the Close button to close the dialog box.

Editing a Document

Many documents that are created need to have changes made to them. These changes may include adding text, called *inserting*, or removing text, called *deleting*. To insert or delete text, you need to be able to move the insertion point to specific locations in a document without erasing the text through which it passes. To move the insertion point without interfering with text, you can use the mouse, the keyboard, or the mouse combined with the keyboard.

Moving the Insertion Point with the Mouse

The mouse can be used to move the insertion point quickly to specific locations in the document. To do this, position the I-beam pointer at the location where you want the insertion point, and then click the left mouse button.

Scrolling with the Mouse

In addition to moving the insertion point to a specific location, the mouse can be used to move the display of text in the document screen. Scrolling in a document changes the text displayed but does not move the insertion point. If you want to move the insertion point to a new location in a document, scroll to the location, position the I-beam pointer in the desired location, and then click the left mouse button.

You can use the mouse with the *horizontal scroll bar* and/or the *vertical scroll bar* to scroll through text in a document. The horizontal scroll bar displays toward the bottom of the Word screen and the vertical scroll bar displays at the right side. Figure 1.9 displays the Word screen with the scroll bars and scroll boxes identified.

Scroll Bars

1.9

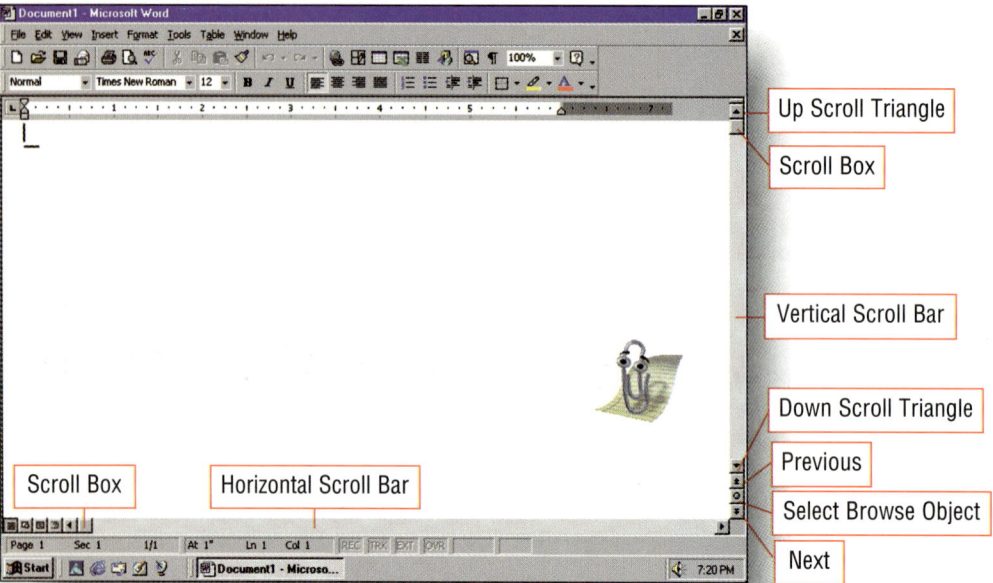

Up Scroll Triangle

Scroll Box

Vertical Scroll Bar

Down Scroll Triangle

Previous

Select Browse Object

Next

Scroll Box

Horizontal Scroll Bar

Click a scroll triangle to scroll the text in the document in the direction indicated on the triangle. The vertical and horizontal scroll bars each contain a scroll box. A scroll box indicates the location of the text in the document screen in relation to the remainder of the document. To scroll up one screen at a time, position the arrow pointer above the scroll box (but below the up scroll triangle) on the vertical scroll bar, and then click the left mouse button. Position the arrow pointer below the scroll box and click the left button to scroll down a screen. If you hold the left button down, the action becomes continuous. You can also position the arrow pointer on the scroll box, hold down the left mouse button, and then drag the scroll box along the scroll bar to reposition text in the document screen.

As you drag the scroll box along the vertical scroll bar in a longer document, page numbers display at the right side of the document screen in a yellow box. (You will notice this when completing exercise 3.)

Moving the Insertion Point to a Specific Page

Along with scrolling options, Word also contains navigation buttons for moving the insertion point to a specific location. Navigation buttons are shown in figure 1.9 and include the Previous button, the Select Browse Object button, and the Next button. The full names of and the task completed by the Previous and Next buttons varies depending on the last navigation completed. Click the Select Browse Object button and a palette of browsing choices displays. You will learn more about the Select Browse Object button in the next section.

Word includes a Go To option that you can use to move the insertion point to a specific page within a document. To move the insertion point to a specific page, you would complete the following steps:

1. Click <u>E</u>dit, expand the menu, and then click <u>G</u>o To; or, double-click the page number at the left side of the Status bar.
2. At the Find and Replace dialog box with the <u>G</u>o To tab selected, key the page number. (If you are using the 10-key pad at the right side of the keyboard, make sure the Num Lock key is on.)
3. Click the Go <u>T</u>o button or press Enter. (The Go <u>T</u>o button displays as the Nex<u>t</u> button until a page number is entered.)
4. Click the Close button to close the Find and Replace dialog box.

Browsing in a Document

The Select Browse Object button located at the bottom of the vertical scroll bar contains options for browsing through a document. Click this button and a palette of browsing choices displays as shown in figure 1.10. Use the options on the palette to move the insertion point to various features in a Word document. Position the arrow pointer on an option in the palette and the option name displays below the options. For example, position the arrow pointer on the last option in the top row and *Browse by Page* displays below the options. When you click the Browse by Page option, the insertion point moves to the next page in the document. Use the other options in the palette to move to the next specified object in the document.

Select Browse
Object

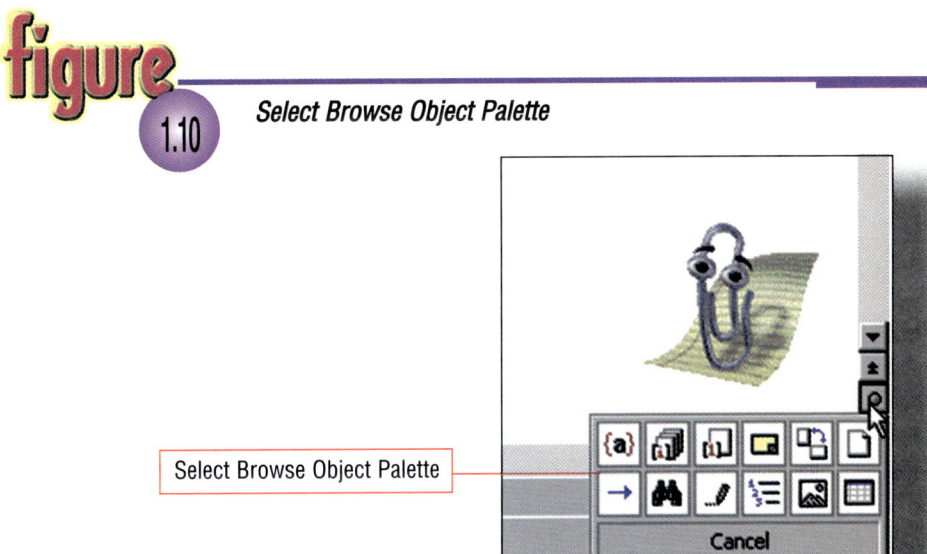

figure

1.10

Select Browse Object Palette

Select Browse Object Palette

exercise 3

Scrolling, Browsing, and Moving the Insertion Point in a Document

1. At a clear document screen, open Word Report 04.
2. Practice moving the insertion point and scrolling and browsing through the document using the mouse by completing the following steps:
   a. Position the I-beam pointer at the beginning of the first paragraph and then click the left mouse button. (This moves the insertion point to the location of the I-beam pointer.)

b. Position the mouse pointer on the down scroll triangle on the vertical scroll bar and then click the left mouse button several times. (This scrolls down lines of text in the document.) With the mouse pointer on the down scroll triangle, hold down the left mouse button and keep it down until the end of the document displays.

c. Position the mouse pointer on the up scroll triangle and hold down the left mouse button until the beginning of the document displays.

d. Position the mouse pointer below the scroll box and then click the left mouse button. Continue clicking the mouse button (with the mouse pointer positioned below the scroll box) until the end of the document displays.

e. Position the mouse pointer on the scroll box in the vertical scroll bar. Hold down the left mouse button, drag the scroll box to the top of the vertical scroll bar, and then release the mouse button. (Notice that the document page numbers display in a yellow box at the right side of the document screen.)

f. Click on the title at the beginning of the document. (This moves the insertion point to the location of the mouse pointer.)

g. Move the insertion point to page 4 by completing the following steps:

1) Click Edit, expand the drop-down menu by clicking the down-pointing arrows that display at the bottom of the menu, and then click Go To; or, double-click the page number at the left side of the Status bar.

2) At the Find and Replace dialog box with the Go To tab selected, make sure *Page* is selected in the Go to what list box, and then key **4** in the Enter page number text box.

Step 2g2

3) Click the Go To button or press Enter.

4) Click the Close button to close the Find and Replace dialog box.

Step 2g3

[Find and Replace dialog box shown: tabs Find, Replace, Go To. "Go to what:" list containing Page, Section, Line, Bookmark, Comment, Footnote, Endnote. "Enter page number:" field showing 4. Text: "Enter + and – to move relative to the current location. Example: +4 will move forward four items." Buttons: Previous, Go To, Close.]

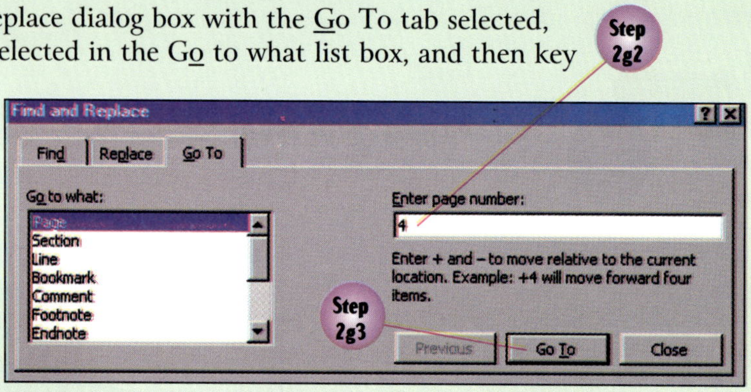

h. Click the Previous Page button located immediately above the Select Browse Object button on the vertical scroll bar. (This moves the insertion point to page 3.)

i. Click the Previous Page button again. (This moves the insertion point to page 2.)

j. Click twice on the Next Page button located immediately below the Select Browse Object button on the vertical scroll bar. (This moves the insertion point to the beginning of page 4.)

k. Move the insertion point to page 1 by completing the following steps:

1) Click the Select Browse Object button located toward the bottom of the vertical scroll bar.

2) At the palette of browsing choices, click the first choice in the bottom row (Go To).

3) At the Find and Replace dialog box with the Go To tab selected, press the Delete key to delete the *4* in the Enter page number text box, and then key **1**.

Step 2k2

Go To

4) Click the Go To button or press Enter.

5) Click the Close button to close the Find and Replace dialog box.

l. Move to the beginning of page 2 by completing the following steps:

1) Click the Select Browse Object button.

2) At the palette of browsing choices, click the last choice in the top row (Browse by Page). (This moves the insertion point to page 2.)

3) Click the Select Browse Object button again and then click the last choice in the top row (Browse by Page). (This moves the insertion point to page 3.)

3. Close Word Report 04.

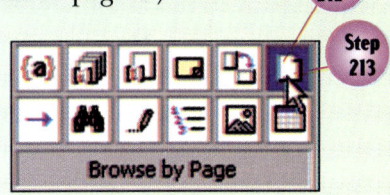

Moving the Insertion Point with the Keyboard

To move the insertion point with the keyboard, use the arrow keys located to the right of the regular keyboard. (You can also use the arrow keys on the numeric keypad. If you use these keys, make sure Num Lock is off.) Use the arrow keys together with other keys to move the insertion point to various locations in the document as shown in figure 1.11.

Insertion Point Movement Commands

To move insertion point	Press
One character left	left arrow
One character right	right arrow
One line up	up arrow
One line down	down arrow
One word to the left	Ctrl + left arrow
One word to the right	Ctrl + right arrow
To end of a line	End
To beginning of a line	Home
To beginning of current paragraph	Ctrl + up arrow
To beginning of previous paragraph	Ctrl + up arrow twice
To beginning of next paragraph	Ctrl + down arrow
Up one screen	Page Up
Down one screen	Page Down
To top of previous page	Ctrl + Page Up
To top of next page	Ctrl + Page Down
To beginning of document	Ctrl + Home
To end of document	Ctrl + End

When moving the insertion point, Word considers a word to be any series of characters between spaces. A paragraph is any text that is followed by a stroke of the Enter key. A page is text that is separated by a soft or hard page break.

If you open a previously saved document, you can move the insertion point to where the insertion point was last located when the document was closed by pressing Shift + F5.

Moving the Insertion Point Using the Keyboard

1. Open Word Report 01.
2. Practice moving the insertion point using the keyboard by completing the following steps:
   a. Press the right arrow key to move the insertion point to the next character to the right. Continue pressing the right arrow key until the insertion point is positioned at the end of the first paragraph.
   b. Press Ctrl + right arrow key to move the insertion point to the next word to the right. Continue pressing Ctrl + right arrow until the insertion point is positioned on the last word of the second paragraph.
   c. Press Ctrl + left arrow key until the insertion point is positioned at the beginning of the document.
   d. Press the End key to move the insertion point to the end of the title.
   e. Press the Home key to move the insertion point to the beginning of the title.
   f. Press Ctrl + Page Down to position the insertion point at the beginning of page 2.
   g. Press Ctrl + Page Up to position the insertion point at the beginning of page 1 (the beginning of the document).
   h. Press Ctrl + End to move the insertion point to the end of the document.
   i. Press Ctrl + Home to move the insertion point to the beginning of the document.
3. Close Word Report 01.

Inserting Text

Once you have created a document, you may want to insert information you forgot or have since decided to include. At the default document screen, Word moves existing characters to the right as you key additional text.

If you want to key over something, switch to the Overtype mode. You can do this by pressing the Insert key or by double-clicking the OVR mode button on the Status bar. When Overtype is on, the OVR mode button displays in black. To turn off Overtype, press the Insert key or double-click the OVR mode button.

Deleting Text

When you edit a document, you may want to delete (remove) text. Commands for deleting text are presented in figure 1.12.

> If you key a character that takes the place of an existing character, deactivate the Overtype mode by pressing the Insert key or double-clicking the OVR button on the Status bar.

figure
1.12
Deletion Commands

Character right of insertion point	Delete key
Character left of insertion point	Backspace key
Text from insertion point to beginning of word	Ctrl + Backspace
Text from insertion point to end of word	Ctrl + Delete

Saving a Document with Save As

Earlier in this chapter, you learned to save a document with the Save button on the Standard toolbar or the Save option from the File drop-down menu. The File drop-down menu also contains a Save As option. The Save As option is used to save a previously created document with a new name.

For example, suppose you create and save a document named Market Funds, and then open it later. If you save the document again with the Save button on the Standard toolbar or the Save option from the File drop-down menu, Word will save the document with the same name. You will not be prompted to key a name for the document. This is because Word assumes that when you use the Save option on a previously saved document, you want to save it with the same name. If you open the document named Market Funds, make some changes to it, and then want to save it with a new name, you must use the Save As option. When you use the Save As option, Word displays the Save As dialog box where you can key a new name for the document.

exercise 5

Editing and Saving a Document

1. Open Word Document 01.
2. Save the document with the name Word C1, Ex 05 using Save As by completing the following steps:
    a. Click File and then Save As.
    b. At the Save As dialog box, key **Word C1, Ex 05**.
    c. Click the Save button or press Enter.
3. Make the following changes to the document:
    a. Change the word *works* in the second sentence of the first paragraph to *operates*.
    b. Delete the words *means of* in the first sentence of the second paragraph and insert the words *method for*.

c. Delete the word *Furthermore* and the comma and space following it that begins the second sentence of the second paragraph. Capitalize the *t* in *the* that now begins the second sentence.

d. Delete the word *therefore* in the second sentence of the second paragraph.

e. Delete the words *over and over* in the second sentence of the second paragraph and insert the words *again and again*.

f. Delete the words *which can wreak havoc with the information stored on them* located at the end of the last sentence of the document.

g. Delete the comma located immediately following the word *telephones* and, if necessary, insert a period.

4. Save the document again with the same name (Word C1, Ex 05) by clicking the Save button on the Standard toolbar or by clicking File and then Save.

5. Print and then close Word C1, Ex 05.

Selecting Text

The mouse and/or keyboard can be used to select a specific amount of text. Once you select the text, you can delete or perform other Word functions involving the selected text. When text is selected, it displays as white text on a black background as shown in figure 1.13.

figure
1.13

Selected Text

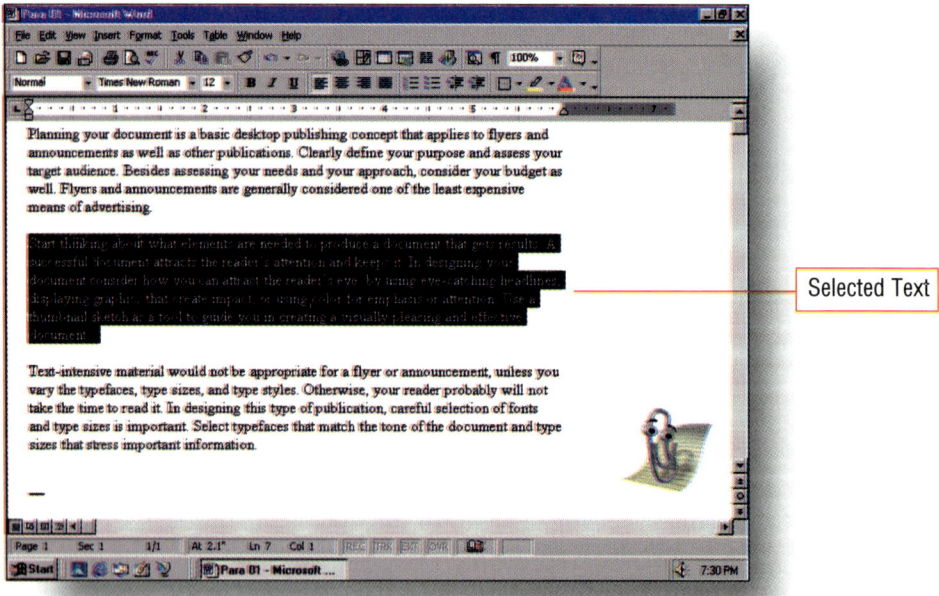

Selected Text

Selecting Text with the Mouse

You can use the mouse to select a word, line, sentence, paragraph, or the entire document. Figure 1.14 indicates the steps to follow to select various amounts of text. To select specific amounts of text such as a line, the instructions in the figure tell you to click in the selection bar. The selection bar is the space at the left side of the document screen between the left edge of the screen and the text. When the mouse pointer is positioned in the selection bar, the pointer turns into an arrow pointing up and to the right (instead of to the left).

figure

1.14   *Selecting with the Mouse*

To select	Complete these steps using the mouse
A word	Double-click the word.
A line of text	Click in the selection bar to the left of the line.
Multiple lines of text	Drag in the selection bar to the left of the lines.
A sentence	Hold down the Ctrl key, then click anywhere in the sentence.
A paragraph	Double-click in the selection bar next to the paragraph or triple-click anywhere in the paragraph.
Multiple paragraphs	Drag in the selection bar.
An entire document	Triple-click in the selection bar.

To select an amount of text other than a word, sentence, or paragraph, position the I-beam pointer on the first character of the text to be selected, hold down the left mouse button, drag the I-beam pointer to the last character of the text to be selected, and then release the mouse button. You can also select all text between the current insertion point and the I-beam pointer. To do this, position the insertion point where you want the selection to begin, hold down the Shift key, click the I-beam pointer at the end of the selection, and then release the Shift key.

To cancel a selection using the mouse, click anywhere in the document screen outside the selected text.

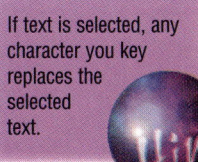

To select text vertically, hold down the Alt key while dragging with the mouse.

Selecting Text with the Keyboard

To select a specific amount of text using the keyboard, use the Extend Selection key, F8, along with the arrow keys. When you press F8, the extend selection mode is turned on and the EXT mode button on the Status bar displays in black letters. (You can also turn on the extend selection mode by double-clicking the EXT mode button on the Status bar.) As you move the insertion point through text, the text is selected. If you want to cancel the selection, press the Esc key, and then press any arrow key (or double-click the EXT mode button on the Status bar and then press any arrow key). You can also select text with the commands shown in figure 1.15.

If text is selected, any character you key replaces the selected text.

figure
1.15 — *Selecting with the Keyboard*

To select	Press
One character to right	Shift + right arrow
One character to left	Shift + left arrow
To end of word	Ctrl + Shift + right arrow
To beginning of word	Ctrl + Shift + left arrow
To end of line	Shift + End
To beginning of line	Shift + Home
One line up	Shift + up arrow
One line down	Shift + down arrow
To beginning of paragraph	Ctrl + Shift + up arrow
To end of paragraph	Ctrl + Shift + down arrow
One screen up	Shift + Page Up
One screen down	Shift + Page Down
To end of document	Ctrl + Shift + End
To beginning of document	Ctrl + Shift + Home
Entire document	Ctrl + A or click Edit, Select All

exercise 6

Selecting and Deleting Text

1. Open Word Document 02.
2. Save the document with Save As and name it Word C1, Ex 06.
3. Make the following changes to the document:
    a. Select the words *and use no cabling at all* and the period that follows located at the end of the last sentence in the first paragraph and then press the Delete key.
    b. Insert a period immediately following the word *signal*.
    c. Delete the heading line containing the text *QWERTY Keyboard* and the blank line below it using the Extend key, F8, by completing the following steps:
        1) Position the insertion point immediately before the *Q* in *QWERTY*.
        2) Press F8 to turn on select.
        3) Press the down arrow key twice. (This selects the heading and the blank line below it.)
        4) Press the Delete key.

d. Complete steps similar to those in c1) through c4) to delete the heading line containing the text *DVORAK Keyboard* and the blank line below it.

e. Begin a new paragraph with the sentence that reads *Keyboards have different physical appearances.* by completing the following steps:

    1) Position the insertion point immediately left of the *K* in *Keyboards* (the first word of the fifth sentence in the last paragraph).

    2) Press the Enter key twice.

f. Delete the last sentence in the last paragraph using the mouse by completing the following steps:

    1) Position the I-beam pointer anywhere in the sentence that begins *All keyboards have modifier keys....*

    2) Hold down the Ctrl key and then click the left mouse button.

    3) Press the Delete key.

g. Delete the last paragraph by completing the following steps:

    1) Position the I-beam pointer anywhere in the last paragraph (the paragraph that reads *Keyboards have different physical appearances.*).

    2) Triple-click the left mouse button.

    3) Press the Delete key.

4. Save the document with the same name (Word C1, Ex 06) by clicking the Save button on the Standard toolbar or clicking <u>F</u>ile and then <u>S</u>ave.

5. Print and then close Word C1, Ex 06.

Using the Undo and Redo Buttons

Undo

Redo

If you make a mistake and delete text that you did not intend to, or if you change your mind after deleting text and want to retrieve it, you can use the Undo or Redo buttons on the Standard toolbar. For example, if you key text and then click the Undo button, the text will be removed. Word removes text to the beginning of the document or up to the point where text had been previously deleted. You can undo text or commands. For example, if you add formatting such as bolding to text and then click the Undo button, the bolding is removed.

If you use the Undo button and then decide you do not want to reverse the original action, click the Redo button. For example, if you select and underline text, and then decide to remove underlining, click the Undo button. If you then decide you want the underlining back on, click the Redo button. Many Word actions can be undone or redone. Some actions, however, such as printing and saving cannot be undone or redone.

You cannot undo a save.

In addition to the Undo and Redo buttons on the Standard toolbar, you can use options from the <u>E</u>dit drop-down menu to undo and redo actions. The first option at the <u>E</u>dit drop-down menu will vary depending on the last action completed. For example, if you click the Numbering button on the Formatting toolbar, and then click <u>E</u>dit on the Menu bar, the first option displays as <u>U</u>ndo Number Default. If you decide you do not want the numbering option on, click the <u>U</u>ndo Number Default option at the <u>E</u>dit drop-down menu. You can also just click the Undo button on the Standard toolbar.

Word maintains actions in temporary memory. If you want to undo an action performed earlier, click the down-pointing triangle to the right of the Undo button. This causes a drop-down menu to display as shown in figure 1.16.

figure

1.16

Undo Drop-Down List

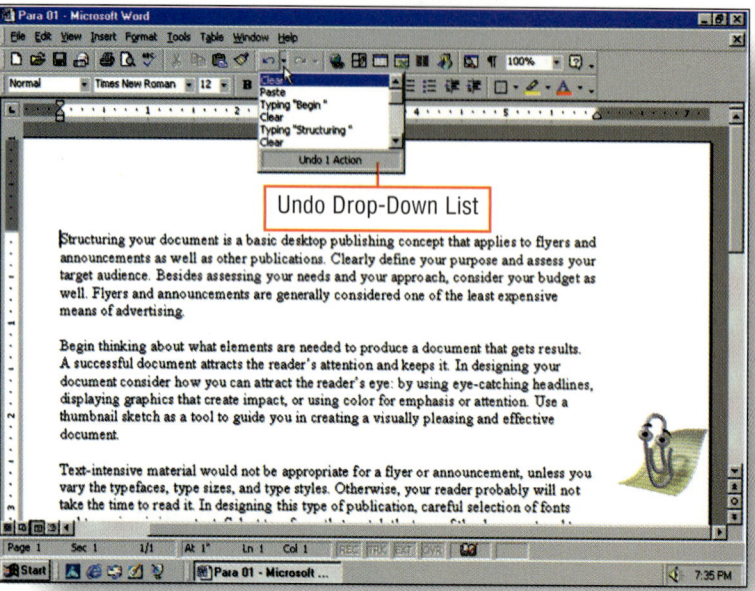

To make a selection from this drop-down menu, click the desired action. Any actions preceding a chosen action are also undone. You can do the same with the actions in the Redo drop-down list. To display the Redo drop-down list, click the down-pointing triangle to the right of the Redo button. To redo an action, click the desired action. Any actions preceding the chosen action are also redone. Multiple actions must be undone or redone in sequence.

Deleting and Restoring Text with the Undo Button

1. Open Word Document 01.
2. Save the document with Save As and name it Word C1, Ex 07.
3. Make the following changes to the document:
   a. Move the insertion point to the end of the document. Press the Backspace key until the last three words of the document (*stored on them.*) are deleted. Be sure to delete the space before *stored*.
   b. Undo the deletion by clicking the Undo button on the Standard toolbar.
   c. Redo the deletion by clicking the Redo button on the Standard toolbar.
   d. Key a period after the word *information* to end the sentence.
   e. Select the first sentence in the first paragraph (the sentence that begins *The most common storage...*) and then delete it.
   f. Select the second paragraph in the document and then delete it.
   g. Undo the two deletions by completing the following steps:
   1) Click the down-pointing triangle to the right of the Undo button.

2) Click the *second* Clear listed in the drop-down menu. (This will redisplay the first sentence in the first paragraph and the second paragraph. The sentence will be selected.)

h. With the first sentence of the first paragraph selected, press the Delete key.

4. Save the document with the same name (Word C1, Ex 07) by clicking the Save button on the Standard toolbar or clicking <u>F</u>ile and then <u>S</u>ave.

5. Print and then close Word C1, Ex 07.

chapter summary

➤ Open Microsoft Word by clicking the Start button on the Taskbar, pointing to <u>P</u>rograms, and then clicking *Microsoft Word*.

➤ The Title bar is the top line of the Word screen and displays the name of the current document. The Menu bar is the second line on the screen and contains a list of options that are used to customize a Word document.

➤ The Standard and Formatting toolbars display below the Menu bar and contain shortcuts for the most popular Word commands. Position the arrow pointer on a button on a toolbar and after one second a ScreenTip displays with the name of the button.

➤ The blinking vertical line is called the insertion point and indicates the position of the next character to be entered at the document screen. The underline symbol is the end-of-document marker and indicates the end of the document.

➤ The mouse pointer displays on the screen as an I-beam called the I-beam pointer or as an arrow pointing up and to the left called the mouse pointer.

➤ The scroll bars appear as gray shaded bars along the right and toward the bottom of the document screen and are used to view various sections of a document.

➤ The Status bar appears as a gray bar below the horizontal scroll bar toward the bottom of the Word screen. It displays such information as the current location of the insertion point and whether certain modes are active.

➤ The Office Assistant is an on-screen Help feature that anticipates the type of help you need, as well as suggesting Help topics related to the work you are doing. The Assistant will also point out ways to perform tasks more easily and provide visual examples and step-by-step instructions for specific tasks.

➤ Word automatically wraps text to the next line as you key information. Press the Enter key only to end a paragraph, create a blank line, or end a short line.

➤ Word contains a feature named AutoCorrect that automatically corrects certain words as they are keyed.

➤ When keying text, the Spell It feature automatically inserts a wavy red line below words not contained in the Spelling dictionary, and the automatic grammar checker inserts a green wavy line below a sentence containing a grammatical error.

➤ Document names can contain a maximum of 255 characters, including the drive letter and folder names, and may include spaces. The following characters cannot be used when naming a document: / \ < > * ? " \ : ; and |.

➤ Drop-down menus and dialog boxes can be removed from the editing window with the mouse or keyboard.

➤ When a document is saved on the disk using the Save or Save As options, the document remains in the document screen. To remove the document from the screen, click File and then Close or click the Close button located at the right side of the Menu bar.

➤ To print a document, open the document and then click the Print button on the Standard toolbar or click File, Print, and then OK.

➤ Be sure to save all needed documents before exiting Word and Windows.

➤ In order to save on or open documents from your data disk, the default folder should be changed. Change the default folder at the Open dialog box or the Save As dialog box or change it permanently at the Options dialog box with the File Locations tab selected.

➤ Open a document by displaying the Open dialog box and then double-clicking the desired document name.

➤ Click the New Blank Document button on the Standard toolbar to display a clear document screen.

➤ The display of toolbars can be turned on or off and toolbars can be moved to different locations on the screen.

➤ Word uses *adaptive* menus containing first-rank and second-rank options. Only the first-rank options are visible when the drop-down menu first displays. To display second-rank options, either click the down-pointing arrows at the bottom of the menu or pause on the menu for a few seconds. If you choose a second-rank option, it is promoted and becomes a first-rank option the next time the drop-down menu is displayed.

➤ The insertion point can be moved throughout the document without interfering with text by using the mouse, the keyboard, or the mouse combined with the keyboard.

➤ The insertion point can be moved by character, word, screen, or page, and from the first to the last character in a document.

➤ The horizontal/vertical scroll bars and the mouse can be used to scroll through a document. The scroll box indicates the location of the text in the document screen in relation to the remainder of the document.

➤ Click the Select Browse Object button located at the bottom of the vertical scroll bar to display options for browsing through a document.

➤ Switch to the Overtype mode if you want to key over something. When Overtype is on, the OVR mode button in the Status bar displays in black.

➤ Text can be deleted by character, word, line, several lines, or partial page using specific keys or by selecting text using the mouse or the keyboard.

➤ A specific amount of text can be selected using the mouse or the keyboard. That text can then be deleted or manipulated in other ways using Word functions.

➤ The selection bar can be used to select specific units of text such as a line. The selection bar is the space at the left side of the document screen between the left edge of the screen and the text.

➤ Use the Undo button on the Standard toolbar if you change your mind after keying, deleting, or formatting text and want to undo the deleting or formatting. Use the Redo button to redo something that had been undone with the Undo button.

commands review

Opening Word

1. Turn on the computer.
2. At the Windows 98 (or Windows 95) screen, position the arrow pointer on the Start button on the Taskbar (located at the bottom left side of the screen), and then click the left mouse button.
3. At the pop-up menu, point to Programs (you do not need to click the mouse button). This causes another menu to display to the right of the first pop-up menu.
4. Move the arrow pointer to *Microsoft Word* and then click the left mouse button.

Saving a Document

1. Click the Save button on the Standard toolbar or click File and then Save.
2. At the Save As dialog box, key the name of the document.
3. Click the Save button or press Enter.

Changing the Default Folder

1. Click the Open button on the Standard toolbar or click File and then Open.
2. At the Open dialog box, click the down-pointing triangle at the right side of the Look in text box.
3. From the drop-down list that displays, click *3¹₂ Floppy (A:)*.
4. Click the Cancel button that displays in the lower right corner of the dialog box.

Changing the Default Folder Permanently

1. Click Tools and then Options.
2. At the Options dialog box, click the File Locations tab.
3. Make sure *Documents* is selected in the File types list box and then click the Modify button.
4. At the Modify Location dialog box, change to the desired folder.
5. Click the OK button.

Closing a Document

1. Click the Close button on the Menu bar or click File and then Close.

Opening a Document

1. Click the Open button on the Standard toolbar or click File and then Open.
2. At the Open dialog box, double-click the document name.

Printing a Document

1. Open the document.
2. Click the Print button on the Standard toolbar.

       or

1. Open the document.
2. Click File and then Print.
3. At the Print dialog box, click OK.

Exiting Word

1. Be sure all needed documents have been saved.
2. Click the Close button on the Title bar or click File and then Exit.

Exiting Windows

1. Click the Start button at the left side of the Taskbar.
2. At the pop-up menu, click Shut Down.
3. At the Shut Down Windows dialog box, make sure *Shut down* is selected, and then click OK.

Scrolling Review

Changing the Display Using the Mouse and the Vertical Scroll Bar

Up one line	Click the up scroll triangle on the vertical scroll bar
Up several lines	Position the arrow pointer as above and then hold down left mouse button
Down one line	Click the down scroll triangle on the vertical scroll bar
Down several lines	Position the arrow pointer as above and then hold down left mouse button
Up one screen	Click with arrow pointer above the scroll box on the scroll bar
Down one screen	Click with arrow pointer below the scroll box on the scroll bar
To beginning of document	Position the arrow pointer on the scroll box, hold down left mouse button, drag the scroll box to the beginning of the scroll bar, and then release the mouse button
To end of document	Position the arrow pointer on the scroll box, hold down left mouse button, drag the scroll box to the end of the scroll bar, and then release the mouse button

Insertion Point Movement Review

Moving the Insertion Point Using the Mouse

To move to a specific location	Move arrow pointer to desired location and then click left mouse button
To move to the next page	Click the Next Page button
To move to the previous page	Click the Previous Page button
To move to a specific page	1. Click Edit and then Go To or double-click the page number at the left side of the Status bar. 2. Key the page number. 3. Click the Go To button or press Enter. 4. Click the Close button.

Moving the Insertion Point Using the Keyboard

To move insertion point	*Press*
One character left	left arrow
One character right	right arrow
One line up	up arrow
One line down	down arrow
One word to the left	Ctrl + left arrow
One word to the right	Ctrl + right arrow
To end of line	End

To beginning of a line	Home
To beginning of current paragraph	Ctrl + up arrow
To beginning of previous paragraph	Ctrl + up arrow twice
To beginning of next paragraph	Ctrl + down arrow
Up one screen	Page Up
Down one screen	Page Down
To top of previous page	Ctrl + Page Up
To top of next page	Ctrl + Page Down
To beginning of document	Ctrl + Home
To end of document	Ctrl + End
To last location when document was closed	Shift + F5

Deletion Commands Review

To delete	*Press*
Character right of insertion point	Delete key
Character left of insertion point	Backspace key
Word before insertion point	Ctrl + Backspace
Word after insertion point	Ctrl + Delete

Selecting Text Review

Selecting Text Using the Mouse

To select text	Position I-beam pointer at the beginning of text to be selected, hold down left mouse button, drag the I-beam pointer to the end of text to be selected, and then release the mouse button

To select	*Complete these steps*
A word	Double-click the word
A line of text	Click in the selection bar to the left of line
Multiple lines of text	Drag in the selection bar to left of lines
A sentence	Hold down Ctrl key and then click anywhere in the sentence
A paragraph	Double-click in the selection bar next to paragraph or triple-click anywhere in the paragraph
Multiple paragraphs	Drag in the selection bar
An entire document	Triple-click in the selection bar
To cancel a selection	Click anywhere outside the selected text in the document screen

Selecting Text Using the Keyboard

To select	*Press*
One character to right	Shift + right arrow
One character to left	Shift + left arrow
To end of word	Ctrl + Shift + right arrow
To beginning of word	Ctrl + Shift + left arrow

To end of line	Shift + End
To beginning of line	Shift + Home
One line up	Shift + up arrow
One line down	Shift + down arrow
To beginning of paragraph	Ctrl + Shift + up arrow
To end of paragraph	Ctrl + Shift + down arrow
One screen up	Shift + Page Up
One screen down	Shift + Page Down
To end of document	Ctrl + Shift + End
To beginning of document	Ctrl + Shift + Home
Entire document	Ctrl + A or click Edit, Select All
To cancel a selection	Press any arrow key

Other Commands Review

Turn on Overtype	Double-click the OVR mode button on the Status bar, or press the Insert key
Undo	Click Undo button on the Standard toolbar
Redo	Click Redo button on the Standard toolbar
Save As	1. Click File and then Save As.
	2. At the Save As dialog box, key the document name.
	3. Click the Save button or press Enter.

thinking offline

Matching: In the space provided at the left, indicate the correct letter or letters that match each description.

- **A** ButtonTip
- **B** Fix It
- **C** Formatting toolbar
- **D** Horizontal scroll bar
- **E** Menu bar
- **F** Office Assistant
- **G** Save As
- **H** Scrolling
- **I** Spell It
- **J** Standard toolbar
- **K** Status bar
- **L** Title bar
- **M** ScreenTip
- **N** Vertical scroll bar

_____ 1. This toolbar contains buttons for working with documents such as the Open button and the Save button.

_____ 2. This toolbar contains buttons for formatting a document such as bold, italics, and underline.

_____ 3. This displays below the horizontal scroll bar and displays the current location of the insertion point.

_____ 4. This displays along the right side of the screen and is used to view various sections of a document.

_____ 5. This displays in the document screen and is an on-screen Help feature that anticipates the type of help you need as well as suggesting Help topics related to the work you are doing.

_____ 6. Doing this in a document changes the text displayed but does not move the insertion point.

_____ 7. This displays at the top of the Word screen and displays the name of the currently open document.

_____ 8. This appears after approximately one second when the mouse pointer is positioned on a button on a toolbar.

_____ 9. Use this option to save a previously created document with a new name.

_____ 10. This feature inserts a wavy red line below words not contained in the Spelling dictionary.

Completion: In the space provided at the right, indicate the correct term, command, or number.

1. This feature automatically corrects certain words as they are being keyed. _____

2. This displays in the document screen as a blinking vertical line. _____

3. This is the second line of the Word screen and contains a list of options that are used to customize a Word document. _____

4. At a blank screen, click this button on the Standard toolbar to open a new blank document. _____

5. Use this keyboard command to move the insertion point to the beginning of the previous page. _____

6. When Overtype is on, this mode button displays in black on the Status bar. _____

7. Press this key on the keyboard to delete the character left of the insertion point. _____

8. Complete these steps using the mouse to select one word. _____

9. Use this keyboard command to select text to the end of the line. _____

10. If you click this button on the Standard toolbar, text you just keyed will be removed. _____

11. Use this keyboard command to move the insertion point to the end of the document. _____

12. Use this keyboard command to select text to the end of the paragraph. _____

13. To select various amounts of text using the mouse, you can click in this bar. _____

working hands-on

Assessment 1

1. Open Windows and then Word.
2. At the clear document screen, change the default folder to the drive where your disk is located. (Check with your instructor to determine if this step is necessary.)
3. At the clear document screen, key the text in figure 1.17. (Correct any errors highlighted by Spell It as they occur and remember to space once after end-of-sentence punctuation.)
4. Save the document in Chapter 01C folder on your disk and name it Word C1, SA 01.
5. Print and then close Word C1, SA 01.

figure

1.17   *Assessment 1*

The primary storage medium used with most personal computers today is the hard drive. Typically, a person uses a hard drive to store the computer's operating system, application programs, fonts, and data files created with the application programs.

Hard drives have large storage capacities, up to several gigabytes. However large or small a hard drive is, at least 10 to 15 percent of its total capacity should be left free. If the hard drive becomes too full, the computer user is likely to experience various difficulties, such as printing problems caused by an inability to spool, or write temporarily to the drive, files that are to be printed.

Assessment 2

1. Open Word Document 03.
2. Save the document with Save As and name it Word C1, SA 02.
3. Make the following changes to the document:
   a. Delete the word *rare* in the first sentence of the first paragraph.
   b. Delete *%* in the second sentence of the second paragraph and then key *percent*.
   c. Delete the word *actually* in the last sentence of the second paragraph.
   d. Delete the word *general* in the last sentence of the second paragraph.
   e. Change the word *primary* in the first sentence of the third paragraph to *main*.

f. Delete the words *in this phase of the expansion* in the second sentence of the third paragraph.
g. Join the first and second paragraphs.
4. Save the document again with the same name (Word C1, SA 02).
5. Print and then close Word C1, SA 02.

Assessment 3

1. Open Word Document 04.
2. Save the document with Save As and name it Word C1, SA 03.
3. Make the following changes to the document:
   a. Delete the words *the ongoing* in the first sentence of the first paragraph.
   b. Delete the last sentence in the first paragraph.
   c. Delete the words *(last year's market catalyst)* in the second sentence of the second paragraph.
   d. Change the word *Moreover* in the first sentence of the third paragraph to *Additionally*.
   e. Insert the word *rapid* after *earlier* in the first sentence of the third paragraph.
   f. Change the word *a* in the second sentence of the third paragraph to *an important*.
   g. Change the word *Plus* in the last sentence of the third paragraph to *Second*.
4. Save the document again with the same name (Word C1, SA 03).
5. Print and then close Word C1, SA 03.

Assessment 4

1. At a clear document screen (click the New Blank Document button), compose a paragraph explaining when you would use the Save As command when saving a document rather than the Save command, and the advantages to Save As.
2. Save the document and name it Word C1, SA 04.
3. Print and then close Word C1, SA 04.

 **Chapter 02C**

Formatting Text and Using Help

PERFORMANCE OBJECTIVES

Upon successful completion of chapter 2, you will be able to:

- Apply bold, italic, and underlining formatting.
- Change the font.
- Adjust character spacing.
- Animate text.
- Turn on/off the display of nonprinting characters.
- Change the alignment of text in paragraphs.
- Change spacing before and after paragraphs.
- Automate formatting with Format Painter.
- Indent text in paragraphs.
- Create numbered and bulleted paragraphs.
- Insert special symbols in a document.
- Change line spacing in a document.
- Apply borders and shading to text.
- Repeat the last action.
- Use the Help feature.

As you work with Word, you will learn a number of commands and procedures that affect how the document appears when printed. The appearance of a document in the document screen and how it looks when printed is called the *format*. Formatting can include such elements as bolding, italicizing, and underlining characters; and inserting special symbols. Text in paragraphs can also be formatted, such as changing text alignment, indenting text, applying formatting with Format Painter, inserting numbers and bullets, changing line spacing, and applying borders and shading.

Microsoft Word contains an on-screen reference manual containing information on features and commands for each program within the suite. In this chapter, you will learn to use the Help feature to display information about Word.

Formatting Characters

Formatting a document can include adding enhancements to characters such as bolding, underlining, and italicizing. A variety of formatting options is displayed in figure 2.1.

Character Formatting

Formatting	Method
Uppercase letters	Press the Caps Lock key
Bold	Press Ctrl + B or click the Bold button on the Formatting toolbar
Underline	Press Ctrl + U or click the Underline button on the Formatting toolbar
Italics	Press Ctrl + I or click the Italic button on the Formatting toolbar

Bold

Underline

Italic

More than one type of character formatting can be applied to the same text. For example, you can both bold and underline a section of text as has been done to the title in figure 2.2. If formatting is applied to text, it can be removed by selecting the text and then clicking the appropriate button on the Formatting toolbar or pressing the shortcut command. For example, to remove underlining from text, you would select the text to which you want the underlining removed, and then click the Underline button on the Formatting toolbar or press Ctrl + U.

All character formatting can be removed from selected text with the shortcut command, Ctrl + spacebar. This removes *all* character formatting. For example, if bold and italics are applied to text, selecting the text and then pressing Ctrl + spacebar will remove both bold and italics.

(Before completing computer exercises, delete the Chapter 01C *folder on your disk. Next, copy the* Chapter 02C *folder from the CD that accompanies this textbook to your disk and then make* Chapter 02C *the active folder.)*

exercise 1

Applying Character Formatting to Text as It Is Keyed

1. At a clear document screen, key the document shown in figure 2.2 with the following specifications:
   a. While keying the document, bold the text shown bolded in the figure by completing the following steps:
      1) Click the Bold button on the Formatting toolbar or press Ctrl + B. (This turns on bold.)
      2) Key the text.
      3) Click the Bold button on the Formatting toolbar or press Ctrl + B. (This turns off bold.)
   b. While keying the document, underline the text shown underlined in the figure by completing the following steps:

        1) Click the Underline button on the Formatting toolbar or press Ctrl + U.
        2) Key the text.
        3) Click the Underline button on the Formatting toolbar or press Ctrl + U.
   c. While keying the document, italicize the text shown in italics in the figure by completing the followings steps:
        1) Click the Italic button on the Formatting toolbar or press Ctrl + I.
        2) Key the text.
        3) Click the Italic button on the Formatting toolbar or press Ctrl + I.
2. Save the document and name it Word C2, Ex 01a.
3. Print Word C2, Ex 01a.
4. With the document still open, make the following changes:
   a. Remove underlining from the title by completing the following steps:
        1) Select the title *COMPUTER MOTHERBOARD*.
        2) Click the Underline button on the Formatting toolbar.
   b. Add underlining to the bolded word *Buses* by completing the following steps:
        1) Select the word *Buses* (do not include the colon).
        2) Click the Underline button on the Formatting toolbar.
   c. Select and then underline each of the other bolded words that begin the remaining paragraphs (*System Clock, Microprocessor, Read-only Memory, Expansion Slots*).
5. Save the document with Save As and name it Word C2, Ex 01b.
6. Print and then close Word C2, Ex 01b.

Exercise 1

COMPUTER MOTHERBOARD

The main circuit board in a computer is called the *motherboard*. The motherboard is a thin sheet of fiberglass or other material with electrical pathways, called *traces*, etched onto it. These traces connect components that are soldered to the motherboard or attached to it by various connectors. Many components are found on the motherboard, including the following:

Buses: The electronic connections that allow communication between components in the computer are referred to as buses.

System Clock: A system clock synchronizes the computer's activities.

Microprocessor: The microprocessor, also called the *processor*, processes data and controls the functions of the computer.

Read-only Memory: The read-only memory (ROM) chip contains the computer's permanent memory in which various instructions are stored.

Expansion Slots: The expansion slots are used to add various capabilities to a computer such as the ability to access files over a network or digitize sound or video.

Changing Fonts

The default font used by Word is 10-point Times New Roman (or 12-point Times New Roman, if you followed the steps presented in chapter 1 on changing the default font). You may want to change this default to some other font for such reasons as changing the mood of a document, enhancing the visual appeal, and increasing the readability of the text. A font consists of three elements—typeface, type size, and type style.

Choosing a Typeface

A *typeface* is a set of characters with a common design and shape. (Word refers to typeface as *font*.) Typefaces may be decorative or plain and are either *monospaced* or *proportional*. A monospaced typeface allots the same amount of horizontal space for each character. Courier is an example of a monospaced typeface. Proportional typefaces allot a varying amount of space for each character. The space allotted is based on the width of the character. For example, the lowercase *i* will take up less space than the uppercase *M*.

Use a serif typeface for text-intensive documents

Proportional typefaces are divided into two main categories: *serif* and *sans serif*. A serif is a small line at the end of a character stroke. Traditionally, a serif typeface is used with documents that are text intensive (documents that are mainly text) because the serifs help move the reader's eyes across the page. A sans serif typeface does not have serifs (*sans* is French for *without*). Sans serif typefaces are often used for headlines and advertisements that are not text intensive. Figure 2.3 shows examples of serif and sans serif typefaces.

As mentioned earlier in chapter 1, space once after end-of-sentence punctuation and after a colon when text is set in a proportional typeface. Proportional typefaces are set closer together and extra white space at the end of a sentence or after a colon is not needed.

figure

2.3

Serif and Sans Serif Typefaces

Serif Typefaces	Sans Serif Typefaces
Bookman Old Style	Arial
Garamond	Eurostile
Goudy Old Style	**Haettenschweiler**
Modern No. 20	**Impact**
Rockwell	Lucinda Sans
Times New Roman	Tahoma

Choosing a Type Size

Type size is divided into two categories: *pitch* and *point size*. Pitch is a measurement used for monospaced typefaces; it reflects the number of characters that can be printed in 1 horizontal inch. (For some printers, the pitch is referred to as *cpi*, or *characters per inch*. For example, the font Courier 10 cpi is the same as 10-pitch Courier.)

Proportional typefaces can be set in different sizes. The size of proportional type is measured vertically in units called *points*. A point is approximately 1/72 of an inch. The higher the point size, the larger the characters. Examples of different point sizes in the Arial typeface are shown in figure 2.4.

Different Point Sizes in Arial

8-point Arial
12-point Arial
18-point Arial
24-point Arial

Choosing a Type Style

Within a typeface, characters may have a varying style. There are four main categories of type styles: normal (for some typefaces, this may be referred to as *light*, *black*, *regular*, or *roman*), bold, italic, and bold italic. Figure 2.5 illustrates the four main type styles in 12 points.

Four Main Type Styles

Tahoma regular   Times New Roman regular
Tahoma bold   **Times New Roman Bold**
Tahoma italic   *Times New Roman Italic*
Tahoma bold italic   ***Times New Roman bold italic***

The term *font* describes a particular typeface in a specific style and size. Some examples of fonts include 10-pitch Courier, 10-point Arial, 12-point Tahoma bold, and 12-point Times New Roman bold italic.

Using the Font Dialog Box

The fonts available display in the Font list box at the Font dialog box. To display the Font dialog box, shown in figure 2.6, click Format and then Font. You can also display the Font dialog box with a shortcut menu. To do this, position the I-beam pointer anywhere within the document screen, click the *right* mouse button, and then click the left mouse button on Font.

figure

2.6

Font Dialog Box

Choose a typeface in this list box. Use the scroll bar at the right side of the box to view various typefaces available.

Choose a type style in this list box. The options in the box may vary depending on the typeface selected.

Choose a type size in this list box; or, select the current measurement in the top box and then key the desired measurement.

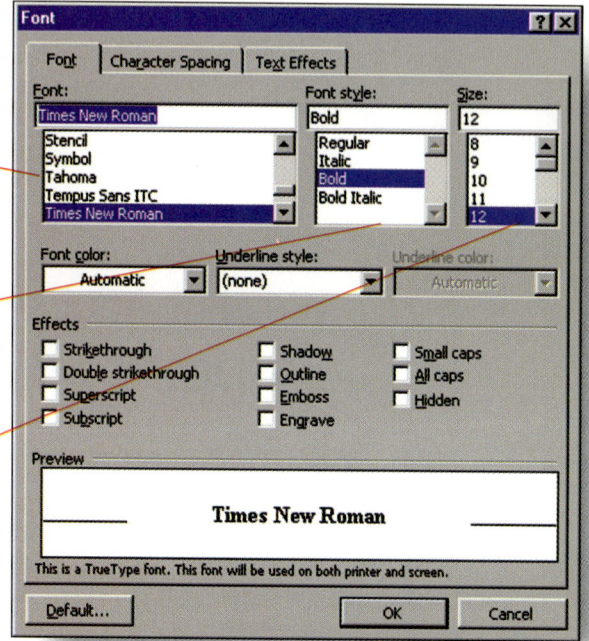

The Font list box at the Font dialog box displays the typefaces (fonts) available with your printer. Figure 2.6 shows the typefaces available with a laser printer (the fonts displayed with your printer may vary from those shown). To select a typeface, select the desired typeface (font), and then click OK or press Enter. The Preview box at the bottom of the dialog box displays the appearance of the selected font.

The Size list box at the Font dialog box displays a variety of common type sizes. Decrease point size to make text smaller or increase point size to make text larger. To select a point size with the mouse, click the desired point size. To view more point sizes, click the down-pointing triangle in the Size scroll bar. You can also key a specific point size. To do this, select the number in the Size text box, and then key the desired point size.

The Font style list box displays the styles available with the selected typeface. As you select different typefaces at the Font dialog box, the list of styles changes in the Font style list box. Choose from a variety of type styles such as regular, bold, italic, or bold and italic.

Make adjustments to character spacing such as expanding or condensing the space between characters with options at the Font dialog box with the Character Spacing tab selected.

Hint

exercise 2

Changing the Font at the Font Dialog Box

1. Open Word Document 01.
2. Save the document with Save As and name it Word C2, Ex 02.
3. Change the typeface to 13-point Bookman Old Style italic by completing the following steps:
   a. Select the entire document. (*Hint: To select the entire document press Ctrl + A or click Edit and then Select All.*)
   b. Display the Font dialog box by clicking Format and then Font.
   c. At the Font dialog box, click the up-pointing triangle at the right side of the Font list box until *Bookman Old Style* displays, and then click *Bookman Old Style*. (If Bookman Old Style is not available, choose another serif typeface such as Galliard BT or Garamond.)

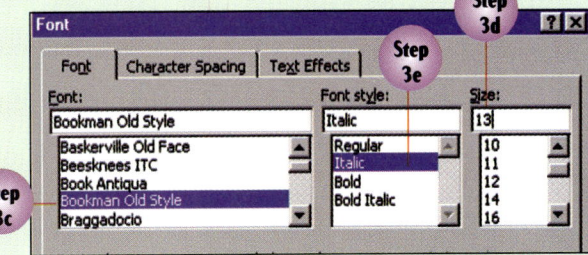

   d. Change the Size option to 13 by selecting the *12* displayed in the Size list box and then keying **13**.
   e. Click *Italic* in the Font style list box.
   f. Click OK or press Enter.
4. At the document screen, deselect the text by clicking anywhere in the document screen outside the selected text.
5. Save the document again with the same name (Word C2, Ex 02).
6. Print and then close Word C2, Ex 02.

In addition to using the Font dialog box to select a typeface, you can use the Font button on the Formatting toolbar. The Font button displays a font name followed by a down-pointing triangle. For example, if your default typeface is Times New Roman, that name displays in the Font button. If you click the down-pointing triangle at the right side of the Font button, a drop-down list displays. Click the desired typeface at this drop-down list.

Font

Font size can be changed with options from the Font Size button on the Formatting toolbar. The Font Size button contains the current point size followed by a down-pointing triangle. To change the type size with the Font Size button, click the down-pointing triangle at the right side of the Font Size button, and then click the desired size at the drop-down list.

Font Size

The Formatting toolbar also contains a Font Color button to change the color of selected text. Click the Font Color button and the selected text changes to the color that displays on the button (below the A). To choose a different color, click the down-pointing triangle at the right side of the button and then click the desired color at the palette of color choices.

Font Color

Changing the Font, Size, and Color Using Buttons on the Formatting Toolbar

1. Open Word Document 02.
2. Save the document with Save As and name it Word C2, Ex 03.
3. Change the typeface to 14-point Arial and the color to Indigo using buttons on the Formatting toolbar by completing the following steps:
   a. Select the entire document. (*Hint: To select the entire document press Ctrl + A or click Edit and then Select All.*)
   b. Click the down-pointing triangle at the right side of the Font button on the Formatting toolbar and then click *Arial* at the drop-down list. (You may need to scroll up the list to display *Arial*.)

   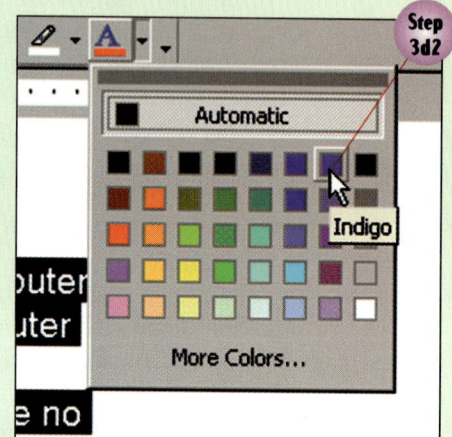

   c. Click the down-pointing triangle at the right side of the Font Size button on the Formatting toolbar and then click *14* at the drop-down list.
   d. Change the font color to Indigo by completing the following steps:
      1) Click the down-pointing triangle at the right side of the Font Color button (the last button on the Formatting toolbar).
      2) At the palette of color choices that displays, click *Indigo* (second color choice from the *right* in the top row).
4. Deselect the text to see what it looks like set in 14-point Arial and in Indigo.
5. Save the document again with the same name (Word C2, Ex 03).
6. Print and then close Word C2, Ex 03.

The Font dialog box contains a variety of underlining options. Click the down-pointing triangle at the right side of the Underline style option box and a drop-down palette of underlining styles displays containing options such as a double line, thick line, dashed line, and so on.

Click the down-pointing triangle at the right side of the Font color text box and a palette of choices displays. Position the arrow pointer on a color and after one second a yellow box displays with the color name. Use this option to change the color of selected text.

Changing the Font and Text Color and Underlining Text

1. Open Word Notice 01.
2. Save the document with Save As and name it Word C2, Ex 04.

3. Change the font and text color by completing the following steps:
   a. Select the entire document.
   b. Display the Font dialog box.
   c. Change the font to 14-point Goudy Old Style bold. (If Goudy Old Style is not available, consider using another serif typeface such as Bookman Old Style or Century Schoolbook.)
   d. With the Font dialog box still displayed, change the text color to Blue by clicking the down-pointing triangle at the right side of the Font color text box, and then clicking *Blue* (sixth color option from the left in the second row).
   e. Click OK or press Enter.
   f. Deselect the text.

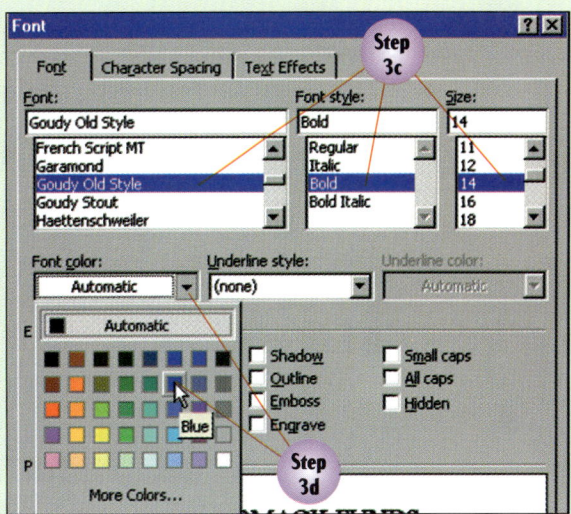

4. Double underline the text *Annual Stockholders' Meeting* by completing the following steps:
   a. Select *Annual Stockholders' Meeting*.
   b. Display the Font dialog box.
   c. Click the down-pointing triangle at the right side of the Underline style option box and then click the double-line option (see figure) at the drop-down list.
   d. Click OK to close the dialog box.

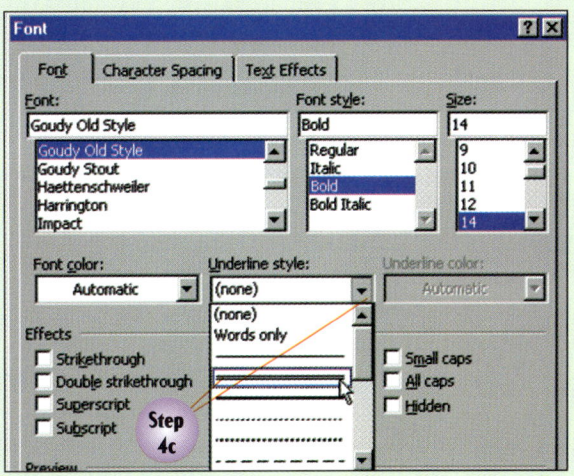

5. Apply a thick underline to the text *6:30 p.m.* by completing the following steps:
   a. Select *6:30 p.m.*
   b. Display the Font dialog box.
   c. Click the down-pointing triangle at the right side of the Underline style option box and then click the thick line option (see figure) that displays below the double-line option.
   d. Click OK to close the dialog box.
   e. Deselect the text
6. Save the document again with the same name (Word C2, Ex 04).
7. Print and then close Word C2, Ex 04.

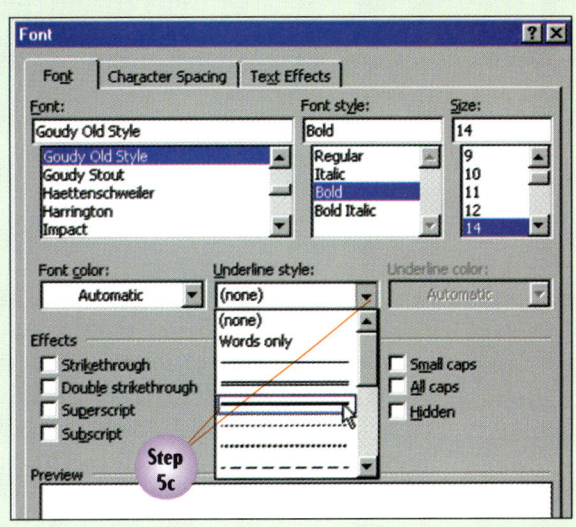

The Effects section of the Font dialog box contains a variety of options that can be used to create different character styles. For example, you can strikethrough text (which has a practical application for some legal documents in which deleted text must be retained in the document), or create superscript and subscript text. With the Hidden option from the Font dialog box, you can include such items as comments, personal messages, or questions in a document. These items can be displayed, printed, or hidden. The Small caps option lets you print small capital letters. This works for some printers, but not all. Additional effects include Double strikethrough, Shadow, Outline, Emboss, Engrave, and All caps.

exercise 5

Changing Text to Small Caps

1. Open Word Notice 01.
2. Save the document with Save As and name it Word C2, Ex 05.
3. Select the entire document and then make the following changes:
   a. Display the Font dialog box and change the font to 14-point Modern No. 20 bold. (Do not close the dialog box.) (If Modern No. 20 is not available, consider using another decorative serif typeface such as Dauphin or BernhardMod BT.)
   b. With the Font dialog box still displayed, change the font color to violet (see the figure).
   c. With the Font dialog box still displayed, click Small caps in the Effects section.
   d. Click OK or press Enter to close the Font dialog box.
   e. Deselect the text.
4. Save the document again with the same name (Word C2, Ex 05).
5. Print and then close Word C2, Ex 05.

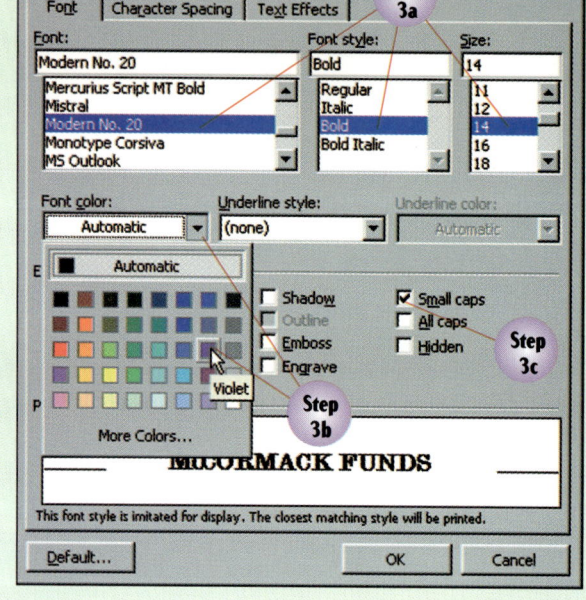

Superscript text is raised slightly above the text line and subscripted text is lowered slightly below the text line. Use the superscript effect for some mathematical equations such as four to the third power (written as 4^3) and use the subscript effect to create some chemical formulas such as H_2O. Create superscript text with the Superscript effect and subscript with the Subscript effect at the Font dialog box. Superscript text can also be created with the shortcut command Ctrl + Shift + =, and subscript text can be created with the shortcut command Ctrl + =.

Applying Superscript Effect to Text and Changing the Font

1. At a clear document screen, key the text shown in figure 2.7 with the following specifications:
   a. Create the first superscript numbers in the document by completing the following steps:
      1) Key text to the point where the superscript number is to appear.
      2) Display the Font dialog box.
      3) At the Font dialog box, click the Superscript check box located in the Effects section.
      4) Click OK to close the Font dialog box.
      5) Key the superscript number.
      6) Turn off Superscript by displaying the Font dialog box, clicking the Superscript check box (this removes the check mark), and then clicking OK to close the dialog box.
   b. Create the second superscript number in the document by completing the following steps:
      1) Key text to the point where the superscript number is to appear.
      2) Press Ctrl + Shift + =.
      3) Key the superscript number.
      4) Press Ctrl + Shift + =.
   c. Finish keying the remainder of the document using either the method described in step a or the one in step b to create the remaining superscript text.
   d. Select the entire document and then change the font to 12-point Bookman Old Style (or a similar serif typeface such as Century Schoolbook or Garamond).
2. Save the document and name it Word C2, Ex 06.
3. Print and then close Word C2, Ex 06.

Exercise 6

The Chinese abacus consisted of pebbles strung on rods inside a frame. The columns represented decimal places (ones place, tens place, hundreds place, and so on). Pebbles in the upper part of an abacus correspond to 5×10^0, or 5, for the first column; 5×10^1, or 50, for the second column; 5×10^2, or 500, for the third column; and so on. Pebbles in the lower part correspond to 1×10^0, or 1, for the first column; 1×10^1, or 10, for the second column; 1×10^2, or 100, for the third column; and so on.

Adjusting Character Spacing

Each typeface is designed with a specific amount of space between characters. This character spacing can be changed with options at the Font dialog box with the Character Spacing tab selected as shown in figure 2.8. To display this dialog box, click Format and then Font. At the Font dialog box, click the Character Spacing tab.

Font Dialog Box with Character Spacing Tab Selected

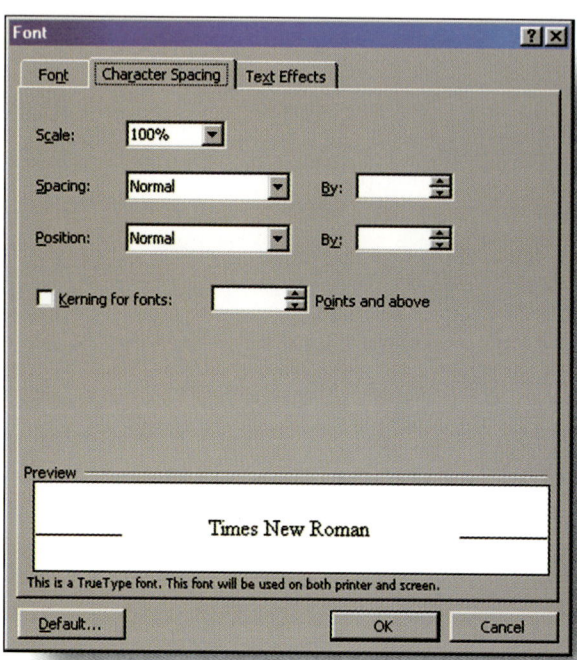

Choose the Scale option to stretch or compress text horizontally as a percentage of the current size. You can choose a percentage from 1 to 600. Expand or condense the spacing between characters with the Position option. Choose either the *Expanded* or *Condensed* option and then enter the desired percentage amount in the By text box. Raise or lower selected text in relation to the baseline with the Spacing option. Choose either the *Raised* or *Lowered* option and then enter the percentage amount in the By text box.

Kerning is a term that refers to the adjustment of spacing between certain character combinations. Kerning provides text with a more evenly spaced look and works only with TrueType or Adobe Type manager fonts. Turn on automatic kerning by inserting a check mark in the Kerning for fonts check box. Specify the beginning point size that you want kerned in the Points and above text box.

Animating Text

Animation effects can be added to text at the Font dialog box with the Text Effects tab selected. To display this dialog box, shown in figure 2.9, click Format and then Font. At the Font dialog box click the Text Effects tab.

figure

2.9

Font Dialog Box with Text Effects Tab Selected

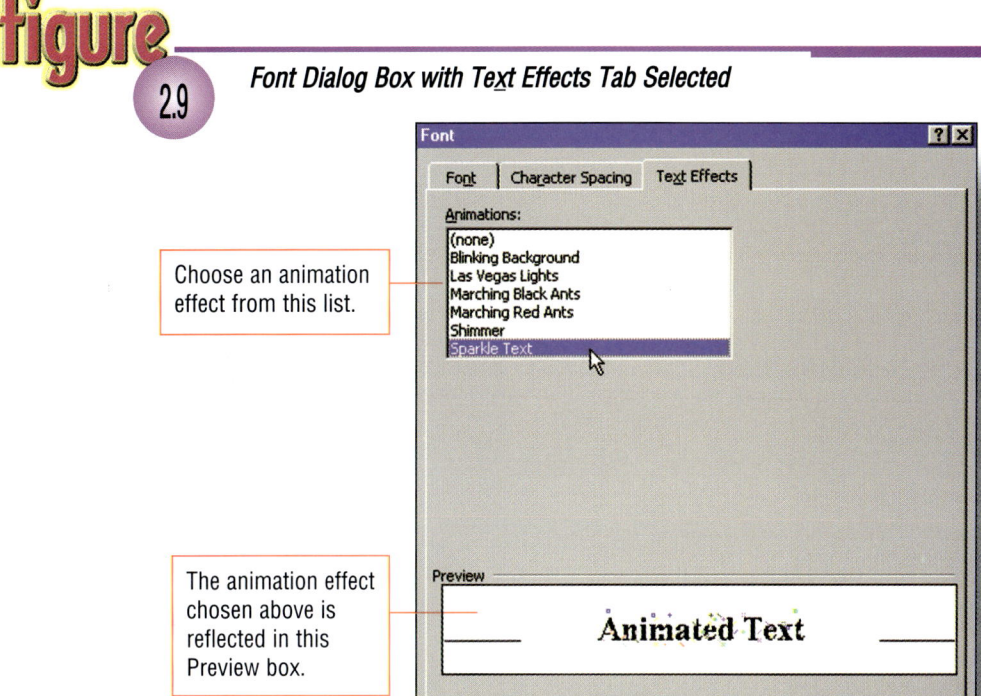

Choose an animation effect from this list.

The animation effect chosen above is reflected in this Preview box.

Animation effects can be added to text, such as a blinking background, a shimmer or sparkle. To add an animation effect, select the text, display the Font dialog box with the Text Effects tab selected, click the desired effect, and then close the Font dialog box. Animation effects added to text display in the screen but do not print.

Apply animation text effects to documents that will be viewed on screen.

exercise 7

Adjusting Character Spacing and Scaling, Turning on Kerning, and Animating Text

1. Open Word Document 02.
2. Save the document with Save As and name it Word C2, Ex 07.
3. Adjust character spacing and turn on kerning by completing the following steps:
   a. Select the entire document.
   b. Click Format and then Font.

c. At the Font dialog box, click the Character Spacing tab.

d. At the Font dialog box with the Character Spacing tab selected, click the down-pointing triangle at the right side of the <u>S</u>pacing option, and then click *Expanded* at the drop-down list. (This inserts *1 pt* in the <u>B</u>y text box.)

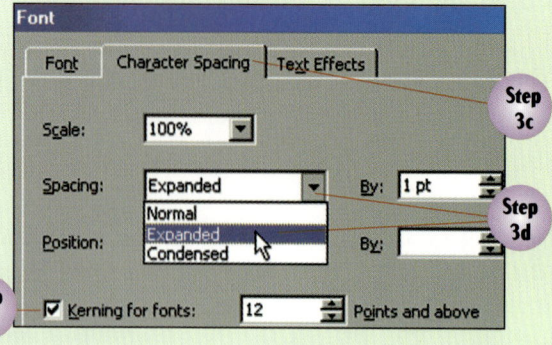

e. Click in the <u>K</u>erning for fonts check box. (This inserts a check mark in the check box and also inserts *12* in the P<u>o</u>ints and above text box.)

f. Click OK to close the dialog box.

g. Deselect the text.

4. Save the document again with the same name (Word C2, Ex 07).

5. Print Word C2, Ex 07.

6. With Word C2, Ex 07 still open, compress text horizontally by completing the following steps:

a. Select the entire document.

b. Click F<u>o</u>rmat and then <u>F</u>ont.

c. At the Font dialog box, click the Character Spacing tab.

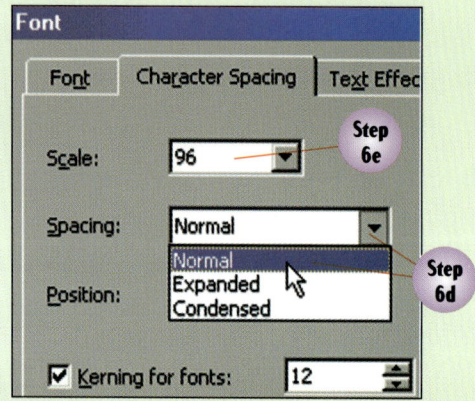

d. At the Font dialog box with the Character Spacing tab selected, click the down-pointing triangle at the right side of the <u>S</u>pacing option, and then click *Normal* at the drop-down list.

e. Select *100%* in the S<u>c</u>ale option text box and then key **96**. (This compresses text to 96 percent of the original horizontal spacing.)

f. Click OK to close the dialog box.

g. Deselect the text.

7. Add a blinking background to the title of the document by completing the following steps:

a. Select the title *COMPUTER KEYBOARDS*.

b. Click F<u>o</u>rmat and then <u>F</u>ont.

c. At the Font dialog box, click the Te<u>x</u>t Effects tab.

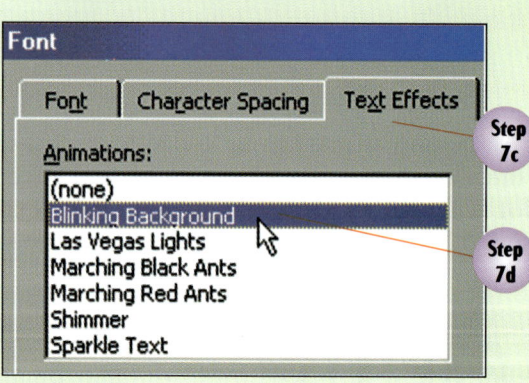

d. Click the *Blinking Background* option in the list box.

e. Click OK to close the dialog box.

8. Save the document again with the same name (Word C2, Ex 07).

9. Print and then close Word C2, Ex 07.

Formatting Paragraphs

Formatting such as changing alignment, indenting text, inserting bullets and numbers, and changing line spacing can be applied to paragraphs. In Word, a paragraph is any amount of text followed by a paragraph mark. A paragraph mark is inserted in a document each time the Enter key is pressed. By default, this paragraph mark is not visible. When changes are made to a paragraph, the formatting changes are inserted in the paragraph mark. If the paragraph mark is deleted, the formatting in the mark is eliminated and the text returns to the default.

Nonprinting characters do not print whether they are displayed or not.

Displaying Nonprinting Characters

When you begin formatting text by paragraph, displaying nonprinting characters can be useful. If you want to remove paragraph formatting from text, delete the paragraph mark. To display the paragraph mark and other nonprinting characters, click the Show/Hide ¶ button on the Standard toolbar. This causes nonprinting characters to display as shown in the document in figure 2.10. Click the Show/Hide ¶ button on the Standard toolbar to turn off the display of nonprinting characters.

¶

Show/Hide ¶

Document with Nonprinting Symbols Displayed

2.10

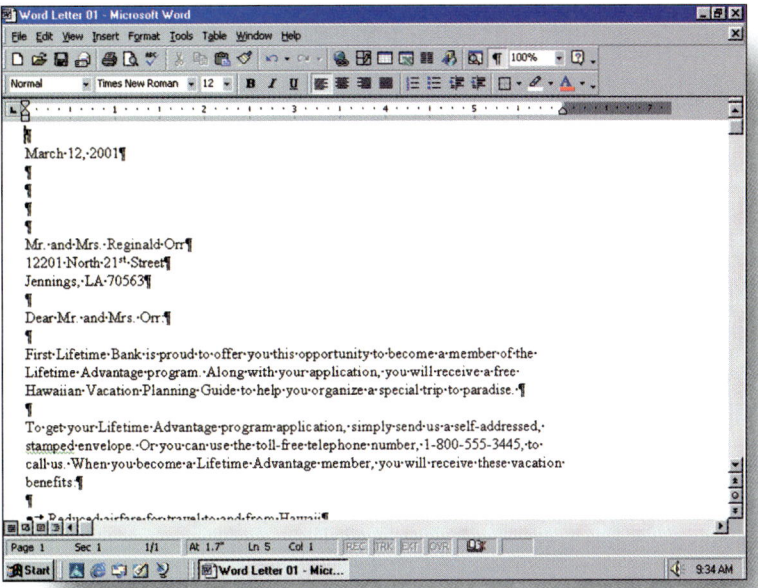

Changing the Alignment of Text in Paragraphs

By default, paragraphs in a Word document are aligned at the left margin and ragged at the right margin. This default alignment can be changed with buttons on the Formatting toolbar or with shortcut commands. Text in a paragraph can be aligned at the left margin, between margins, at the right margin, or at the left and right margins. Figure 2.11 illustrates the different paragraph alignments.

figure

2.11

Paragraph Alignments

Left Aligned Text

Center Aligned Text

Right Aligned Text

Fully Aligned Text

Use the buttons on the Formatting toolbar or the shortcut commands shown in figure 2.12 to change the alignment of text in paragraphs.

figure

2.12

Paragraph Alignment Buttons and Commands

To align text	Button	Shortcut command
at the left margin		Ctrl + L
between margins		Ctrl + E
at the right margin		Ctrl + R
at the left and right margins		Ctrl + J

You can change the alignment of text in paragraphs before you key the text or you can change the alignment of existing text. If you change the alignment before keying text, the alignment formatting is inserted in the paragraph mark. As you key text and press Enter, the paragraph formatting is continued. For example, if you press Ctrl + E to turn on center aligning, key text for the first paragraph, and then press Enter, the center alignment formatting is still active and the insertion point displays in the middle of the left and right margins.

Align Left

To return paragraph alignment to the default (left aligned), click the Align Left button on the Formatting toolbar or press Ctrl + L. You can also return all paragraph formatting to the default by pressing Ctrl + Q. This shortcut command returns all paragraph formatting (not just alignment) to the default settings.

To change the alignment of existing text in a paragraph, position the insertion point anywhere within the paragraph. The entire paragraph does not have to be selected. To change the alignment of several adjacent paragraphs in a document, select a portion of the first paragraph through a portion of the last paragraph. Only a portion of the first and last paragraphs needs to be selected.

Using AutoComplete

Microsoft Word and other Office applications include an AutoComplete feature that inserts an entire item when you key a few identifying characters. For example, key the letters *Mond* and *Monday* displays in a ScreenTip above the letters. Press the Enter key or press F3 and Monday is inserted in the document. When entering Thursday in exercise 8, key the first four characters (Thur) and then press the Enter key.

exercise 8

Changing Paragraph Alignment to Center

1. At a clear document screen, turn on the display of nonprinting characters by clicking the Show/Hide ¶ button on the Standard toolbar.
2. Key the text shown in figure 2.13.
3. Make the following changes to the document:
   a. Select the entire document.
   b. With the entire document still selected, change the font to 16-point Arial bold and the font color to Blue.
   c. With the entire document still selected, change the alignment of paragraphs to center by clicking the Center button on the Formatting toolbar.
   d. Deselect the text by clicking in the document screen outside the selected text.
4. Click the Show/Hide ¶ button on the Standard toolbar to turn off the display of nonprinting characters.
5. Save the document and name it Word C2, Ex 08.
6. Print and then close Word C2, Ex 08.

figure
2.13   *Exercise 8*

McCORMACK FUNDS

McCormack LifeLine Trust Annuities Seminar

Thursday, March 15

8:30 a.m. to 11:30 a.m.

Conference Room C

exercise 9

Changing Paragraph Alignment to Justified

1. Open Word Document 02.
2. Save the document with Save As and name it Word C2, Ex 09.
3. Change the alignment of the text in paragraphs to justified by selecting the entire document and then clicking the Justify button on the Formatting toolbar.
4. Save the document again with the same name (Word C2, Ex 09).
5. Print and then close Word C2, Ex 09.

Changing Alignment at the Paragraph Dialog Box

Paragraph alignment can also be changed at the Paragraph dialog box with the Indents and Spacing tab selected as shown in figure 2.14. To change the alignment of text in a paragraph, display the Paragraph dialog box by clicking Format and then Paragraph. At the Paragraph dialog box with the Indents and Spacing tab selected, click the down-pointing triangle in the Alignment option box. From the drop-down menu that displays, click an alignment option, and then click OK or press Enter.

2.14 *Paragraph Dialog Box with Indents and Spacing Tab Selected*

Change paragraph alignment by clicking this down-pointing triangle and then clicking the desired alignment at the drop-down list.

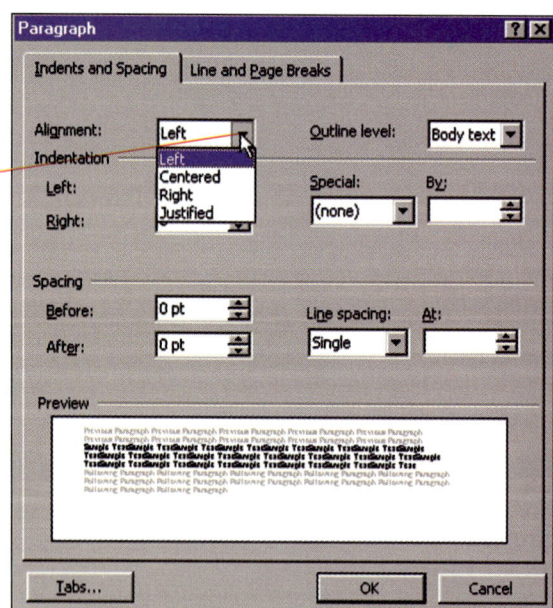

Changing Paragraph Alignment to Justified Using the Paragraph Dialog Box

1. Open Word Document 01.
2. Save the document with Save As and name it Word C2, Ex 10.
3. Change the alignment of text in paragraphs to justified using the Paragraph dialog box by completing the following steps:

   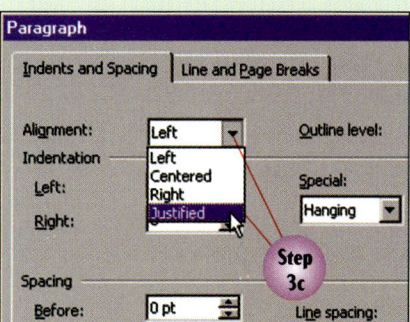

   a. Select the entire document.
   b. Click Format and then Paragraph.
   c. At the Paragraph dialog box, click the down-pointing triangle at the right of the Alignment option box, and then click *Justified*.
   d. Click OK or press Enter.
   e. Deselect the text.
4. Save the document again with the same name (Word C2, Ex 10).
5. Print and then close Word C2, Ex 10.

Using Shortcut Menus

Word provides shortcut menus that display commands related to the text or item of selected text or the positioning of the insertion point. Another method for displaying the Paragraph dialog box is to use a shortcut menu. To do this, position the insertion point in the text that you want formatted and then click the *right* button on the mouse. At the shortcut menu that displays, click Paragraph. This displays the Paragraph dialog box.

Some keyboards include a Shortcut Menu key (an image of a menu) located in the bottom row of the keyboard to the right of the space bar. When pressed, this key will display a shortcut menu with the Paragraph option.

Changing Paragraph Alignment to Right Using a Shortcut Menu

1. At a clear document screen, turn on the display of nonprinting characters.
2. Change the alignment of text to Right by completing the following steps:
   a. Position the I-beam pointer anywhere in the document screen and then click the *right* mouse button.
   b. At the shortcut menu that displays, click Paragraph.
   c. At the Paragraph dialog box, change the setting in the Alignment option box to *Right*.
   d. Click OK or press Enter.
3. Key the first line of text shown in figure 2.15 and then press Enter. Key the remaining

lines of text. (Each time you press Enter, the formatting from the previous paragraph is carried to the next paragraph.)

4. Select the entire document and then change the font to 14-point Arial bold.
5. Save the document and name it Word C2, Ex 11.
6. Turn off the display of nonprinting characters.
7. Print and then close Word C2, Ex 11.

figure

2.15   *Exercise 11*

McCORMACK FUNDS
5499 Fourth Street
New York, NY 10223
(212) 555-2277

Spacing before and after Paragraphs

Spacing before and after paragraphs in a document can be increased or decreased with options at the Paragraph dialog box. To increase or decrease spacing before a paragraph, display the Paragraph dialog box, select the current measurement in the Before text box (in the Spacing section), and then key a new measurement. Complete similar steps to increase or decrease spacing after paragraphs except choose the After option. You can also click the up- or down-pointing triangles to the right of the Before or After options to increase or decrease the measurement. Word uses a point measurement for spacing before and after paragraphs. Enter or display a higher point measurement to increase the spacing or enter or display a lower point measurement to decrease the spacing.

exercise 12

Spacing before Paragraphs

1. Open Word List.
2. Save the document with Save As and name it Word C2, Ex 12.
3. Make the following changes to the document:
   a. Select the entire document and then change the font to 12-point Bookman Old Style (or a similar serif typeface).
   b. With the document still selected, change the alignment of the paragraphs to Center.
   c. Select the title *LIFETIME REAL ESTATE ACCOUNT* and then change the font to 14-point Arial bold.

d. Add 6 points of spacing before certain paragraphs by completing the following steps:

1) Select from *Investment Practices of the Account* through *Expense Deductions*.
2) With the text selected, display the Paragraph dialog box.
3) At the Paragraph dialog box, click once on the up-pointing triangle at the right side of the Before option (in the Spacing section). (This changes the measurement in the text box to *6 pt.*)
4) Click OK to close the dialog box.

4. Save the document again with the same name (Word C2, Ex 12).
5. Print and then close Word C2, Ex 12.

Formatting with Format Painter

The Standard toolbar contains a button that can be used to copy character formatting to different locations in the document. This button is called the Format Painter and displays on the Standard toolbar as a paintbrush. To use the Format Painter button, position the insertion point on a character containing the desired character formatting, click the Format Painter button, and then select text to which you want the character formatting applied. When you click the Format Painter button, the mouse I-beam pointer displays with a paintbrush attached. If you want to apply character formatting a single time, click the Format Painter button once. If, however, you want to apply the character formatting in more than one location in the document, double-click the Format Painter button. If you have double-clicked the Format Painter button, turn off the feature by clicking the Format Painter button once.

Format Painter

exercise 13

Formatting Headings with the Format Painter

1. Open Word Report 01.
2. Save the document with Save As and name it Word C2, Ex 13.
3. Make the following changes to the document:
    a. Select the entire document and then change the font to 12-point Garamond (or a similar serif typeface such as Bookman Old Style or New Century Schoolbook).
    b. Select the title, *GRAPHICS SOFTWARE*, and then change the font to 14-point Arial bold.
    c. Use the Format Painter button to center the three headings in the report and

change the font for the headings to 14-point Arial bold by completing the
following steps:
1) Position the insertion point next to any character in the title *GRAPHICS
   SOFTWARE*.
2) Double-click the Format Painter button on the Standard toolbar.
3) Select the heading *Early Painting and Drawing Programs*.
4) Select the heading *Developments in Painting and Drawing Programs*.
5) Select the heading *Painting and Drawing Programs Today*.
6) Click once on the Format Painter button on the Standard toolbar. (This turns
   the feature off.)
7) Deselect the heading.

4. Save the document again with the same name (Word C2, Ex 13). (The formatting you
   apply to this document may create a page break in an undesirable location. You will
   learn how to control page breaks in chapter 3.)
5. Print and then close Word C2, Ex 13.

Indenting Text in Paragraphs

By now you are familiar with the word wrap feature of Word, which ends lines
and wraps the insertion point to the next line. To indent text from the left
margin, or the left and right margins, or to create numbered items, use indent
buttons on the Formatting toolbar, shortcut commands, options from the
Paragraph dialog box, markers on the Ruler, or the Alignment button on the Ruler.
Indent markers on the Ruler are identified in figure 2.16. Refer to figure 2.17 for
methods for indenting text in a document.

figure

2.16 **Ruler and Indent Markers**

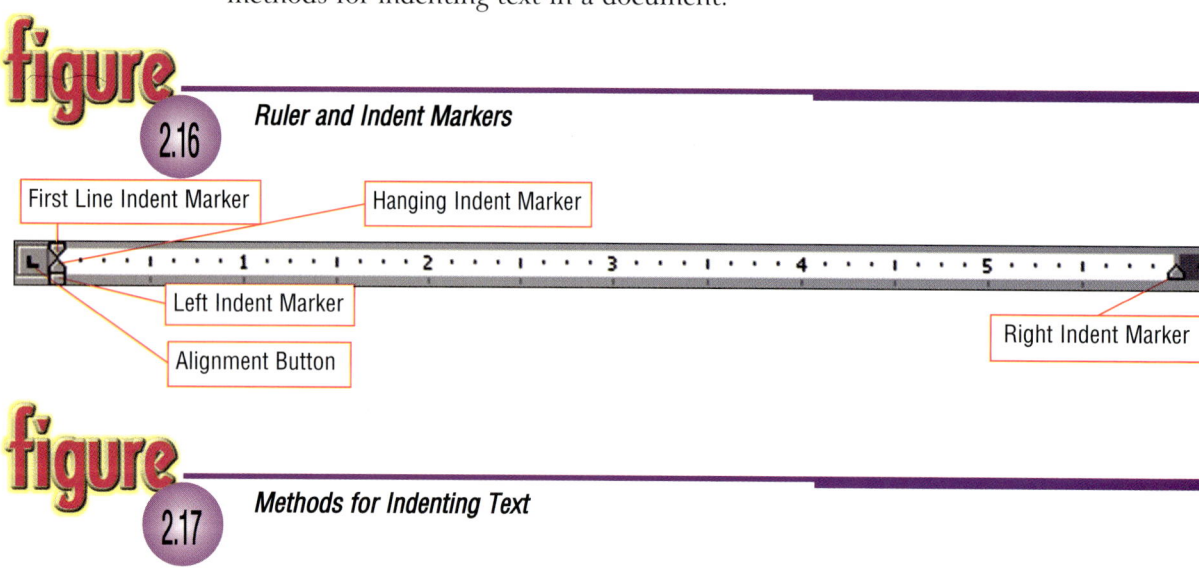

First Line Indent Marker
Hanging Indent Marker
Left Indent Marker
Alignment Button
Right Indent Marker

figure

2.17 **Methods for Indenting Text**

Indent	Methods for Indenting
First line of paragraph	• Press the Tab key. • Display Paragraph dialog box, click down-pointing triangle to the right of the <u>S</u>pecial text box, click *First line*, and then click OK.

	• Drag the first line indent marker on the Ruler.
	• Click the Alignment button located at the left side of the Ruler until the First Line Indent button displays and then click on the Ruler at the desired location.
Text from left margin	• Click the Increase Indent button on the Formatting toolbar to increase indent or click the Decrease Indent button to decrease the indent.
	• Press Ctrl + M to increase indent or press Ctrl + Shift + M to decrease indent.
	• Display the Paragraph dialog box, key the desired indent measurement in the <u>L</u>eft text box, and then click OK.
	• Drag the left indent marker on the Ruler.
Text from left and right margins	• Display the Paragraph dialog box, key the desired indent measurement in the <u>L</u>eft text box and the <u>R</u>ight text box, and then click OK.
	• Drag the left indent marker and the right indent marker on the Ruler.
All lines of text except the first (called a hanging indent)	• Press Ctrl + T. (Press Ctrl + Shift + T to remove hanging indent.)
	• Display the Paragraph dialog box, click the down-pointing triangle to the right of the <u>S</u>pecial text box, click *Hanging*, and then click OK.
	• Click the Alignment button located at the left side of the Ruler until the Hanging Indent button displays and then click on the Ruler at the desired location.

Indents can be set on the Ruler using the left indent marker, the right indent marker, first line indent marker, and hanging indent marker. A first-line indent and a hanging indent can also be set on the Ruler using the Alignment button. The Alignment button displays at the left side of the Ruler. Click this button to display the desired alignment (such as First Line Indent and Hanging Indent) and then click on the Ruler at the location where you want to set the indent.

Indenting the First Line of Paragraphs Using the First Line Indent Button

1. Open Word Document 03.
2. Save the document with Save As and name it Word C2, Ex 14.
3. Indent the first line of each paragraph 0.25 inches by completing the following steps:
   a. Select the entire document.
   b. Click the Alignment button located at the left side of the Ruler until the First Line Indent button displays.

c. Click on the 0.25-inch mark on the Ruler.
d. Deselect the text
4. Save the document again with the same name (Word C2, Ex 14).
5. Print and then close Word C2, Ex 14.

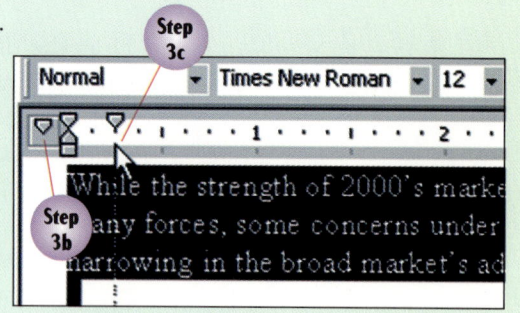

exercise 15

Indenting Text from the Left Margin

1. Open Word Ch 02, Ex 01a. (You created this document in exercise 1.)
2. Save the document with Save As and name it Word C2, Ex 15.
3. Indent the second paragraph in the document to the first tab setting by completing the following steps:
   a. Position the insertion point anywhere in the second paragraph (begins with *Buses:*).
   b. Click the Increase Indent button on the Formatting toolbar.
4. Indent the third paragraph by completing the following steps:
   a. Position the insertion point anywhere in the third paragraph (begins with *System Clock:*).
   b. Click F_ormat and then _Paragraph.
   c. At the Paragraph dialog box with the Indents and Spacing tab selected, select *0"* in the Left text box, and then key **0.5**.
   d. Click OK or press Enter.

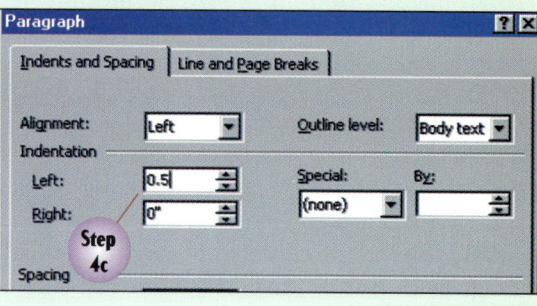

5. Indent the remaining three paragraphs in the document by completing the following steps:
   a. Make sure the Ruler is displayed. (If not, click _View, expand the drop-down menu [if necessary], and then click _Ruler.)
   b. Select from the fourth paragraph (begins with *Microprocessor:*) to the end of the document.
   c. Position the arrow pointer on the left indent marker on the Ruler, hold down the left mouse button, drag the marker to the 0.5-inch mark on the Ruler, and then release the mouse button.
   d. Deselect the text. (To do this with the mouse, click anywhere in the text outside the selected text.)

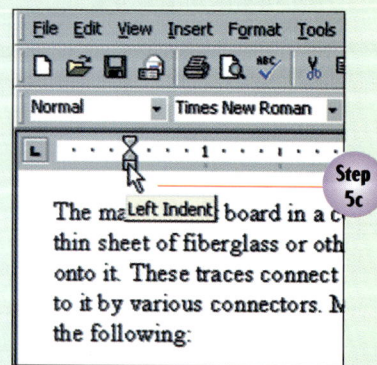

6. Save the document again with the same name (Word C2, Ex 15).
7. Print and then close Word C2, Ex 15.

Indenting Text from the Left and Right Margins

1. At a clear document screen, key the document shown in figure 2.18. Bold and center align the title as shown.
2. After keying the document, indent the second paragraph of the document from the left and right margins by completing the following steps:
   a. Make sure the Ruler is displayed.
   b. Position the insertion point anywhere in the second paragraph (begins with *I deeply care about…*).
   c. Position the arrow pointer on the left indent marker on the Ruler, hold down the left mouse button, drag the marker to the 0.5-inch mark on the Ruler, and then release the mouse button.
   d. Position the arrow pointer on the right indent marker on the Ruler, hold down the left mouse button, drag the marker to the 5.5-inch mark on the Ruler, and then release the mouse button.
3. Indent the fourth paragraph in the document from the left and right margins by completing the following steps:
   a. Position the insertion point anywhere within the fourth paragraph (begins with *I plan to increase…*).
   b. Click Format and then Paragraph.
   c. At the Paragraph dialog box with the Indents and Spacing tab selected, select the *0"* in the Left text box, and then key **0.5**.
   d. Click the up-pointing triangle at the right of the Right text box until *0.5"* displays in the text box.
   e. Click OK or press Enter.
4. Select all the paragraphs in the document (excluding the title) and then change the paragraph alignment to justified.
5. Save the document and name it Word C2, Ex 16.
6. Print and then close Word C2, Ex 16.

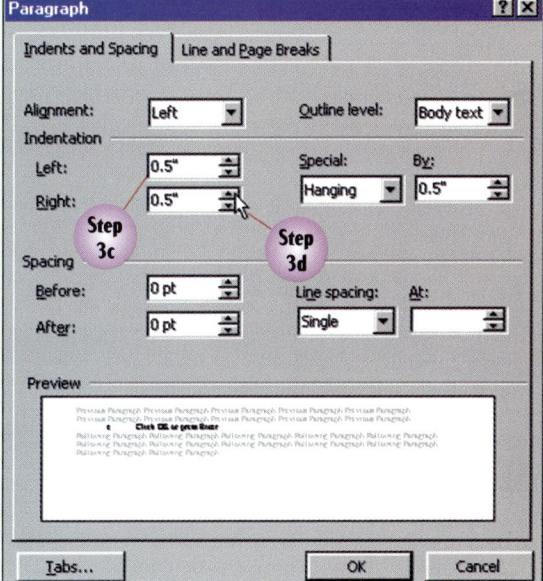

figure
2.18
Exercise 16

McCORMACK FUNDS APPOINTS NEW CEO

On September 3, 2001, Kelly Millerton became Chief Executive Officer of McCormack Funds. Ms. Millerton has been with McCormack Funds for twelve years. She began her career as the Director of Marketing and has held the position of Chief Operating Officer for the past three years. When asked about her appointment, Ms. Millerton stated:

I deeply care about McCormack Funds and our shareholders and am committed to keeping the company strong and providing a wide range of high-quality investments.

Ms. Millerton's commitment to the strength of the company is apparent in the ambitious nature of her goals. When asked what specific goals she has for McCormack Funds, she stated:

I plan to increase the assets under management by the company and its subsidiaries from their present level of $41 billion to an amount over $100 billion by the year 2002. To do this, McCormack Funds has to continue to provide both topnotch investment products and superior service, but also must expand our expertise to a broader level.

exercise 17

Creating Hanging Paragraphs

1. Open Word Bibliography.
2. Save the document with Save As and name it Word C2, Ex 17.
3. Create a hanging indent for the first two paragraphs by completing the following steps:
   a. Select at least a portion of the first and second paragraphs.
   b. Position the arrow pointer on the hanging indent marker on the Ruler.
   c. Hold down the left mouse button, drag the marker to the 0.5-inch mark on the Ruler, and then release the mouse button.
4. Create a hanging indent for the third paragraph by completing the following steps:
   a. Position the insertion point anywhere in the third paragraph.
   b. Click the Alignment button located at the left

side of the Ruler until the Hanging Indent button displays.

   c. Click on the 0.5-inch mark on the Ruler.

5. Create a hanging indent for the fourth paragraph by completing the following steps:

   a. Position the insertion point anywhere in the fourth paragraph.

   b. Press Ctrl + T.

6. Create a hanging indent for the fifth paragraph by completing the following steps:

   a. Position the insertion point somewhere in the fifth paragraph.

   b. Click Format and then Paragraph.

   c. At the Paragraph dialog box with the Indents and Spacing tab selected, click the down-pointing triangle to the right of the Special text box, and then click *Hanging* at the drop-down menu.

   d. Click OK or press Enter.

7. Select the entire document and then change to a serif typeface (other than Times New Roman) in 12-point size.

8. Save the document again with the same name (Word C2, Ex 17).

9. Print and then close Word C2, Ex 17.

Creating Numbered and Bulleted Paragraphs

If you key **1.**, press the space bar, key a paragraph of text, and then press Enter, Word will indent the number approximately 0.25 inches and then hang indent the text in the paragraph approximately 0.5 inches from the left margin. Additionally, *2.* will be inserted 0.25 inches from the left margin at the beginning of the next paragraph. This is part of Word's AutoFormat feature. (If this feature is not activated, you can turn it on by clicking Tools and then AutoCorrect. At the AutoCorrect dialog box, click the AutoFormat As You Type tab. Click in the Automatic numbered lists check box to insert a check mark and then click OK.) Continue keying numbered items and Word will insert the next number in the list. To turn off numbering, press the Enter key twice or click the Numbering button on the Formatting toolbar. (You can also remove all paragraph formatting from a paragraph, including automatic numbering, by pressing Ctrl + Q.)

    If you press Enter twice between numbered paragraphs, the automatic number is removed. To turn it back on, key the next number in the list (and the period) followed by a space, key the paragraph of text, and then press Enter. Word will automatically indent the number and hang indent the text.

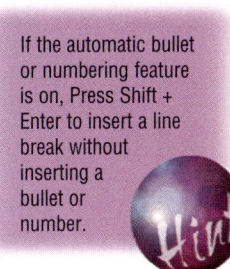

If the automatic bullet or numbering feature is on, Press Shift + Enter to insert a line break without inserting a bullet or number.

Creating Numbered Paragraphs

1. At a clear document screen, key the text shown in figure 2.19. When keying the numbered paragraph, complete the following steps:
   a. Key **1.** and then press the space bar.
   b. Key the paragraph of text and then press Enter. (This moves the insertion point down to the next line, inserts *2.* indented 0.25 inches from the left margin, and also indents the first paragraph of text approximately 0.5 inches from the left margin.)
   c. Continue keying the remaining text. (Remember, you do not need to key the paragraph number and period—these are automatically inserted.)
2. Save the document and name it Word C2, Ex 18.
3. Print and then close Word C2, Ex 18.

Exercise 18

FREQUENTLY ASKED QUESTIONS

1. What influence did the Jacquard loom have on the subsequent development of computers?
2. Why is Charles Babbage known as the "father of the computer"?
3. What is a transistor, and what effect did its invention have on electronics in general and on computers in particular?
4. What are the main components of a computer, and what do they do?
5. How do computers encode information?
6. What is the motherboard of a computer, and what does it contain?
7. What are the main types of memory in a computer, and how do they differ from one another?
8. What are the major types of printers, and how do they differ from one another?

If you do not want automatic numbering in a document, turn the feature off at the AutoCorrect dialog box with the AutoFormat As You Type tab selected as shown in figure 2.20. To display this dialog box, click <u>T</u>ools and then <u>A</u>utoCorrect. At the AutoCorrect dialog box, click the AutoFormat As You Type tab. To turn off automatic numbering, remove the check mark from the *Automatic numbered lists* option.

figure

2.20

AutoCorrect Dialog Box with AutoFormat As You Type Tab Selected

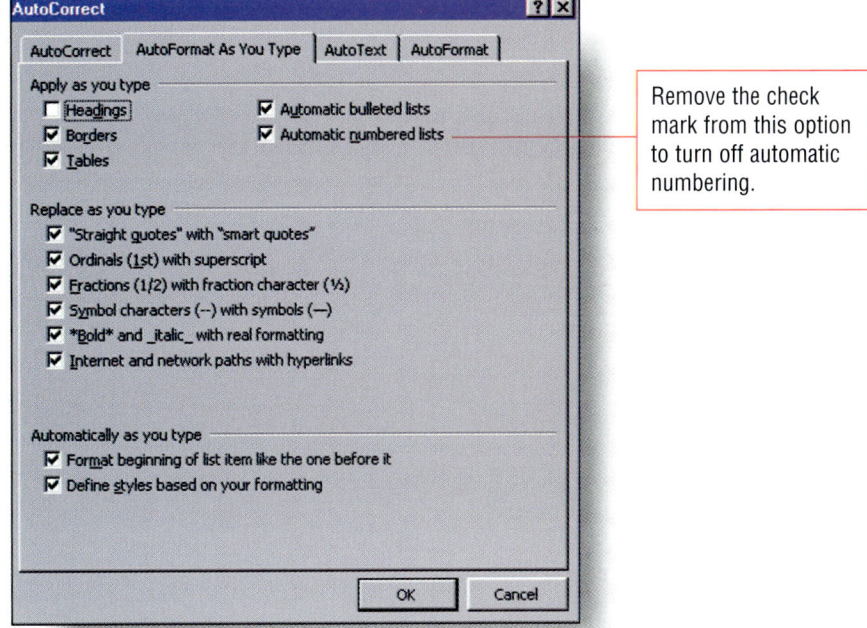

Remove the check mark from this option to turn off automatic numbering.

You can also automate the creation of numbered paragraphs with the Numbering button on the Formatting toolbar. To use this button, key the text (do not key the number) for each paragraph to be numbered, select the paragraphs to be numbered, and then click the Numbering button on the Formatting toolbar.

In addition to automatically numbering paragraphs, Word's AutoFormat feature will create bulleted paragraphs. (If this feature is not activated, you can turn it on by clicking Tools and then AutoCorrect. At the AutoCorrect dialog box, click the AutoFormat As You Type tab. Click in the Automatic bulleted lists check box to insert a check mark, and then click OK.)

Figure 2.21 shows an example of bulleted paragraphs. Bulleted lists with hanging indents are automatically created when a paragraph begins with the symbol *, >, or -. Key one of the symbols, press the space bar, key text, and then press Enter. The AutoFormat feature inserts a bullet indented 0.25 inches from the left margin and indents the text following the bullet 0.5 inches. The type of bullet inserted depends on the type of character entered. For example, if you use the asterisk (*) symbol, a round bullet is inserted. An arrow bullet is inserted if the greater than symbol (>) is used.

Numbering

figure
2.21

Bulleted Paragraphs

- This is a paragraph preceded by a bullet. A bullet is used to indicate a list of items or topics.
- This is another paragraph preceded by a bullet. Bulleted paragraphs can be easily created by keying certain symbols before the text or with the Bullets button on the Formatting toolbar.

exercise 19

Creating Bullets

1. At a clear document screen, key the text shown in figure 2.22 with the following specifications:
   a. Bold and center the title in uppercase letters as shown in figure 2.22.
   b. Key the first paragraph in the figure and then create the bulleted paragraphs by completing the following steps:
      1) With the insertion point positioned at the left margin of the first paragraph to contain a bullet, key the greater than symbol (>).
      2) Press the space bar once.
      3) Key the text of the first bulleted paragraph (the text that begins *Loads during start-up....*).
      4) Press the Enter key once and then continue keying the text after the bullets.
   c. After keying the last bulleted paragraph, press the Enter key twice (this turns off bullets), and then key the last paragraph shown in the figure.
2. Save the document and name it Word C2, Ex 19.
3. Print and then close Word C2, Ex 19.

figure
2.22

Exercise 19

COMPUTER OPERATING SYSTEM

The most important piece of software used on a personal computer system is its *operating system*, or OS. The OS performs a number of interdependent functions such as the following:

> Loads during start-up, recognizes the CPU and devices connected to it, such as keyboards, monitors, hard drives, and floppy disk drives
> Manages the operations of the CPU and of devices connected to it
> Creates a *user interface*, an environment displayed on the computer screen with which the user interacts when working at the computer
> Creates and updates a file system, or *directory*, for each storage device that is attached to the computer; this directory shows the location of each file on each storage device and thus enables the user to access programs and documents
> Supports operations performed from within other programs, such as opening and closing programs, calling resources such as fonts and sounds, and saving and printing documents

Without an OS, a computer is just a paperweight. The OS brings the system to life and gives the system its character. When a person starts a computer, instructions built into the machine's ROM look for an OS, first on any disk inserted into a floppy disk drive at start-up and then on the system's primary hard drive. When found, the OS is loaded, in part, into the computer's RAM, where it remains until the computer is turned off.

Bullets can be applied to existing text by selecting the text and then clicking the Bullets button on the Formatting toolbar. Insert bullets to selected text by clicking the Bullets button on the Formatting toolbar.

Bullets

exercise 20

Using the Bullets and Numbering Buttons

1. Open Word List.
2. Save the document with Save As and name it Word C2, Ex 20.
3. Add bullets to text by completing the following steps:
   a. Select text from *The Real Estate Account* through *Expense Deductions*.
   b. Click the Bullets button on the Formatting toolbar.
   c. Deselect the text.
4. Save the document with the same name (Word C2, Ex 20).
5. Print Word C2, Ex 20.
6. With the document still open, change the bullets to numbers by completing the following steps:
   a. Select text from *The Real Estate Account* through *Expense Deductions*.
   b. Click the Numbering button on the Formatting toolbar.
   c. Deselect the text.
7. Save the document again with the same name (Word C2, Ex 20).
8. Print and then close Word C2, Ex 20.

In addition to the Bullets and Numbering buttons on the Formatting toolbar, you can also use options from the Bullets and Numbering dialog box to number paragraphs or insert bullets. To display this dialog box, click Format and then Bullets and Numbering. The Bullets and Numbering dialog box contains three tabs: Bulleted, Numbered, and Outline Numbered. Figure 2.23 shows the Bullets and Numbering dialog box with each tab selected. Select the Bulleted tab if you want to insert bullets before selected paragraphs and select the Numbered tab to insert numbers.

At the Bullets and Numbering dialog box with the Outline Numbered tab displayed, you can specify the type of numbering for paragraphs at the left margin, first tab setting, second tab setting, and so on. (The options that display with *Heading 1*, *Heading 2*, or *Heading 3* are not available unless the text to be numbered has been formatted with a Heading style. You will learn more about styles in chapter 5.)

figure
2.23

Bullets and Numbering Dialog Box with Each Tab Selected

Click a bulleting option to select it and then click OK or double-click the desired option.

Click a numbering option to select it and then click OK or double-click the desired option.

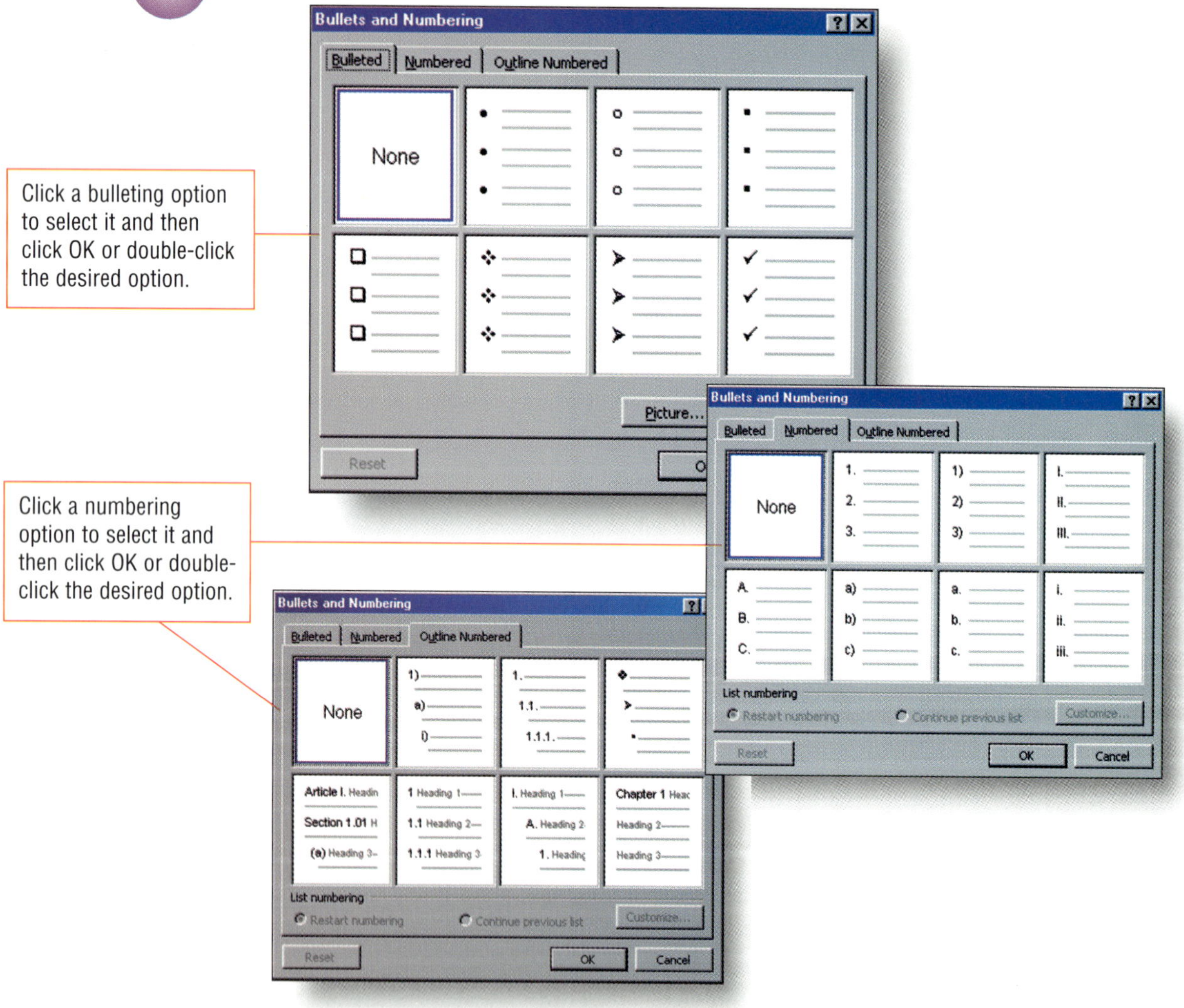

exercise 21

Numbering Paragraphs Using the Bullets and Numbering Dialog Box

1. Open Word List.
2. Save the document with Save As and name it Word C2, Ex 21.
3. Number the paragraphs in the document using the Bullets and Numbering dialog box by completing the following steps:

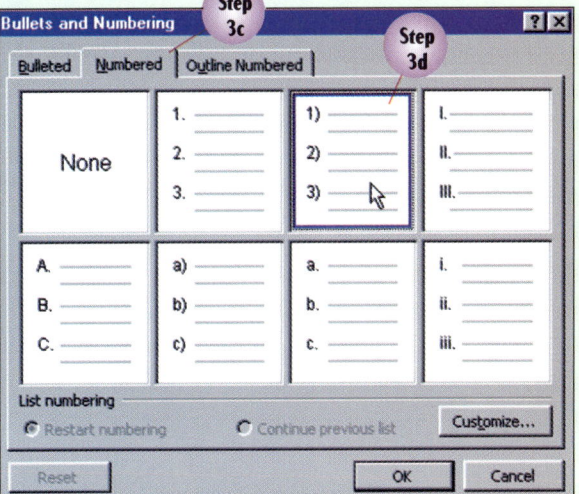

   a. Select the paragraphs in the document *excluding* the title and the blank lines below the title.
   b. Click F̲ormat and then Bullets and N̲umbering.
   c. At the Bullets and Numbering dialog box, click the N̲umbered tab.
   d. Click the third numbering option box in the top row.
   e. Click OK or press Enter.
4. Add *Annuity Contracts* between paragraphs 4 and 5 by completing the following steps:
   a. Position the insertion point immediately to the right of the last letter in *Role of Account*.
   b. Press Enter. (This moves the insertion point a double space below the previous paragraph.)
   c. Key **Annuity Contracts**.
5. Select and then delete *Investment Practices of the Account* (paragraph 2).
6. Select the entire document and then change to a sans serif typeface in 12-point size (you determine the typeface).
7. Save the document again with the same name (Word C2, Ex 21).
8. Print and then close Word C2, Ex 21.

exercise 22

Creating an Outline Numbered List

1. Open Word Agenda.
2. Save the document with Save As and name it Word C2, Ex 22.
3. Apply outline numbering to the document by completing the following steps:
   a. Select the paragraphs in the document *excluding* the title, subtitle, and blank lines below the subtitle.
   b. Click F̲ormat and then Bullets and N̲umbering.

   c. At the Bullets and Numbering dialog box, click the Outline Numbered tab.

   d. Click the second option from the left in the top row.

   e. Click OK or press Enter to close the dialog box.

   f. Deselect the text.

4. Save the document again with the same name (Word C2, Ex 22).

5. Print Word C2, Ex 22.

6. With the document still open, make the following changes:

   a. Delete *Sponsors* in the Education section.

   b. Move the insertion point immediately right of the last letter in *Personal Lines* (in the Sales and Marketing section), press the Enter key, and then key **Production Report**.

7. Select the entire document and then change to a serif typeface of your choosing (other than Times New Roman).

8. Save the document again with the same name (Word C2, Ex 22).

9. Print and then close Word C2, Ex 22.

Creating Ordinals

Word's AutoFormat feature automatically formats ordinal numbers. For example, if you key **1st** and then press the space bar, Word will correct it to 1st. Word automatically changes the font size of the *st* and formats the letters as superscript text. This automatic feature will change other ordinal numbers such as 2nd, 3rd, 4th, and so on.

Creating Ordinals

1. At a clear document screen, key the text shown in figure 2.24. Let Word's AutoFormat feature insert the bullets (key an asterisk and then press the space bar before the first bulleted paragraph) and automatically change the formatting of the ordinal numbers.

2. Save the document and name it Word C2, Ex 23.

3. Print and then close Word C2, Ex 23.

2.24

NOTES ON CHANGING CONTRACT

After reading the contract prepared by Neimi and Gleason, I recommend the following changes:

- Delete the 1st paragraph in the 2nd section.
- Add a paragraph between the 2nd and 3rd paragraphs in the 4th section that fully describes the responsibilities of the contract holder.
- Remove the words *and others* in the 4th paragraph of the 6th section.

Inserting Symbols

Many of the typefaces (fonts) include special symbols such as bullets, publishing symbols, and letters with special punctuation (such as É, ö, and ñ). To insert a symbol, display the Symbol dialog box with the <u>S</u>ymbols tab selected as shown in figure 2.25 by clicking <u>I</u>nsert and then <u>S</u>ymbol. At the Symbol dialog box, double-click the desired symbol, and then click Close; or click the desired symbol, click <u>I</u>nsert, and then click Close.

2.25

Symbol Dialog Box with Symbols Tab Selected

Click this down-pointing triangle to display a list of fonts. Choose the font that contains the desired symbol.

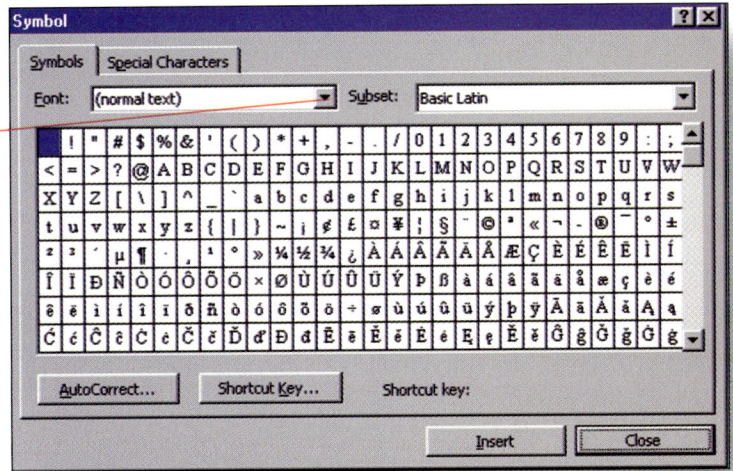

Changing the Font for Symbols

At the Symbol dialog box with the <u>S</u>ymbols tab selected, you can change the font with the <u>F</u>ont option. When you change the font, different symbols display in the dialog box. To change the font, display the Symbol dialog box with the <u>S</u>ymbols tab selected, click the down-pointing triangle to the right of the <u>F</u>ont text box, and then click the desired font at the drop-down list.

exercise 24

Creating Special Symbols

1. At a clear document screen, create the document shown in figure 2.26 by completing the following steps:

   a. Key the text in the document to the point where the ® symbol is to be inserted and then complete the following steps:

      1) Click <u>I</u>nsert and then <u>S</u>ymbol.
      2) At the Symbol dialog box with the <u>S</u>ymbols tab selected, click the down-pointing triangle at the right side of the <u>F</u>ont text box, and then click *(normal text)* at the drop-down list. (You may need to scroll up to see this option. Skip this step if *(normal text)* is already selected.)
      3) Double-click the ® symbol (approximately the third symbol from the *right* in the fourth row).
      4) Click the Close button.

   b. Key the text in the memo to the point where the ó is to be inserted and then complete the following steps:

      1) Click <u>I</u>nsert and then <u>S</u>ymbol.
      2) At the Symbol dialog box with the <u>S</u>ymbols tab selected, make sure <u>F</u>ont displays as *(normal text)*.
      3) Double-click the ó symbol (approximately the eleventh symbol from the left in the seventh row).
      4) Click the Close button.

   c. Key the text in the memo to the point where the ñ is to be inserted and then complete the following steps:

      1) Click <u>I</u>nsert and then <u>S</u>ymbol.
      2) At the Symbol dialog box, make sure the <u>F</u>ont is *(normal text)*, and then double-click the ñ symbol (approximately the ninth symbol from the left in the seventh row).
      3) Click the Close button.

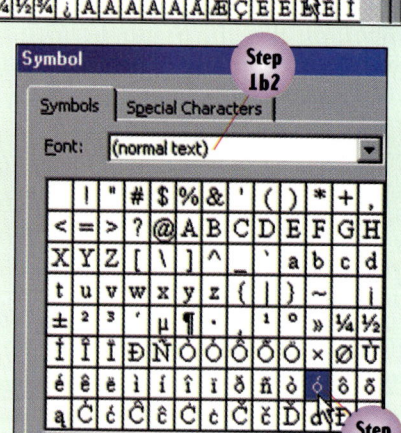

4) Repeat these steps when you key the other occurrences of Viña.

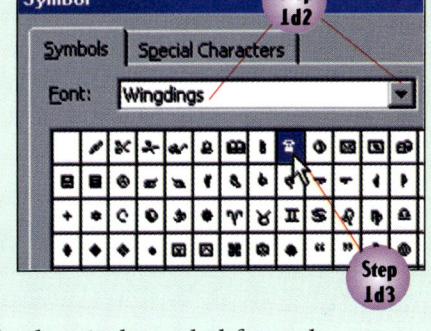

d. Key the text in the memo to the point where the first bullet (☎) is to be inserted and then complete the following steps:
   1) Click Insert and then Symbol.
   2) At the Symbol dialog box, change the font to *Wingdings*. To do this, click the down-pointing triangle at the right side of the Font text box, click the down scroll triangle until *Wingdings* displays, and then click it.
   3) Double-click the ☎ symbol (approximately the ninth symbol from the left in the top row).
   4) Click the Close button.

e. Press the Tab key, key the text following the first bullet, and then press Enter. (If the automatic bulleting feature is on, Word inserts another bullet.)

f. Key the remaining text following the bullets. (The bullets will be automatically inserted.)

g. After keying the text following the last bullet, press Enter twice. (This turns off the automatic bullets.)

h. Key the remainder of the text in the document.

2. Save the document and name it Word C2, Ex 24.

3. Print and then close Word C2, Ex 24.

Exercise 24

ENHANCED SERVICES

New Options in Retirement

"You can now change the source of your annuity income from any MIRA® account to any other MIRA account," states Concepción Viña, Fund Manager for retirement accounts. In addition, Viña states that retirees receiving annuity income through the graduated payment method can now switch to the standard payment method.

Automated Telephone Service Improvements

Access to your accumulation is now available 24 hours a day, 7 days a week through the Automated Telephone Service. You can use this service to:

☎   Find out your last premium paid

☎ Set up future accumulation transfers
☎ Make multiple transfers in the same call
☎ Get a confirmation statement automatically

Faster Cash Withdrawals

You can get cash from a supplemental retirement annuity or a preferred personal annuity. "Often, this cash can be available the next business day," states Viña.

Changing Line Spacing

By default, the word wrap feature single spaces text. There may be occasions when you want to change to another spacing, such as line and a half or double. Line spacing can be changed with shortcut commands or options from the Paragraph dialog box. Figure 2.27 illustrates the shortcut commands to change line spacing.

figure 2.27
Line Spacing Shortcut Commands

Press	To change line spacing to
Ctrl + 1*	single spacing
Ctrl + 2	double spacing
Ctrl + 5	1.5 line spacing

(*Use the numbers on the keyboard, not the numeric keypad.)

Changing Line Spacing

1. Open Word Document 02.
2. Save the document with Save As and name it Word C2, Ex 25.
3. Change the line spacing for all paragraphs to 1.5 line spacing by completing the following steps:
   a. Select the entire document.

b. Press Ctrl + 5.
4. Change the alignment of all paragraphs to justified.
5. Save the document again with the same name (Word C2, Ex 25).
6. Print and then close Word C2, Ex 25.

Line spacing can also be changed at the Paragraph dialog box. At the Paragraph dialog box, you can change line spacing with the Line spacing option or the At option. If you click the down-pointing triangle to the right of the Line spacing text box at the Paragraph dialog box, a drop-down list displays with a variety of spacing options. For example, to change the line spacing to double you would click *Double* at the drop-down list. You can key a specific line spacing measurement in the At text box at the Paragraph dialog box. For example, to change the line spacing to double, key **2** in the At text box.

exercise 26

Changing Line Spacing at the Paragraph Dialog Box

1. Open Word Document 03.
2. Save the document with Save As and name it Word C2, Ex 26.
3. Change the line spacing to double using the Paragraph dialog box by completing the following steps:
   a. Select the entire document.
   b. Click Format and then Paragraph.
   c. At the Paragraph dialog box, make sure the Indents and Spacing tab is selected, and then click the down-pointing triangle to the right of the Line spacing text box (this box contains the word *Single*).
   d. From the drop-down list that displays, click *Double*.
   e. Click OK or press Enter to close the dialog box.
   f. Click outside the selected text to deselect it.

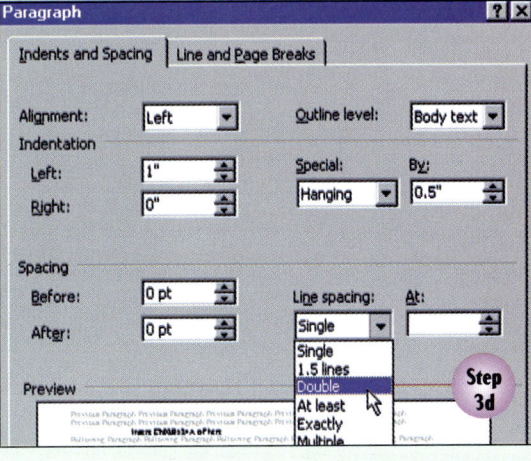

4. Save the document again with the same name (Word C2, Ex 26).
5. Print Word C2, Ex 26.
6. With Word C2, Ex 26 still open, change the line spacing to 1.3 by completing the following steps:
   a. Select the entire document.
   b. Click Format and then Paragraph.
   c. At the Paragraph dialog box, make sure the Indents and Spacing tab is selected.

d. Click in the <u>A</u>t text box and then key **1.3**.

e. Click OK or press Enter to close the dialog box.

f. Click outside the text to deselect it.

7. Save the document again with the same name (Word C2, Ex 26).

8. Print and then close Word C2, Ex 26.

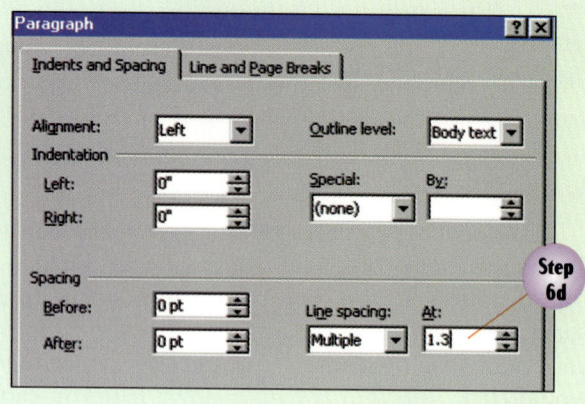

Step 6d

Repeating the Last Action

Another method for repeating the last action is pressing F4.

Use the Format Painter feature to copy character formatting to different locations in a document. If you want to apply other types of formatting, such as paragraph formatting, to a document, consider using the Repeat command. To use the Repeat command, apply the desired formatting, move the insertion point to the next location where you want the formatting applied, click <u>E</u>dit, expand the drop-down menu, and then click <u>R</u>epeat; or press Ctrl + Y.

exercise 27

Formatting Using the Repeat Command

1. Open Word Report 01.

2. Save the document with Save As and name it Word C2, Ex 27.

3. Make the following changes to the document:

   a. Select the entire document.

   b. Change the line spacing to single.

   c. Bold the headings *Early Painting and Drawing Programs, Developments in Painting and Drawing Programs,* and *Painting and Drawing Programs Today*.

4. Apply paragraph formatting and repeat the formatting by completing the following steps:

   a. Position the insertion point anywhere in the heading *Early Painting and Drawing Programs*.

   b. Click F<u>o</u>rmat and then <u>P</u>aragraph.

   c. At the Paragraph dialog box, click twice on the up-pointing triangle at the right side of the <u>B</u>efore option (in the Spacing section). (This changes the measurement in the text box to *12 pt*.)

   d. Click once on the up-pointing triangle at the right side of the Aft<u>e</u>r option. (This changes the measurement in the text box to *6 pt*.)

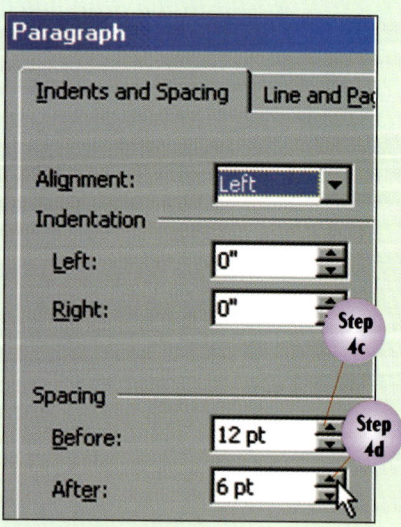

Step 4c

Step 4d

e. Click OK to close the Paragraph dialog box.

f. Repeat the paragraph formatting for the second heading by completing the following steps:

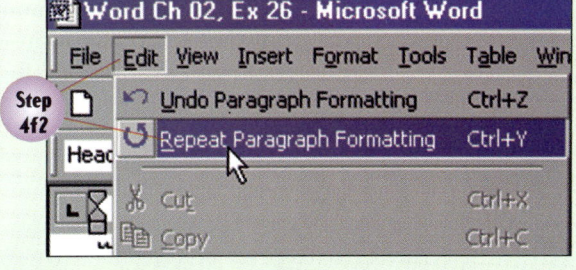

1) Position the insertion point anywhere in the heading *Developments in Painting and Drawing Programs*.

2) Click Edit, expand the drop-down menu, and then click Repeat Paragraph Formatting.

g. Repeat the paragraph formatting for the third heading by positioning the insertion point anywhere in the heading *Painting and Drawing Programs Today* and then pressing Ctrl + Y.

5. Move the insertion point to any character in the title *GRAPHICS SOFTWARE* and then insert 12 points of space after the paragraph.

6. Save the document again with the same name (Word C2, Ex 27).

7. Print and then close Word C2, Ex 27.

Applying Borders and Shading

Every paragraph you create in Word contains an invisible frame. A border that appears around this frame can be applied to a paragraph. A border can be added to specific sides of the paragraph or to all sides. The type of border line and thickness of the line can be customized. In addition, you can add shading and fill within the border.

When a border is added to a paragraph of text, the border expands and contracts as text is inserted or deleted from the paragraph. You can create a border around a single paragraph or a border around selected paragraphs.

Creating a Border with the Border Button

One method for creating a border is to use options from the Border button on the Formatting toolbar. The name of the button changes depending on the border choice that was previously selected at the button drop-down palette. When Word is first opened, the button name displays as Outside Border. Click the down-pointing triangle at the right side of the button and a palette of border choices displays as shown in figure 2.28.

figure

2.28

Border Palette

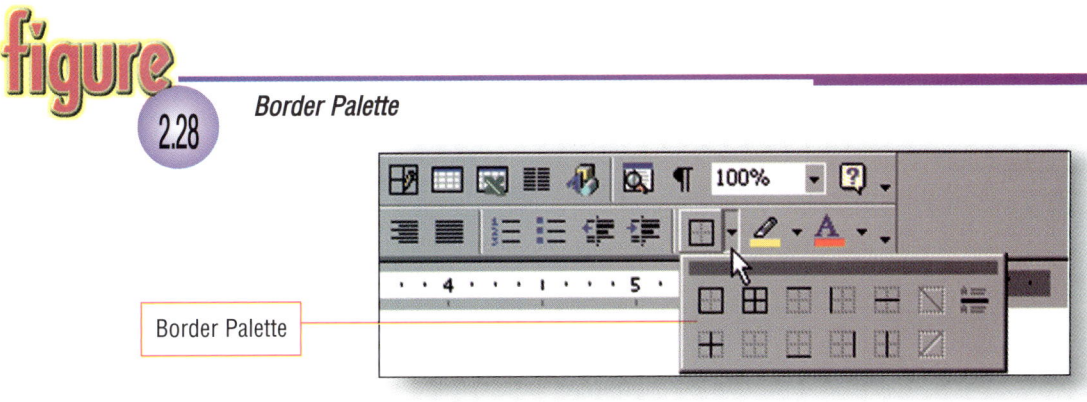

Border Palette

Click the option that will insert the desired border. For example, to insert a border at the bottom of the paragraph, click the Bottom Border option (third option from the left in the bottom row). Clicking an option will add the border to the paragraph where the insertion point is located. To add a border to more than one paragraph, select the paragraphs first and then click the desired option.

Adding Borders to Paragraphs of Text

1. Open Word Document 03.
2. Save the document with Save As and name it Word C2, Ex 28.
3. Create a border around the first paragraph by completing the following steps: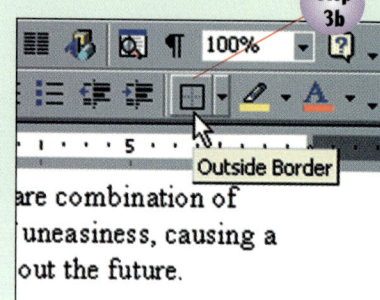
   a. Position the insertion point anywhere in the first paragraph.
   b. Position the mouse pointer on the Border button on the Formatting toolbar and wait for the ScreenTip to display. Make sure the ScreenTip displays as Outside Border and then click the button. (If this is not the name for the button, click the down-pointing triangle at the right side of the button and then click the Outside Border option [first option in the first row].)
4. Complete steps similar to those in 3 to add a border to the second paragraph.
5. Complete steps similar to those in 3 to add a border to the third paragraph.
6. Save the document again with the same name (Word C2, Ex 28).
7. Print Word C2, Ex 28.
8. With the document still open, remove the borders by completing the following steps:
   a. Select the three paragraphs in the document. (You do not have to select all the text in the first and last paragraphs, just a portion.)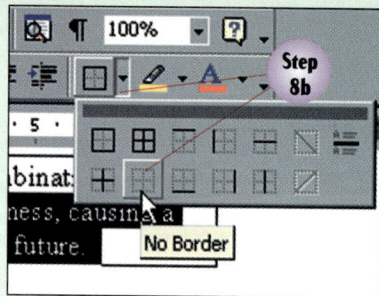
   b. Click the down-pointing triangle at the right side of the Border button on the Formatting toolbar and then click the No Border option (second option from the left in the bottom row). (This removes the borders from the three paragraphs.)
   c. Deselect the text.
9. Add a border around and between the paragraphs by completing the following steps:
   a. Select from the middle of the first paragraph to somewhere in the middle of the third paragraph.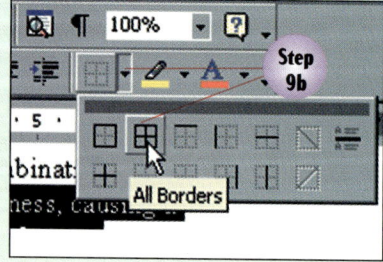
   b. Click the down-pointing triangle at the right side of the Border button and then click the All Borders option (second option from the left in the top row).
   c. Deselect the text.
10. Save the document again with the same name (Word C2, Ex 28).
11. Print and then close Word C2, Ex 28.

Adding Borders and Shading

As you learned in the previous section, borders can be added to a paragraph or selected paragraphs with options from the Border button on the Formatting toolbar. If you want to customize the line creating the border or add shading, use options from the Borders and Shading dialog box. To display this dialog box, shown in figure 2.29, click Format and then Borders and Shading.

Borders and Shading Dialog Box with the Borders Tab Selected

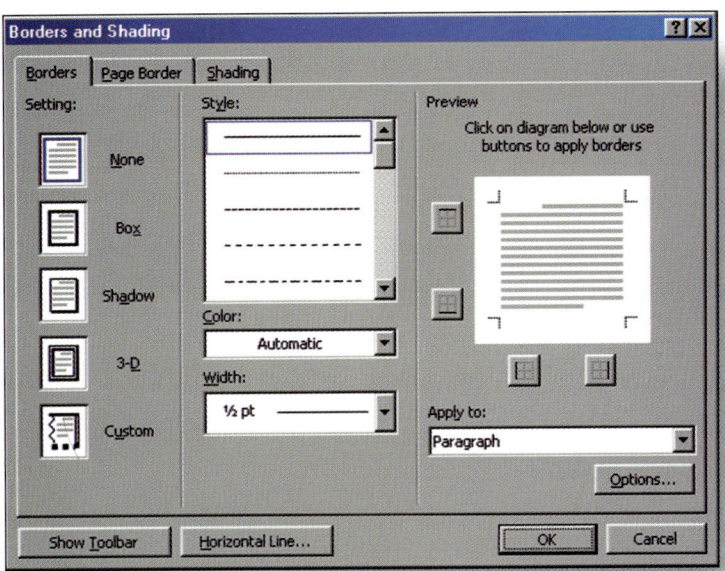

The buttons in the Setting section of the dialog box contain a visual display of line options. For example, click the Box button to insert a border around the paragraph (or selected paragraphs). Click the 3-D button to insert a border with a shadow, creating a three-dimensional look.

With the options in the Style list box, you can change the line style by clicking the desired style in the list box. The default line color is black. This can be changed to a different color by clicking the down-pointing triangle at the right side of the Color text box and then clicking the desired color at the drop-down list. If the desired color is not visible, scroll down the list. The default line width is ½ point. The line width can be changed by clicking the down-pointing triangle at the right side of the Width text box and then clicking the desired width at the pop-up list.

The diagram in the Preview section offers another method for inserting border lines. Specify where you want a border line to appear by clicking the desired location on the diagram. For example, if you want to insert a border at the bottom of the paragraph (or selected paragraphs), click the bottom portion of the diagram in the Preview section. This adds a border line to the diagram. You can also click a button in the Preview section that displays the desired border. For example, to add a border at the right side of the paragraph (or selected paragraphs), click the button that displays at the bottom of the diagram at the right side.

The Apply to option has a setting of *Paragraph*. This specifies to what the border and shading will apply. Click the Options button and options display for setting the desired distance between the edge of the border and the text.

Adding a Customized Border to a Document

1. Open Word Notice 01.
2. Save the document with Save As and name it Word C2, Ex 29.
3. Make the following changes to the document:
   a. With the insertion point at the beginning of the document, press the Enter key twice.
   b. Select the entire document and then change the font to 18-point Mistral bold and the text color to Dark Red. (If Mistral is not available, choose a fancy, decorative typeface.)
   c. With the entire document still selected, add a dark blue shadow border by completing the following steps:
      1) Click Format and then Borders and Shading.
      2) At the Borders and Shading dialog box with the Borders tab selected, click the Shadow button.
      3) Click the down-pointing triangle at the right side of the Width text box and then click the *6 pt* line at the pop-up list.
      4) Click the down-pointing triangle at the right side of the Color text box and then click *Dark Blue* at the drop-down list.
      5) Click OK or press Enter.
4. Deselect the text.
5. Save the document again with the same name (Word C2, Ex 29).
6. Print and then close Word C2, Ex 29.

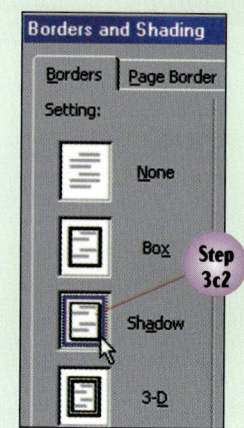

Adding Shading

With choices from the Borders and Shading dialog box with the Shading tab selected, shown in figure 2.30, you can add shading to the border around text. Fill color choices display in the upper left corner of the dialog box. To add a fill, click the desired color in this section. If you want to add a pattern, click the down-pointing triangle at the right side of the Style text box and then click the desired pattern at the drop-down list. If a pattern is added inside a border, the color of the pattern can be changed with the Color option. Click the down-pointing triangle at the right side of the Color text box and then click the desired color at the drop-down list.

The Preview area of the Borders and Shading dialog box with the Shading tab selected displays how the border shading and/or pattern will display.

figure

2.30

Borders and Shading Dialog Box with Shading Tab Selected

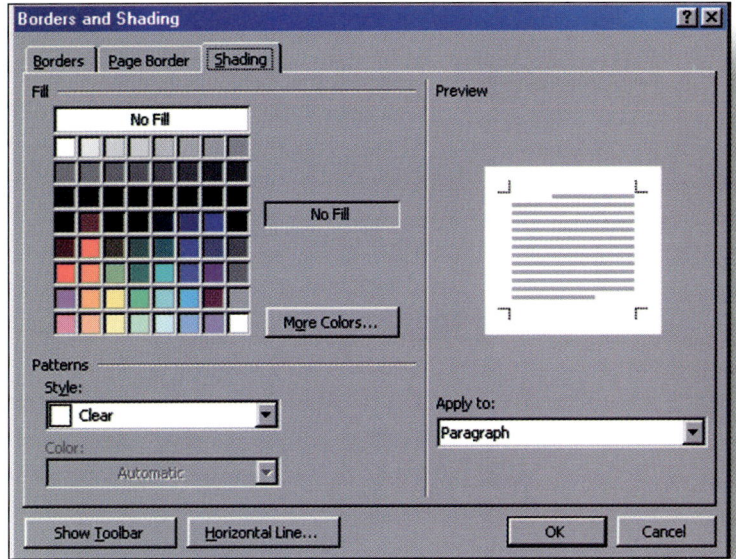

exercise 30

Adding Borders and Shading to Paragraphs of Text

1. Open Word Document 03.
2. Save the document with Save As and name it Word C2, Ex 30.
3. Create a border around all the paragraphs in the document that is 3 points thick and contains 25% shading by completing the following steps:

   a. Select all paragraphs in the document.
   b. Click Format and then Borders and Shading.
   c. At the Borders and Shading dialog box with the Borders tab selected, click the Box button located at the left side of the dialog box.
   d. Click the down-pointing triangle at the right side of the Width text box and then click *3 pt* at the pop-up list.
   e. Make sure that *Automatic* is selected in the Color text box. If not, click the down-pointing triangle at the right side of the Color text box and then click *Automatic* at the drop-down list. (This option is located at the beginning of the list.)
   f. Click the Shading tab.
   g. Click the Light Turquoise color in the Fill section of the dialog box.
   h. Click the down-pointing triangle at the right side of the Style list box and then click *5%* at the drop-down list.
   i. Click OK to close the dialog box.

Step 3f

Step 3g

Step 3h

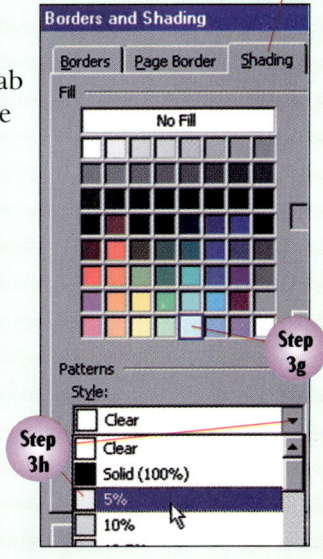

4. Deselect the text.
5. Save the document again with the same name (Word C2, Ex 30).
6. Print and then close Word C2, Ex 30.

Using Help

Word's Help feature is an on-screen reference manual containing information about all Word features and commands. Word's Help feature is similar to the Windows Help and the Help features in Excel, PowerPoint, and Access. Get help using the Office Assistant or turn off the Assistant and get help from the Microsoft Word Help dialog box.

Getting Help from the Office Assistant

Press F1 to display the yellow box above the Office Assistant.

The Office Assistant will provide information about specific topics. To get help using the Office Assistant, click the Office Assistant or click Help and then Microsoft Word Help. This causes a box to display above the Office Assistant as shown in figure 2.31. (If the Office Assistant is not visible, click the Microsoft Word Help button on the Standard toolbar.)

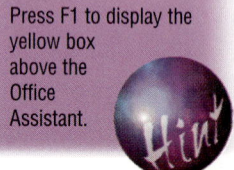

2.31

Office Assistant Help Box

Microsoft
Word Help

Show

Forward

When the help box displays above the Office Assistant, the text *Type your question here, and then click Search* displays in the text box below the question *What would you like to do?* This text is already selected, so key a question about a specific Word feature, and then click the Search button. The Office Assistant will display a list of related topics. At this list, click the desired topic and information will display in a Microsoft Word Help dialog box. After reading the information, click the Close button located in the upper right corner of the dialog box (contains an X).

The Microsoft Word Help dialog box contains a toolbar with the buttons shown in figure 2.32. Click the Show button to expand the dialog box and display three tabs—Contents, Answer Wizard, and Index. If you move to various help items, click the

Back button to return to the previous window. The Forward button is dimmed until the Back button has been clicked. When the Forward button is active, click the button to move forward to a help item. Send the Help information to the printer by clicking the Print button. Click the Options button and a drop-down menu displays with many of the same features as the buttons. For example, there is a Show Tabs option that will expand the dialog box, and Back and Forward options that do the same thing as the Back and Forward buttons. Additional options include Home, Stop, Refresh, Internet Options, and Print.

Back

Print

Options

Microsoft Word Help Dialog Box Toolbar

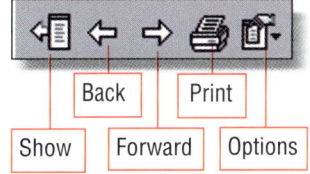

Show   Back   Forward   Print   Options

exercise 31

Using the Office Assistant to Learn How to Automatically Insert Arrows

1. At a clear document screen, use the Office Assistant to read information about automatically inserting arrows by completing the following steps:

   a. Make sure the Office Assistant is visible. If it is not, click Help and then Show the Office Assistant.
   b. Click the Office Assistant.
   c. At the yellow box that displays above the Office Assistant, key **How do I automatically insert an arrow in a document?**
   d. Click the Search button.
   e. At the list that displays in the yellow box, click *Insert symbols and special characters*. (When you position the arrow pointer on the topic, the pointer turns into a hand.)
   f. At the Microsoft Word Help dialog box, click *Automatically insert an arrow, face, or other symbol* in the *What do you want to do?* section.
   g. Read the information about automatically inserting arrows and faces and then print the information by clicking the Print button on the dialog box toolbar, and then clicking OK at the Print dialog box.
   h. Click on *turn on AutoCorrect* that displays in blue and underlined in the Microsoft Word Help dialog box. (This displays information about turning on AutoCorrect.)

What would you like to do?

- Insert symbols and special characters — Step 1e
- Troubleshoot printed forms and forms that users view in Word
- Ways to add text to drawing objects and pictures
- Troubleshoot text in drawing objects
- Use a text box to add a callout or label
- ▼ See more...

How do I automatically insert an arrow in a document? — Step 1c

Options   Search

i. After reading the information on AutoCorrect, click the Back button on the dialog box toolbar.

j. Click the Close button located in the upper right corner of the dialog box (contains an X).

2. If necessary, remove the Office Assistant yellow box by clicking in the document screen outside the yellow box.

Using the Expanded Microsoft Word Help Dialog Box

The Microsoft Word Help dialog box toolbar contains a Show button. Click the Show button and the dialog box expands as shown in figure 2.33. Three tabs display in the expanded dialog box—Contents, Answer Wizard, and Index.

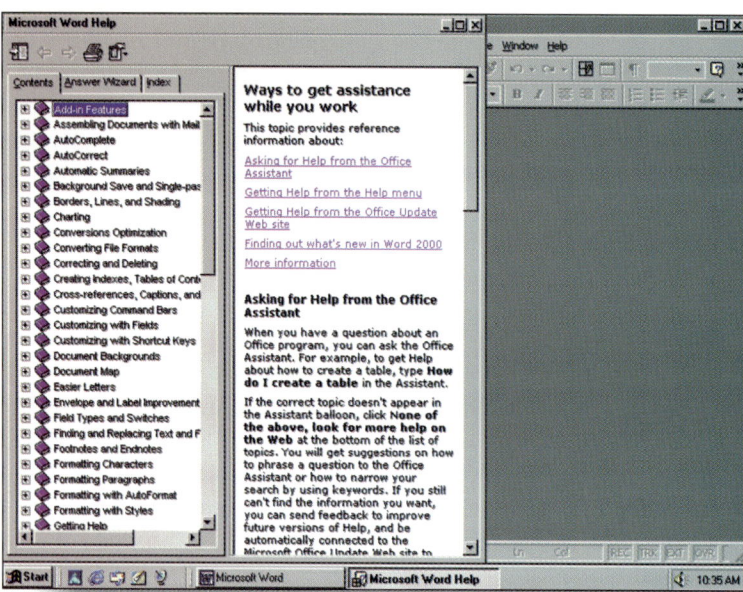

Expanded Microsoft Word Help Dialog Box

Select the Contents tab at the expanded Microsoft Word Help dialog box and a variety of categories display preceded by an icon of a closed book. Most of these categories contain additional categories. To display these additional categories, double-click a category. This causes the *closed book* icon to change to an *open book* icon and the additional categories to display below the selected category.

Click the Answer Wizard tab and a text box displays preceded by the question "What would you like to do?" Key your question in the text box and then click the Search button. This displays a list of categories in the Select topic to display list box. Click a topic in the list box, and information about the topic displays at the right side of the dialog box.

With the Index tab selected, enter a keyword in the Type keywords list box, and then click the Search button. Topics related to the keyword display in the

Choose a topic list box. Click a topic in this list box and information about that topic displays at the right side of the dialog box. You can also scroll through the Or choose keywords list box to display the desired topic. The topics in this list box are alphabetized.

Hiding/Turning Off the Office Assistant

To hide the Office Assistant, click Help and then Hide the Office Assistant. Redisplay the Office Assistant by clicking the Microsoft Word Help button on the Standard toolbar or by clicking Help and then Show the Office Assistant.

The Office Assistant can also be turned off. To do this, click the Office Assistant and then click the Options button that displays in the yellow box. At the Office Assistant dialog box that displays as shown in figure 2.34, click the Use the Office Assistant option to remove the check mark, and then click OK.

figure

2.34   *Office Assistant Dialog Box*

Remove the check mark from this check box to turn off the Office Assistant.

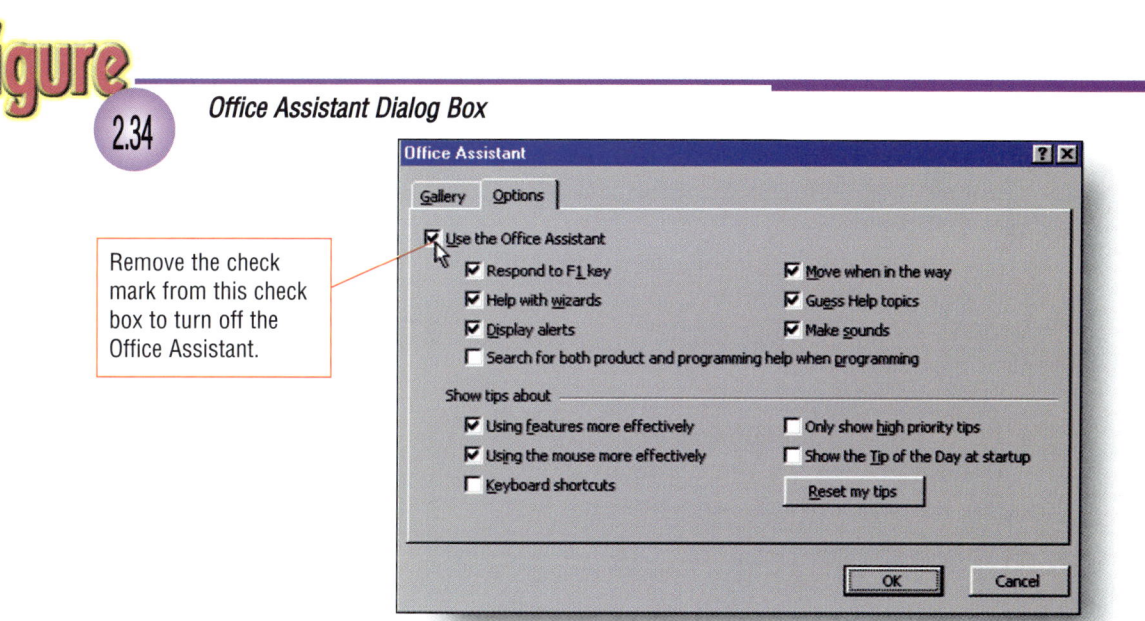

exercise

Turning Off the Office Assistant and Using Help

1. At a clear document screen, turn off the Office Assistant by completing the following steps:
    a. Make sure the Office Assistant is visible.
    b. Click the Office Assistant.
    c. Click the Options button in the yellow box.
    d. At the Office Assistant dialog box, click the Use the Office Assistant option (this removes the check mark).
    e. Click OK to close the dialog box.

2. Use the Help feature with the <u>C</u>ontents tab selected to find information on formatting characters by completing the following steps:

   a. Click <u>H</u>elp on the Menu bar and then click Microsoft Word <u>H</u>elp.

   b. At the Microsoft Word Help dialog box, click the <u>C</u>ontents tab. (Skip this step if the <u>C</u>ontents tab is already selected.)

   c. Double-click *Formatting* in the <u>C</u>ontents list box. (This displays subcategories below *Formatting*.)

   d. Double-click *Formatting Characters* in the <u>C</u>ontents list box. (This displays subcategories below *Formatting Characters*.)

   e. Click a subcategory topic that interests you and then read the information about the subcategory that displays at the right side of the dialog box.

   f. Click several other subcategories that interest you and read the information about each subcategory.

3. Use the Help feature with the <u>A</u>nswer Wizard tab selected to search for information on indenting paragraphs by completing the following steps:

   a. Click the <u>A</u>nswer Wizard tab.

   b. Key **How do I indent text in paragraphs?** in the <u>W</u>hat would you like to do? text box and then click the <u>S</u>earch button.

   c. At the list of topics that displays in the Select <u>t</u>opic to display list box, click *Indent paragraphs*.

   d. Look at the topics that display at the right side of the dialog box and then click a topic that interests you.

   e. After reading information about the topic, click the Back button on the dialog box toolbar.

   f. Click the topic *About paragraph alignment* in the Select <u>t</u>opic to display list box.

   g. Read the information that displays at the right side of the dialog box.

4. Use the Help feature with the <u>I</u>ndex tab selected to search for information on line spacing by completing the following steps:

   a. Click the <u>I</u>ndex tab.

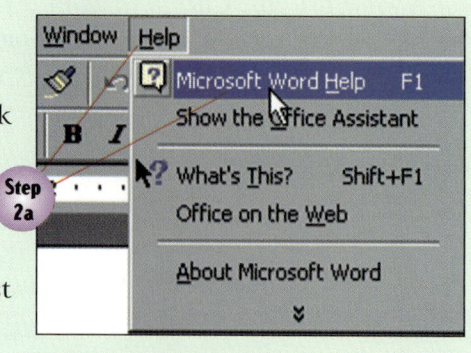

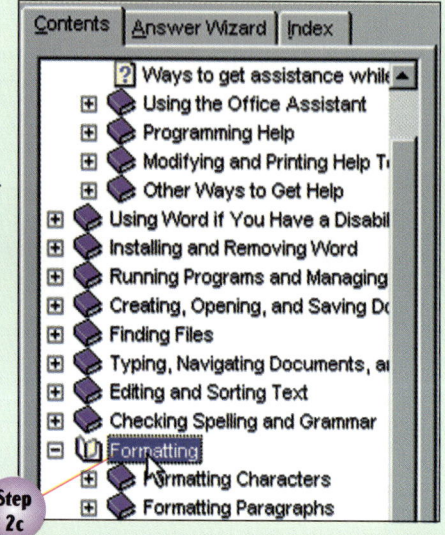

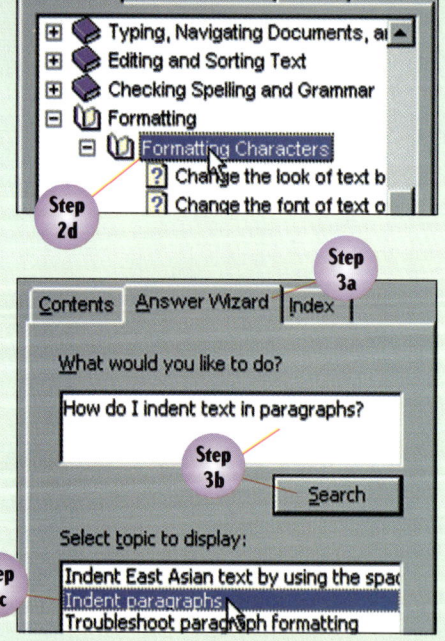

b. Key **line space** in the Type keywords text box and then click the Search button.

c. Click the topic *About line spacing* that displays in the Choose a topic list box.

d. Read the information that displays at the right side of the dialog box.

5. Click the Close button that displays in the upper right corner of the dialog box (contains an X) to close the Microsoft Word Help dialog box.

6. Turn on the display of the Office Assistant by clicking Help and then Show the Office Assistant.

7. Click in the document screen to remove the yellow box above the Office Assistant.

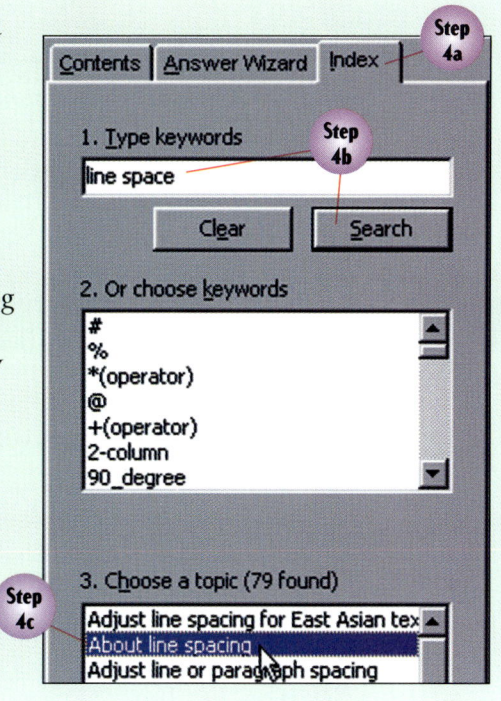

Using Additional Help Features

Click the Help option on the Menu bar, expand the drop-down menu, and a variety of help features are available. You have already learned about the Microsoft Word Help option and the Hide the Office Assistant (or Show the Office Assistant) option. The drop-down menu contains a number of other options.

Choose the What's This option to point to a specific item and display information about that item. For example, to display information about a button on a toolbar, click Help and then What's This. This causes the mouse pointer to display with a question mark attached. Click a button on a toolbar and the name of the button along with information about the button displays in a yellow box. You can also use this option to display information on what formatting has been applied to specific text. To do this, click Help and then What's This. Click specific text in the document and a gray box displays containing information on paragraph formatting and font formatting.

Click Office on the Web from the Help drop-down menu and you are connected to the Microsoft Office Update web site. From this site, you can get answers to the most frequently asked questions about Word. You can also get up-to-date tips, templates, clip art, and Help files.

If you have been a WordPerfect user and would like information on how to carry out a command in Word, click Help, expand the drop-down menu, and then click WordPerfect Help.

Word contains a self-repairing feature that will find and fix errors in Word. To run this feature, click Help, expand the drop-down menu, and then click Detect and Repair. This displays the Detect and Repair dialog box with a message telling you that during the process you may be asked to provide the installation source

Click Help, About Microsoft Word, and then click the System Info button to display information about your computer such as your processor type, operating system, memory, and hard disk space.

and to exit or open applications. Click the <u>S</u>tart button to begin the detect and repair process.

The last option at the <u>H</u>elp drop-down menu, <u>A</u>bout Microsoft Word, displays information such as the release date, license number, and system information. You can also display information about Microsoft's technical support such as a listing of support telephone numbers.

Using What's This and Displaying System Information

1. At a clear document screen, use the What's This feature by completing the following steps:
   a. Click <u>H</u>elp and then What's <u>T</u>his. (This causes the mouse pointer to display with a question mark attached.)
   b. Click the Bold button on the Formatting toolbar. (This causes a yellow box to display with information on the Bold button.)
   c. Click in the document screen outside the yellow box. (This removes the box.)
   d. Click <u>H</u>elp and then What's <u>T</u>his.
   e. Click the Select Browse Object button (displays towards the bottom of the vertical scroll bar). (This causes a yellow box to display with information on the Select Browse Object.)
   f. Click in the document screen outside the yellow box. (This removes the box.)
2. Read information about Word by completing the following steps:
   a. Click <u>H</u>elp and then <u>A</u>bout Microsoft Word.
   b. At the About Microsoft Word dialog box, click the <u>S</u>ystem Info button that displays in the lower right corner of the dialog box.
   c. At the Microsoft System Information dialog box, read the information, then exit the dialog box by clicking <u>F</u>ile (on the dialog box menu bar) and then E<u>x</u>it.
   d. At the About Microsoft Word dialog box, click the <u>T</u>ech Support button that displays in the lower right corner of the dialog box.
   e. Read the information that displays in the Microsoft Word Help dialog box and then click the Close button that displays in the upper right corner of the dialog box (contains an X).
   f. At the About Microsoft Word dialog box, click OK.

Using ScreenTips

ScreenTips

Word includes a ScreenTips feature that is available in every dialog box and displays as a button containing a question mark. This button displays in the upper right corner of dialog boxes. To use the ScreenTips feature, click the ScreenTips button, and then click an item in the dialog box. Word will display an explanation about the particular item. Click inside the dialog box outside the explanation box to remove it.

exercise 34

Using ScreenTips

1. At a clear document screen, display information about specific items in the Paragraph dialog box by completing the following steps:
   a. Display the Paragraph dialog box.
   b. Click the ScreenTips button. (This button is located in the upper right corner of the dialog box and contains a question mark.)
   c. Move the arrow pointer (displays with a question mark attached) to the Alignment option and then click the left mouse button. (This displays a yellow box containing information on alignment.)
   d. Click the ScreenTips button and then click the Line spacing option.
   e. Close the Paragraph dialog box.
2. Display information about specific options (you choose the options) in the Font dialog box by completing steps similar to those in step 1.
3. Close the Font dialog box.

chapter summary

➤ The appearance of a document in the document screen and how it looks when printed is called the format.

➤ Text can be bolded, italicized, and underlined with buttons on the Formatting toolbar or with shortcut commands. Do this as text is keyed or apply the features later by selecting the text then choosing the desired feature.

➤ You can remove all character formatting from selected text by pressing Ctrl + spacebar.

➤ A font consists of three parts: typeface, type style, and type size.

➤ A typeface is a set of characters with a common design and shape. Typefaces are either monospaced, allotting the same amount of horizontal space to each character, or proportional, allotting a varying amount of space for each character.

➤ A type style is a variation of style within a certain typeface. There are four main kinds of type styles: normal, bold, italic, and bold italic.

➤ Type size is measured in pitch or point size. Pitch is the number of characters per inch—the higher the pitch, the smaller the characters. Point size is a vertical measurement—the higher the point size, the larger the characters.

➤ Change the font at the Font dialog box or use the Font button on the Formatting toolbar. Click the Font Size button on the Formatting toolbar to change the font size or click the Font Color button to change the text color.

➤ The Effects section of the Font dialog box contains a variety of options that can be used to create different character styles such as Strikethrough, Double strikethrough, Superscript, Subscript, Shadow, Outline, Emboss, Engrave, Small caps, All caps, and Hidden.

➤ Adjust character spacing and turn on kerning with options at the Font dialog box with the Character Spacing tab selected.

➤ Animate text in the screen with options at the Font dialog box with the Text Effects tab selected.

➤ To turn on or off the display of nonprinting characters such as paragraph marks, click the Show/Hide ¶ button on the Standard toolbar.

➤ In Word, a paragraph is any amount of text followed by a paragraph mark (a stroke of the Enter key). Word inserts into the paragraph mark any paragraph formatting that is turned on before the text is keyed.

➤ To remove paragraph formatting from text, delete the paragraph mark or remove all paragraph formatting by pressing Ctrl + Q.

➤ By default, paragraphs in a Word document are aligned at the left margin and ragged at the right margin. This default alignment can be changed with buttons on the Formatting toolbar, at the Paragraph dialog box, or with shortcut commands for left, center, right, or fully aligned.

➤ Increase or decrease space before or after a paragraph or selected paragraphs with the Before and After options at the Paragraph dialog box.

➤ Use the Format Painter button (displays on the Standard toolbar as a paintbrush) to copy character formatting already applied to text to different locations in the document.

➤ The first line of text in a paragraph can be indented by pressing the Tab key, with an option from the Paragraph dialog box, or with the first-line indent marker on the Ruler.

➤ All lines of text in a paragraph can be indented to a tab setting or to a specific measurement from the left margin with an option from the Paragraph dialog box or with the left indent marker on the Ruler.

➤ Text in paragraphs can be indented from the left and the right margins with options at the Paragraph dialog box or with the left and right indent markers on the Ruler.

➤ In a hanging paragraph, the first line of the paragraph remains at the left margin, while the remaining lines are indented to the first tab setting. Hanging paragraphs can be created with a shortcut command, with options from the Paragraph dialog box, with the hanging indent marker on the Ruler, or with the Hanging Indent button.

➤ Word's AutoFormat feature will automatically format numbered and bulleted lists as well as create ordinal numbers.

➤ Bulleted lists with hanging indents are automatically created when a paragraph begins with *, >, or -. The type of bullet inserted depends on the type of character entered.

➤ Paragraphs can also be numbered with the Numbering button on the Formatting toolbar and bullets can be inserted before paragraphs with the Bullets button. Numbers or bullets can also be inserted with options at the Bullets and Numbering dialog box.

➤ Many of the typefaces (fonts) include special symbols such as bullets and publishing symbols. Insert a symbol in a document at the Symbols dialog box.

➤ Line spacing can be changed with shortcut commands or options from the Paragraph dialog box.

➤ Repeat the last action by clicking Edit, expanding the drop-down menu, and then clicking Repeat; or by pressing Ctrl + Y.

➤ Every paragraph created in Word contains an invisible frame. A border that appears around this frame can be added to a paragraph.

➤ Use options from the Border button on the Formatting toolbar to insert borders around a paragraph or selected paragraphs.

➤ Use options at the Borders and Shading dialog box with the <u>B</u>orders tab selected to add a customized border to a paragraph or selected paragraphs.

➤ Use options at the Borders and Shading dialog box with the <u>S</u>hading tab selected to add shading or a pattern to a paragraph of text or selected paragraphs.

➤ Word's Help feature is an on-screen reference manual containing information about all Word features and commands.

➤ To get help from the Office Assistant, click the Assistant, key a question, and then click the <u>S</u>earch button.

➤ Some Help information displays in the Microsoft Word Help dialog box. This dialog box contains a toolbar with the following buttons—Show, Forward, Back, Print, and Options.

➤ The expanded Microsoft Word Help dialog box displays with three tabs—<u>C</u>ontents, <u>A</u>nswer Wizard, and <u>I</u>ndex.

➤ <u>H</u>ide the Office Assistant by clicking <u>H</u>elp and then Hide the <u>O</u>ffice Assistant. Redisplay the Office Assistant by clicking the Microsoft Word Help button on the Standard toolbar or by clicking <u>H</u>elp and then Show the <u>O</u>ffice Assistant.

➤ Turn off the Office Assistant for the entire Word session by clicking the Office Assistant and then clicking the <u>O</u>ptions button. At the Office Assistant dialog box, click the <u>U</u>se the Office Assistant option to remove the check mark, and then click OK.

➤ Additional options from the <u>H</u>elp drop-down menu include: What's <u>T</u>his, Office on the <u>W</u>eb, Word<u>P</u>erfect Help, Detect and <u>R</u>epair, and <u>A</u>bout Microsoft Word.

➤ Use the ScreenTips button in any dialog box to read information about specific items in the dialog box.

commands review

	Mouse	Keyboard
Uppercase function		Caps Lock Key
Bold	Click Bold button on Formatting toolbar	Ctrl + B
Italics	Click Italic button on Formatting toolbar	Ctrl + I
Underline	Click Underline button on Formatting toolbar	Ctrl + U
Remove all character formatting from selected text		Ctrl + space bar
Display Font dialog box	F<u>o</u>rmat, <u>F</u>ont	F<u>o</u>rmat, <u>F</u>ont
Turn on/off display of nonprinting characters	Click Show/Hide *f* button on Standard toolbar	
Align text at the left margin	Click Align Left button on Formatting toolbar	Ctrl + L
Align text between margins	Click Center button on Formatting toolbar	Ctrl + E
Align text at the right margin	Click Align Right button on Formatting toolbar	Ctrl + R
Align text at the left and right margins	Click Justify button on Formatting toolbar	Ctrl + J
Return all paragraph formatting to normal		Ctrl + Q

	Mouse	Keyboard
Paragraph dialog box	F̲ormat, P̲aragraph	
Format Painter	Click Format Painter button on Standard toolbar	
Indent first line of a paragraph	At the Paragraph dialog box, click S̲pecial, then *First line*; or drag first-line indent marker on Ruler to desired measurement; or change to the First Line Indent button and then click on Ruler at desired measurement	Tab key
Indent left margin of all lines of text in a paragraph or selected paragraphs	At the Paragraph dialog box, key indent measurement in the L̲eft text box; or drag left indent marker on Ruler to desired measurement; or click Increase Indent button on Formatting toolbar	Ctrl + M
Decrease indent of text in a paragraph	Decrease number in the L̲eft text box at the Paragraph dialog box; or drag left indent marker on Ruler to desired measurement; or click Decrease Indent button on Formatting toolbar	Ctrl + Shift + M
Indent left and right margins of paragraph	At the Paragraph dialog box, key indent measurement in the L̲eft and R̲ight text boxes; or drag left indent marker on Ruler to desired measurement, and then drag right indent marker to desired measurement	
Create a hanging paragraph	At the Paragraph dialog box, key the desired indent measurement in the L̲eft text box, click S̲pecial, then *Hanging*; or drag hanging indent marker on Ruler to desired measurement; or change to the Hanging Indent button and then click on Ruler at desired measurement	Ctrl + T
Create numbered/bulleted paragraphs	Select paragraphs, click Numbering or Bullets button on Formatting toolbar; or display the Bullets and Numbering dialog box	
Bullets and Numbering dialog box	F̲ormat, Bullets and N̲umbering	F̲ormat, Bullets and N̲umbering
Display Symbol dialog box	Insert, S̲ymbol	Insert, S̲ymbol
Change to single spacing		Ctrl + 1
Change to double spacing		Ctrl + 2
Change to 1.5 line spacing		Ctrl + 5
Change line spacing at Paragraph dialog box	Click the up/down pointing triangle to the right of At box; key measurement in A̲t box; or click Li̲ne Spacing	
Repeat the last action	E̲dit, expand drop-down menu, R̲epeat	Ctrl + Y
Display Borders and Shading dialog box	Format, B̲orders and Shading	F̲ormat, B̲orders and Shading
Microsoft Word Help dialog box	Click Office Assistant, key question, click S̲earch button, and then click desired topic; or turn off Office Assistant and then click H̲elp and then Microsoft Word H̲elp	
Office Assistant dialog box	Click Office Assistant and then click O̲ptions button	

thinking offline

Matching: In the space provided at the left, indicate the correct letter <u>or letters</u> that match each description.

- **A** Arial
- **B** Century Schoolbook
- **C** Garamond
- **D** italic
- **E** font
- **F** pitch
- **G** point
- **H** proportional
- **I** sans serif
- **J** serif
- **K** subscript
- **L** super script
- **M** Times New Roman
- **N** type size
- **O** type style
- **P** typeface

_____ 1. This kind of typeface does not have a small line at the end of each character stroke.

_____ 2. This term refers to a particular typeface in a specific style and size.

_____ 3. This is a set of characters with a common design and shape.

_____ 4. This term refers to text that is lowered slightly below the regular line of text.

_____ 5. With this type of measurement, the higher the number, the larger the characters.

_____ 6. These are examples of different typefaces.

_____ 7. This term refers to text that is raised slightly above the regular line of text.

Completion: In the space provided at the right, indicate the correct term, symbol, or command.

1. To use the Format Painter to apply formatting to several locations in a document, do this to the Format Painter button.   _____

2. Change the font of selected text with this button on the Formatting toolbar.   _____

3. This is the shortcut command to bold text.   _____

4. This is the shortcut command to underline text.   _____

5. This keyboard command removes all character formatting from selected text.   _____

6. Word inserts paragraph formatting into this mark.   _____

7. To turn on or off the display of nonprinting characters, click this button on the Standard toolbar.   _____

8. This is the Word default paragraph alignment.   _____

9. You can return all paragraph formatting to normal with this keyboard command.   _____

10. In this kind of paragraph, the first line remains at the left margin and the remaining lines are indented to the first tab setting.   _____

11. Insert spacing before or after paragraphs with options at this dialog box.   _____

12. The number 2nd is referred to as this. _____

13. Automate the creation of bulleted paragraphs with the Bullets button on this toolbar. _____

14. At the Paragraph dialog box, change line spacing with the Line spacing option or this. _____

15. This is the shortcut command to change line spacing to 2. _____

16. This is the shortcut command to repeat the last action. _____

17. The Border button is located on this toolbar. _____

18. Click this option on the Menu bar and then click Borders and Shading to display the Borders and Shading dialog box. _____

19. Click this button, located in the Setting section of the Borders and Shading dialog box, to add a border that has a three-dimensional look to paragraphs. _____

20. Display the Office Assistant dialog box by clicking the Office Assistant and then clicking this button. _____

21. Click this button on the Microsoft Word Help dialog box toolbar to expand the dialog box. _____

22. Click this tab at the expanded Microsoft Word Help dialog box to display a variety of categories preceded by an icon of a closed book. _____

23. In the space provided below, list the steps you would complete to insert the symbol ✂ into a document. (*Hint: The* ✂ *symbol is located in the* Wingdings *font.*)

_____

_____

24. In the space provided below, list the steps you would complete to change the line spacing to 1.25.

_____

_____

working hands-on

Assessment 1

1. At a clear document screen, key the document shown in figure 2.35. Bold, italicize, and underline the text as shown.
2. After keying the document, make the following changes:
   a. Change the line spacing to 1.5 for the two paragraphs in the body of the document.
   b. Change the paragraph alignment to justified for the two paragraphs in the body of the document.

3. Save the document and name it Word C2, SA 01.
4. Print and then close Word C2, SA 01.

Assessment 1

RATES REDUCED

As a result of anticipated lower claims costs and other expected cost savings, premiums for LongLife insurance policies have been reduced, **effective February 1, 2001**. The new, lower premiums will apply to both existing and new policies. Policy benefits will remain the same.

The actual rate of reduction will vary depending on the policyholder's age and plan option. If you are between the ages of 45 and 64 and have a policy with a *periodic* inflation option, your premium reduction will be between 13 and 32 percent! Premiums of a colleague in the same age bracket with an *automatic* inflation option will be reduced by between 5 and 29 percent! Reductions may be higher or lower at other ages.

Assessment 2

1. Open Word Document 03.
2. Save the document with Save As and name it Word C2, SA 02.
3. Make the following changes:
   a. Add a title to the document by completing the following steps:
      1) With the insertion point positioned on the first character in the document, press the Enter key twice.
      2) Press the up arrow key twice. (This moves the insertion point to the beginning blank line.)
      3) Click the Center button on the Formatting toolbar and then click the Bold button.
      4) Key **ECONOMIC GAINS**.
   b. Select and then bold the following text in the document:
      1) *25%* (located in the second paragraph)
      2) *5000* (located in the second paragraph)
      3) *economic slowdown* (located in the third paragraph)
   c. Select and then italicize the following text in the document:
      1) *strength* (located in the first paragraph)
      2) *second half of 2000* (located in the second paragraph)
      3) *third-quarter 2000 earnings* (located in the third paragraph)
   d. Select the entire document and then compress text horizontally to 97 percent of the original horizontal spacing.
   e. Deselect the text.
4. Save the document again with the same name (Word C2, SA 02).
5. Print and then close Word C2, SA 02.

Assessment 3

1. Open Word Report 03.
2. Save the document with Save As and name it Word C2, SA 03.
3. Make the following changes to the document:
   a. Select the entire document and then change the font to 12-point Garamond (or a similar serif typeface).
   b. Select the title *NETWORK TOPOLOGIES* and then change the font to 18-point Tahoma bold (or a similar sans serif typeface).
   c. Use Format Painter to center and change the formatting to 18-point Tahoma bold for the three headings *Linear Bus Networks*, *Star Networks*, and *Ring Networks*.
4. Save the document again with the same name (Word C2, SA 03).
5. Print and then close Word C2, SA 03.

Assessment 4

1. Open Word Document 05.
2. Save the document with Save As and name it Word C2, SA 04.
3. Make the following changes to the document:
   a. Select the entire document and then change the font to 12-point Century Schoolbook (or a similar serif typeface).
   b. Select the title *ARE YOU PREPARING FOR RETIREMENT?* and then change the font to 14-point Century Schoolbook bold (or the serif typeface you chose in step 3a).
   c. Select from the second paragraph (that begins *Living longer than ever,...*) to the end of the document and then add the following:
      1) Add paragraph numbering.
      2) Add 3 points of spacing before paragraphs. (To do this, select the current measurement in the Before text box at the Paragraph dialog box, and then key **3**.)
   d. Move the insertion point to the end of the document, and then add the following text:

      The Growth Account® is a registered trademark of McCormack Funds.
      Edited by Anya Volochëk

4. Save the document again with the same name (Word C2, SA 04).
5. Print and then close Word C2, SA 04.

Assessment 5

1. At a clear document screen, key the document shown in figure 2.36.
2. After keying the text in the document, make the following changes to the document:
   a. Select the entire document and then change the font to 13-point Bookman Old Style.
   b. Select the title and then change the font to 18-point Bookman Old Style bold.
   c. Select the heading *Choices and Changes* and then change the font to 16-point Bookman Old Style bold.
3. Save the document and name it Word C2, SA 05.
4. Print and then close Word C2, SA 05.

figure

2.36 *Assessment 5*

GENERAL MATTERS

Choices and Changes

As long as your annuity fund certificate permits, you can choose or change any of the following:

> an annuity starting date;
> an income option;
> a transfer;
> a method of payment for death benefits;
> a date when the commuted value of an annuity becomes payable;
> an annuity partner, beneficiary, or other person named to receive payments;
> a cash withdrawal or other distribution; and
> a repurchase.

You have to make your choices or changes via a written notice satisfactory to us and received at our home offices. Transfers between accounts can currently be made by telephone. You can change the terms of a transfer, cash withdrawal, repurchase, or other cash distribution only before they are scheduled to take place.

Assessment 6

1. At a clear document screen, key the document shown in figure 2.37.
2. After keying the text in the document, make the following changes to the document:
   a. Select the paragraphs of text in the body of the document (all paragraphs except the title and the blank line below the title).
   b. With the paragraphs of text selected, change the paragraph alignment to justified.
   c. Select the paragraphs that begin with bolded words and then indent the text 0.5 inches from the left margin.
3. Save the document and name it Word C2, SA 06.
4. Print Word C2, SA 06.
5. With the document still open, select the paragraphs that begin with the bolded words, and then indent 0.5 inches from the right margin (the left margin should already be indented 0.5 inches).
6. Save the document again with the same name (Word C2, SA 06).
7. Print and then close Word C2, SA 06.

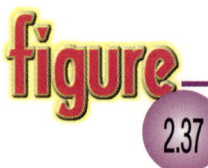

figure 2.37 *Assessment 6*

TOTAL RETURN CHARTS

The total return charts for the annuity accounts represent past performance. The value of your accumulation may rise or fall. The units you own may be worth more or less than their original price upon redemption. The following terms are used in the total return charts:

Average annual total return: The average rate that an investment grew each year over a specified period of time.

Annual total return: The rate at which an investment grew during a given twelve-month period ending December 31. In some cases, only part-year results are available if, for example, an account began operations during a year, or if a current year is not yet completed.

Accumulation units: The value of a single unit as it stood on March 31. The total return charts show how the value of accumulation units has fluctuated over time.

Accumulative rates: The compounded total growth of an investment over an extended period of time (not just a year).

As you read the total return charts, remember that past performance is no guarantee of future results. Historical information can, however, help you decide which accounts may meet your risk-tolerance and growth expectations.

Assessment 7

1. At a clear document screen, create the document shown in figure 2.38 with the following specifications:
   a. Change the line spacing to double.
   b. Center, bold, and italicize text as indicated.
   c. Create hanging paragraphs as indicated.
   d. Change the paragraph alignment for all paragraphs to justified.
2. Save the document and name it Word C2, SA 07.
3. Print and then close Word C2, SA 07.

figure
2.38

Assessment 7

BIBLIOGRAPHY

Amaral, Howard G. (1998). *Economic Growth in America*, 2nd edition (pp. 103-112).

Denver, CO: Goodwin Publishing Group.

Cuevas, Roxanne A. (1999). *Establishing a Stock Portfolio* (pp. 18-35). Los Angeles, CA:

North Ridge, Inc.

Forsyth, Stuart M. (1999). *International Investing* (pp. 23-31). San Francisco, CA:

Roosevelt & Carson Publishing.

Gudroe, Andrea G. (2000). *Global Economics*, 3rd edition (pp. 67-72). Phoenix, AZ:

Desert Palm Press.

Assessment 8

1. At a clear document screen, create the document shown in figure 2.39.
2. After keying the document, insert numbering before each paragraph in the document (except the title and the blank line below the title).
3. Save the document and name it Word C2, SA 08.
4. Print Word C2, SA 08.
5. Make the following changes to the document:
   a. Delete *External fund raising*.
   b. Change *Internal fund raising* so it reads *Fund raising*.
   c. Add *Corporate* between the fourth and fifth paragraphs.
6. Save the document again with the same name (Word C2, SA 08).
7. Print and then close Word C2, SA 08.

figure

2.39

Assessment 8

COMMUNITY CONNECTIONS PROJECT

Mission statement
Project planning
Education
Government
Private business
External fund raising
Internal fund raising
Environmental issues
Recommendations
Evaluation

Assessment 9

1. Open Word Document 02.
2. Save the document with Save As and name it Word C2, SA 09.
3. Make the following changes to the document:
   a. Select the entire document, change to a serif typeface other than Times New Roman, and then deselect the text.
   b. Select the heading *QWERTY Keyboard* and the paragraph that follows it, and then add a double line border of your choosing and light green shading.
   c. Select the heading *DVORAK Keyboard* and the paragraph that follows it, and apply the same border and shading as in step 3b. *(Hint: Use the Repeat command.)*
4. Save the document again with the same name (Word C2, SA 09).
5. Print and then close Word C2, SA 09.

Assessment 10

1. Use the Office Assistant to help you find information about AutoFormat. (Key the question **What changes will AutoFormat make?** in the text box below the question *What would you like to do?* At the list that displays in the yellow box, click *Format a document automatically*.) Make sure you learn about what AutoFormat automatically formats in a document and also learn about the dialog box where you can make changes to AutoFormat. Print this information.
2. After reading about and experimenting with the AutoFormat feature, write a description of the feature that includes the following:
   a. Create a title for the description that is keyed in all capital letters and is centered and bolded.
   b. List the steps to display the dialog box where you can make changes to AutoFormat.
   c. List three changes that Word can make automatically.
   d. Consider adding enhancements to the document such as bold and/or italics, and bullets and/or numbering.
3. Save the completed description and name it Word C2, SA 10.
4. Print and then close Word C2, SA 10.

Chapter 03C

Enhancing the Visual Display and Clarity of Documents

3

PERFORMANCE OBJECTIVES

Upon successful completion of chapter 3, you will be able to:

- Set, clear, and move tabs on the Ruler and at the Tabs dialog box.
- Change the document view.
- Change the top, bottom, left, and right margins in a document.
- Insert a hard page break in a document.
- Preview a document.
- Vertically align text in a document.
- Format text into newspaper columns.
- Complete a spelling check on text in a document.
- Complete a grammar check on text in a document.
- Add words to and delete words from the AutoCorrect dialog box.
- Display synonyms and antonyms for specific words using the Thesaurus.

Formatting can be applied to a document such as setting tabs, changing the document margins, and inserting page breaks. In this chapter, you will learn to apply these types of formatting along with formatting text into newspaper columns, completing a spelling check on text in a document, improving the grammar of text in a document by completing a grammar check, and using the Thesaurus to find synonyms and related words for a specific word.

Manipulating Tabs

When you work with a document, Word offers a variety of default settings such as margins and line spacing. One of these defaults is a left tab set every 0.5 inches. In some situations, these default tabs are appropriate; in others, you may want to create your own. Two methods exist for setting tabs. Tabs can be set on the Ruler or at the Tabs dialog box.

Manipulating Tabs on the Ruler

Use the Ruler to set, move, and delete tabs. By default, the Ruler displays below the Formatting Toolbar as shown in figure 3.1. If the Ruler is not displayed, turn on the display by clicking <u>V</u>iew, expanding the drop-down menu, and then clicking <u>R</u>uler.

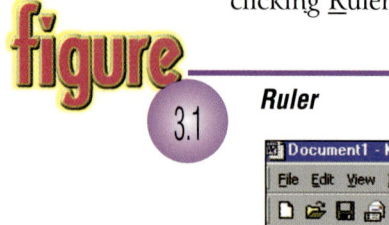

Ruler

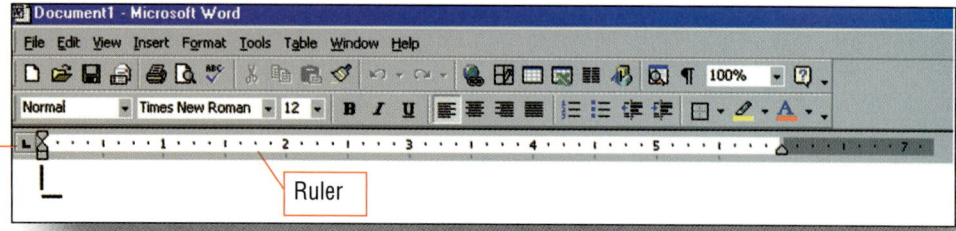

Alignment Button

Ruler

The Ruler displays left tabs set every 0.5 inches. These default tabs are indicated by tiny vertical lines along the bottom of the Ruler. With a left tab, text aligns at the left edge of the tab. The other types of tabs that can be set on the Ruler are center, right, decimal, and bar.

Alignment

The small button at the left side of the Ruler is called the Alignment button. (You used this button in chapter 2 to indent the first line of text in a paragraph and to create a hanging indent.) Each time you click the Alignment button, a different tab or paragraph alignment symbol displays. Figure 3.2 shows the tab alignment symbols and what type of tab each will set.

Tab Alignment Symbols

L	=	left tab
⊥	=	center tab
⅃	=	right tab
⊥·	=	decimal tab
I	=	bar tab

The columns displayed in figure 3.3 show text aligned at different tabs. The text in the first column in figure 3.3 was keyed at a left tab. The second column of text was keyed at a center tab, the third column at a right tab, and the fourth column at a decimal tab. (Refer to figure 3.7 for an example of a bar tab.)

figure

3.3 *Examples of Left, Center, Right, and Decimal Tabs*

Valencia	Washington	Olympia	22.908
Yang	Oregon	Salem	1,655.05555
Nicholson	California	Sacramento	623.5

Setting Tabs

To set a left tab on the Ruler, make sure the left alignment symbol **L** displays in the Alignment button. Position the arrow pointer just below the tick mark (the marks on the Ruler) where you want the tab symbol to appear and then click the left mouse button. When you set a tab on the Ruler, any default tabs to the left are automatically deleted by Word. Set a center, right, decimal, or bar tab on the Ruler in a similar manner.

Before setting a tab on the Ruler, click the Alignment button at the left side of the Ruler until the appropriate tab symbol is displayed, and then set the tab. If you change the tab symbol in the Alignment button, the symbol remains until you change it again or you exit Word. If you exit then reenter Word, the tab symbol returns to the default of left tab.

(Before completing computer exercises, delete the Chapter 02C *folder on your disk. Next, copy the* Chapter 03C *folder from the CD that accompanies this textbook to your disk and then make* Chapter 03C *the active folder.)*

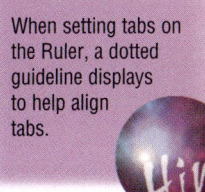

When setting tabs on the Ruler, a dotted guideline displays to help align tabs.

exercise

Setting Left Tabs on the Ruler

1. At a clear document screen, key the document shown in figure 3.4 by completing the following steps:
   a. Key the heading **TORRES ENTERPRISES**, centered and bolded.
   b. Press Enter twice. (Be sure to return the paragraph alignment back to left and turn off bold.)
   c. Set left tabs at the 1.25-inch mark and the 3.5-inch mark on the Ruler by completing the following steps:
      1) Click the Show/Hide ¶ button on the Standard toolbar to turn on the display of nonprinting characters.
      2) Make sure the Ruler is displayed.
      3) Make sure the left tab symbol displays in the Alignment button at the left side of the Ruler.
      4) Position the arrow pointer below the 1.25-inch mark on the Ruler and then click the left mouse button.

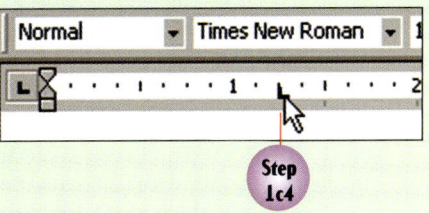

Step
1c4

5) Position the arrow pointer below the 3.5-inch tick mark on the Ruler and then click the left mouse button.

d. Key the text in columns as shown in figure 3.4. Press the Tab key before keying each column entry. (Make sure you press Tab before keying the text in the first column as well as the second column.)

e. Click the Show/Hide ¶ button on the Standard toolbar to turn off the display of nonprinting characters.

2. Save the document and name it Word C3, Ex 01.

3. Print and then close Word C3, Ex 01.

figure
3.4

Exercise 1

TORRES ENTERPRISES

Michele Yabe   Manager
Jason Edmondson   Assistant Manager
Kimberly Pascual   Supervisor
Eduardo Ross   Training Specialist
Troy Zimmerman   Administrative Assistant

When you press the Enter key, the insertion point is moved down to the next line and a paragraph mark is inserted in the document. Paragraph formatting is stored in this paragraph mark. For example, if you make changes to tab settings, these changes are inserted in the paragraph mark. In some situations, you may want to start a new line but not a new paragraph. To do this, press Shift + Enter. Word inserts a line break symbol (visible when nonprinting characters have been turned on) and moves the insertion point to the next line.

If you change tab settings and then create columns of text using the New Line command, Shift + Enter, the tab formatting is stored in the paragraph mark at the end of the columns. If you want to make changes to the tab settings for text in the columns, position the insertion point anywhere within the columns (all the text in the columns does not have to be selected), and then make the changes.

If you want to set a tab at a specific measurement on the Ruler, hold down the Alt key, position the arrow pointer at the desired position, and then hold down the left mouse button. This displays two measurements on the Ruler. The first measurement displays the location of the arrow pointer on the Ruler in relation to the left edge of the page. The second measurement is the distance from the location of the arrow pointer on the Ruler to the right margin. With the left mouse button held down, position the tab symbol at the desired location, and then release the mouse button and the Alt key.

Position the insertion point in any paragraph of text and tabs for the paragraph appear on the Ruler.

Setting Left, Center, and Right Tabs on the Ruler

1. At a clear document screen, key the document shown in figure 3.5 by completing the following steps:
   a. Key the heading **WORKSHOPS** centered and bolded.
   b. Press Enter three times. (Be sure to return the paragraph alignment back to left and turn off bold.)
   c. Set a left tab at the 0.5-inch mark, a center tab at the 3.5-inch mark, and a right tab at the 5.5-inch mark by completing the following steps:
      1) Click the Show/Hide ¶ button on the Standard toolbar to turn on the display of nonprinting characters.
      2) Make sure the Ruler is displayed.
      3) Make sure the left tab symbol displays in the Alignment button at the left side of the Ruler.
      4) Position the arrow pointer below the 0.5-inch tick mark on the Ruler. Hold down the Alt key and then the left mouse button. Make sure the first measurement on the Ruler

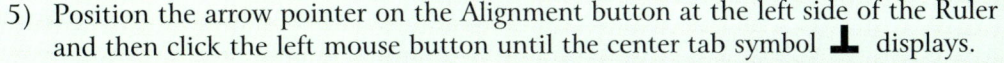

      displays as 0.5" and then release the mouse button and the Alt key.
      5) Position the arrow pointer on the Alignment button at the left side of the Ruler and then click the left mouse button until the center tab symbol ⊥ displays.
      6) Position the arrow pointer below the 3.5-inch tick mark on the Ruler. Hold down the Alt key and then the left mouse button. Make sure the first measurement on the Ruler displays as 3.5" and

      then release the mouse button and the Alt key.
      7) Position the arrow pointer on the Alignment button at the left side of the Ruler and then click the left mouse button until the right tab symbol ⌐ displays.
      8) Position the arrow pointer below the 5.5-inch tick mark on the Ruler. Hold down the Alt key and then the left mouse button. Make sure the first measurement

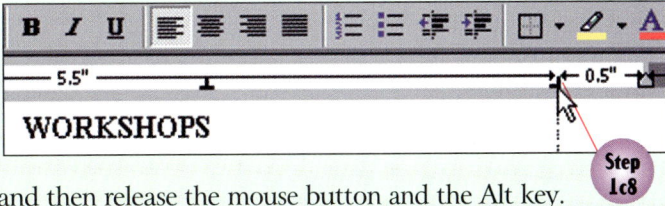

      on the Ruler displays as 5.5" and then release the mouse button and the Alt key.
   d. Key the text in columns as shown in figure 3.5. Press the Tab key before keying each column entry and press Shift + Enter twice after keying the text in the third column. (This moves the insertion point a double space below the text and inserts the New Line command.)
2. Save the document and name it Word C3, Ex 02.
3. Print and then close Word C3, Ex 02.

figure
3.5
Exercise 2

WORKSHOPS

Quality Management	February 5	$150
Staff Development	February 12	130
Streamlining Production	March 1	115
Managing Records	March 27	90

Moving Tabs

After a tab has been set on the Ruler, it can be moved to a new location. To move a single tab, position the arrow pointer on the tab symbol on the Ruler, hold down the left mouse button, drag the symbol to the new location on the Ruler, and then release the mouse button.

Deleting Tabs

To delete a tab from the Ruler, position the arrow pointer on the tab symbol you want deleted, hold down the left mouse button, drag the symbol down into the document screen, and then release the mouse button.

exercise 3

Moving and Deleting Tabs on the Ruler

1. Open Word Tab 01.
2. Save the document with Save As and name it Word C3, Ex 03.
3. Move the tab settings so the columns are more balanced by completing the following steps:
   a. Select only the text in columns (do not include any blank lines above the columns of text).
   b. Position the arrow pointer on the left tab symbol at the 0.5-inch mark, hold down the left mouse button, drag the left tab symbol to the 1.25-inch mark on the Ruler, and then release the mouse button. (*Hint: Use the Alt key to help you precisely position the tab symbol.*)
   c. Position the arrow pointer on the decimal tab symbol at the 3.5-inch mark, hold down the left mouse button, drag the decimal tab symbol into the document screen, and then release the mouse button. (This deletes the tab and merges the second column of text with the first column.)

d. Click the Alignment button at the left side of the Ruler until the right tab symbol displays.

e. Position the arrow pointer on the 4.75-inch mark on the Ruler and then click the left mouse button. (*Hint: Use the Alt key to help you precisely position the tab symbol.*)

f. Deselect the text.

4. Save the document again with the same name (Word C3, Ex 03).

5. Print and then close Word C3, Ex 03.

Manipulating Tabs at the Tabs Dialog Box

Use the Tabs dialog box shown in figure 3.6 to set tabs at a specific measurement. You can also use the Tabs dialog box to set tabs with preceding leaders and clear one tab or all tabs. To display the Tabs dialog box, click Format, expand the drop-down menu, and then click Tabs.

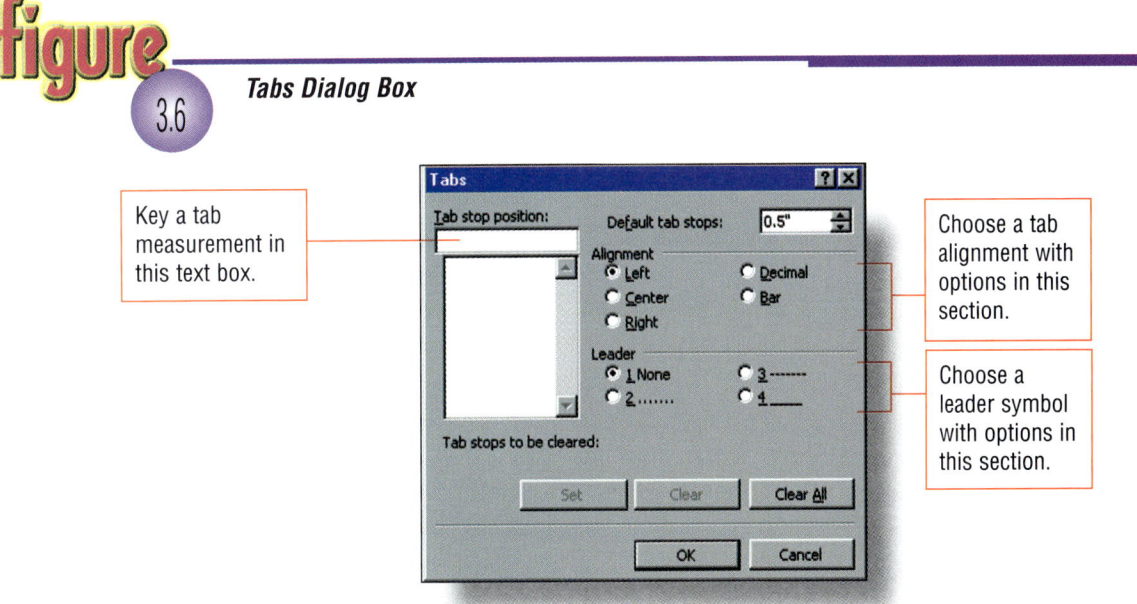

figure

3.6 **Tabs Dialog Box**

Key a tab measurement in this text box.

Choose a tab alignment with options in this section.

Choose a leader symbol with options in this section.

Clearing Tabs

At the Tabs dialog box, you can clear an individual tab or all tabs. To clear all tabs, click the Clear All button. To clear an individual tab, specify the tab position, and then click the Clear button.

Setting Tabs

At the Tabs dialog box, you can set a left, right, center, or decimal tab as well as a bar. (For an example of a bar tab, refer to figure 3.7.) You can also set a left, right, center, or decimal tab with preceding leaders. To change the type of tab at the

Tabs dialog box, display the dialog box, and then click the desired tab in the Alignment section. Key the desired measurement for the tab in the <u>T</u>ab stop position text box.

Setting Left Tabs and a Bar Tab at the Tabs Dialog Box

1. At a clear document screen, key the document shown in figure 3.7 by completing the following steps:
   a. Key the title **TRAINING DATES** bolded and centered, press the Enter key twice, and then change the paragraph alignment back to Left.
   b. Display the Tabs dialog box and then set left tabs and a bar tab by completing the following steps:
      1) Click F<u>o</u>rmat, expand the drop-down menu, and then click <u>T</u>abs.
      2) Make sure <u>L</u>eft is selected in the Alignment section of the dialog box. (If not, click <u>L</u>eft.)
      3) Key **1.75** in the <u>T</u>ab stop position text box. (The insertion point should automatically be positioned in the <u>T</u>ab stop position text box. If not, click in the text box.)
      4) Click the <u>S</u>et button.
      5) Key **3.5** in the <u>T</u>ab stop position text box and then click the <u>S</u>et button.
      6) Key **3** in the <u>T</u>ab stop position text box, click <u>B</u>ar in the Alignment section, and then click the <u>S</u>et button.
      7) Click OK to close the Tabs dialog box.
   c. Key the text in columns as shown in figure 3.7. Press the Tab key before keying each column entry. (The vertical line between columns will appear automatically. You need only key the dates. Do not press Enter after keying the date *February 27*.)
2. Save the document and name it Word C3, Ex 04.
3. Print and then close Word C3, Ex 04.

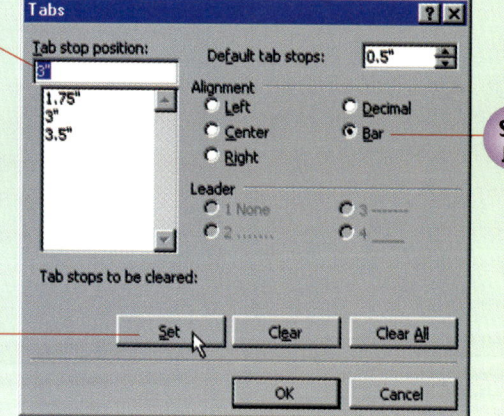

Step 1b6

Step 1b6

Step 1b6

Exercise 4

3.7

TRAINING DATES

January 9	February 6
January 17	February 12
January 22	February 15
January 30	February 27

Setting Leader Tabs

The four types of tabs can also be set with leaders. Leaders are useful in a table of contents or other material where you want to direct the reader's eyes across the page. Figure 3.8 shows an example of leaders. Leaders can be periods (.), hyphens (-), or underlines (_). To add leaders to a tab, click the type of leader desired in the Leader section of the Tabs dialog box.

Set a tab with leaders at the Tabs dialog box. *Hint*

exercise 5

Setting a Left Tab and a Right Tab with Dot Leaders

1. At a clear document screen, create the document shown in figure 3.8 by completing the following steps:
    a. Change the font to 12-point Tahoma. (If your printer does not support Tahoma, choose a similar sans serif typeface such as Univers.)
    b. Center and bold the title *TABLE OF CONTENTS*.
    c. Press Enter three times. (Be sure to return the alignment of the paragraph back to left and turn off bold.)
    d. Change the line spacing to 2.
    e. Set a left tab and a right tab with dot leaders by completing the following steps:
        1) Click Format and then Tabs.
        2) At the Tabs dialog box, make sure Left is selected in the Alignment section of the dialog box. (If not, click Left.)
        3) Make sure the insertion point is positioned in the Tab stop position text box, key **1**, and then click the Set button.
        4) Key **5** in the Tab stop position text box.
        5) Click Right in the Alignment section of the dialog box.
        6) Click 2....... in the Leader section of the dialog box and then click the Set button.
        7) Click OK or press Enter.
    f. Key the text in columns as shown in figure 3.8. Press the Tab key before keying each column entry.

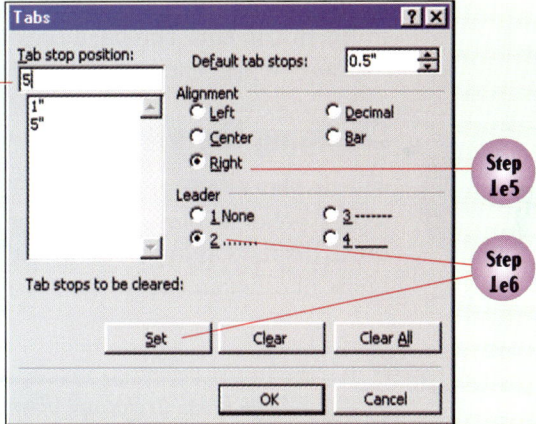
Step 1e4
Step 1e5
Step 1e6

2. Save the document and name it Word C3, Ex 05.
3. Print and then close Word C3, Ex 05.

figure

3.8

Exercise 5

View the positioning of elements on a page in Print Preview.

The insertion point remains where it was in the preceding view when you change to a different view

Preparing Multiple-Paged Documents

Word assumes that you are using standard-sized paper, which is 8.5 inches wide and 11 inches long. By default, a Word document contains 1-inch top and bottom margins and 1.25-inch left and right margins. With the default top and bottom margins of 1 inch, a total of 9 inches of text will print on a page (1 inch for the top margin, 9 inches of printed text, and then 1 inch for the bottom margin). As you create long documents, you will notice that when the insertion point nears 9.8 inches (or approximately Line 45 [this number may vary]) a page break is inserted in the document. The page break is inserted at the next line (at the 10-inch measurement). The line below the page break is the beginning of the next page.

Changing the View

The display of a page break will change depending on the view. At the Normal view, a page break displays as a row of dots. Change to the Print Layout view and a page break displays as an actual break in the page. Figure 3.9 shows an example of a page break in a document in the Normal view and another in the Print Layout view.

figure

3.9

Page Break in Normal View

> The pixelization problem in painting programs was resolved in two ways. First, as the
>
> RAM and storage capacities of personal computers grew, raster image-processing programs were
>
> created that could handle images with a greater number of dots per inch. Today's high-end raster
>
> image programs can handle full-screen images at 2400 dpi or higher in 16.7 million different
>
> colors. Another solution to the pixelization problem was the development of antialiasing,
>
> whereby pixels along the edge of an image are progressively lightened or darkened to produce

Page break in Normal view

Chapter Three

Page Break in Print Layout View

The pixelization problem in painting programs was resolved in two ways. First, as the RAM and storage capacities of personal computers grew, raster image-processing programs were created that could handle images with a greater number of dots per inch. Today's high-end raster

Page break in Print Layout view

image programs can handle full-screen images at 2400 dpi or higher in 16.7 million different colors. Another solution to the pixelization problem was the development of antialiasing, whereby pixels along the edge of an image are progressively lightened or darkened to produce

To change to the Print Layout view, click <u>V</u>iew and then <u>P</u>rint Layout or click the Print Layout View button at the left side of the horizontal scroll bar. (The Print Layout View button is the third button from the left side of the screen before the horizontal scroll bar.) To change back to the Normal view, click <u>V</u>iew and then <u>N</u>ormal or click the Normal View button at the left side of the horizontal scroll bar. (The Normal View button is the first button from the left.)

When you are working in a document containing more than one page of text, the Status bar displays the page where the insertion point is positioned and will also display the current page followed by the total number of pages in a document. For example, if the insertion point is positioned somewhere on page 3 of a 12-page document (with one section), the left side of the Status bar will display *Page 3   Sec 1   3/12*. The *3/12* indicates that the insertion point is positioned on page 3 in a document containing 12 pages.

Print Layout View

Normal View

Changing Margins

The default margin settings are displayed in the Page Setup dialog box shown in figure 3.10. To display the Page Setup dialog box, click <u>F</u>ile and then Page Set<u>u</u>p or double-click a gray area at the top of the Ruler. At the Page Setup dialog box, make sure the <u>M</u>argins tab is selected.

To change margins in a document, display the Page Setup dialog box, select the current measurement in the <u>T</u>op, <u>B</u>ottom, <u>L</u>eft, or Ri<u>g</u>ht text boxes, key the new measurement for the margin, and then click OK or press Enter. As you make changes to the margin measurements at the Page Setup dialog box, the sample page in the Preview box illustrates the adjustments to the margins. You can also click the up- and down-pointing triangles after each margin option to increase or decrease the margin measurement.

Margin changes are applied to the entire document until the document is divided into sections.

figure

3.10

Page Setup Dialog Box with _Margins_ Tab Selected

Notice the default settings for the top, bottom, left, and right margins.

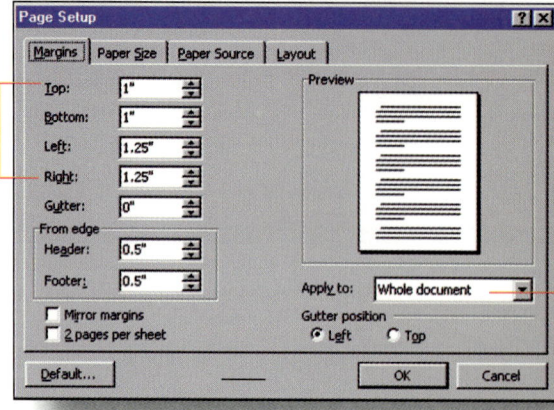

If you want margin changes to affect the entire document, leave the Apply to option set at *Whole document*. If you want margin changes to affect the document from the insertion point to the end of the document, change the Apply to option to *This point forward*.

Most printers contain a required margin (between one-quarter and three-eighths of an inch) because printers cannot print to the edge of the page.

If you want the new margins to affect the entire document, position the insertion point anywhere within the document, and then make margin changes at the Page Setup dialog box. You can also specify that margin changes affect the text in a document from the position of the insertion point to the end of the document. To do this, click the down-pointing triangle at the right of the Apply to option box in the Page Setup dialog box, and then click *This point forward* at the drop-down list.

Inserting a Section Break

By default, changes made to margins in a document are applied to all text in the document. If you want margin changes to apply to specific text in a document, select the text first. Text in a document can also be divided into sections. When a document is divided into sections, each section can be formatted separately. For example, different margin settings can be applied to each section in a document. Insert a section break at the Break dialog box. Display this dialog box by clicking Insert and Break.

exercise 6

Changing Margins and View

1. Open Word Report 01.
2. Save the report with Save As and name it Word C3, Ex 06.
3. Change the top margin to 1.5 inches and the left and right margins to 1 inch by completing the following steps:
   a. Click File and then Page Setup or double-click a gray area at the top of the Ruler.
   b. At the Page Setup dialog box, click the Margins tab.
   c. Click the up-pointing triangle after the Top option until *1.5"* displays in the Top text box.
   d. Click the down-pointing triangle after the Left option until *1"* displays in the Left text box.
   e. Click the down-pointing triangle after the Right option until *1"* displays in the Right text box.
   f. Click OK or press Enter.

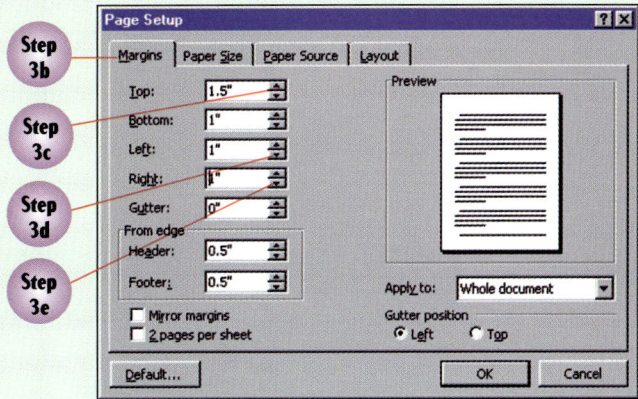

Step 3b

Step 3c

Step 3d

Step 3e

4. Make the following changes to the document:
   a. Select the title *GRAPHICS SOFTWARE* and then change the font to 18-point Arial bold.
   b. Select the heading *Early Painting and Drawing Programs* and then change the font to 14-point Arial bold.
   c. Use Format Painter to change the formatting to 14-point Arial bold for the remaining two headings, *Developments in Painting and Drawing Programs* and *Painting and Drawing Programs Today*.
5. Change the document view by completing the following steps:
   a. Change to Print Layout view by clicking the Print Layout View button located at the left side of the horizontal scroll bar (third button from the left).
   b. Scroll through the document and notice how page breaks appear in the document.
   c. Change back to Normal view by clicking View and then Normal.
6. Save the document again with the same name (Word C3, Ex 06).
7. Print and then close Word C3, Ex 06.

Inserting Hard Page Breaks

Word's default settings break each page after Line 45 (approximately 9.8 inches). Word automatically inserts page breaks in a document as you edit it. Since Word does this automatically, you may find that page breaks sometimes occur in undesirable locations. To remedy this, you can insert your own page break. A page break inserted automatically by Word is called a *soft page break* and a break inserted by you is called a *hard page break*.

To insert a hard page break, position the insertion point where you want the break to occur, click Insert and then Break. At the Break dialog box, make sure Page break is selected, and then click OK or press Enter. You can also insert a hard page break by positioning the insertion point in the document where you want the break to occur and then pressing Ctrl + Enter.

A hard page break displays in the Normal view as a line of dots with the words *Page Break* in the middle of the line. A hard page break displays in the same manner as a soft page break in the Print Layout view.

Soft page breaks automatically adjust if text is added to or deleted from a document. A hard page break does not adjust and is therefore less flexible than a soft page break. If you add or delete text from a document with a hard page break, check the break to determine whether it is still in a desirable location.

A hard page break can be deleted from a document. To delete a hard page break position the insertion point on the page break and then press the Delete key.

Inserting Hard Page Breaks

1. Open Word Report 01.
2. Save the document with Save As and name it Word C3, Ex 07.
3. Make the following changes to the document:
   a. Change the left and right margins to 1 inch.
   b. Insert a hard page break at the beginning of the heading *Developments in Painting and Drawing Programs* by completing the following steps:
      1) Position the insertion point at the beginning of the heading *Developments in Painting and Drawing Programs*.
      2) Press Ctrl + Enter.
   c. Insert a hard page break at the beginning of the remaining heading *Painting and Drawing Programs Today*.
4. Save the document again with the same name (Word C3, Ex 07).
5. Print and then close Word C3, Ex 07.

Previewing a Document

Press Ctrl + F2 to display Print Preview.

Print Preview

Before printing a document, viewing the document may be useful. Word's Print Preview feature displays the document on the screen as it will appear when printed. With this feature, you can view a partial page, single page, multiple pages, or zoom in on a particular area of a page.

To view a document, click File and then Print Preview or click the Print Preview button on the Standard toolbar. (The Print Preview button is the sixth button from the left on the Standard toolbar.) In Print Preview, the page where the insertion point is located displays on the screen. Figure 3.11 shows a document in Print Preview and figure 3.12 identifies the buttons on the Print Preview toolbar.

figure 3.11

Document in Print Preview

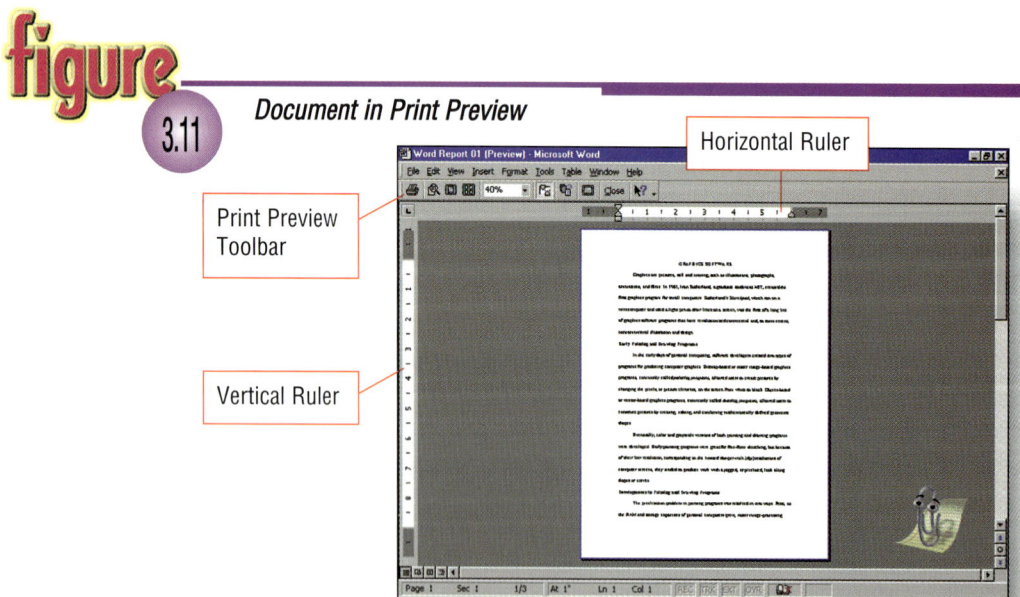

Horizontal Ruler

Print Preview Toolbar

Vertical Ruler

 figure

3.12 *Print Preview Toolbar Buttons*

Click this button	Named	To do this
	Print	Send the current document to the printer.
	Magnifier	Toggle the mouse pointer between a magnifying glass, which is used to view the document, and the normal mouse pointer, which is used to edit the document.
	One Page	Display individual pages in the document.
	Multiple Pages	Display multiple pages in the document (up to 18 pages).
42%	Zoom	Change viewing by percentage option or to Page Width, Text Width, Whole Page, or Two Pages.
	View Ruler	Turn the display of the Ruler on or off.
	Shrink to Fit	Try to "shrink" the contents of the last page in the document onto the previous page if there is only a small amount of text on the last page.
	Full Screen	Toggle the screen display between the normal display and full screen display, which removes everything from the Print Preview screen except the document and the Print Preview toolbar.
Close	Close Preview	Close Print Preview and return to document screen.
▶?▾	Context Sensitive Help	Display context-sensitive help.

   While in Print Preview, you can move through a document using the insertion point movement keys, the horizontal and vertical scroll bars, and/or the Page Up and Page Down keys.

exercise 8

Viewing a Document with Print Preview

1. Open Word Report 01.
2. View the document by completing the following steps:

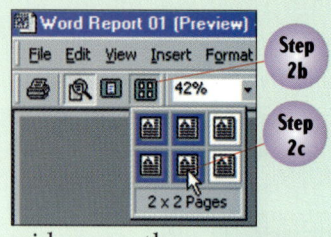

a. Click File and then Print Preview or click the Print Preview button on the Standard toolbar.
b. Click the Multiple Pages button on the Print Preview Toolbar. (This causes a grid to appear immediately below the button.)
c. Position the arrow pointer in the upper left portion of the grid, move the arrow pointer down and to the right until the message at the bottom of the grid displays as *2 x 2 Pages,* and then click the mouse button.

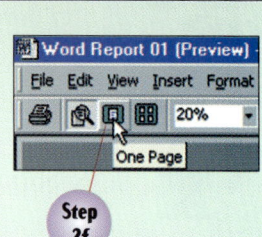

d. Click the Full Screen button on the Print Preview toolbar. This displays only the pages in the document and the Print Preview toolbar.
e. Click the Full Screen button again to restore the screen display.
f. Click the One Page button on the Print Preview toolbar.
g. Click the down-pointing triangle at the right of the Zoom button and then click *50%* at the drop-down list.
h. Click the down-pointing triangle at the right of the Zoom button and then click *75%* at the drop-down list.
i. Click the One Page button on the Print Preview toolbar.
j. Click the Close button on the Print Preview toolbar.
3. Close Word Report 01.

Vertically Aligning Text

Text in a Word document is aligned at the top of the page by default. This alignment can be changed using the Vertical alignment option at the Page Setup dialog box with the Layout tab selected as shown in figure 3.13. Display this dialog box by clicking File and then Page Setup. At the Page Setup dialog box, click the Layout tab.

figure

3.13

Page Setup Dialog Box with Layout Tab Selected

Click this down-pointing triangle to display a list of vertical alignment options.

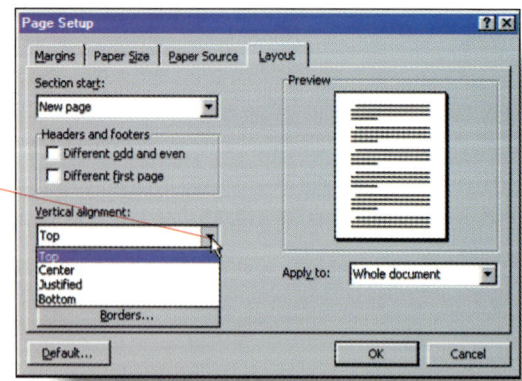

The <u>V</u>ertical alignment option from the Page Setup dialog box contains four choices—*Top*, *Center*, *Justified*, and *Bottom*. The default setting is *Top*, which aligns text at the top of the page. Choose *Center* if you want text centered vertically on the page. The *Justified* option will align text between the top and the bottom margins. The *Center* option positions text in the middle of the page vertically, while the *Justified* option adds space between paragraphs of text (not within) to fill the page from the top to bottom margins. If you center or justify text, the text does not display centered or justified on the screen in the Normal view but it does display centered or justified in the Print Layout view. Choose the *Bottom* option to align text in the document vertically along the bottom of the page.

Vertically Aligning Text in a Document

1. Open Word C3, Ex 02.
2. Save the document with Save As and name it Word C3, Ex 09.
3. Change to the Print Layout view by clicking <u>V</u>iew and then <u>P</u>rint Layout or clicking the Print Layout View button located at the left side of the screen before the horizontal scroll bar.
4. Vertically center the text in the document by completing the following steps:
   a. Click <u>F</u>ile and then Page Set<u>u</u>p.
   b. At the Page Setup dialog box, click the <u>L</u>ayout tab. (Skip this step if the <u>L</u>ayout tab is already selected.)
   c. Click the down-pointing triangle at the right side of the <u>V</u>ertical alignment option box and then click *Center* at the drop-down list.
   d. Click OK to close the dialog box.

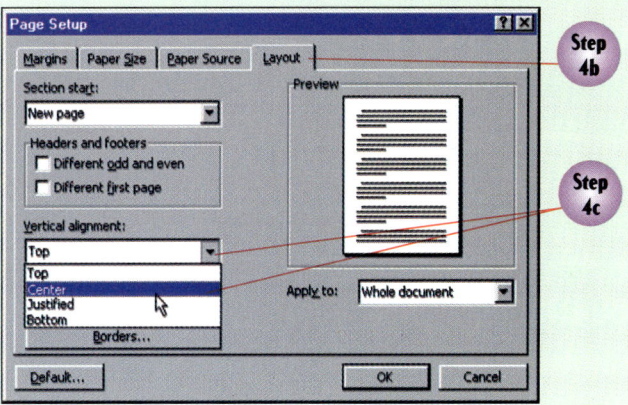

5. Display the document in Print Preview by clicking the Print Preview button on the Standard toolbar.
6. After viewing the document, click the <u>C</u>lose button on the Print Preview toolbar.
7. Save the document again with the same name (Word C3, Ex 09).
8. Print and then close Word C3, Ex 09.

Using the Click and Type Feature

In chapter 2, you learned to change paragraph alignment with buttons on the Formatting toolbar, shortcut commands, or options at the Paragraph dialog box. Another method for changing paragraph alignment is to use the *click and type* feature. Before using this feature, you must change to the Print Layout view.

In Print Layout view, hover the mouse pointer between the left and right margins (at approximately the three-inch mark on the Ruler). After a few seconds, four short horizontal lines display below the I-beam pointer. These horizontal lines represent center alignment. Double-click the mouse button and the insertion point is moved to the center of the margins and the Center button on the Formatting toolbar is activated.

You can change to right alignment in a similar manner. Hover the mouse pointer near the right margin and after a few seconds horizontal lines display at the left side of the I-beam pointer. These horizontal lines represent right alignment and are similar in appearance to the lines on the Align Right button on the Formatting toolbar. With the right alignment lines displayed at the left side of the I-beam pointer, double-click the left mouse button.

If the alignment lines are not displayed near the I-beam pointer and you double-click the left mouse button, a left tab is set at the position of the insertion point. If you want to change the alignment and not set a tab, be sure the alignment lines display near the I-beam pointer before double-clicking the mouse button. To change to left alignment, hover the mouse pointer near the left margin. When horizontal lines display representing left alignment, double-click the left mouse button.

Using Click and Type to Align Text

1. At a clear document screen, create the document shown in figure 3.14 by completing the following steps:
   a. If necessary, change to the Print Layout view by clicking <u>V</u>iew and then <u>P</u>rint Layout.
   b. Position the I-beam pointer between the left and right margins at about the 3-inch mark on the horizontal ruler and the 2½-inch mark on the vertical ruler.
   c. When the center alignment lines display below the I-beam pointer, double-click the left mouse button.
   d. Key the centered text shown in figure 3.14.
   e. After keying the centered text, press Enter twice then change to right alignment by completing the following steps:
      1) Position the I-beam pointer near the right margin at approximately the 4-inch mark on the vertical ruler until the right alignment lines display at the left side of the I-beam pointer. (You may need to scroll down the document to display the 4-inch mark on the vertical ruler.)
      2) Double-click the left mouse button.
   f. Key the right aligned text shown in figure 3.14.
2. Make the following changes to the document:
   a. Select the centered text and then change the font to 14-point Arial bold and the line spacing to Double.

b. Select the right aligned text and then change the font to 8-point Arial bold.
   c. Deselect the text.
3. Save the document and name it Word C3, Ex 10.
4. Print and then close Word C3, Ex 10.

Exercise 10

MICROSOFT EXCEL TRAINING
Developing Financial Spreadsheets
Tuesday, October 16, 2001
Training Center
9:00 a.m. - 3:30 p.m.

Sponsored by
Cell Systems

Inserting the Date and Time

The current date and/or time can be inserted in a document with options from
the Date and Time dialog box shown in figure 3.15. To display this dialog box,
click Insert and then Date and Time.

Date and Time Dialog Box

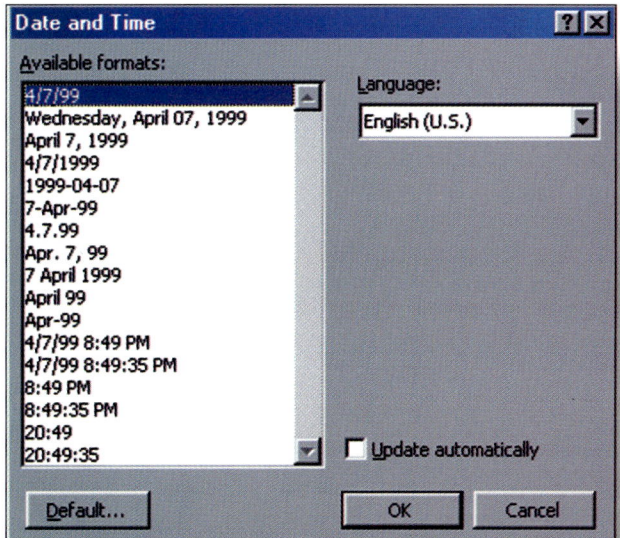

The Date and Time dialog box contains a list of date and time options in the Available formats list box. Click the desired date or time format, then click OK or press Enter.

The date can also be inserted in a document with the shortcut command, Alt + Shift + D. When you press Alt + Shift + D, the date is inserted in figures (such as 10/1/01). Press Alt + Shift + T to insert the current time in the document. The time is inserted in figures followed by AM or PM (such as 2:33 PM).

The date and/or time is inserted in the document as regular text. The date and/or time can also be inserted in a document as a field. If a date is inserted in a document as a field, the date is automatically updated if the document is opened on a different day. If the time is inserted as a field, the time is automatically updated when the document is opened again. To insert the date and/or time as a field, click the Update automatically check box that displays towards the bottom of the Date and Time dialog box.

Inserting the Date and Time Automatically

1. Open Word Document 05.
2. Save the document with Save As and name it Word C3, Ex 11.
3. Make the following changes to the document:
   a. Bold the title *ARE YOU PREPARING FOR RETIREMENT?*.
   b. Select from the paragraph that begins *Living longer than ever...* through the last paragraph in the document (do not include the blank lines at the end of the document) and then click the Bullets button on the Formatting toolbar.
   c. Move the insertion point to the end of the document (at the beginning of a blank line) and then complete the following steps:
      1) Key **Date:** and then press the space bar once.
      2) Press Alt + Shift + D. (This inserts the current date.)
      3) Press the Enter key.
      4) Key **Time:** and then press the space bar once.
      5) Press Alt + Shift + T. (This inserts the current time.)
4. Print Word C3, Ex 11.
5. Change the current date format by completing the following steps:
   a. Delete the current date.
   b. Click Insert and then Date and Time.
   c. At the Date and Time dialog box, click the fourth option in the Available formats list box.
   d. Click OK or press Enter.
6. Save the document again with the same name (Word C3, Ex 11).
7. Print and then close Word C3, Ex 11.

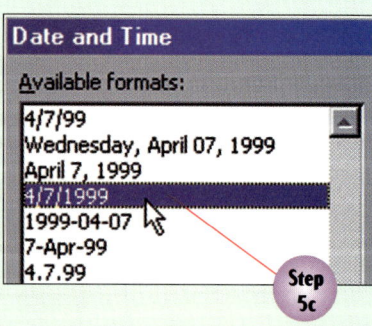

Highlighting Text

As people read information in books, magazines, periodicals, papers, and so on, they may highlight important information with a highlighting pen. A highlighting pen creates a colored background through which the text can be read. This colored background draws the reader's eyes to the specific text.

Word provides a button on the Formatting toolbar that lets you highlight text in a document using the mouse. With this highlighting feature, you can select and highlight specific text in a document with a variety of colors. To use this feature, click the Highlight button on the Formatting toolbar, and then select the desired text using the mouse. When the Highlight button is activated, the I-beam pointer displays with a pen attached. Continue selecting text you want highlighted and when completed, click once on the Highlight button to deactivate it.

The default highlighting color is yellow. You can change this color by clicking the down-pointing triangle to the right of the Highlight button. From the drop-down list of colors that displays, click the desired color. This changes the color of the small rectangle below the pen on the Highlight button. If you are using a noncolor printer, highlighted text will print with a gray background. To remove highlighting from text, change the highlighting color to *None*, activate the Highlight button, and then select the highlighted text.

exercise 12

Highlighting Text in a Document

1. Open Word Document 04.
2. Save the document with Save As and name it Word C3, Ex 12.
3. Highlight text in the document by completing the following steps:
   a. Click the Highlight button on the Formatting toolbar.
   b. Select the sentence *While an agreement would be positive for the financial markets, the uncertainty surrounding the budget discussion is a lingering concern.* that displays in the first paragraph.
   c. Click the Highlight button to deactivate it.
4. Change the highlighting color and then highlight text in the document by completing the following steps:
   a. Click the down-pointing triangle to the right of the Highlight button on the Formatting toolbar.
   b. From the drop-down list of colors, click the Turquoise color.
   c. Select the sentence *While the sign of healthy cyclical rotation to other sections such as financial services and consumer non-durables has been noticed, no group has yet emerged as a clear leader.* that displays at the end of the second paragraph.
   d. Click the Highlight button to deactivate it.
5. Save the document again with the same name (Word C3, Ex 12).

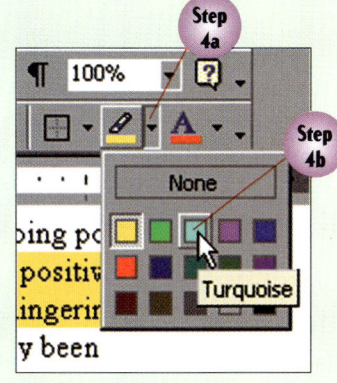

Step 4a

Step 4b

6. Print Word C3, Ex 12.
7. Remove highlighting from text in the document by completing the following steps:
   a. Click the down-pointing triangle to the right of the Highlight button on the Formatting toolbar.
   b. From the drop-down list that displays, click *None* (ScreenTip displays with *No Highlight*).
   c. Select the sentence *While an agreement would be positive for the financial markets, the uncertainty surrounding the budget discussion is a lingering concern.* that displays in the first paragraph.
   d. Select the sentence *While the sign of healthy cyclical rotation to other sections such as financial services and consumer non-durables has been noticed, no group has yet emerged as a clear leader.* that displays at the end of the second paragraph.
   e. Return the highlight color to yellow.
   f. Click the Highlight button to deactivate it.
8. Save the document again with the same name (Word C3, Ex 12).
9. Print and then close Word C3, Ex 12.

Creating Newspaper Columns

When preparing a document containing text, an important point to consider is the readability of the document. Readability refers to the ease with which a person can read and understand groups of words. The line length of text in a document can enhance or detract from the readability of text. If the line length is too long, the reader may lose his or her place on the line and have a difficult time moving to the next line below. To improve the readability of some documents such as newsletters or reports, you may want to set the text in columns.

Text can be set in two different types of columns in Word. One type, called newspaper columns, is commonly used for text in newspapers, newsletters, and magazines. The other type, called side-by-side columns, is used for text that you want to keep aligned horizontally. Side-by-side columns are created using the Tables feature (covered in chapter 6).

Newspaper columns contain text that flows up and down in the document, as shown in figure 3.16. When the first column on the page is filled with text, the insertion point moves to the top of the next column on the same page. When the last column on the page is filled with text, the insertion point moves to the beginning of the first column on the next page.

Columns

Create newspaper columns using the Columns button on the Standard toolbar or using options from the Columns dialog box. The formatting for newspaper columns can be established before the text is keyed or it can be applied to existing text. A document can include as many columns as there is room for on the page. Word determines how many columns can be included on the page based on the page width, the margin widths, and the size and spacing of the columns.

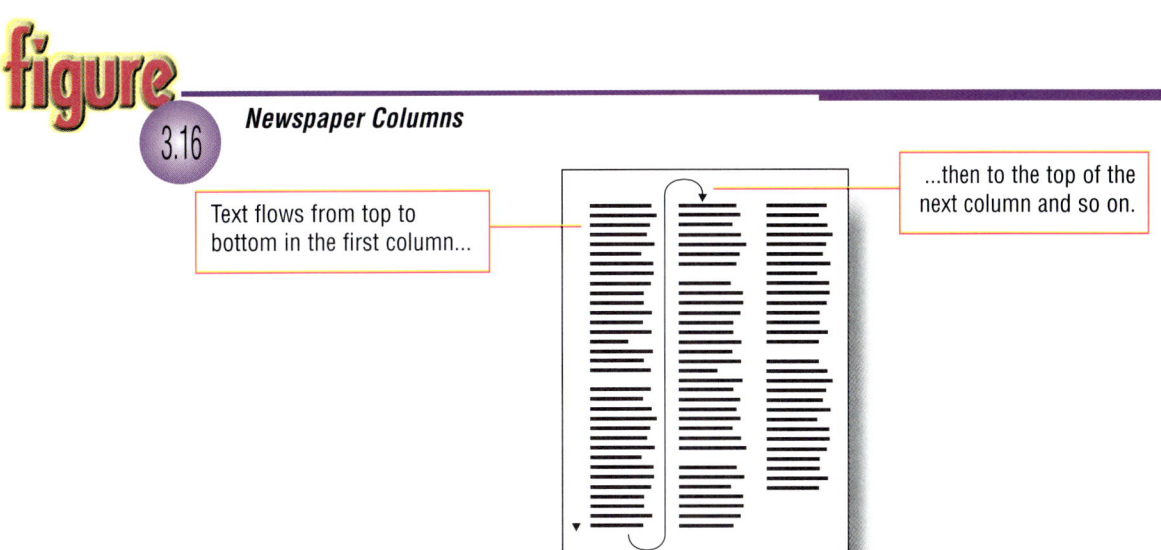

figure

3.16

Newspaper Columns

Text flows from top to bottom in the first column...

...then to the top of the next column and so on.

Formatting Sections

Changes in columns affect the entire document or the section of the document in which the insert point is positioned. If you want to create different numbers or styles of columns in a document, divide the document into sections. There are three methods for inserting a section break in a document.

One method is to use the Break dialog box. Display this dialog box by clicking Insert and Break. In the Section break types section of the Break dialog box, choose to insert a section break that begins a new page or choose to insert a continuous section break. A continuous section break displays in the Normal view as a double line of dots across the screen with the words *Section Break (Continuous)* inserted in the middle. In the Print Layout view, a section break does not display on the screen. However, the section number where the insertion point is located displays in the Status bar as Sec followed by the number. A section break that begins a new page displays as a double row of dots across the screen with the words *Section Break (Next Page)* inserted in the middle. In the Print Layout view, a section break that begins a new page displays as a new page.

Another method for inserting a section break in a document is to use the Columns dialog box and specify that text is to be formatted into columns from the location of the insertion point forward in the document. The third method is to select the text first and then apply column formatting.

Creating Newspaper Columns with the Columns Button

To create newspaper columns using the Columns button on the Standard toolbar, click the Columns button. This causes a grid to display as shown in figure 3.17. Move the mouse down and to the right until the desired number of columns displays with a blue background on the Columns grid and then click the mouse button.

Columns Grid

3.17

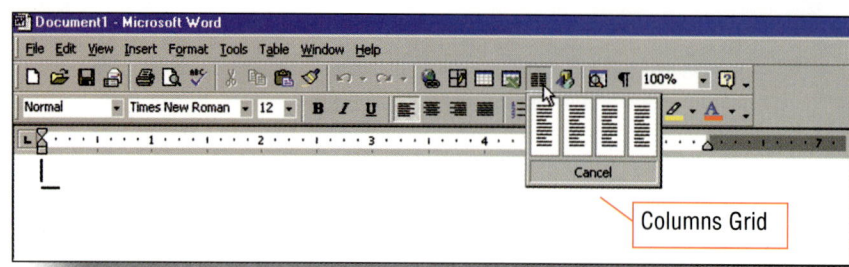

Columns Grid

If a document contains a title and you want that title to span both columns, position the insertion point at the left margin at the first line of text that will begin the columns and then click Insert and then Break. At the Break dialog box shown in figure 3.18, click Continuous, and then click OK or press Enter.

Break Dialog Box

3.18

Click Continuous to insert a continuous section break

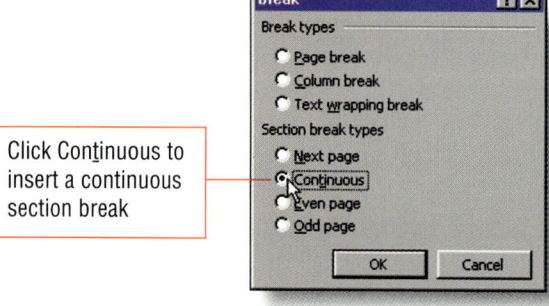

In addition to using the method just described, you could also format the text in a document into columns and not the title by selecting the text in the document (excluding the title), and then using the Columns button on the Standard toolbar to create the columns. A third method is explained in the next section on creating columns with options from the Columns dialog box.

In Normal view, text displays in a single column at the left side of the document screen. If you want to view columns as they will appear when printed, change to the Print Layout view.

Formatting Text into Newspaper Columns Using the Columns Button

1. Open Word Report 01.
2. Save the document with Save As and name it Word C3, Ex 13.
3. Make the following changes to the document:
   a. Change to the Print Layout view.
   b. Select the title and then change the font to 18-point Times New Roman bold.
   c. Select the text in the document from the beginning of the first paragraph (begins with *Graphics are pictures...*) to the end of the document. With the text selected, make the following changes:
      1) Change the font to 11-point Times New Roman.
      2) Change the line spacing to single.
      3) Set a left tab on the Ruler at the 0.25-inch mark.
      4) Format the text into two newspaper columns by clicking the Columns button on the Standard toolbar, moving the arrow pointer down and to the right until two columns display with a blue background on the Columns grid (and *2 Columns* displays below the grid), and then clicking the mouse button again.
      5) Deselect the text.
      6) Insert six points of space before and after each of the three headings in the document (*Early Painting and Drawing Programs, Developments in Painting and Drawing Programs* and *Painting and Drawing Programs Today*). *(Hint: Do this with the Before and After options at the Paragraph dialog box.)*

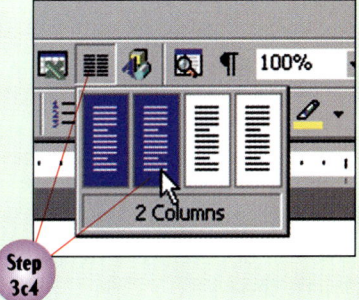

Step 3c4

4. Save the document again with the same name (Word C3, Ex 13).
5. Print and then close Word C3, Ex 13.

Creating Newspaper Columns with the Columns Dialog Box

The Columns dialog box can be used to create newspaper columns that are equal or unequal in width. To display the Columns dialog box shown in figure 3.19, click Format, expand the drop-down menu, and then click Columns.

figure

3.19

Columns Dialog Box

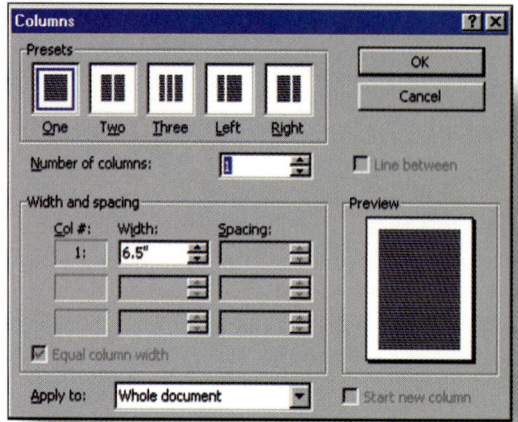

At the Columns dialog box, you can choose from a number of preset columns, choose your own number of columns, specify the width and spacing of specific columns, insert a line between columns, and specify where column formatting is to apply.

Formatting Text into Uneven Newspaper Columns with a Line Between

1. Open Word Report 02.
2. Save the document with Save As and name it Word C3, Ex 14.
3. Delete the section 2 portion of the document by completing the following steps:
   a. Select the text in the document from the beginning of the title *SECTION 2: COMPUTERS IN ENTERTAINMENT* (located on page 2) to the end of the document.
   b. Press the Delete key.
4. Make the following changes to the document:
   a. Select the entire document and then change the font to 12-point Bookman Old Style (or a similar serif typeface).
   b. Select the title *SECTION 1: COMPUTERS IN COMMUNICATION* and then change the font to 14-point Arial bold.
   c. Select the heading *Telecommunications* and then change the font to 12-point Arial bold.
   d. Use Format Painter to apply 12-point Arial bold to the two remaining headings (*Publishing* and *News Services*).
   e. Select the text from the beginning of the first paragraph to the end of the document and then make the following changes:
      1) Change the line spacing to single.
      2) Set a left tab on the Ruler at the 0.25-inch mark.
   f. Insert 6 points of space above and below each of the three headings (*Telecommunications*, *Publishing*, and *News Services*).

5. Format the text of the report into uneven columns with a line between by completing the following steps:

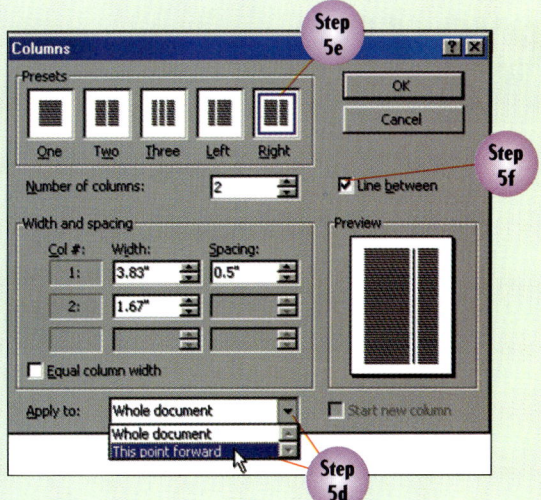

Step 5e
Step 5f
Step 5d

   a. Change to the Print Layout view.
   b. Position the insertion point at the left margin of the first paragraph.
   c. Click Format, expand the drop-down menu, and then click Columns.
   d. At the Columns dialog box, click the down-pointing triangle at the right side of the Apply to text box, and then click *This point forward* at the drop-down list.
   e. Click the Right option in the Presets section of the Columns dialog box.
   f. Click the Line between check box.
   g. Click OK or press Enter.
   h. If the heading *News Services* displays at the top of the second column, remove the six points of space before the heading. (If the heading moves to the bottom of the first column, position the insertion point at the beginning of the heading, and then press the Enter key. This should move the heading to the top of the second column.)

6. Save the document again with the same name (Word C3, Ex 14).
7. Print and then close Word C3, Ex 14.

Inserting a Column and/or Page Break

When formatting text into columns, Word automatically breaks the columns to fit the page. At times, column breaks may appear in an undesirable location. For example, a heading may appear at the bottom of the column, while the text after the heading begins at the top of the next column. You can insert a column break by positioning the insertion point where you want the column to end and begin a new page by pressing Ctrl + Shift + Enter. You can also insert a column break by positioning the insertion point at the location where the new column is to begin, and then clicking Insert and then Break. At the Break dialog box, click Column break, and then click OK or press Enter.

Editing Text in Columns

To move the insertion point in a document using the mouse, position the arrow pointer where desired, and then click the left button. On the keyboard, the left and right arrow keys move the insertion point in the direction indicated within the column. When the insertion point gets to the end of the line within the column, it moves down to the beginning of the next line within the same column.

You can use the mouse or the keyboard to move the insertion point between columns. If you are using the mouse, position the I-beam pointer where desired, and then click the left button. If you are using the keyboard, press Alt + up arrow to move the insertion point to the top of the previous column, or press Alt + down arrow to move the insertion point to the top of the next column.

Editing Text in Newspaper Columns

1. Open Word C3, Ex 13.
2. Save the document with Save As and name it Word C3, Ex 15.
3. Make the following changes to the report:
   a. Change the left and right margins to 1 inch.
   b. Select the entire document and then change the font to 11-point Bookman Old Style (or a similar serif typeface).
   c. Change the spacing between the two columns by completing the following steps:
      1) Position the insertion point somewhere in the first paragraph.
      2) Click Format and then Columns.
      3) At the Columns dialog box, click the down-pointing triangle at the right side of the Spacing text box (located in the Width and spacing section) until *0.3"* displays.
      4) Click OK or press Enter to close the dialog box.
   d. Select the title and then change the font to 16-point Tahoma bold.
   e. Select the heading *Early Painting and Drawing Programs* and then change the font to 11-point Tahoma bold.
   f. Use Format Painter to apply 11-point Tahoma bold to the two remaining headings.
   g. If the heading *Developments in Painting and Drawing Programs* displays at the top of the second column, remove the six points of space before the heading. (If the heading moves to the bottom of the first column, position the insertion point at the beginning of the heading, and then press the Enter key. This should move the heading to the top of the second column.)

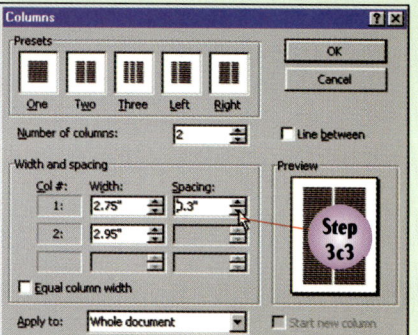

4. Save the document again with the same name (Word C3, Ex 15).
5. Print and then close Word C3, Ex 15.

Removing Column Formatting

To remove column formatting using the Columns button, position the insertion point in the section containing columns, or select the text in columns. Click the Columns button on the Standard toolbar and then click the first column in the Columns grid. To remove column formatting using the Columns dialog box, position the insertion point in the section containing columns, or select the text in columns, and then click Format and then Columns. At the Columns dialog box, click One in the Presets section, and then click OK or press Enter.

Checking the Spelling and Grammar of a Document

Word includes writing tools to help create a thoughtful and well-written document. Two of these tools are a spelling checker and a grammar checker. The

spelling checker finds misspelled words and offers replacement words. It also finds duplicate words and irregular capitalizations. When you spell check a document, the spelling checker compares the words in your document with the words in its dictionary. If a match is found, the word is passed over. If there is no match for the word, the spelling checker will stop, select the word, and offer replacements.

The grammar checker will search a document for errors in grammar, style, punctuation, and word usage. The spelling checker and the grammar checker can help you create a well-written document but do not replace the need for proofreading. You would complete the following steps to complete a spelling and grammar check:

1. Click the Spelling and Grammar button on the Standard toolbar or click Tools and then Spelling and Grammar.
2. If a spelling error is detected, the misspelled word is selected and a Spelling and Grammar dialog box similar to the one shown in figure 3.20 displays. The sentence containing the misspelled word is displayed in the Not in Dictionary: text box. If a grammatical error is detected, the sentence containing the error is selected and the Spelling and Grammar dialog box similar to the one shown in figure 3.21 displays.
3. If a misspelled word is selected, replace the word with the correct spelling, tell Word to ignore it and continue checking the document, or add the word to a custom dictionary. If a sentence containing a grammatical error is selected, the grammar checker displays the sentence in the top text box in the Spelling and Grammar dialog box. Choose to ignore or change errors found by the grammar checker.
4. When the spelling and grammar check is completed, the Office Assistant displays the message *The spelling and grammar check is complete.* Click anywhere in the document screen outside the message box to remove the box.

Spelling and
Grammar

Complete a spelling and grammar check on a portion of a document by selecting the text first and then clicking the Spelling and Grammar button.

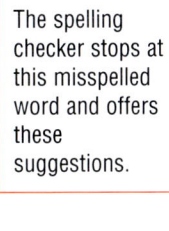

figure

3.20

Spelling and Grammar Dialog Box with Spelling Error Selected

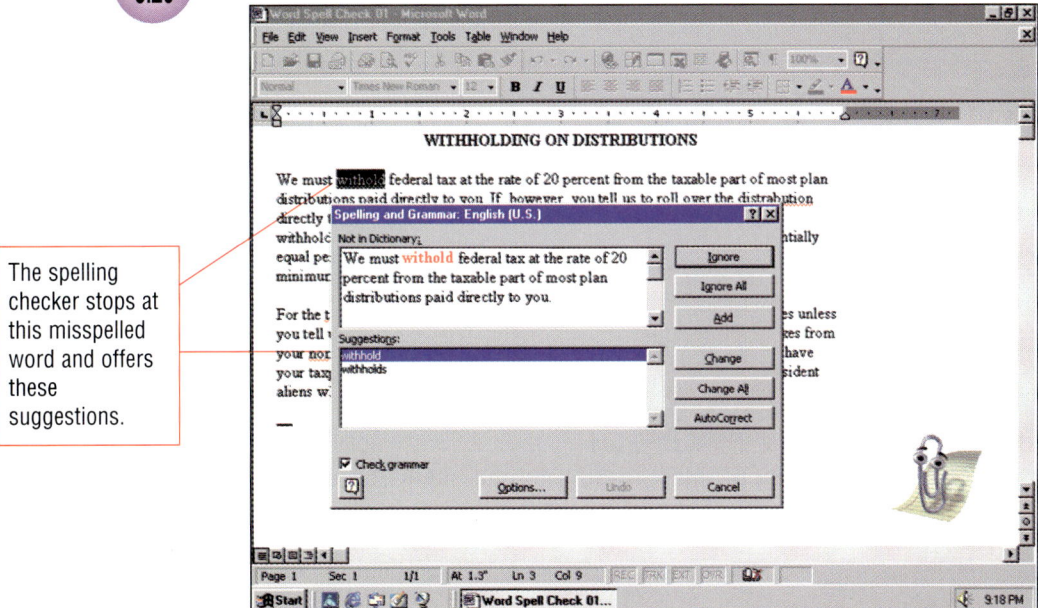

The spelling checker stops at this misspelled word and offers these suggestions.

Spelling and Grammar Dialog Box with Grammar Error Selected

The grammar checker selects this sentence and offers this suggestion to correct the grammar.

The Office Assistant provides information on the grammar rule.

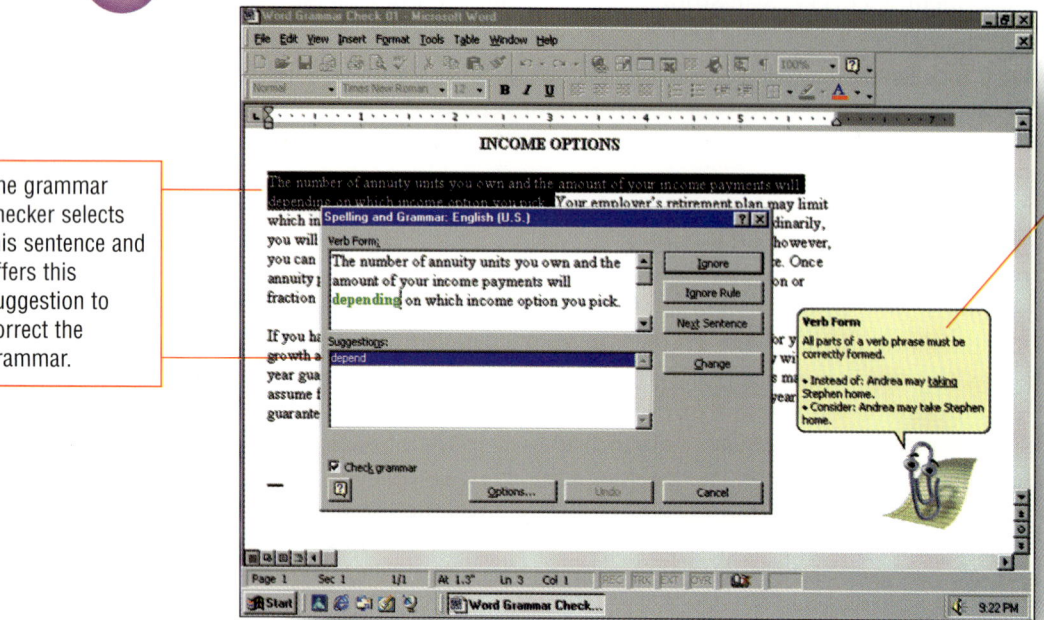

When a word is selected during a spelling and grammar check, you need to determine if the word should be corrected or if it should be ignored. Word provides buttons at the right side and bottom of the Spelling and Grammar dialog box to make decisions. The buttons will change depending on whether a misspelled word is selected or a sentence containing a grammatical error. Figure 3.22 describes the buttons and the functions performed by the buttons.

Spelling and Grammar Checking Buttons

Button	Function
Ignore	During spell checking, skips that occurrence of the word; in grammar checking, leaves the currently selected text as written.
Ignore All	During spell checking, skips that occurrence of the word and all other occurrences of the word in the document.
Ignore Rule	During grammar checking, leaves the currently selected text as written and also ignores the current rule for the remainder of the grammar check in the document.

Add	Adds the selected word to the main spelling checker dictionary.
Change	Replaces the selected word in the sentence with the selected word in the Suggestions list box.
Change All	Replaces the selected word in the sentence with the selected word in the Suggestions list box and all other occurrences of the word in the document.
AutoCorrect	Inserts the selected word and the correct spelling of the word in the AutoCorrect dialog box.
Undo Edit	Reverses the most recent spelling and grammar action.
Next Sentence	Accepts manual changes made to a sentence and then continues grammar checking.
Options	Displays a dialog box with options for customizing a spelling and grammar check.

By default, the spelling and grammar in a document is checked. You can turn off the grammar checker and perform only a spelling check. To do this, click the Check grammar option at the Spelling and Grammar dialog box (located in the lower left corner) to remove the check mark.

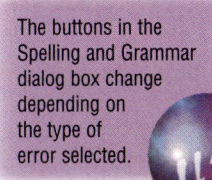
The buttons in the Spelling and Grammar dialog box change depending on the type of error selected.

exercise 16

Spell Checking a Document

1. Open Word Spell Check 01.
2. Save the document with Save As and name it Word C3, Ex 16.
3. Perform a spelling check by completing the following steps:
   a. Click the Spelling and Grammar button on the Standard toolbar (the seventh button from the left).
   b. The spelling checker selects the word *withold*. The proper spelling is selected in the Suggestions list box so click the Change All button. (Because this word is misspelled in other locations in the document, clicking the Change All button will change the other misspellings.)
   c. The spelling checker selects the word *distrabution*. The proper spelling is selected in the Suggestions list box so click the Change button. (Click the Change button because the word is only misspelled once.)
   d. The spelling checker selects the word *imployer*. The proper spelling is selected in the Suggestions list box so click the Change button.
   e. The spelling checker selects the word *fedaral*. The proper spelling is selected in the Suggestions list box so click the Change All button.
   f. The spelling checker selects *yaers*. The proper spelling is selected in the Suggestions list box so click the Change button.
   g. The spelling checker selects *taxible*. The proper spelling is selected in the Suggestions list box so click the Change button.

h. If the spelling checker selects *noneligible*, click Ignore All to skip the word (it is spelled properly).

i. The spelling checker selects the word *identificatoin*. The proper spelling is selected in the Suggestions list box so click the Change button.

j. The Office Assistant displays the message, *The spelling and grammar check is complete.* Click in the document screen outside this message to remove the message.

4. Save the document again with the same name (Word C3, Ex 16).

5. Print and then close Word C3, Ex 16.

Editing while Spell Checking

When spell checking a document, you can temporarily leave the Spelling and Grammar dialog box, make corrections in the document, and then resume spell checking. For example, suppose while spell checking you notice a sentence that you want to change. To correct the sentence, move the I-beam pointer to the location in the sentence where the change is to occur, click the left mouse button, and then make changes to the sentence. To resume spell checking, click the Resume button, which was formerly the Ignore button.

Spell Checking a Document with Words in Uppercase and with Numbers

1. Open Word Spell Check 02.

2. Save the document with Save As and name it Word C3, Ex 17.

3. Check spell checking options by completing the following steps:

a. Click Tools and then Options.

b. At the Options dialog box, click the Spelling & Grammar tab.

c. Make sure there is a check mark in the Ignore words in UPPERCASE check box. (If there is no check mark, click in the check box before Ignore words in UPPERCASE to insert one.)

d. Make sure there is a check mark in the Ignore words with numbers check box. (If there is no check mark, click in the check box before Ignore words with numbers to insert one.)

e. Click OK or press Enter to close the dialog box.

4. Perform a spelling check by completing the following steps:

a. Click the Spelling and Grammar button on the Standard toolbar.

b. The spelling checker selects the word *beigin*. The proper spelling is selected in the Suggestions list box so click the Change button (or Change All button).

c. The spelling checker selects the word *aney*. The proper spelling of the word is selected in the Suggestions list box so click the Change button (or Change All button).

d. The grammar checker selects *the distribution is because you are disabled* and displays information on capitalization. Click the Ignore Rule button to tell the grammar checker to ignore the rule.

e. The spelling checker selects *seperated*. The proper spelling is selected in the Suggestions list box so click the Change button (or Change All button).

    f.   The spelling checker selects *annuty*. The proper spelling is selected in the Suggestio_n_s list box so click the *C*hange button (or Change A*l*l button).

    g.   The spelling checker selects *searies*. The proper spelling is selected in the Suggestio_n_s list box so click the *C*hange button (or Change A*l*l button).

    h.   The spelling checker selects *gros*. The proper spelling is selected in the Suggestio_n_s list box so click the *C*hange button (or Change A*l*l button).

    i.   The spelling checker selects *laess*. The proper spelling *less* is not selected in the Suggestio_n_s list box but it is one of the words suggested. Click *less* in the Suggestio_n_s list box, and then click the *C*hange button.

    j.   The grammar checker selects *you are required to make a payment to someone besides yourself under a MIRA plan.* and displays information on commonly confused words. Click the I*g*nore Rule button to tell the grammar checker to ignore the rule.

    k.   When the spelling and grammar check is completed, click outside the Office Assistant message box to remove the message box.

  5. Save the document again with the same name (Word C3, Ex 17).

  6. Print and then close Word C3, Ex 17.

Checking the Grammar and Style of a Document

Word includes a grammar checking feature that you can use to search a document for grammar, style, punctuation, and word usage. Like the spelling checker, the grammar checker does not find every error in a document and may stop at correct phrases. The grammar checker can help you create a well-written document but does not replace the need for proofreading.

    To complete a grammar check (as well as a spelling check) on a document, click the Spelling and Grammar button on the Standard toolbar or click *T*ools, and then *S*pelling and Grammar. (At the Spelling and Grammar dialog box, make sure there is a check mark in the Chec*k* grammar check box.) The grammar checker selects the first sentence with a grammatical error and displays the sentence in the top text box in the dialog box. The grammar rule that is violated is displayed above the text box and the Office Assistant displays information about the grammar rule. Choose to ignore or change errors found by the grammar checker. When the grammar checker is done, the open document is displayed on the screen. The changes made during the check are inserted in the document. By default, a spelling check is completed on a document during a grammar check.

Read grammar suggestions carefully. Some suggestions may not be valid and a problem identified by the grammar checker may not be a problem. *Hint*

Checking Grammar in a Document

  1. Open Word Grammar Check 01.

  2. Save the document with Save As and name it Word C3, Ex 18.

  3. Perform a grammar check by completing the following steps:

    a.   Click the Spelling and Grammar button on the Standard toolbar.

    b.   The grammar checker selects the sentence *The number of annuity units you own and the amount of your income payments will depending on which income option you pick.* and

displays *depend* in the Suggestions list box. The Office Assistant displays information on verb form. Read this information and then click the Change button.

c. The grammar checker selects the sentence *Once annuity payments start, you cannot change the income option for the accumulation or fraction of accumulation on which their based.* and displays *they're* in the Suggestions list box. The Office Assistant displays information on commonly confused words. Read this information and then click the Change button.

d. The grammar checker selects the sentence *If your married, McCormack Funds may assume for you a survivor annuity with half-benefit to annuity partner and a 10-year guaranteed period, with your spouse as your annuity partner.* and displays *you're* in the Suggestions list box. The Office Assistant displays information on commonly confused words. (This is the same information displayed in the previous step.) Click the Change button to change *your* to *you're*.

e. The Office Assistant displays a message box telling you that the spelling and grammar check is completed. Click in the document screen outside this box to remove the box.

4. Save the document again with the same name (Word C3, Ex 18).

5. Print and then close Word C3, Ex 18.

Changing Grammar Checking Options

If you click the Options button in the Spelling and Grammar dialog box, the Spelling and Grammar dialog box displays with options for customizing the grammar checking. One of the options is Show readability statistics. Insert a check mark in this option and readability statistics about the document will display when grammar checking is completed. Most of the readability information is self-explanatory. The last two statistics included, however, are described in figure 3.23.

figure
3.23

Readability Statistics

Flesch Reading Ease	The Flesch reading ease is based on the average number of syllables per word and the average number of words per sentence. The higher the score, the greater the number of people who will be able to understand the text in the document. Standard writing generally scores in the 60-70 range.
Flesch-Kincaid Grade Level	This is based on the average number of syllables per word and the average number of words per sentence. The score indicates a grade level. Standard writing is generally written at the seventh- or eighth-grade level.

Changing Writing Style

At the Spelling and Grammar dialog box (as well as the Options dialog box with the Spelling & Grammar tab selected), you can specify a writing style. The default writing style is *Standard*. This can be changed to *Casual, Formal, Technical,* or *Custom*. Choose the writing style that matches the document you are checking. For example, if you are checking a scientific document, change the writing style to *Technical*. If you are checking a short story, consider changing the writing style to *Casual*. To change the writing style, click the down-pointing triangle at the right of the <u>W</u>riting style text box, and then click the desired style at the drop-down list.

Changing Grammar Checking Options, Then Grammar Checking a Document

1. Open Word Document 05.
2. Save the document with Save As and name it Word C3, Ex 19.
3. Change grammar checking options by completing the following steps:
    a. Click <u>T</u>ools and then <u>O</u>ptions.
    b. At the Options dialog box, click the Spelling & Grammar tab.
    c. At the Options dialog box with the Spelling & Grammar tab selected, click the Show <u>r</u>eadability statistics. (This inserts a check mark in the option.)
    d. Click the down-pointing triangle at the right of the <u>W</u>riting style text box and then click *Formal* at the drop-down list.
    e. Click OK to close the dialog box.

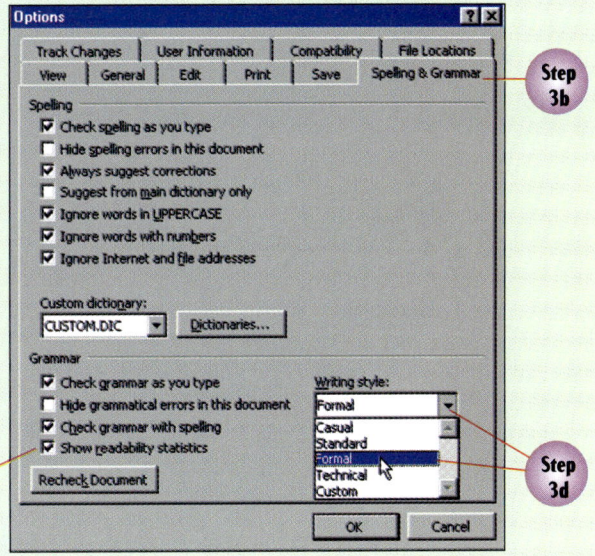

4. Complete a grammar check on the document by completing the following steps:
    a. Click the Spelling and Grammar button on the Standard toolbar.
    b. The grammar checker selects the sentence *That is all changing—here's why.*, displays *here is* in the Suggesti<u>o</u>ns list box, and the Office Assistant displays information about contraction use. Read this information and then click the <u>C</u>hange button to change *here's* to *here is*.

c. The grammar checker selects the sentence *Your house is not expected to skyrocket in value as in past years.* and displays *Passive Voice (no suggestions)* in the Suggestions list box. Read the information on passive voice displayed by the Office Assistant. Leave the sentence as written and continue grammar checking by clicking the Ne<u>x</u>t Sentence button.

d. The grammar checker selects the sentence *By the time you are ready to retire, your nest egg may seem substantial—but it isn't going to buy what it would buy today.*, displays *time,* in the Suggestions list box, and the Office Assistant displays information about comma use. This sentence is correct as written so click the <u>I</u>gnore button

e. The grammar checker again selects the sentence *By the time you are ready to retire, your nest egg may seem substantial—but it isn't going to buy what it would buy today.* and displays *is not* in the Suggestions list box; the Office Assistant displays information about contraction use. Click the <u>C</u>hange button to change *isn't* to *is not.*

f. If the grammar checker selects the same sentence again and displays information about comma use, click the <u>I</u>gnore button.

g. The grammar checker displays the Readability Statistics for the document. Read these statistics and then click OK to close the dialog box.

5. Change the checking options back to the default by completing the following steps:
   a. Click <u>T</u>ools and then <u>O</u>ptions.
   b. At the Options dialog box, click the Spelling & Grammar tab.
   c. At the Options dialog box with the Spelling & Grammar tab selected, click the Show <u>r</u>eadability statistics. (This removes the check mark from the check box.)
   d. Click the down-pointing triangle at the right of the <u>W</u>riting style text box and then click *Standard* at the drop-down list.
   e. Click OK to close the dialog box.

6. Make the following changes to the document:
   a. Select the entire document and then change to a serif typeface (other than Times New Roman) in 12-point size.
   b. Select the title *ARE YOU PREPARING FOR RETIREMENT?* and then change the font to 14-point Arial bold.
   c. Select from the second paragraph (that begins *Living longer than ever...*) to the end of the document and then click the Bullets button on the Formatting toolbar.

7. Save the document again with the same name (Word C3, Ex 19).

8. Print and then close Word C3, Ex 19.

Customizing AutoCorrect

Earlier in this chapter, you learned that during a spelling check a selected word can be added to AutoCorrect. You can add, delete, or change words at the AutoCorrect dialog box. To display the AutoCorrect dialog box with the AutoCorrect tab selected as shown in figure 3.24, click <u>T</u>ools and then <u>A</u>utoCorrect. Several options display at the beginning of the AutoCorrect dialog box. If a check appears in the check box before the option, the option is active.

figure
3.24

AutoCorrect Dialog Box

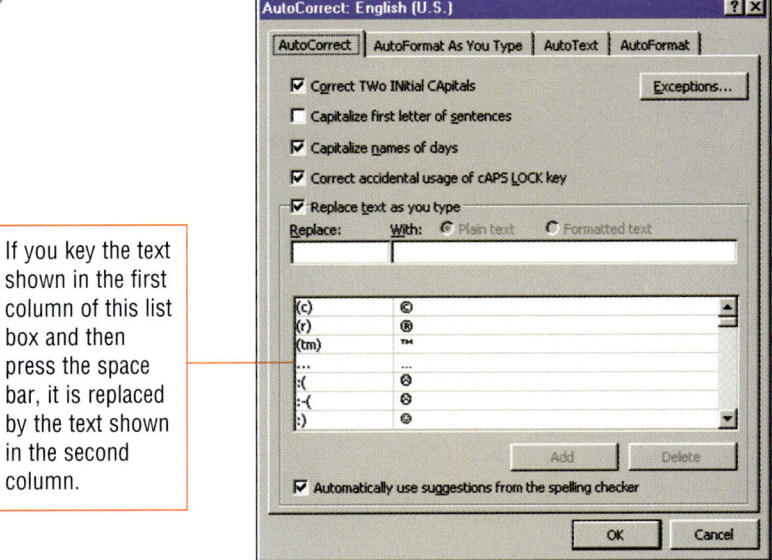

If you key the text shown in the first column of this list box and then press the space bar, it is replaced by the text shown in the second column.

Adding a Word to AutoCorrect

Commonly misspelled words or typographical errors can be added to AutoCorrect. For example, if you consistently key *oopen* instead of *open*, you can add *oopen* to AutoCorrect and tell it to correct it as *open*. To do this, you would display the AutoCorrect dialog box, key *oopen* in the Replace text box, key *open* in the With text box, and then click the Add button. The next time you key *oopen* and then press the space bar, AutoCorrect changes it to *open*.

Deleting a Word from AutoCorrect

A word that is contained in AutoCorrect can be deleted. To delete a word, display the AutoCorrect dialog box, click the desired word in the list box (you may need to click the down-pointing triangle to display the desired word), and then click the Delete button.

Adding Text to and Deleting Text from AutoCorrect

1. At a clear document screen, add words to AutoCorrect by completing the following steps:
   a. Click Tools and then AutoCorrect.
   b. At the AutoCorrect dialog box with the AutoCorrect tab selected, make sure the insertion point is positioned in the Replace text box. If not, click in the Replace text box.

c. Key **dtp**.
d. Press the Tab key (this moves the insertion point to the <u>W</u>ith text box) and then key **desktop publishing**.
e. Click the <u>A</u>dd button. (This adds *dtp* and *desktop publishing* to the AutoCorrect and also selects *dtp* in the <u>R</u>eplace text box.)
f. Key **particuler** in the Replace text box. (When you begin keying *particuler*, *dtp* is automatically deleted.)
g. Press the Tab key and then key **particular**.
h. Click the <u>A</u>dd button.
i. With the insertion point positioned in the Replace text box, key **populer**.
j. Press the Tab key and then key **popular**.
k. Click the <u>A</u>dd button.
l. With the insertion point positioned in the Replace text box, key **tf**.
m. Press the Tab key and then key **typeface**.
n. Click the <u>A</u>dd button.
o. Click OK or press Enter.

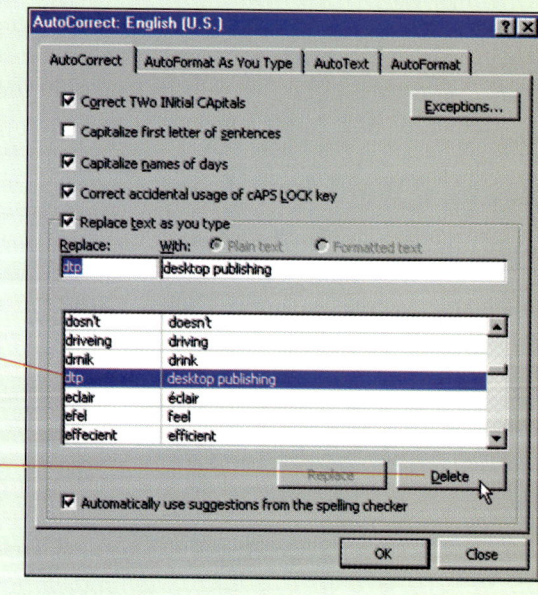

2. Key the text shown in figure 3.25. (Key the text exactly as shown. AutoCorrect will correct words as you key.)
3. Save the document and name it Word C3, Ex 20.
4. Print Word C3, Ex 20.
5. Delete the words you added to AutoCorrect by completing the following steps:
   a. Click <u>T</u>ools and then <u>A</u>utoCorrect.
   b. At the AutoCorrect dialog box, click *dtp* in the list box. (Click the down-pointing triangle in the list box scroll bar until *dtp* is visible and then click *dtp*.)
   c. Click the <u>D</u>elete button.
   d. Click the *particuler* option in the list box.
   e. Click the <u>D</u>elete button.
   f. Click the *populer* option in the list box.
   g. Click the <u>D</u>elete button.
   h. Click the *tf* option in the list box.
   i. Click the <u>D</u>elete button.
   j. Click OK or press Enter.
6. Close Word C3, Ex 20.

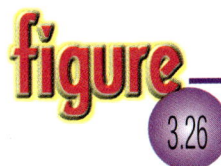

figure 3.25

Exercise 20

CHOOSING A TYPEFACE

A tf is a set of characters with a common general design and shape. One of teh most important considerations in establishing a particuler mood or feeling in a document is the tf. For example, a decorative tf may be chosen for invitations or menus, while a simple block-style tf may be chosen for headlines or reports. Choose a tf that reflects the contents, your audience expectations, and the image you want to project.

There are many typefaces, adn new designs are created on a regular basis. The most populer tf for typewriters is Courier. There are a variety of typefaces populer with dtp programs including Arial, Bookman, Century Schoolbook, Garamond, Helvetica, and Times New Roman.

Using the Thesaurus

Word offers a Thesaurus program that can be used to find synonyms, antonyms, and related words for a particular word. Synonyms are words that have the same or nearly the same meaning. When using the Thesaurus, Word may display antonyms for some words. Antonyms are words with opposite meanings. With the Thesaurus, you can improve the clarity of business documents.

To use the Thesaurus, position the insertion point next to any character in the word for which you want to find a synonym or antonym, click Tools, expand the drop-down menu, point to Language, and then click Thesaurus. At the Thesaurus dialog box shown in figure 3.26, select the desired synonym (or antonym) in the Replace with Synonym list box, and then click the Replace button.

figure 3.26

Thesaurus Dialog Box

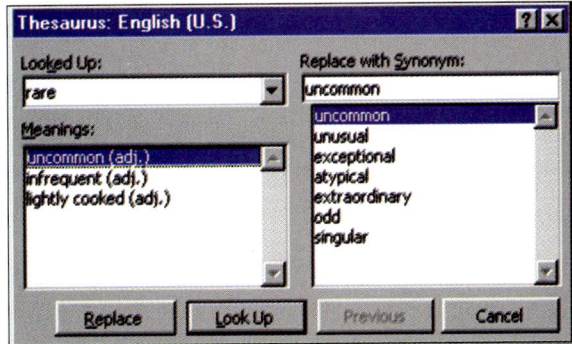

At the Thesaurus dialog box, a list of words displays in the Meanings list box. Depending on the word you are looking up, the words in the Meanings list box may display followed by *(n.)* or *(adj)*. You might also see the words *Antonym*, and *Related Words*. The first word in the Meanings list box is selected by default and synonyms for that word are displayed in the Replace with Synonym list box. You can view synonyms in the Replace with Synonym list box for the words shown in the Meanings list box by clicking the desired word.

Displaying Synonyms Using a Shortcut Menu

Another method for displaying synonyms for a word is to use a shortcut menu. To do this, position the mouse pointer on the word and then click the *right* mouse button. At the shortcut menu that displays, point to Synonyms, and then click the desired synonym at the side menu. Figure 3.27 shows synonyms in the shortcut menu side menu for the word *expectation*. Click the Thesaurus option at the bottom of the side menu to display the Thesaurus dialog box.

Shortcut Menu Synonyms Side Menu

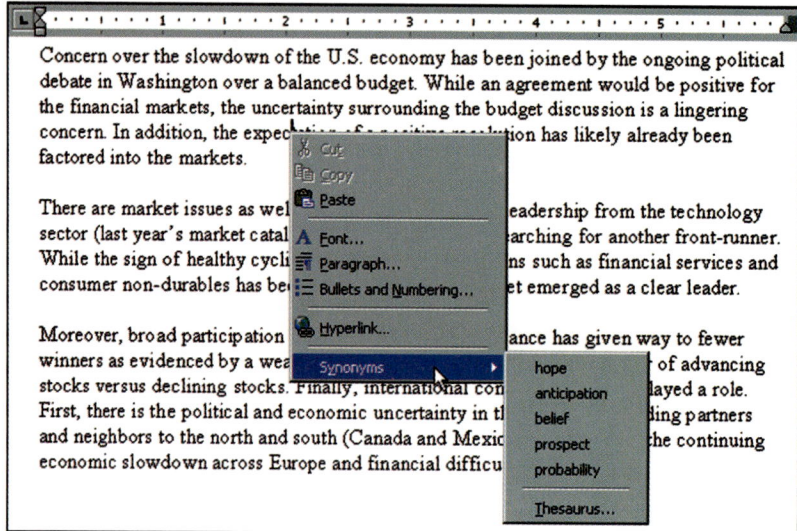

Changing Words Using the Thesaurus

1. Open Word Document 03.
2. Save the document with Save As and name it Word C3, Ex 21.
3. Change the word *rare* in the first paragraph to *unusual* using the Thesaurus by completing the following steps:

a. Position the insertion point anywhere in the word *rare* (located in the first paragraph).

b. Click <u>T</u>ools, expand the drop-down menu, point to <u>L</u>anguage, and then click <u>T</u>hesaurus.

c. At the Thesaurus dialog box, click *unusual* in the Replace with <u>S</u>ynonym list box, and then click the <u>R</u>eplace button.

4. Follow similar steps to make the following changes using the Thesaurus:

a. Change *uneasiness* in the first paragraph to *nervousness*.

b. Change *relatively* in the second paragraph to *comparatively*.

5. Change *phase* in the third paragraph to *stage* using a shortcut menu by completing the following steps:

a. Position the mouse pointer on the word *phase* located in the second sentence of the third paragraph.

b. Click the *right* mouse button.

c. At the shortcut menu that displays, point to Sy<u>n</u>onyms and then click *stage* at the side menu.

6. Save the document again with the same name (Word C3, Ex 21).

7. Print and then close Word C3, Ex 21.

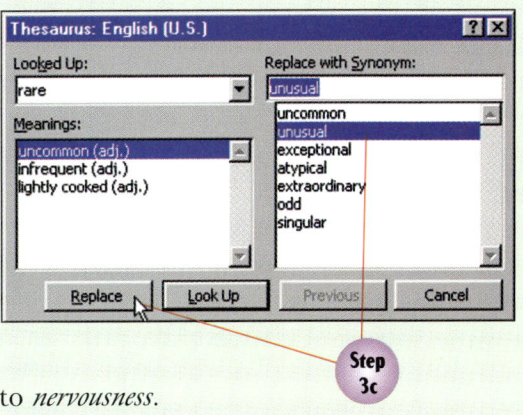

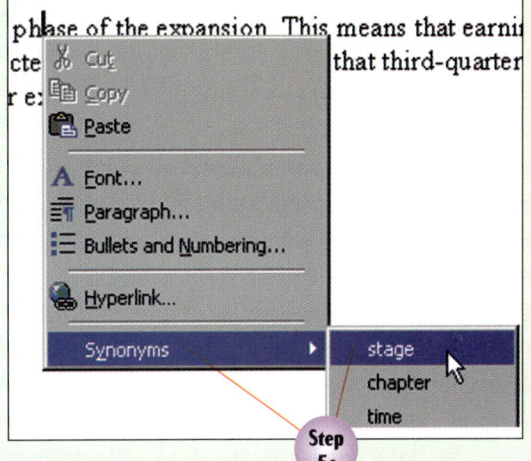

chapter summary

➤ By default, tabs are set every 0.5 inches. These settings can be changed on the Ruler or at the Tabs dialog box.

➤ Use the Alignment button at the left side of the Ruler to select a left, right, center, or decimal tab. When you set a tab on the Ruler, any tabs to the left are automatically deleted.

➤ Turning on the display of nonprinting characters, such as those for paragraphs and tabs, is useful when creating tabbed text.

➤ After a tab has been set on the Ruler, it can be moved or deleted using the mouse pointer.

➤ At the Tabs dialog box, you can set any of the four types of tabs as well as a bar tab at a specific measurement. You can also set tabs with preceding leaders and clear one tab or all tabs. Preceding leaders can be periods, hyphens, or underlines.

➤ Change to the Print Layout view by clicking <u>V</u>iew and then <u>P</u>rint Layout or by clicking the Print Layout View button at the left side of the horizontal scroll bar. Change back to the Normal view by clicking <u>V</u>iew and then <u>N</u>ormal or clicking the Normal View button at the left side of the horizontal scroll bar.

- By default, a Word document contains 1.25-inch left and right margins and 1-inch top and bottom margins.

- Word inserts a page break at approximately 10 inches from the top of each page. With the default 1-inch top and bottom margins, this allows a total of 9 inches to be printed on a standard page. The page break displays as a row of dots in the Normal view and as an actual break in the page in Print Layout view.

- The page break that Word inserts automatically is a soft page break. A page break that you insert is a hard page break.

- With Word's Print Preview feature, you can view a partial page, single page, multiple pages, or zoom in on a particular area of a page. With buttons from the Print Preview toolbar at the top of the Print Preview screen, you can change the display of the document, send a document to the printer, and turn the display of the rulers on or off.

- Vertically align text in a document with the Vertical alignment option at the Page Setup dialog box with the Layout tab selected.

- Use the click and type feature to center, right align, and left align text.

- Insert the current date and/or time with options at the Date and Time dialog box or with shortcut commands.

- Highlight text in a document by clicking the Highlight button on the Formatting toolbar and then selecting the text. A variety of highlighting colors is available.

- Newspaper columns can be created with the Columns button on the Standard toolbar or with options at the Columns dialog box.

- In the Normal view, text will display in a single column at the left side of the document screen. Change to the Print Layout view to view columns as they will appear when printed.

- Options at the Columns dialog box let you change the spacing between columns, apply columns formatting from the point of the insertion point forward, insert a line between columns, or start a new column.

- To move the insertion point in a document with columns using the mouse, position the mouse pointer where desired, and then click the left button. To move the insertion point with the keyboard, use the arrow keys.

- Column formatting can be removed with the Columns button on the Standard toolbar or at the Columns dialog box.

- Word includes a spelling and grammar checker.

- The spelling checker matches the words in your document with the words in its dictionary. If a match is not found, the word is selected and possible corrections are suggested.

- When checking the spelling and/or grammar in a document, you can temporarily leave the Spelling and Grammar dialog box, make corrections in the document, and then resume checking.

- With the grammar checker, you can search a document for correct grammar, style, punctuation, and word usage.

- When a grammar error is detected, the Office Assistant displays information about the specific error.

- Commonly misspelled words, typographical errors, or abbreviations can be added to or deleted from the AutoCorrect dialog box.

- The Thesaurus finds synonyms, antonyms, and related words for a particular word.

commands review

	Mouse	Keyboard
Display the Ruler	View, Ruler	View, Ruler
New Line command		Shift + Enter
Tabs dialog box	Format, Tabs	Format, Tabs
Print Layout view	Click Print Layout View button at left side of horizontal scroll bar	View, Print Layout
Normal view	Click Normal View button at left side of horizontal scroll bar	View, Normal
Insert a hard page break	Insert, Break, Page Break	Ctrl + Enter
Print Preview	Click Print Preview button on Standard toolbar or click File, Print Preview	File, Print Preview
Page Setup dialog box	File, Page Setup or double-click a gray area at top of the Ruler	File, Page Setup
Display Columns dialog box	Format, Columns	Format, Columns
Insert a column break	Insert, Break, Column break	Ctrl + Shift + Enter
Spelling and Grammar dialog box	Click Spelling and Grammar button on Standard toolbar	Tools, Spelling and Grammar
AutoCorrect dialog box	Tools, AutoCorrect	Tools, AutoCorrect
Thesaurus dialog box	Tools, Language, Thesaurus	Tools, Language, Thesaurus
Insert date/time	Insert, Date and Time, click desired selection, click OK	Alt + Shift + D (date)
Highlight text	Click Highlight button on Formatting toolbar, select text	Alt + Shift + T (time)

thinking offline

Completion: In the space provided at the right, indicate the correct term, symbol, or command.

1. By default, each tab is set apart from the other by this measurement. _____

2. These are the four types of tabs that can be set on the Ruler. _____
   _____
   _____
   _____

3. This is the default tab type. _____

4. When setting tabs on the Ruler, choose the tab type with this button.

5. Press these keys on the keyboard to insert a New Line command.

6. Tabs can be set on the Ruler or here.

7. To remove all previous tabs, click this button at the Tabs dialog box.

8. This is the default left and right margin measurement.

9. Press these keys on the keyboard to insert a hard page break.

10. This view displays the document on the screen as it will appear when printed.

11. Vertically align text with the Vertical alignment option at the Page Setup dialog box with this tab selected.

12. This is the shortcut command to insert the current date.

13. The Columns button is located on this toolbar.

14. Change to this view to display columns as they will appear when printed.

15. To complete a spelling and grammar check, click this button on the Standard toolbar.

16. When spell checking a document, click this button at the Spelling and Grammar dialog box to skip all occurrences of the selected word.

17. This is the default writing style that the grammar checker uses when checking grammar in a document.

18. This feature finds synonyms, antonyms, and related words for a particular word.

19. In the space provided below, list the steps you would complete to add the letters *hs* and the replacement words *holographic system* at the AutoCorrect dialog box.

working hands-on

Assessment 1

1. At a clear document screen, complete the following steps:
    a. Change the font to 12-point Arial.
    b. Key the document shown in figure 3.28. For the text in columns, set a left tab at the 1-inch mark, the 2.5-inch mark, and the 4-inch mark on the Ruler.
    c. Change the vertical alignment for text to *Center*.
2. Save the document and name it Word C3, SA 01.
3. Print Word C3, SA 01.
4. With the document still open, select the text in columns and then move the tab at the 1-inch mark on the Ruler to the 0.75-inch mark, the tab at the 2.5-inch mark to the 2.75-inch mark, and the tab on the 4-inch mark to the 4.5-inch mark.
5. Save the document again with the same name (Word C3, SA 01).
6. Print and then close Word C3, SA 01.

figure 3.28   *Assessment 1*

SOFTWARE TRAINING SCHEDULE

Word	April 9	8:30 - 11:30 a.m.
PowerPoint	April 11	1:00 - 3:30 p.m.
Excel	May 8	8:30 - 11:30 a.m.
Access	May 10	1:00 - 3:30 p.m.

Assessment 2

1. At a clear editing window, key the document shown in figure 3.29 with the following specifications:
    a. Change the font to 12-point Century Schoolbook (or a similar serif typeface such as Bookman Old Style or Garamond).
    b. Bold and center the title as shown.
    c. Before keying the text in columns, display the Tabs dialog box, and then set left tabs at the 0.5-inch mark and the 1-inch mark, and a right tab with dot leaders at the 5.5-inch mark.
2. Save the document and name it Word C3, SA 02.
3. Print and then close Word C3, SA 02.

Assessment 2

TABLE OF CONTENTS

Assessment 3

1. Open Word C3, SA 02.
2. Save the document with Save As and name it Word C3, SA 03.
3. Select the text in columns and then move the tab symbols on the Ruler as follows:
    a. Move the left tab symbol at the 1-inch mark to the 1.5-inch mark.
    b. Move the left tab symbol at the 0.5-inch mark to the 1-inch mark.
    c. Move the right tab symbol at the 5.5-inch mark to the 5-inch mark.
4. Save the document again with the same name (Word C3, SA 03).
5. Print and then close Word C3, SA 03.

Assessment 4

1. Open Word Report 03.
2. Save the document with Save As and name it Word C3, SA 04.
3. Make the following changes to the report:
    a. Change the left and right margins to 1 inch.
    b. Set the title *NETWORK TOPOLOGIES* in 16-point Times New Roman bold.
    c. Set the three headings in the document (*Linear Bus Networks*, *Star Networks*, and *Ring Networks*) in 14-point Times New Roman bold.
    d. Select the text from the beginning of the first paragraph (begins with *A network's layout...*) to the end of the document and then make the following changes:

1) Change the line spacing to single.
2) Set a left tab at the 0.25-inch mark on the Ruler.
3) Format the selected text into two columns.

   e. Insert six points of space before and after each of the three headings in the document (*Linear Bus Networks*, *Star Networks*, and *Ring Networks*).

4. Save the document again with the same name (Word C3, SA 04).
5. Print and then close Word C3, SA 04.

Assessment 5

1. Open Word C3, SA 04.
2. Save the document with Save As and name it Word C3, SA 05.
3. Make the following changes to the document:
   a. Change the left and right margins to 1.25 inches.
   b. Change the width between the columns to 0.3 inches and insert a line between the columns.
4. Save the document again with the same name (Word C3, SA 05).
5. Print and then close Word C3, SA 05.

Assessment 6

1. Open Word Spell Check 03.
2. Save the document with Save As and name it Word C3, SA 06.
3. Complete a spelling check on the document.
4. After completing the spell check, make the following changes to the document:
   a. Set the entire document in a serif typeface of your choosing (other than Times New Roman).
   b. Set the title and two headings in a sans serif typeface.
   c. Move the insertion point to the end of the document. Insert the current date, press the Enter key, and then insert the current time.
5. Save the document again with the same name (Word C3, SA 06).
6. Print and then close Word C3, SA 06.

Assessment 7

1. Open Word Grammar Check 02.
2. Save the document with Save As and name it Word C3, SA 07.
3. Display the Options dialog box with the Spelling & Grammar tab selected, change the writing style to *Formal*, and then close the dialog box.
4. Complete a grammar check on the document. You determine what to change and what to leave as written. Not all sentences selected by the grammar checker contain errors. After the grammar checking is completed, proofread the document and make any necessary changes not selected by the grammar checker.
5. Make the following changes to the document:
   a. Set the entire document in a serif typeface of your choosing (other than Times New Roman).
   b. Set the title in a larger sans serif font.
   c. Double-space the paragraph in the document and change the alignment of the paragraph to justified.
6. Save the document again with the same name (Word C3, SA 07).
7. Display the Options dialog box with the Spelling & Grammar tab selected, change the writing style to *Standard*, and then close the dialog box.
8. Print and then close Word C3, SA 07.

Assessment 8

1. In some Word documents, especially documents with left and right margins wider than 1 inch, the right margin may appear quite ragged. If the paragraph alignment is changed to justified, the right margin will appear even, but there will be extra space added throughout the line. In these situations, hyphenating long words that fall at the end of the text line provides the document with a more balanced look. Use Word's Help feature to learn how to automatically hyphenate words in a document.
2. Open Word Report 01.
3. Save the document with Save As and name it Word C3, SA 08.
4. Automatically hyphenate words in the document, limiting the consecutive hyphens to 2. *(Hint: Specify the number of consecutive hyphens at the Hyphenation dialog box.)*
5. Save the document again with the same name (Word C3, SA 08).
6. Print and then close Word C3, SA 08.

 **Chapter 04C**

Working with Multiple Documents

PERFORMANCE OBJECTIVES

Upon successful completion of chapter 4, you will be able to:

- **Create a folder.**
- **Copy, move, rename, delete, and print documents.**
- **Move and copy blocks of text within a document.**
- **Move and copy blocks of text between documents.**
- **Print specific pages in a document.**
- **Print multiple copies of a document.**
- **Print envelopes and labels.**
- **Change paper size and orientation.**
- **Send a Word document by e-mail.**

Almost every company that conducts business maintains a filing system. The system may consist of documents, folders, and cabinets; or it may be a computerized filing system where information is stored on tapes and disks. Whatever type of filing system a business uses, daily maintenance of files is important to a company's operation. In this chapter, you will learn to maintain files (documents) in Word, including such activities as copying, moving, renaming, and printing documents, and creating additional file folders.

Some documents may need to be heavily revised, and these revisions may include deleting, moving, or copying blocks of text. This kind of editing is generally referred to as *cut and paste*. Cutting and pasting can be done within the same document, or, text can be selected and then moved or copied to another document.

In chapter 1, you learned to print a document with the Print button on the Standard toolbar or through the Print dialog box. By default, one copy of all pages of the currently open document is printed. In this chapter, you will learn to customize a print job with selections from the Print dialog box and to change the paper size and orientation.

Maintaining Documents

Many file (document) management tasks can be completed at the Open and Save As dialog boxes. These tasks can include copying, moving, printing, and renaming documents; opening multiple documents; opening a document as read only; and creating a new folder. To display the Open dialog box, shown in figure 4.1, click the Open button on the Standard toolbar or click <u>F</u>ile and then <u>O</u>pen. To display the Save As dialog box, click <u>F</u>ile and then Save <u>A</u>s.

Open Dialog Box

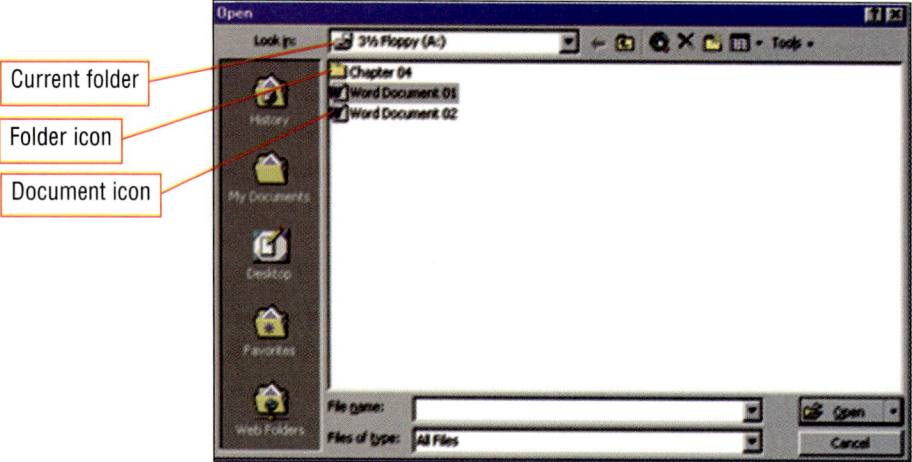

Current folder

Folder icon

Document icon

Some document maintenance tasks such as creating a folder and deleting documents are performed by using buttons on the Open dialog box or Save As dialog box toolbar. Figure 4.2 displays the Open dialog box toolbar buttons.

Open Dialog Box Toolbar Buttons

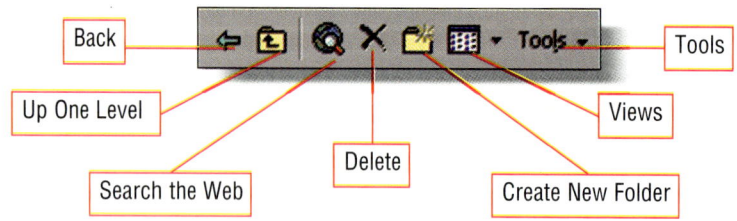

Back

Up One Level

Search the Web

Delete

Create New Folder

Views

Tools

If possible, do all your work in Microsoft Office on the hard drive or network drive. Use a floppy disk primarily for transporting and archiving documents.

Creating a Folder

In Word, documents are grouped logically and placed in *folders*. A folder can be created within a folder. The main folder on a disk or drive is called the *root* folder. Additional folders can be created as a branch of this root folder.

At the Open or Save As dialog boxes, a document displays in the list box preceded by a *document* icon , and a folder is preceded by a *folder* icon .

Create a new folder by clicking the Create New Folder button located on the dialog box toolbar at the Open dialog box or Save as dialog box. At the New Folder dialog box shown in figure 4.3, key a name for the folder, and then click OK or press Enter. The new folder becomes the active folder.

Create New Folder

If you want to make the previous folder the active folder, click the Up One Level button on the dialog box toolbar. Clicking this button changes to the folder that was up one level from the current folder. After clicking the Up One Level button, the Back button becomes active. Click this button and the previously active folder becomes active again.

Up One Level

A folder name can contain a maximum of 255 characters. Numbers, spaces, and symbols can be used in the folder name, except those symbols explained in chapter 1 in the *Naming a Document* section.

Back

(Before completing computer exercises, delete the Chapter 03C *folder on your disk. Next, copy the* Chapter 04C *folder from the CD that accompanies this textbook to your disk and then make* Chapter 04C *the active folder.)*

New Folder Dialog Box

4.3

Key a folder name in this text box and then press Enter or click OK.

Creating a Folder

1. Create a folder named *Documents* on your disk by completing the following steps:
   a. Display the Open dialog box and open the *Chapter 04C* folder on your disk.
   b. Click the Create New Folder button (located on the dialog box toolbar).
   c. At the New Folder dialog box, key **Documents**.
   d. Click OK or press Enter. (The *Documents* folder is now the active folder.)
   e. Change back to the *Chapter 04C* folder by clicking the Up One Level button on the dialog box toolbar.
2. Click the Cancel button to close the Open dialog box.

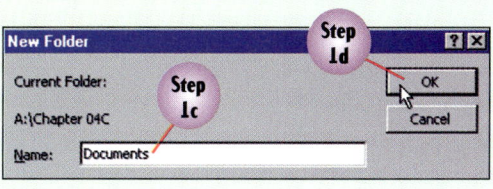

Selecting Documents

Document management tasks can be completed on one document or selected documents. For example, you can move one document to a different folder, or you can select several documents and move them at one time. Selected documents can be deleted, copied, moved, or printed.

To select one document, display the Open dialog box, and then click the desired document. To select several adjacent documents (documents displayed next to each other) using the mouse, you would complete the following steps:

1. Display the Open dialog box.
2. Click the first document to make it active.
3. Position the arrow pointer on the last document to be selected, hold down the Shift key, and then click the left mouse button.

You can also select documents that are not adjacent in the Open dialog box. To do this with the mouse, you would complete the following steps:

1. Display the Open dialog box.
2. Click the first document you want selected.
3. Hold down the Ctrl key.
4. Click each document you want selected.
5. When all desired documents are selected, release the Ctrl key.

When the Open dialog box is displayed, the first document in the Look in list box is automatically selected. Before selecting documents, deselect the first document (unless this first document is to be included with the other selected documents). To deselect the first document, position the arrow pointer anywhere in a clear portion of the Look in list box (not on a document name), and then click the left mouse button.

Deleting Documents and Folders

At some point, you may want to delete certain documents from your data disk or any other disk or folder in which you may be working. If you use Word on a regular basis, you should establish a system for deleting documents. The system you choose depends on the work you are doing and the amount of folder or disk space available. To delete a document, display the Open or Save As dialog box, select the document, and then click the Delete button on the dialog box toolbar. At the dialog box asking you to confirm the deletion, click Yes.

You can also delete a document by displaying the Open dialog box, selecting the document to be deleted, clicking the Tools button on the dialog box toolbar, and then clicking Delete at the drop-down menu. Another method for deleting a document is to display the Open dialog box, right-click the document to be deleted, and then click Delete at the shortcut menu.

If your disk is full, use Save As to save the document to a different drive or folder.

Delete

Tools

exercise 2

Deleting a Document

1. Delete a document by completing the following steps:
   a. Display the Open dialog box with *Chapter 04C* the active folder.
   b. Click Word Document 06 to select it.
   c. Click the Delete button on the dialog box toolbar.
   d. At the question asking if you want to delete the items, click <u>Y</u>es.
2. Close the Open dialog box.

exercise 3

Deleting Selected Documents

1. Delete selected documents by completing the following steps:
   a. Display the Open dialog box with *Chapter 04C* the active folder.
   b. Click Word Report 02.
   c. Hold down the Shift key and then click Word Report 04.
   d. Click the Too<u>l</u>s button on the dialog box toolbar.
   e. At the drop-down menu that displays, click <u>D</u>elete.
   f. At the question asking if you are sure you want to delete the items, click <u>Y</u>es.
   g. At the message telling you that Word Report 02 is a read-only file and asking if you are sure you want to delete it, click the Yes to <u>A</u>ll button.
2. Close the Open dialog box.

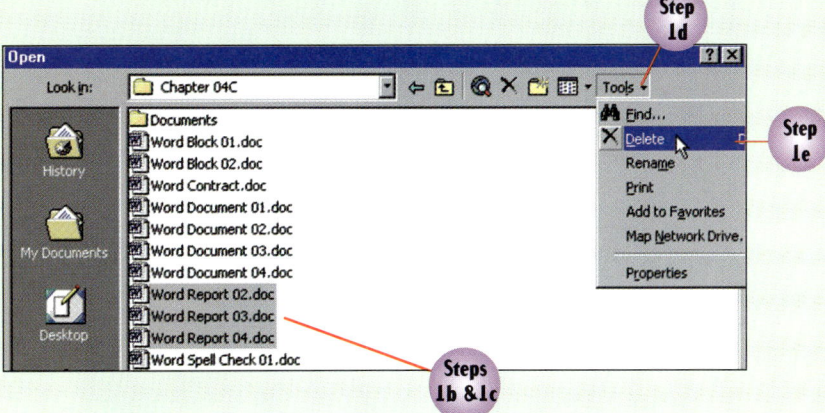

A folder and all its contents can be deleted at the Open or Save As dialog box. Delete a folder and its contents in the same manner as deleting a document or selected documents.

Deleting to the Recycle Bin

Documents deleted from your data disk are deleted permanently. (There are recovery programs, however, that will help you recover deleted text. If you accidentally delete a document or documents from a disk, do not do anything more with the disk until you can run a recovery program.) Documents deleted from the hard drive are automatically sent to the Windows Recycle Bin. If you accidentally delete a document to the Recycle Bin, it can be easily restored. To free space on the drive, empty the Recycle Bin on a periodic basis. Restoring a document from or emptying the contents of the Recycle Bin is done at the Windows desktop (not in Word). To empty the Recycle Bin, you would complete the following steps:

Minimize

1. Display the Windows desktop. (If you are just beginning, turn on the computer, and Windows will open. If you are currently working in Word, click the Minimize button at the right side of the Title bar. (The Minimize button contains the single underline symbol (_). Be sure to click the Minimize button on the Title bar and not the one just below it on the Menu bar.)
2. At the Windows desktop, double-click the *Recycle Bin* icon (located at the left side of the desktop).
3. At the Recycle Bin dialog box, shown in figure 4.4, click File and then Empty Recycle Bin.
4. At the question asking if you are sure you want to delete these items, click Yes.

4.4

Recycle Bin Dialog Box

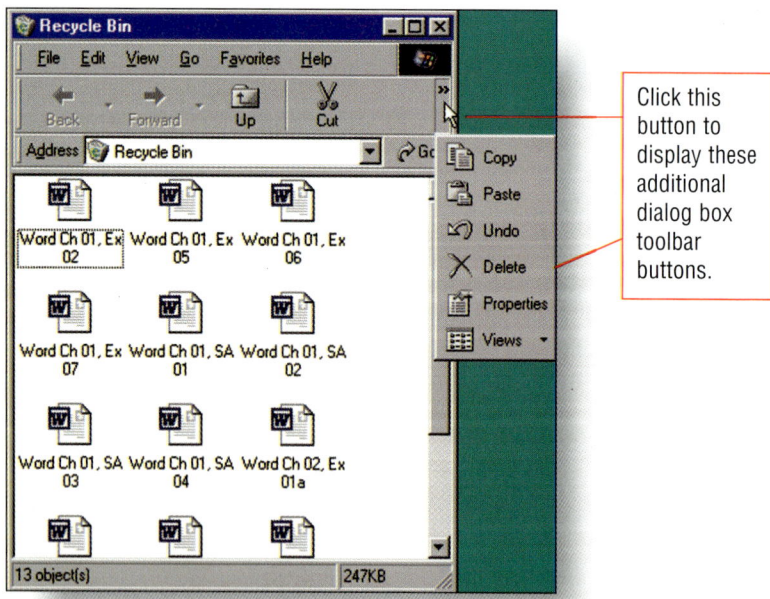

Click this button to display these additional dialog box toolbar buttons.

If you want to empty only specific documents from the Recycle Bin, hold down the Ctrl key while clicking the documents to be emptied. Position the arrow pointer on one of the selected documents, click the *right* mouse button, and then click the left mouse button on <u>D</u>elete. At the question asking if you want to delete the selected documents, click <u>Y</u>es. You can also delete selected documents by expanding the Recycle Bin dialog box toolbar (click the right-pointing arrows that display at the right side of the toolbar—see figure 4.4) and then clicking the Delete button.

A document or selected documents can also be restored from the Recycle Bin. To do this, you would complete the following steps:

1. At the Windows desktop, double-click the Recycle Bin icon.
2. At the Recycle Bin dialog box, click the document to be restored. (If you are restoring more than one document, hold down the Ctrl key while clicking the desired documents.)
3. Click <u>F</u>ile and then <u>R</u>estore.

At the Recycle Bin dialog box, you can also restore a document by positioning the arrow pointer on the document to be restored, clicking the *right* mouse button, and then clicking the left mouse button on R<u>e</u>store.

If you minimized the Word program by clicking the Minimize button, you can maximize (display the Word screen) the Word program at the desktop by clicking the Microsoft Word button located on the Taskbar (at the bottom of the screen).

Copying Files

In previous chapters, you opened a document from the data disk and saved it with a new name on the same disk. This process makes an exact copy of the document, leaving the original on the disk. You copied documents and saved the new document in the same folder as the original document. You can also copy a document into another folder and use the document's original name or give it a different name, or select documents at the Open dialog box and copy them to the same folder or into a different folder. To copy a document into another folder, you would complete the following steps:

1. Open the document you want to copy.
2. Display the Save As dialog box.
3. At the Save As dialog box, change to the desired folder. To do this, click the down-pointing triangle to the right of the Save <u>i</u>n text box, and then click the desired folder at the drop-down menu.
4. Click the <u>S</u>ave button in the lower right corner of the dialog box.

The Open and Save As dialog boxes contain an Up One Level button (located on the dialog box toolbar). Use this button if you want to change to the folder that is up one level from the current folder.

Saving a Copy of an Open Document

1. Open Word Document 02.
2. Save the document with Save As and name it Keyboards. (Make sure *Chapter 04C* is the active folder.)
3. Save a copy of the Keyboards document in the *Documents* folder created in exercise 1 by completing the following steps: (If your system does not contain this folder, check with your instructor to determine if there is another folder you can use.)
   a. With Keyboards still open, display the Save As dialog box.
   b. At the Save As dialog box, change to the *Documents* folder. To do this, double-click *Documents* at the beginning of the list box (folders are listed before documents).
   c. Click the <u>S</u>ave button located in the lower right corner of the dialog box.
4. Close Keyboards.
5. Change back to the *Chapter 04C* folder by completing the following steps:
   a. Display the Open dialog box.
   b. Click the Up One Level button located on the dialog box toolbar.
   c. Click Cancel to close the Open dialog box.

A document can be copied to another folder without opening the document first. To do this, use the <u>C</u>opy and <u>P</u>aste options from a shortcut menu at the Open (or Save As) dialog box.

Copying a Document at the Open Dialog Box

1. Copy Word Document 01 to the *Documents* folder by completing the following steps:
   a. Display the Open dialog box with *Chapter 04C* the active folder.
   b. Position the arrow pointer on Word Document 01, click the *right* mouse button, and then click <u>C</u>opy at the shortcut menu.
   c. Change to the *Documents* folder by double-clicking *Documents* at the beginning of the list box.
   d. Position the arrow pointer in any white area (not on a document name) in the list box, click the *right* mouse button, and then click <u>P</u>aste at the shortcut menu.
2. Change back to the *Chapter 04C* folder by clicking the Up One Level button located on the dialog box toolbar.
3. Close the Open dialog box.

A document or selected documents can be copied into the same folder. When you do this, Word names the document(s) "Copy of xxx" (where xxx is the current document name). You can copy one document or selected documents into the same folder.

Copying Selected Documents into the Same Folder

1. Copy documents into the same folder by completing the following steps:
   a. Display the Open dialog box with *Chapter 04C* the active folder.
   b. Select Word Document 03, Word Document 04, and Word Document 05. (To do this, click Word Document 03, hold down the Shift key, and then click Word Document 05.)
   c. Position the arrow pointer on one of the selected documents, click the *right* mouse button, and then click <u>C</u>opy at the shortcut menu.
   d. Position the arrow pointer in any white area in the list box, click the *right* mouse button, and then click <u>P</u>aste at the shortcut menu. (In a few seconds, Word will redisplay the Open dialog box with the following documents added: Copy of Word Document 03, Copy of Word Document 04, and Copy of Word Document 05.)
2. Close the Open dialog box.

Copying Selected Documents into a Different Folder

1. Copy several documents to the *Documents* folder by completing the following steps:
   a. Display the Open dialog box with *Chapter 04C* the active folder.
   b. Select Word Document 02, Word Document 04, and Word Document 05 by completing the following steps:
      1) Click once on Word Document 02. (This selects the document.)
      2) Hold down the Ctrl key, click Word Document 04, click Word Document 05, and then release the Ctrl key.
   c. Position the arrow pointer on one of the selected documents, click the *right* mouse button, and then click <u>C</u>opy at the shortcut menu.
   d. Double-click the folder named *Documents*. (This folder is located at the beginning of the list box.)
   e. When the *Documents* folder displays, position the arrow pointer in any white area in the list box, click the *right* mouse button, and then click <u>P</u>aste at the shortcut menu.
   f. Click the Up One Level button to change back to the *Chapter 04C* folder.
2. Close the Open dialog box by clicking the Cancel button.

Sending Documents to a Different Drive or Folder

With the <u>C</u>opy and <u>P</u>aste options from the shortcut menu at the Open or Save As dialog box, you can copy documents to another folder or drive. With the Send <u>T</u>o option, you can quickly send a copy of a document to another drive or folder. To use this option, position the arrow pointer on the document you want copied, click the *right* mouse button, position the arrow pointer on Send <u>T</u>o (this causes a side menu to display), and then click the desired drive or folder.

Cutting and Pasting a Document

A document can be removed from one folder or disk and inserted in another folder or on a disk using the Cut and Paste options from the shortcut menu at the Open dialog box. To do this you would display the Open dialog box, position the arrow pointer on the document to be removed (cut), click the *right* mouse button, and then click Cut at the shortcut menu. Change to the desired folder, position the arrow pointer in a white area in the list box, click the *right* mouse button, and then click Paste at the shortcut menu.

Cutting and Pasting a Document

1. Save and move a document into a different folder by completing the following steps:
   a. Open Word Document 04.
   b. Save the document with Save As and name it Economic Outlook.
   c. Close Economic Outlook.
   d. Move Economic Outlook to the *Documents* folder by completing the following steps:
      1) Display the Open dialog box with *Chapter 04C* the active folder.
      2) Position the arrow pointer on Economic Outlook, click the *right* mouse button, and then click Cut at the shortcut menu.
      3) Double-click *Documents* to make it the active folder.
      4) Position the arrow pointer in the white area in the list box, click the *right* mouse button, and then click Paste at the shortcut menu.
   e. Click the Up One Level button to make the *Chapter 04C* folder the active folder.
2. Close the Open dialog box.

Renaming Documents

At the Open dialog box, use the Rename option from the Tools drop-down menu to give a document a different name. The Rename option changes the name of the document and keeps it in the same folder. To use Rename, display the Open dialog box, click once on the document to be renamed, click the Tools button on the dialog box toolbar and then click the Rename Option. This causes a black border to surround the document name and the name to be selected. Key the desired name and then press Enter.

You can also rename a document by right-clicking the document name at the Open dialog box and then clicking Rename at the shortcut menu. Key the desired name for the document and then press the Enter key.

Renaming a Document

1. Rename a document located in the *Documents* folder by completing the following steps:
   a. Display the Open dialog box with *Chapter 04C* the active folder.
   b. Double-click *Documents* to make it the active folder.
   c. Click once on Word Document 05 to select it.
   d. Click the Tools button on the dialog box toolbar.
   e. At the drop-down menu that displays, click Rename.
   f. Key **Retirement** and then press the Enter key. (Depending on your system setup, you may need to key **Retirement.doc**.)
   g. At the message asking if you are sure you want to change the name of the read-only file, click Yes.
   h. Complete steps similar to those in 1c through 1g to rename Word Document 04 to Stock Market (or Stock Market.doc).
   i. Click the Up One Level button.
2. Close the Open dialog box.

Deleting a Folder and Its Contents

As you learned earlier in this chapter, a document or selected documents can be deleted. In addition to documents, a folder (and all its contents) can be deleted. Delete a folder in the same manner as a document is deleted.

Deleting a Folder and Its Contents

1. Delete the *Documents* folder and its contents by completing the following steps:
   a. Display the Open dialog box with *Chapter 04C* the active folder.
   b. Click once on the *Documents* folder to select it.
   c. Click the Delete button on the dialog box toolbar.
   d. At the question asking if you want to remove the folder and its contents, click Yes.
   e. At the message telling you that Word Document 01 is a read-only file and asking if you are sure you want to delete it, click the Yes to All button.
2. Close the Open dialog box.

Opening Documents

A document or selected documents can be opened at the Open dialog box. To open one document, display the Open dialog box, position the arrow pointer on the desired document, click the *right* mouse button, and then click Open at the shortcut menu. To open more than one document, select the documents in the Open dialog box, position the arrow pointer on one of the selected documents, click the *right* mouse button, and then click Open at the shortcut menu.

Closing Documents

If more than one document is open, all open documents can be closed at the same time. To do this, hold down the Shift key, click <u>F</u>ile and then <u>C</u>lose All. Holding down the Shift key before clicking <u>F</u>ile causes the <u>C</u>lose option to change to <u>C</u>lose All.

Opening and Closing Several Documents

1. Open several documents by completing the following steps:
   a. Display the Open dialog box with *Chapter 04C* the active folder.
   b. Select Word Document 01, Word Document 02, Word Document 03, and Word Document 04.
   c. Position the arrow pointer on one of the selected documents, click the *right* mouse button, and then click the left mouse button on <u>O</u>pen.
2. Close the open documents by completing the following steps:
   a. Hold down the Shift key.
   b. Click <u>F</u>ile and then <u>C</u>lose All.

Printing Documents

Up to this point, you have opened a document and then printed it. With the <u>P</u>rint option from the Too<u>l</u>s drop-down menu or the <u>P</u>rint option from the shortcut menu at the Open dialog box, you can print a document or several documents without opening them.

Printing Documents

1. Display the Open dialog box with *Chapter 04C* the active folder.
2. Select Word Document 03, Word Document 04, and Word Document 05.
3. Click the Too<u>l</u>s button on the dialog box toolbar.
4. At the drop-down menu that displays, click <u>P</u>rint.

Working with Blocks of Text

When cutting and pasting, you work with blocks of text. A block of text is a portion of text that you have selected. (Chapter 1 explained the various methods for selecting text.) A block of text can be as small as one character or as large as an entire page or document. Once a block of text has been selected, it can be deleted, moved to a new location, or copied and pasted within a document or to other open documents.

Deleting a Block of Text

Word offers different methods for deleting text from a document. To delete a single character, you can use either the Delete key or the Backspace key. To delete more than a single character, select the portion of text to be deleted, and then choose one of the following options:

- Press Delete.
- Click the Cut button on the Standard toolbar.
- Click Edit and then click Cut.

If you press Delete, the text is deleted permanently. (You can, however, restore deleted text with the Undo Typing option from the Edit menu or with the Undo or Redo buttons on the Standard toolbar.) The Cut button on the Standard toolbar and the Cut option from the Edit drop-down menu will delete the selected text and insert it in the *Clipboard*. Word's Clipboard is a temporary area of memory. The Clipboard holds text while it is being moved or copied to a new location in the document or to a different document. Text inserted in the Clipboard stays there until other text is inserted. Delete selected text with the Delete key if you do not need it again. Use the other methods if you might want to insert deleted text in the current document or a different document.

Moving a Block of Text

Word offers a variety of methods for moving text. After you have selected a block of text, move the text with buttons on the Standard toolbar or options from the Edit drop-down menu. To move a block of selected text from one location to another using buttons on the Standard toolbar, you would complete the following steps:

1. Select the text.
2. Click the Cut button on the Standard toolbar.
3. Position the insertion point at the location where the selected text is to be inserted.
4. Click the Paste button on the Standard toolbar.

To move a block of selected text from one location to another using options from the Edit menu, you would complete the following steps:

1. Select the text.
2. Click Edit and then click Cut.
3. Position the insertion point at the location where the selected text is to be inserted.
4. Click Edit and then Paste.

In addition to the methods just described, a block of selected text can also be moved with the mouse. There are two methods for moving text with the mouse. You can use the mouse to drag selected text to a new location or use a shortcut menu.

To drag selected text to a new location, you would complete the following steps:

1. Select the text to be moved with the mouse.
2. Move the I-beam pointer inside the selected text until it becomes an arrow pointer.
3. Hold down the left mouse button, drag the arrow pointer (displays with a gray box attached) to the location where you want the selected text inserted, and then release the button.
4. Deselect the text.

Cut

Undo

Redo

Consider using the Cut button rather than the Delete key to delete text. If you want to bring back the deleted text, position the insertion point and then click the Paste button.

Paste

If you drag and then drop selected text in the wrong location, immediately click the Undo button.

When you hold down the left mouse button and drag the mouse, the arrow pointer displays with a small gray box attached. In addition, the insertion point displays as a grayed vertical bar. When the insertion point (grayed vertical bar) is located in the desired position, release the mouse button. The selected text is removed from its original position and inserted in the new location.

To move selected text with a shortcut menu, you would complete the following steps:

1. Select the text to be moved with the mouse.
2. Move the I-beam pointer inside the selected text until it becomes an arrow pointer.
3. Click the *right* mouse button.
4. At the shortcut menu that displays, click Cut.
5. Position the insertion point where the text is to be inserted.
6. Click the *right* mouse button to display the shortcut menu and then click Paste.

The Clipboard contents are deleted when the computer is turned off. Save text you want permanently as a separate document.

When selected text is cut from a document and inserted in the Clipboard, it stays in the Clipboard until other text is inserted in the Clipboard. For this reason, you can paste text from the Clipboard more than just once. For example, if you cut text to the Clipboard, you can paste this text in different locations within the document or other documents as many times as desired.

exercise 13

Moving Selected Text

1. Open Word Document 03.
2. Save the document with Save As and name it Word C4, Ex 13.
3. Move the following text in the document:
   a. Move the second paragraph above the first paragraph by completing the following steps:
      1) Select the second paragraph including the blank line below the paragraph.
      2) Click the Cut button on the Standard toolbar.
      3) Position the insertion point at the beginning of the first paragraph.
      4) Click the Paste button on the Standard toolbar.
   b. Move the third paragraph above the second paragraph by completing the following steps:
      1) Select the third paragraph including the blank line below the paragraph.
      2) Click Edit and then click Cut. (This may display the Clipboard toolbar. You will learn about this toolbar later in this chapter.)
      3) Position the insertion point at the beginning of the second paragraph.
      4) Click Edit and then Paste.
   c. Move the first paragraph to the end of the document using the mouse by completing the following steps:

1) Using the mouse, select the first paragraph including the blank line below the paragraph.
2) Move the I-beam pointer inside the selected text until it becomes an arrow pointer.
3) Hold down the left mouse button, drag the arrow pointer (displays with a small gray box attached) a double space below the last paragraph (make sure the insertion point, which displays as a grayed vertical bar, is positioned a double space below the last paragraph), and then release the mouse button.
4) Deselect the text.
5) If necessary, press Enter to create space between paragraphs. (Skip this step if the paragraphs are already separated by a double space.)

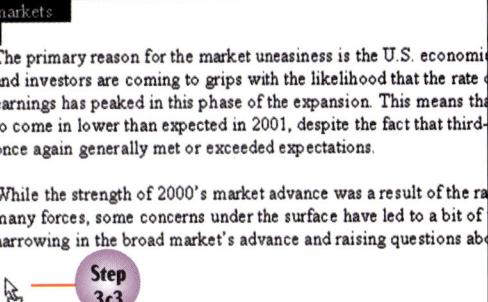

d. If the Clipboard toolbar is displayed, close it.
4. Save the document again with the same name (Word C4, Ex 13).
5. Print and then close Word C4, Ex 13.

Copying a Block of Text

Copying selected text can be useful in documents that contain repetitive portions of text. You can use this function to insert duplicate portions of text in a document instead of rekeying the text. After you have selected a block of text, copy the text to a different location with buttons on the Standard toolbar or options from the Edit drop-down menu. To copy text with the buttons on the Standard toolbar, you would complete the following steps:

1. Select the text to be copied.
2. Click the Copy button on the Standard toolbar.
3. Move the insertion point to the location where the copied text is to be inserted.
4. Click the Paste button on the Standard toolbar.

Copy

To copy text with options from the Edit drop-down menu, you would complete the following steps:

1. Select the text to be copied.
2. Click Edit and then click Copy.
3. Move the insertion point to the location where the copied text is to be inserted.
4. Click Edit and then Paste.

exercise 14

Copying Selected Text with Buttons on the Standard Toolbar

1. Open Word Block 01.
2. Save the document with Save As and name it Word C4, Ex 14.
3. Select the entire document and then change the font to 14-point Goudy Old Style bold (or a similar serif typeface).
4. Copy the text in the document to the end of the document by completing the following steps:
   a. Select all the text in the document including two blank lines below the text.
   b. Click the Copy button on the Standard toolbar.
   c. Move the insertion point to the end of the document.
   d. Click the Paste button on the Standard toolbar.
5. Copy the text again at the end of the document. To do this, position the insertion point at the end of the document, and then click the Paste button on the Standard toolbar. (This inserts a copy of the text from the Clipboard.)
6. Save the document with the same name (Word C4, Ex 14).
7. Print and then close Word C4, Ex 14.

The mouse can also be used to copy a block of text in a document to a new location. To do this, you would complete the following steps:

1. Select the text with the mouse.
2. Move the I-beam pointer inside the selected text until it becomes an arrow pointer.
3. Hold down the left mouse button and hold down the Ctrl key. Drag the arrow pointer (displays with a small gray box and a box containing a plus symbol) to the location where you want the copied text inserted (make sure the insertion point, which displays as a grayed vertical bar, is positioned in the desired location), and then release the mouse button and then the Ctrl key.
4. Deselect the text.

If you select a block of text and then decide you selected the wrong text or you do not want to do anything with the block, you can deselect it. If you are using the mouse, click the left mouse button outside the selected text. If you are using the keyboard, press an arrow key to deselect text. If you selected with the Extend mode (F8), press Esc and then press an arrow key to deselect text.

exercise 15

Copying Selected Text Using the Mouse

1. Open Word Block 02.
2. Save the document with Save As and name it Word C4, Ex 15.

3. Copy the text in the document using the mouse by completing the following steps:
   a. Select all the text with the mouse and include two blank lines below the text. (Consider turning on the display of nonprinting characters.)
   b. Move the I-beam pointer inside the selected text until it becomes an arrow pointer.
   c. Hold down the Ctrl key and then the left mouse button. Drag the arrow pointer (displays with a small gray box and a box with a plus symbol inside) to the end of the document immediately above the end-of-document marker (make sure the insertion point, which displays as a grayed vertical bar, is positioned immediately above the end-of-document marker), then release the mouse button and then the Ctrl key.
   d. Deselect the text.

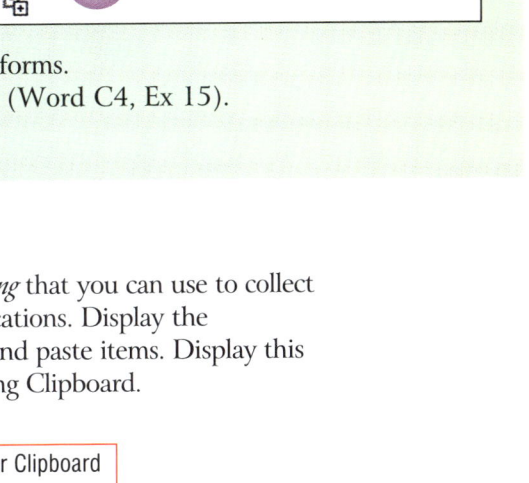

4. Select both forms using the mouse (including two blank lines below the second form) and then copy the selected forms to the end of the document.
5. Make sure all forms fit on one page. If the forms do not fit on one page, consider deleting any extra blank lines between forms.
6. Save the document again with the same name (Word C4, Ex 15).
7. Print and then close Word C4, Ex 15.

Collecting and Pasting Multiple Items

Office 2000 includes a new feature called *collecting and pasting* that you can use to collect up to 12 different items and then paste them in various locations. Display the Clipboard toolbar shown below when you want to collect and paste items. Display this toolbar by right-clicking an existing toolbar and then clicking Clipboard.

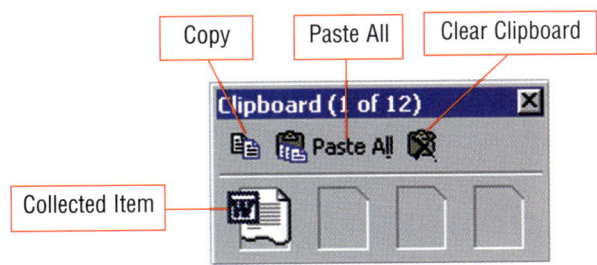

Select text or an object you want to copy and then click the Copy button on the Clipboard toolbar. Continue selecting text or items and clicking the Copy button. To insert an item, position the insertion point in the desired location and then click the button on the Clipboard representing the item. Position the insertion point on a button and a ScreenTip displays with information on the item. If the item is text, the first 50 characters display. When all desired items are inserted, click the Clear Clipboard button to remove any remaining items.

Usually, if you cut or copy any two items consecutively, the Clipboard toolbar automatically displays. If you close the Clipboard toolbar three times in a row without clicking a button on the toolbar, the Clipboard toolbar will no longer appear automatically. To display the Clipboard toolbar, right-click any currently displayed toolbar, and then click Clipboard. You can also click <u>V</u>iew, point to <u>T</u>oolbars, and then click Clipboard. When you display the Clipboard toolbar and then click a button on the toolbar, the count is reset, and from that point on the Clipboard toolbar appears automatically again.

Collecting and Pasting Paragraphs of Text

1. Open Word Contract.
2. Display the Clipboard toolbar by right-clicking an existing toolbar and then clicking Clipboard at the drop-down list. (If there are any items in the Clipboard, click the Clear Clipboard button.)
3. Select paragraph 2 in the *TRANSFERS AND MOVING EXPENSES* section and then click the Copy button on the Clipboard toolbar.
4. Select and then copy each of the following paragraphs:
   a. Paragraph 4 in the *TRANSFERS AND MOVING EXPENSES* section.
   b. Paragraph 1 in the *SICK LEAVE* section.
   c. Paragraph 3 in the *SICK LEAVE* section.
   d. Paragraph 5 in the *SICK LEAVE* section.
5. Paste the paragraphs by completing the following steps:
   a. Click the New Blank Document button on the Standard toolbar.
   b. Key **CONTRACT NEGOTIATION ITEMS** centered and bolded.
   c. Press Enter twice, turn off bold, and return the paragraph alignment back to Left.
   d. Click the button on the Clipboard representing paragraph 2. (When the paragraph is inserted in the document, the paragraph number changes.)
   e. Click the button on the Clipboard representing paragraph 4.
   f. Click the button on the Clipboard representing paragraph 3.
   g. Click the button on the Clipboard representing paragraph 5.
6. Click the Clear Clipboard button on the Clipboard toolbar.
7. Select the numbered paragraphs and then click the Numbering button on the Formatting toolbar. (This properly renumbers the paragraphs.)
8. Deselect the text and then close the Clipboard toolbar.
9. Save the document and name it Word C4, Ex 16.
10. Print and then close Word C4, Ex 16.
11. Close Word Contract without saving the changes.

Step 5d

Clipboard (5 of 12)
Paste All
2. Employees transferring to anot

Inserting One Document into Another

Some documents may contain standard information—information that remains the same. For example, a legal document, such as a will, may contain text that is standard and appears in all wills. Repetitive text can be saved as a separate

document and then inserted into an existing document whenever needed. Insert a separate document into an existing document by displaying the Insert File dialog box and double-clicking the desired document. To display the Insert File dialog box shown in figure 4.5, click Insert, expand the drop-down menu, and then click File.

Insert File Dialog Box

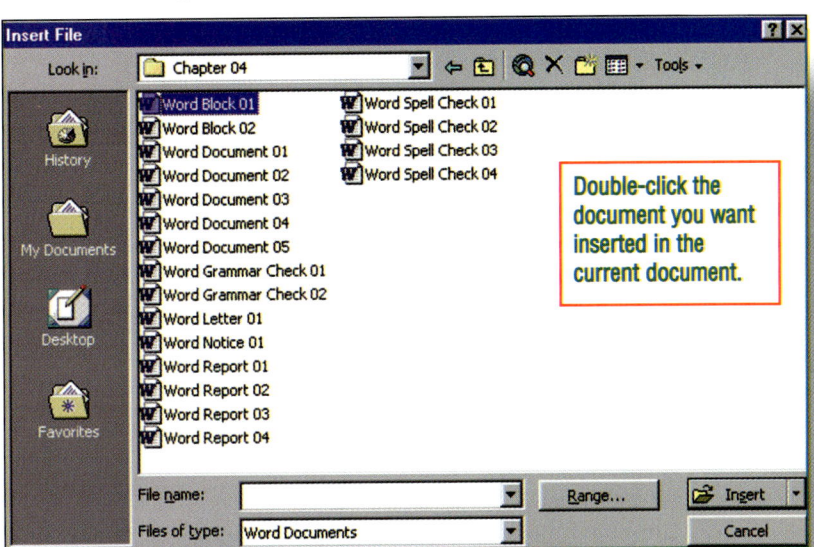

Saving Selected Text and Inserting One Document into Another

1. Open Word Document 04.
2. Select the first paragraph and then save it as a separate document named Budget by completing the following steps:
   a. Select the first paragraph in the document.
   b. Click the Copy button on the Standard toolbar.
   c. Click the New Blank Document button on the Standard toolbar (first button on the left).
   d. At the clear document screen, click the Paste button on the Standard toolbar.
   e. Save the document and name it Budget.
   f. Close the Budget document.
3. Close Word Document 04 without saving any changes.
4. At a clear document screen, key the title and the first paragraph of text shown in figure 4.6. After keying the first paragraph of text, press Enter twice and then insert the Budget document by completing the following steps:

a. Click Insert, expand the drop-down menu, and then click File.
   b. At the Insert File dialog box, double-click Budget.
5. Move the insertion point a double space below the last paragraph and then key the last paragraph shown in figure 4.6.
6. Save the document and name it Word C4, Ex 17.
7. Print and then close Word C4, Ex 17.

Exercise 17

LOOKING FORWARD

The basic, underlying conditions that have driven the markets thus far, such as moderate growth with low inflation and falling interest rates, remain firmly in place. Importantly, continued low inflation and lackluster economic growth have set the stage for further interest rate cuts, and rates do indeed have room to move even lower, particularly if the current administration and Congress can reach a compromise on a balanced budget.

[Insert *Budget* document here.]

Even beyond the core fundamentals in the U.S. economy, there are clear reasons to be optimistic over the longer term, including reasonable stock valuations, stable labor costs, rising savings rates from baby boomers, increasing demand for U.S. exports in light of expanding economies overseas, and U.S. superiority in the technologies of the future.

Working with Windows

Word operates within the Windows environment created by the Windows 98 program. However, when working in Word, a *window* refers to the document screen. The Windows 98 program creates an environment in which various software programs are used with menu bars, scroll bars, and icons to represent programs and files. With the Windows 98 program, you can open several different software programs and move between them quickly. Similarly, using windows in Word, you can open several different documents and move between them quickly.

Opening Multiple Windows

With multiple documents open, you can move the insertion point between them. You can move or copy information between documents or compare the contents of several documents. The maximum number of documents (windows) that you can have open at one time depends on the memory of your computer system and the amount of text in each document. When you open a new window, it is placed on top of the original window. Once multiple windows are opened, you can resize the windows to see all or a portion of them on the screen.

When a document is open, a button displays on the taskbar. This button represents the open document and contains a document icon, and the document name. (Depending on the length of the document name and the size of the button, not all of the name may be visible.) Another method for determining what documents are open is to click the <u>W</u>indow option on the Menu bar. This displays a drop-down menu similar to the one shown in figure 4.7. (The number of documents and document names displayed at the bottom of the menu will vary.)

Window Drop-Down Menu

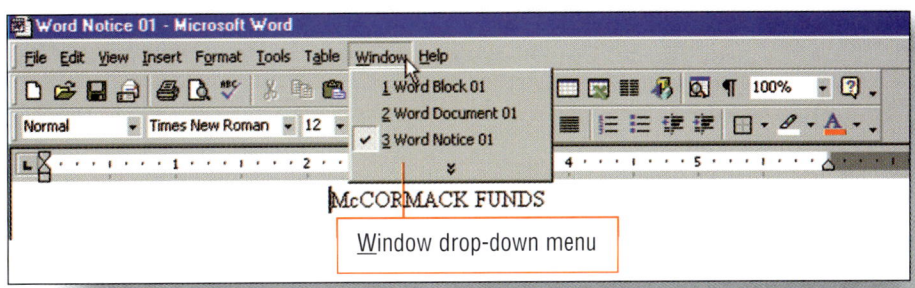

Window drop-down menu

The open document names display at the bottom of the menu. The document name with the check mark in front of it is the *active* document. The active document is the document containing the insertion point. To make one of the other documents active, click the desired document name. When you change the active document, the Window menu is removed and the new active document displays.

Closing Multiple Windows

All open documents can be closed at the same time. To do this, hold down the Shift key, and then click <u>F</u>ile on the Menu bar. This causes the <u>F</u>ile drop-down menu to display with the <u>C</u>lose option changed to <u>C</u>lose All. Click the <u>C</u>lose All option and all open documents will be closed.

Opening and Closing Multiple Windows

(Note: If you are using Word on a network system that contains a virus checker, you may not be able to open multiple documents at once. Continue by opening each document individually.)

1. Open several documents at the same time by completing the following steps:
   a. Display the Open dialog box.
   b. Click the document named Word Block 01.
   c. Hold down the Ctrl key, click Word Document 01, and then click Word Notice 01.
   d. Release the Ctrl key.
   e. Position the arrow pointer on one of the selected documents, click the *right* mouse button, and then click the left mouse button on <u>O</u>pen.

2. Make Word Document 01 the active document by clicking the button on the Taskbar containing the name Word Document 01.
3. Make Word Block 01 the active document by clicking <u>W</u>indow and then clicking <u>1</u>.
4. Close all open documents by holding down the Shift key, clicking <u>F</u>ile, and then clicking <u>C</u>lose All.

Arranging Windows

If you have more than one document open, you can use the <u>A</u>rrange All option from the <u>W</u>indow drop-down menu to view a portion of all open documents. To do this, click <u>W</u>indow, expand the menu, and then click <u>A</u>rrange All. Figure 4.8 shows a document screen with four documents open that have been arranged.

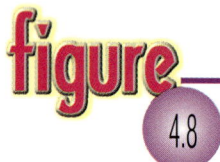

Arranged Documents

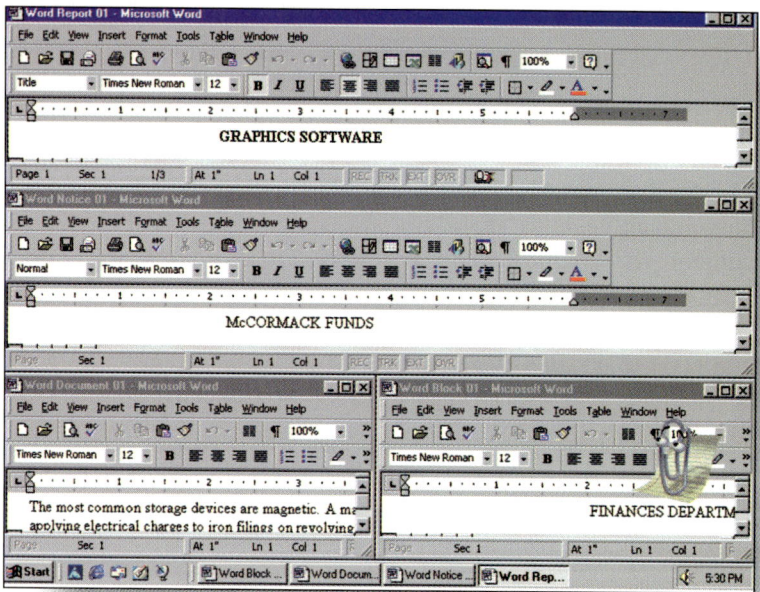

Arranging Windows

1. Open the following documents: Word Block 01, Word Document 01, Word Notice 01, and Word Report 01.
2. Arrange the windows by clicking <u>W</u>indow, expanding the drop-down menu, and then clicking <u>A</u>rrange All.

3. Make Word Block 01 the active document by positioning the arrow pointer on the title bar for Word Block 01 and then clicking the left mouse button.
4. Close Word Block 01.
5. Make Word Notice 01 active and then close it.
6. Close the remaining documents.

Maximizing, Restoring, and Minimizing Documents

Maximize

Minimize

Restore

Use the Maximize and Minimize buttons in the upper right corner of the active document window to change the size of the window. The Maximize button is the button in the upper right corner of the active document immediately to the left of the Close button. (The Close button is the button containing the X.) The Minimize button is located immediately to the left of the Maximize button.

If you arrange all open documents and then click the Maximize button in the active document, the active document expands to fill the document screen. In addition, the Maximize button changes to the Restore button. To return the active document back to its size before it was maximized, click the Restore button. If you click the Minimize button in the active document, the document is reduced and a button displays on the Taskbar representing the document. To maximize a document that has been minimized, click the button on the Taskbar representing the document.

You can minimize all open programs by right-clicking an empty spot on the Taskbar and then clicking Minimize All Windows.

Minimizing, Maximizing, and Restoring Documents

1. Open Word Block 02.
2. Maximize Word Block 02 by clicking the Maximize button at the right side of the Title bar. (The Maximize button is the button at the right side of the Title bar, immediately left of the Close button.)
3. Open Word Document 03.
4. Open Word Report 01.
5. Arrange the windows.
6. Make Word Block 02 the active window.
7. Minimize Word Block 02 by clicking the Minimize button in the upper right corner of the active window.
8. Make Word Document 03 the active document and then minimize Word Document 03.
9. Restore Word Document 03 by clicking the button on the Taskbar representing the document.
10. Restore Word Block 02.
11. Make Word Report 01 the active document and then close it.
12. Close Word Document 03.
13. Maximize Word Block 02 by clicking the Maximize button at the right side of the Title bar.
14. Close Word Block 02.

Cutting and Pasting Text Between Windows

With several documents open, you can easily move, copy, and/or paste text from one document to another. To move, copy, and/or paste text between documents, use the cutting and pasting options you learned earlier in this chapter together with the information about windows.

exercise 21

Copying Selected Text from One Open Document to Another

1. Open Word Document 03.
2. Save the document with Save As and name it Word C4, Ex 21.
3. With Word C4, Ex 21 still open, open Word Document 04.
4. With Word Document 04 the active document, copy the first two paragraphs in the document and paste them into Word C4, Ex 21 by completing the following steps:
   a. Select the first two paragraphs in Word Document 04.
   b. Click the Copy button on the Standard toolbar.
   c. Deselect the text.
   d. Make Word C4, Ex 21 the active document.
   e. Position the insertion point a double space below the last paragraph and then click the Paste button on the Standard toolbar.
5. Make Word Document 04 the active document and then close it. (This displays Word C4, Ex 21.)
6. With Word C4, Ex 21 displayed, make the following changes to the document:
   a. Key the title **ECONOMIC OUTLOOK** at the beginning of the document, centered and in bold.
   b. Select the entire document and then change the font to 12-point Garamond (or a similar serif typeface).
7. Save the document again with the same name (Word C4, Ex 21).
8. Print and then close Word C4, Ex 21.

Printing Documents

Save a document before printing it.

In chapter 1, you learned to print the document displayed in the document screen at the Print dialog box. By default, one copy of all pages of the currently open document prints. With options at the Print dialog box, you can specify the number of copies to print and also specific pages for printing. To display the Print dialog box shown in figure 4.9, click File and then Print.

Print Dialog Box

4.9

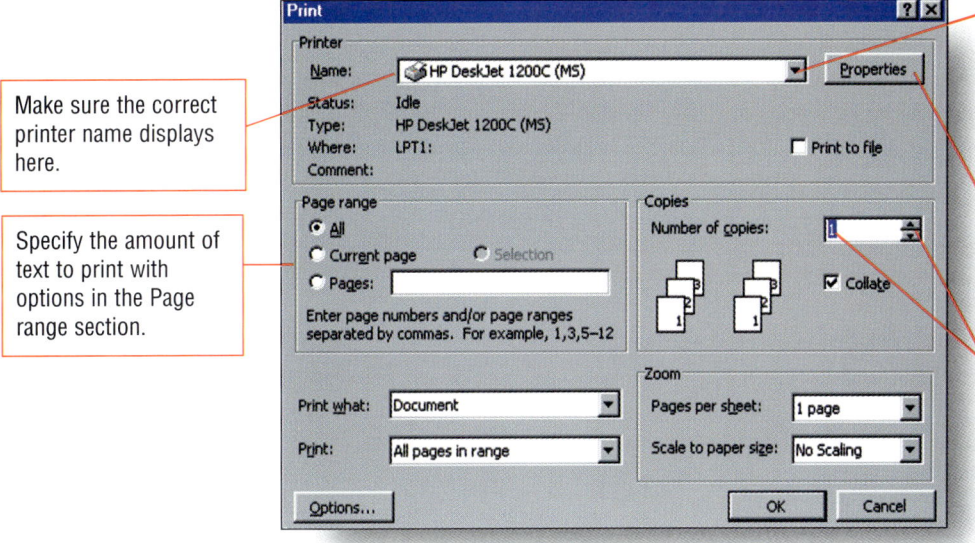

Make sure the correct printer name displays here.

Specify the amount of text to print with options in the Page range section.

Click this down-pointing triangle to display a list of installed printers.

Click this button to set options for the selected printer such as paper size, layout, orientation, paper source, and paper quality.

Print multiple copies of a document by increasing this number.

If you want to cancel the current print job, double-click the *Print Status* icon on the Status bar (located at the far right side). Depending on how much of the document has been sent to the printer, this may or may not stop the printing of the entire document.

Printing Specific Text or Pages

The Page range section of the Print dialog box contains settings you can use to specify the amount of text you want printed. At the default setting of <u>A</u>ll, all pages of the current document are printed. Choose the Curr<u>e</u>nt page option to print the page where the insertion point is located. If you want to select and then print a portion of the document, choose the <u>S</u>election option at the Print dialog box. This prints only the text that has been selected in the current document. (This option is dimmed unless text is selected in the document.)

With the Pa<u>g</u>es option, you can identify a specific page, multiple pages, and/or a range of pages. If you want specific multiple pages printed, use a comma (,) to indicate *and* and use a hyphen (-) to indicate *through*. For example, to print pages 2 and 5, you would key **2,5** in the Pa<u>g</u>es text box. To print pages 6 through 10, you would key **6-10**.

Click the <u>P</u>roperties button at the Print dialog box to display a dialog box with options for specifying the paper size, orientation, and paper source.

Hint

Printing Specific Pages

1. Open Word Report 01.
2. Save the document with Save As and name it Word C4, Ex 22.
3. Make the following changes to the document:
   a. Change the top, left, and right margins to 1.5 inches.
   b. Set the entire document in 13-point Bookman Old Style (or a similar serif typeface).
   c. Set the title *GRAPHICS SOFTWARE* in 14-point Arial bold.
   d. Set the first heading *Early Painting and Drawing Programs* in 13-point Arial bold.
   e. Use Format Painter to set the two remaining headings in the report in 13-point Arial bold.
   f. Check the page breaks in the document and, if necessary, adjust the page breaks. (Consider inserting your own hard page break with Ctrl + Enter if Word breaks a page in an undesirable location.)
4. Save the document again with the same name (Word C4, Ex 22).
5. Print pages 1 and 3 of the report by completing the following steps:
   a. Display the Print dialog box by clicking File and then Print.
   b. At the Print dialog box, click Pages.
   c. Key **1,3** in the Pages text box.
   d. Click OK or press Enter.
6. Close Word C4, Ex 22.

Printing Multiple Copies

If you want to print more than one copy of a document, use the Number of copies option from the Print dialog box. If you print several copies of a document containing multiple pages, Word prints the pages in the document collated. For example, if you print two copies of a three-page document, pages 1, 2, and 3 are printed, and then the pages are printed a second time. Printing pages collated is helpful but takes more printing time. To speed up the printing time, you can tell Word <u>not</u> to print the pages collated. To do this, remove the check mark from the Collate option at the Print dialog box. With the check mark removed, Word will print all copies of the first page, and then all copies of the second page, and so on.

Printing Multiple Copies of a Document

1. Open Word Document 02.
2. Print three copies of the document by completing the following steps:
   a. Display the Print dialog box.
   b. Key **3**. (The insertion point is automatically positioned in the Number of copies text box when the Print dialog box displays.)
   c. Click OK or press Enter.
3. Close Word Document 02.

Printing Envelopes

Word automates the creation of envelopes with options at the Envelopes and Labels dialog box with the Envelopes tab selected as shown in figure 4.10. Key the delivery address in the Delivery address text box and the return address in the Return address text box. If you open the Envelopes and Labels dialog box in a document containing a name and address, the name and address are automatically inserted in the Delivery address text box in the dialog box.

At the Envelopes and Labels dialog box, you can send the envelope directly to the printer by clicking the Print button, or you can insert the envelope in the current document by clicking the Add to Document button.

figure
4.10

Envelopes and Labels Dialog Box with Envelopes Tab Selected

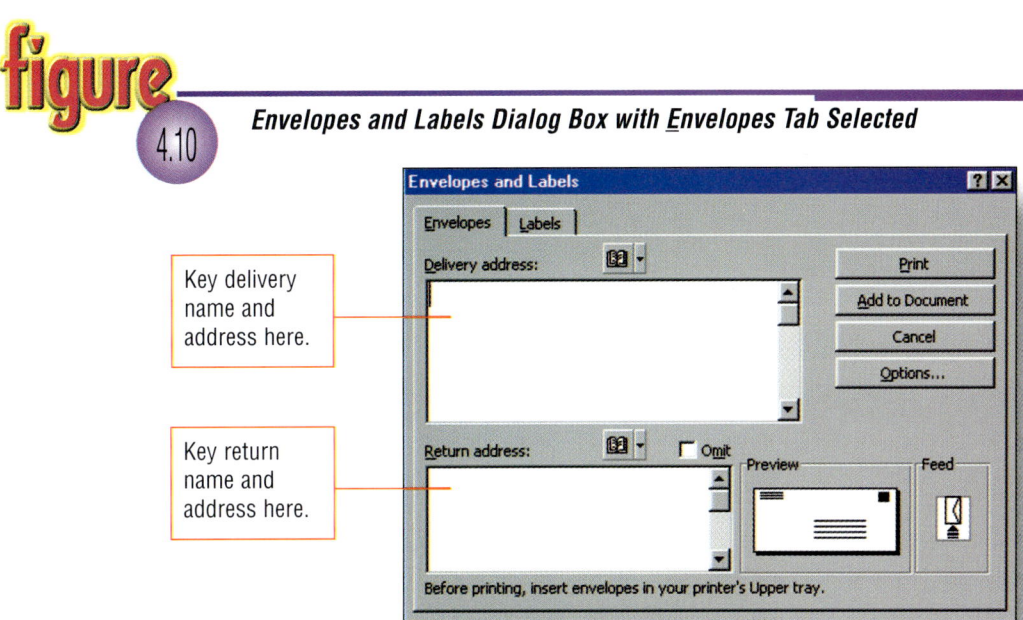

Key delivery name and address here.

Key return name and address here.

If you enter a return address before printing the envelope, Word will display the question *"Do you want to save the new return address as the default return address?"* At this question, click Yes if you want the current return address available for future envelopes. Click No if you do not want the current return address used as the default. If a default return address displays in the Return address section of the dialog box, you can tell Word to omit the return address when printing the envelope by clicking the Omit check box to remove the check mark.

The Envelopes and Labels dialog box contains a Preview sample box and a Feed sample box. The Preview sample box shows how the envelope will appear when printed and the Feed sample box shows how the envelope should be inserted into the printer. (This will vary for different printers.)

exercise 24

Printing an Envelope

1. At a clear document screen, create an envelope that prints the delivery address and return address shown in figure 4.11 by completing the following steps:
   a. Click Tools and then Envelopes and Labels.
   b. At the Envelopes and Labels dialog box with the Envelopes tab selected, key the delivery address shown in figure 4.11 (the one containing the name *Mr. Gregory Watanabe*). (Press the Enter key to end the line containing the name and the line containing the street address. Do not press Enter after keying the city, state, and zip code because that will cause an extra page to print.)
   c. Click in the Return address text box. (If there is any text in the Return Address text box, select and then delete it.)
   d. Key the return address shown in figure 4.11 (the one containing the name *Mrs. Wendy Steinberg*).
   e. Click the Add to Document button.
   f. At the message *"Do you want to save the new return address as the default return address?"*, click No.
2. Save the document and name it Word C4, Ex 24.
3. Print and then close Word C4, Ex 24. *(Note: Manual feed of the envelope may be required. Please check with your instructor.)*

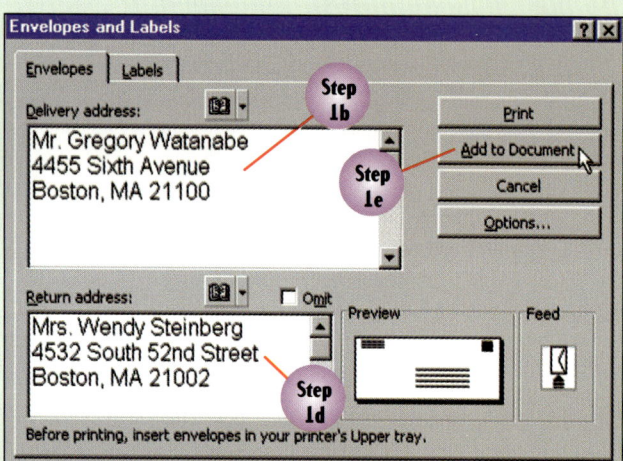

Exercise 24

Mrs. Wendy Steinberg
4532 South 52nd Street
Boston, MA 21002

Mr. Gregory Watanabe
4455 Sixth Avenue
Boston, MA 21100

Creating an Envelope in an Existing Document

1. Open Word Letter 01.
2. Create and print an envelope for the document by completing the following steps:
    a. Click Tools and then Envelopes and Labels.
    b. At the Envelopes and Labels dialog box (with the Envelopes tab selected), make sure the delivery address displays properly in the Delivery address section.
    c. If any text displays in the Return address section, insert a check mark in the Omit check box (located to the right of the Return address option. (This tells Word not to print the return address on the envelope.)
    d. Click the Print button.
3. Close Word Letter 01.

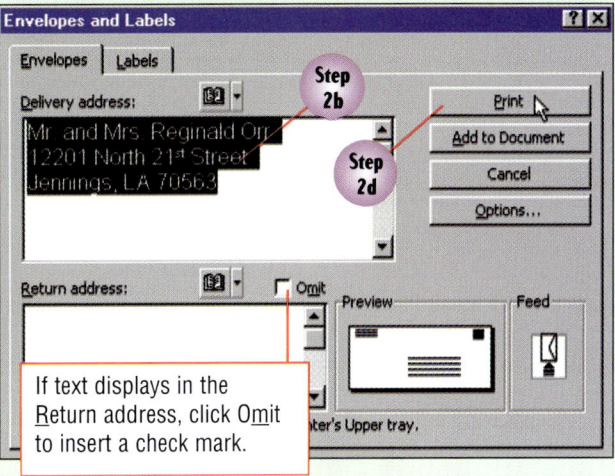

If text displays in the Return address, click Omit to insert a check mark.

Printing Labels

Use Word's labels feature to print text on mailing labels, file labels, disk labels, or other types of labels. Word includes a variety of predefined labels that can be purchased at an office supply store. To create a sheet of mailing labels with the same name and address using the default options, display the Envelopes and Labels dialog box with the Labels tab selected as shown in figure 4.12. Key the desired address in the Address text box and then click the New Document button to insert the mailing label in a new document or click the Print button to send the mailing label directly to the printer.

Envelopes and Labels Dialog Box with Labels Tab Selected

4.12

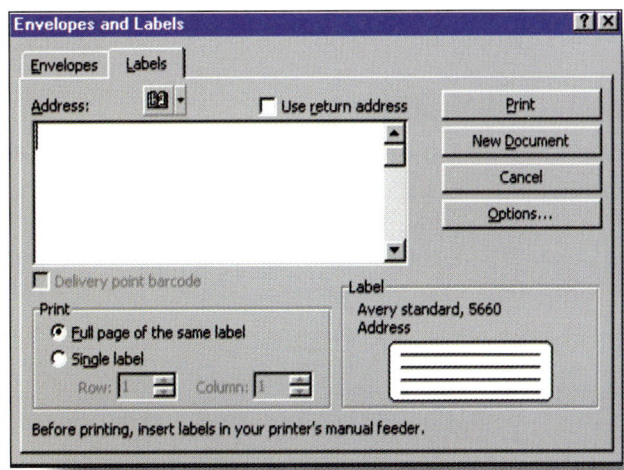

exercise 26

Creating Mailing Labels

1. Open Word Letter 01.
2. Create mailing labels with the delivery address by completing the following steps:
    a. Click Tools and then Envelopes and Labels.
    b. At the Envelopes and Labels dialog box, click the Labels tab.
    c. Make sure the delivery address displays properly in the Address section.
    d. Click the New Document button.
3. Save the mailing label document and name it Word C4, Ex 26.
4. Print and then close Word C4, Ex 26.
5. Close Word Letter 01.

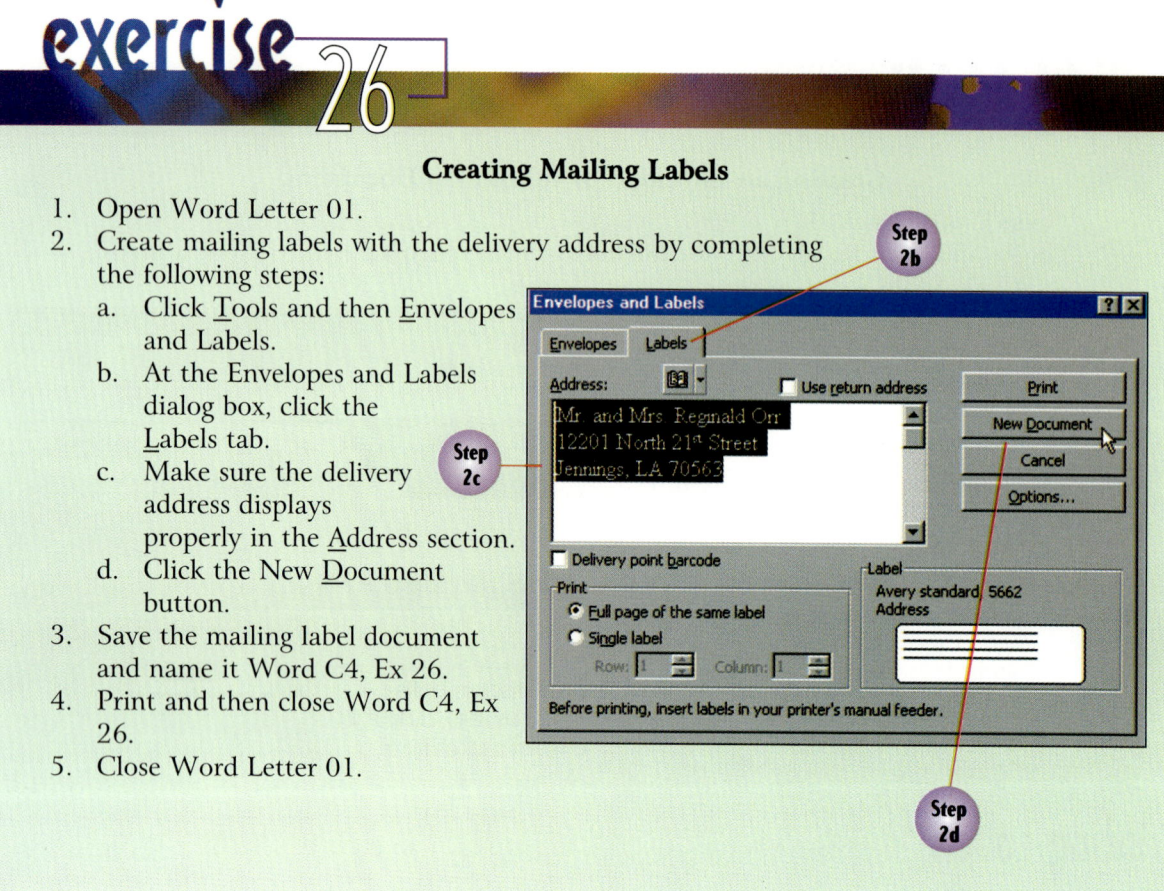

Step 2b

Step 2c

Step 2d

If you open the Envelopes and Labels dialog box (with the Labels tab selected) in a document containing a name and address, the name and address are automatically inserted in the Address section of the dialog box. To enter different names in each of the mailing labels, start at a clear document screen, display the Envelopes and Labels dialog box with the Labels tab selected, and then click the New Document button. The Envelopes and Labels dialog box is removed from the screen and the document screen displays with label forms. The insertion point is positioned in the first label form. Key the name and address in this label and then press the Tab key to move the insertion point to the next label. Pressing Shift + Tab will move the insertion point to the preceding label.

Changing Label Options

Click the Options button at the Envelopes and Labels dialog box with the Labels tab selected and the Label Options dialog box displays as shown in figure 4.13.

figure

4.13

Label Options Dialog Box

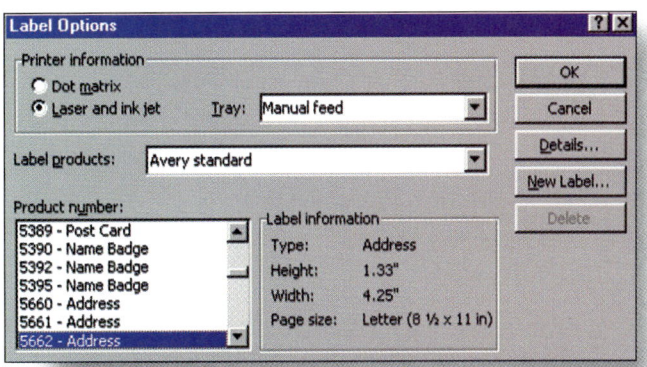

At the Label Options dialog box, choose the type of printer, the desired label product, and the product number. This dialog box also displays information about the selected label such as type, height, width, and paper size. When you select a label, Word automatically determines label margins. If, however, you want to customize these default settings, click the Details button at the Label Options dialog box.

exercise 27

Creating Customized Mailing Labels

1. At a clear document screen, create mailing labels by completing the following steps:
   a. Click Tools and then Envelopes and Labels.
   b. Make sure the Labels tab is selected. (If not, click Labels.)
   c. Click the Options button.
   d. At the Label Options dialog box, make sure *Avery standard* displays in the Label products text box.
   e. Click the down-pointing triangle at the right side of the Product number list box until *5662 - Address* is visible and then click *5662 - Address*.

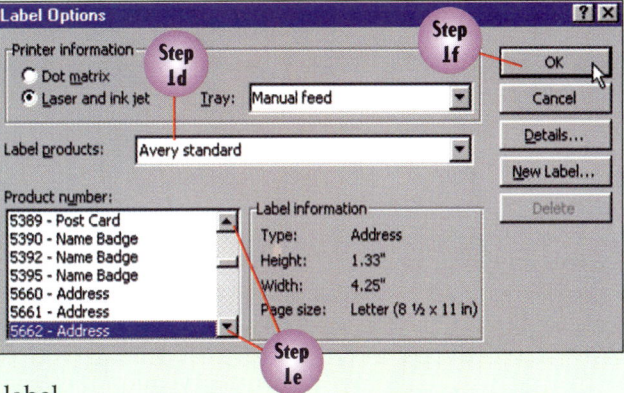

   f. Click OK or press Enter.
   g. At the Envelopes and Labels dialog box, click the New Document button.
   h. At the document screen, key the first name and address shown in figure 4.14 in the first label.
   i. Press Tab to move the insertion point to the next label and then key the second name and address shown in figure 4.14. Continue in this manner until all names and addresses have been keyed.
2. Save the document and name it Word C4, Ex 27.
3. Print and then close Word C4, Ex 27.
4. At the clear document screen, close the document screen without saving changes.

Exercise 27

Mr. David Lowry
12033 South 152ⁿᵈ Street
Houston, TX 77340

Ms. Marcella Santos
394 Apple Blossom
Friendswood, TX 77533

Mr. and Mrs. Al Sasaki
1392 Pioneer Drive
Baytown, TX 77903

Mrs. Jackie Rhyner
29039 107ᵗʰ Avenue East
Houston, TX 77302

Changing Paper Size and Orientation

Word assumes that you are printing on standard stationery—8.5 inches wide by 11 inches long. If you need to print text on different size stationery, change the paper size at the Page Setup dialog box with the Paper Size tab selected as shown in figure 4.15.

Page Setup Dialog Box with Paper Size Tab Selected

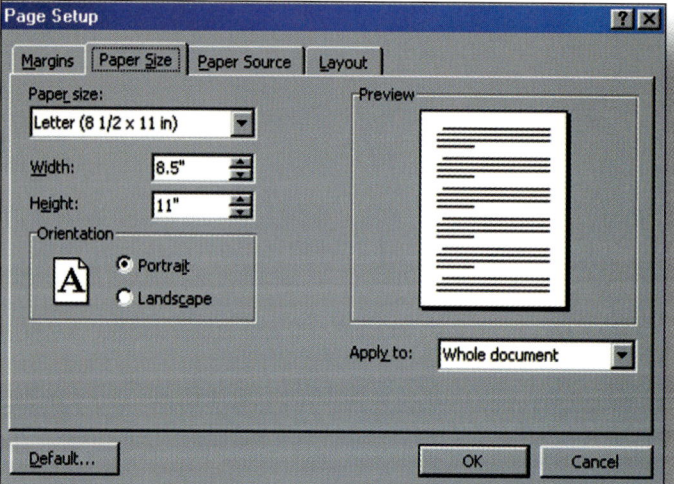

Word provides several predefined paper sizes. The number and type of paper sizes will vary depending on the selected printer. Use the predefined paper sizes if they are the necessary sizes. If the predefined sizes do not include what you need, create your own paper size with the Custom size option. If you choose the Custom size option at the Page Setup dialog box, you can enter the desired measurements for the width and height of the paper size.

Word provides two orientations for paper sizes—portrait and landscape. Figure 4.16 illustrates how text appears on the page in portrait and landscape orientations.

figure

4.16

Portrait and Landscape Orientations

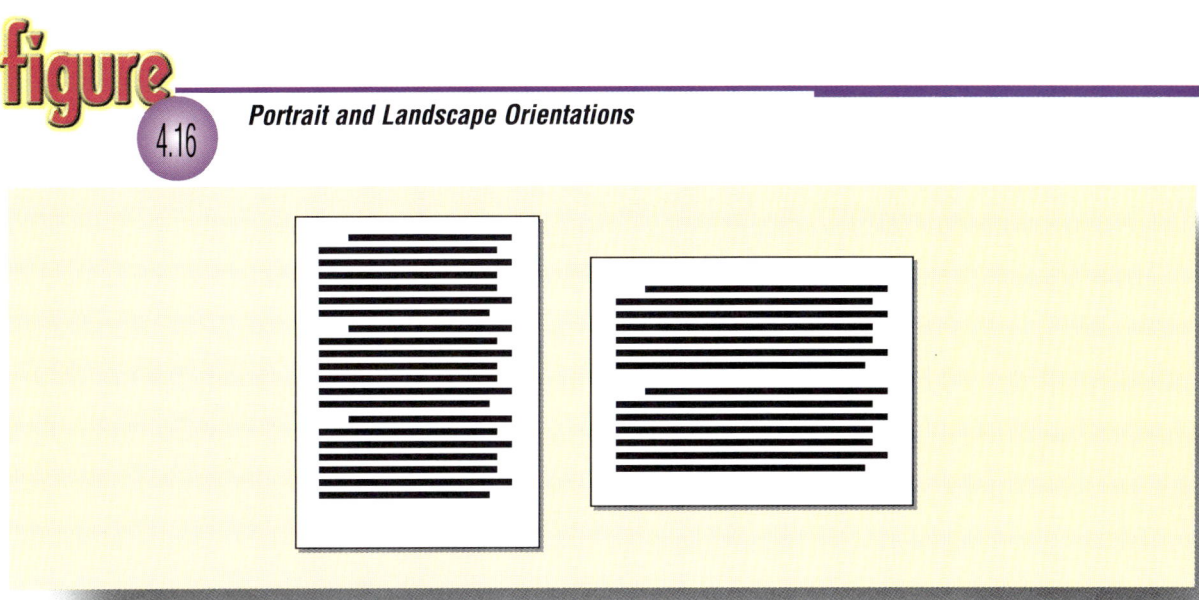

By default, the change in paper size will affect the entire document. At the Page Setup dialog box, the Apply to option has a default setting of *Whole document*. This can be changed to *This point forward*. At this setting, the paper size change will affect text from the current position of the insertion point to the end of the document.

exercise

Changing to a Predesigned Paper Size

(Note: Check with your instructor before completing this exercise. Your printer may not be capable of printing on legal-sized stationery.)

1. Open Word Report 01.
2. Save the document with Save As and name it Word C4, Ex 28.
3. Change the paper size to Legal by completing the following steps:
   a. Click File and then Page Setup.
   b. At the Page Setup dialog box, click the Paper Size tab. (Skip this step if the Paper Size tab is already selected.)
   c. Click the down-pointing triangle at the right of the Paper size option and then click *Legal (8 1/2 x 14 in)* at the drop-down list. (This paper size may be listed as *Legal 8.5 x 14 in* or *US Legal.*)
   d. Click OK or press Enter.

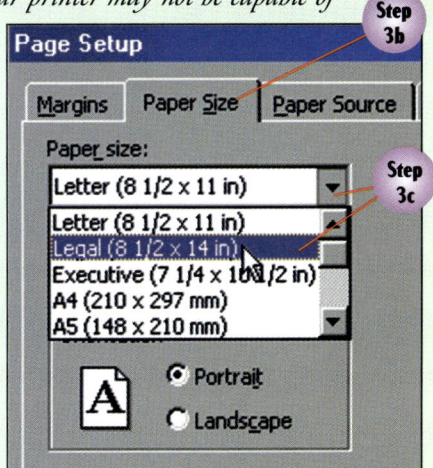

Step 3b

Step 3c

4. Save the document again with the same name (Word C4, Ex 28).
5. Print and then close Word C4, Ex 28. (Check with your instructor before printing to see if your printer is capable of printing legal-sized documents.)

Changing to Landscape Orientation

1. Open Word Document 02.
2. Save the document with Save As and name it Word C4, Ex 29.
3. Change margins and page orientation by completing the following steps:
   a. Display the Page Setup dialog box with the Margins tab selected.
   b. Change the left and right margins to 1.5 inches.
   c. Click the Paper Size tab.
   d. At the Page Setup dialog box with the Paper Size tab selected, click Landscape in the Orientation section.
   e. Click OK to close the dialog box.
4. Save the document again with the same name (Word C4, Ex 29).
5. Print and then close Word C4, Ex 29.

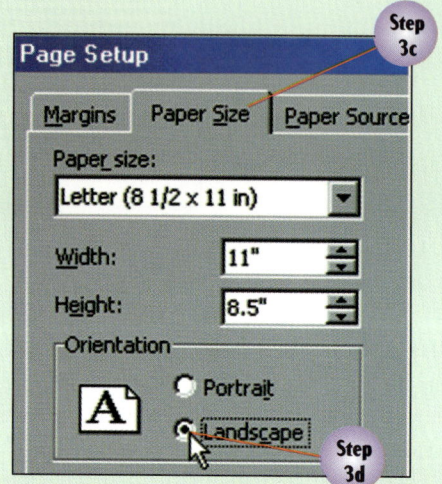

Sending a Word Document by E-Mail

Computers within a company can be connected by a private network referred to as an "intranet." With an intranet, employees within a company can send a Word document by e-mail. To send a Word document by e-mail, you will need to have Outlook available on your system. System configurations can be quite varied and you may find that your screen does not exactly match what you see in the figure in this section. Steps in exercise 30 may need to be modified to accommodate your system.

To send a document by e-mail, open the document in Word, and then click the E-mail button on the Standard toolbar. (You can also click File, point to Send To, and then click Mail Recipient.) This displays the e-mail header below the Formatting toolbar as shown in figure 4.17. When the e-mail header displays, Outlook is automatically opened.

At the e-mail header, fill in the recipient information and then click the Send a Copy button. Word sends a copy of the document to the recipient and closes the e-mail header. The original document remains open for editing. When the document is saved, the e-mail information is saved with the document.

The e-mail header contains buttons you can use to customize the e-mail message. Buttons are available for sending a copy of a document, selecting a name from an address book, establishing a priority level, and specifying delivery options.

figure
4.17

E-mail Header

E-mail Header

In the next exercise, you will send the e-mail to your instructor. If your system is not networked and your computer is not part of an intranet system, skip step 3d (clicking the Send a Copy button).

exercise 30

Creating and Printing an Outlook E-mail Message

(Note: Before completing this exercise, check to see if you can send e-mail messages. If you cannot, consider completing all the steps in the exercise except step 3d.)

1. Open Word Contract.
2. Save the document with Save As and name it Word C4, Ex 30.
3. Send Word C4, Ex 30 by e-mail by completing the following steps:
   a. Click the E-mail button on the Standard toolbar.
   b. At the e-mail header, key your instructor's name in the To... text box. (Depending on how the system is configured, you may need to key your instructor's e-mail address.)
   c. Click the down-pointing triangle at the right side of the Set Priority button and then click High Priority at the drop-down list.
   d. Click the Send a Copy button.
4. Save the document again with the same name (Word C4, Ex 30).
5. Close the Word C4, Ex 30 document.

chapter summary

➤ A new folder can be created at the Open dialog box or the Save As dialog box.

➤ One document or several documents can be selected at the Open dialog box. A document or selected documents can be copied, moved, renamed, deleted, printed, or opened.

➤ A copy of a document can be made by opening the document and then saving it with a different name. A document can also be copied with the Copy option from the Open dialog box shortcut menu. A document or selected documents can be copied to the same folder or to a different folder. If a document is copied to the same folder, Word adds *Copy of* before the document name.

➤ Use the Cut and Paste options from the Open dialog box shortcut menu to move a document from one folder to another.

➤ Use the Rename option from the Open dialog box Tools drop-down menu or the shortcut menu to give a document a different name.

➤ Documents and/or folders can be deleted with the Delete button on the Open or Save As dialog box toolbar or the Delete option from the shortcut menu. Documents deleted from the hard drive are sent to the Windows Recycle Bin. Documents can be emptied or recovered from the Recycle Bin at the Windows desktop.

➤ Several documents can be opened at one time at the Open dialog box. All open documents can be closed at the same time by holding down the Shift key, then clicking File and then Close All.

➤ A document or selected documents can be printed at the Open dialog box.

➤ Deleting, moving, or copying blocks of text within a document is generally referred to as *cutting and pasting*. A block of text can be as small as one character or as large as an entire page or document.

➤ When deleting a block of text, use the Delete key if you do not need that text again; use the Cut button on the Standard toolbar or the Cut option from the Edit drop-down menu if you might want to insert the deleted text in the current or a different document.

➤ Selected text can be copied in a document or a different document using the Copy and Paste buttons on the Standard toolbar or the Copy and Paste options from the Edit drop-down menu.

➤ With the collect and paste feature, you can collect up to 12 items and then paste them in various locations.

➤ Insert one document into another by displaying the Insert File dialog box and then double-clicking the desired document.

➤ When working in Word for Windows, a window refers to the document screen.

➤ You can open multiple documents and copy or move text between documents.

➤ Each open document fills the entire editing window. Move among the open documents by clicking the button on the Taskbar representing the desired document or by clicking Window and then clicking the desired document name. The active document is the document containing the insertion point.

➤ Use the Arrange All option from the Window drop-down menu to view a portion of all open documents.

- Use the Minimize, Maximize, and Restore buttons in the upper right corner of the window to reduce or increase the size of the active window.
- With several documents open, you can easily move, copy, and/or paste text from one document to another.
- The options available at the Print dialog box can help to customize a print job.
- To cancel a print job, double-click the Print Status icon on the Status bar (located at the right side).
- The Page range section of the Print dialog box contains settings you can use to specify the amount of text you want printed. With the Pages option, you can identify a specific page, multiple pages, and/or a range of pages for printing.
- If you want to print more than one copy of a document, use the Number of copies option from the Print dialog box.
- Create and print an envelope with options at the Envelopes and Labels dialog box.
- Use Word's labels feature to print text on mailing labels, file labels, disk labels, or other types of labels. These additional options are available at the Label Options dialog box: Printer information, Label products (to choose the type of label), and Details (to change label margins).
- The default paper size is 8.5 inches wide by 11 inches long. Paper size can be changed at the Page Setup dialog box with the Paper Size tab selected.
- Word provides two page orientations—portrait and landscape. Change the page orientation at the Page Setup dialog box with the Paper Size tab selected.
- When computers are connected by an intranet, a Word document can be sent by e-mail. Click the E-mail button on the Standard toolbar to display the e-mail header.

commands review

	Mouse/Keyboard
Open dialog box	File, Open; or click Open button on Standard toolbar
Save As dialog box	File, Save As
Minimize Word	Click Minimize button at right side of Title bar
Close all open documents	Hold Shift key, click File, Close All
Delete selected text permanently	Press Delete
Delete selected text and insert it in the Clipboard	Edit, Cut; or click Cut button on Standard toolbar
Insert text from Clipboard to new location	Edit, Paste; or click Paste button on Standard toolbar
Copy selected text	Edit, Copy, move insertion point to new location, then Edit, Paste; or click Copy button on Standard toolbar, move insertion point to new location, and then click Paste button
Deselect text	Click left mouse button outside selected text; or press any arrow key

	Mouse/Keyboard
Save selected text as separate document	Edit, Copy or click Copy button on Standard toolbar; click New Blank Document button on Standard toolbar; click Edit, Paste or click Paste button on Standard toolbar; then save in the normal manner
Display Clipboard toolbar	Right-click any displayed toolbar and then click Clipboard
Insert document into another	With insertion point at the desired location for the standard text, click Insert, File, then double-click the desired document
Arrange all open documents	Window, Arrange All
Minimize a document	Click Minimize button
Maximize a document	Click Maximize button
Display Print dialog box	File, Print
Display Envelopes and Labels dialog box	Tools, Envelopes and Labels
Display the Page Setup dialog box	File, Page Setup
Display e-mail header	Click E-mail button on Standard toolbar; or click File, point to Send To, then click Mail Recipient

thinking offline ....

Completion: In the space provided at the right, indicate the correct term, command, or number.

1. A new folder can be created with this button at the Open or Save As dialog box.

2. Click this button at the Open or Save As dialog box to change to the folder that is up one level from the current folder.

3. To display the Open dialog box shortcut menu, display the Open dialog box, position the arrow pointer on a document, and then click this mouse button.

4. To select documents at the Open dialog box that are not adjacent using the mouse, hold down this key while clicking the desired documents.

5. A document can be copied to another folder without opening the document using the Copy option and this option from the Open dialog box shortcut menu.

6. To close all open documents at once, hold down this key, click File and then click Close All.

7. When a document or selected documents are deleted from the hard drive, the documents are sent to this bin.

8. This choice from the Window drop-down menu causes each open document to appear in a separate window with no windows overlapping.

9. If more than one document is open, this word describes the document where the insertion point is located.

_____

10. Do this if you want a document to fill the editing window.

_____

11. To print pages 1 through 4 in a document, key this in the Pages text box at the Print dialog box.

_____

12. Word provides two page orientations—portrait and this.

_____

13. Click the E-mail button on this toolbar to display the e-mail header.

_____

14. In the space provided below, list the steps you would complete to open several consecutive documents at one time.

_____

_____

15. In the space provided below, list the steps you would complete to print pages 2 through 8 and page 12 of the open document.

_____

_____

16. In the space provided below, list the steps you would complete to save the second paragraph of a document named Loan Agreement as a separate document named Disclosure.

_____

_____

working hands-on

Assessment 1

1. Display the Open dialog box with *Chapter 04C* the active folder and then create a new folder named *Checking Tools*.
2. Copy (be sure to use the Copy option and not the Cut option) all documents that begin with *Word Spell Check* and *Word Grammar Check* into the *Checking Tools* folder.
3. With the *Checking Tools* folder as the active folder, rename the following documents:
   a. Rename Word Spell Check 01 to Plans. (Depending on your system setup, you may need to rename it to Plans.doc.)
   b. Rename Word Spell Check 02 to Total Return. (Depending on your system setup, you may need to rename it to Total Return.doc.)
4. Make *Chapter 04C* the active folder and then close the Open dialog box.

Assessment 2

1. Display the Open dialog box and then delete the *Checking Tools* folder and all documents contained within it.

2. Delete the following documents:
   Copy of Word Document 03
   Copy of Word Document 04
   Copy of Word Document 05
3. Close the Open dialog box.

Assessment 3

1. Open Word Report 01.
2. Save the document with Save As and name it Word C4, SA 03.
3. Make the following changes to the report:
   a. Select the entire document and then change to a serif typeface other than Times New Roman (you determine the typeface) and change the line spacing to single.
   b. Select and then delete the last sentence in the document.
   c. Move the section titled *Painting and Drawing Programs Today* above the section titled *Developments in Painting and Drawing Programs*.
   d. Set the title and three headings in a larger, bold, sans serif typeface.
   e. Change the top, left, and right margins to 1.5 inches.
4. Save the document again with the same name (Word C4, SA 03).
5. Print and then close Word C4, SA 03.

Assessment 4

1. At a clear document screen, create the document shown in figure 4.18. Double-space between lines and triple-space after the last line in the document.
2. Make the following changes to the document:
   a. Change the font for the entire document to 14-point Copperplate Gothic Bold. (If this font is not available, choose Bookman Old Style.)
   b. Select and then copy the text a triple space below the original text.
   c. Paste the text two more times. (There should be a total of four forms when you are done, and they should fit on one page.)
3. Save the document and name it Word C4, SA 04.
4. Print and then close Word C4, SA 04.

figure

4.18

Assessment 4

> ### NEWS FLASH!!
>
> ### LIFETIME ANNUITY FUNDS WORKSHOP TODAY!
>
> **Friday, October 20, 2001**
>
> **North Bay Conference Hall**

Assessment 5

1. Open Word Block 01, Word Document 01, Word Notice 01, and Word Spell Check 01.
2. Make Word Notice 01 the active document.
3. Make Word Block 01 the active document.
4. Arrange all the windows.
5. Make Word Spell Check 01 the active document and then minimize it.
6. Minimize the remaining documents.
7. Restore Word Block 01 by clicking the button on the Taskbar representing the document.
8. Restore Word Document 01.
9. Restore Word Notice 01.
10. Restore Word Spell Check 01.
11. Close Word Spell Check 01.
12. Close Word Notice 01.
13. Close Word Document 01.
14. Maximize Word Block 01.
15. Close Word Block 01.

Assessment 6

1. Open Word Document 03 and Word Document 04.
2. Make Word Document 03 the active document and then save it with Save As and name it Word C4, SA 06.
3. Make the following changes to the open documents:
    a. Select and then delete the last paragraph of text in Word C4, SA 06.
    b. Copy the first two paragraphs in Word Document 04 and then paste them at the end of Word C4, SA 06.
    c. Check the spacing of paragraphs in Word C4, SA 06 and make sure there is a blank line between each paragraph.
4. Make sure Word C4, SA 06 is the active document and then make the following changes:
    a. Add the title *ECONOMIC GROWTH IN THE 90s* at the beginning of the document, making it bold and centered.
    b. Set the entire document in a serif typeface (other than Times New Roman).
5. Save the document again with the same name (Word C4, SA 06).
6. Print and then close Word C4, SA 06.
7. Close Word Document 04.

Assessment 7

1. Open Word Document 01.
2. Print two copies of the document, displaying the Print dialog box only once.
3. Close Word Document 01.

Assessment 8

1. Open Word Report 01.
2. Save the document with Save As and name it Word C4, SA 08.
3. Make the following changes to the document:
   a. Select the entire document and then change the font to 13-point Century Schoolbook.
   b. Set the title in 16-point Century Schoolbook bold.
   c. Set the three headings in 14-point Century Schoolbook bold. (*Hint: Use Format Painter.*)
   d. Change the top, bottom, left, and right margins to 1.5 inches.
   e. Change the page orientation to landscape.
4. Save the document again with the same name (Word C4, SA 08).
5. Print page 2 of the report.
6. Close Word C4, SA 08.

Assessment 9

1. At a clear document screen, create an envelope with the text shown in figure 4.19.
2. Save the envelope document and name it Word C4, SA 09.
3. Print and then close Word C4, SA 09.

Assessment 9

Dr. Roseanne Holt
21330 Cedar View Drive
Logan, UT 84598

        Mr. Gene Mietzner
        4559 Corrin Avenue
        Smithfield, UT 84521

Assessment 10

1. Create mailing labels with the names and addresses shown in figure 4.20. Use the Avery standard, 5660 – Address label.
2. Save the document and name it Word C4, SA 10.
3. Print and then close Word C4, SA 10.
4. At the clear document screen, close the document screen without saving changes.

Assessment 10

Ms. Susan Lutovsky	Mr. Leonard Krueger	Mr. and Mrs. Jim Kiel
1402 Mellinger Drive	13290 North 120th	413 Jackson Street
Fairhope, OH 43209	Canton, OH 43291	Avondale, OH 43887
Mr. Vince Kiley	Mrs. Irene Hagen	Ms. Helga Gundstrom
14005 288th South	12930 147th Avenue East	P.O. Box 3112
Canton, OH 43287	Canton, OH 43296	Avondale, OH 43887

Assessment 11

1. Use Word's Help feature to learn how to create a postnet bar code and a FIM-A code for an envelope. Print the information.
2. After reading about and experimenting with creating a postnet bar code and a FIM-A code, write a description of the features that includes the following:
   a. Create a title for the description that is keyed in all capital letters and is centered and bolded.
   b. Describe the purpose of the postnet bar code and the FIM-A code.
   c. Set the document in a serif typeface (other than Times New Roman).
   d. Set the document title in a sans serif typeface.
3. Save the completed description and name it Word C4, SA 11.
4. Print and then close Word C4, SA 11.
5. At a clear document screen, create an envelope that contains the addresses shown in figure 4.21. Add a postnet bar code and a FIM-A code to the envelope.
6. Save the envelope document and name it Word C4, Envelope.
7. Print and then close Word C4, Envelope.

Assessment 11

Ms. Candace Bryner
2604 Linden Boulevard
Montgomery, AL 36334

Mr. Chad Frazier
610 Valley Avenue
Montgomery, AL 36336

Chapter 05C

Formatting Documents

5

PERFORMANCE OBJECTIVES

Upon successful completion of chapter 5, you will be able to:

- Create, format, edit, and delete a header or footer.
- Create a different header or footer on the first page of a document.
- Create a header or footer for odd pages and another for even pages.
- Create a header or footer for different sections in a document.
- Insert page numbering in a document.
- Create a document using a Word template and a Wizard.
- Apply styles to text in a document.
- Display a document in Outline view.
- Assign headings in an outline and collapse and expand an outline.

In a Word document, text can be created that prints at the top of every page and/or the bottom of every page and page numbering can be added to documents. Word contains a variety of features to automate the formatting of documents such as find and replace, styles, templates, and outlining.

Working with Headers and Footers

Text that appears at the top of every page is called a *header* and text that appears at the bottom of every page is referred to as a *footer*. Headers and footers are common in manuscripts, textbooks, reports, and other publications.

Creating a Header or Footer

With the <u>H</u>eader and Footer option from <u>V</u>iew, you can create a header or a footer. When you click <u>V</u>iew and then <u>H</u>eader and Footer, Word automatically changes to the Print Layout view, dims the text in the document, inserts a pane where the header or footer is entered, and also inserts the Header and Footer toolbar. Figure 5.1 shows a document with a header pane and the Header and Footer toolbar displayed. Figure 5.2 identifies the buttons on the Header and Footer toolbars.

figure 5.1

Header Pane and Header and Footer Toolbar

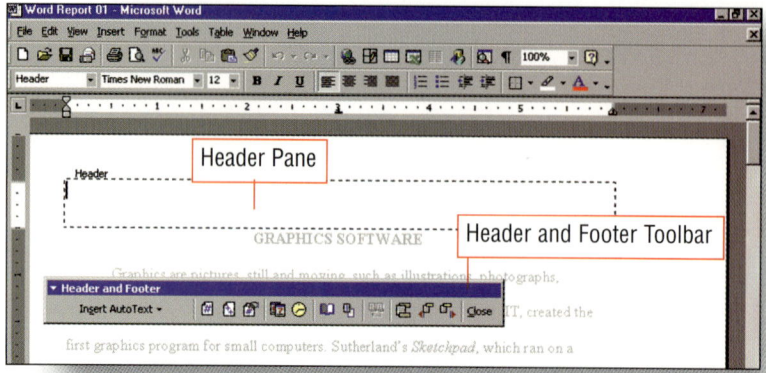

Header Pane

Header and Footer Toolbar

Consider inserting a header or footer in any document longer than one page in length.

Hint

figure 5.2

Header and Footer Toolbar Buttons

Click this button	Named	To do this
Insert AutoText ▾	Insert AutoText	Insert AutoText into header/footer.
	Insert Page Number	Insert page number in header/footer.
	Insert Number of Pages	Prints the total number of pages in the active document.
	Format Page Number	Format the page numbers in the current section.
	Insert Date	Insert date in header/footer.
	Insert Time	Insert time in header/footer.
	Page Setup	Display Page Setup dialog box.
	Show/Hide Document Text	Turn on/off the display of document text.
	Same as Previous	Link/Unlink header/footer to or from previous section.
	Switch Between Header and Footer	Switch between the header pane and the footer pane.
	Show Previous	Show previous section's header/footer.
	Show Next	Show next section's header/footer.
Close	Close Header and Footer	Close header/footer pane.

By default, the insertion point is positioned in the header pane. Key the header text in the header pane. If you are creating a footer, click the Switch Between Header and Footer button on the Header and Footer toolbar. This displays a footer pane where footer text is keyed.

Header and footer text can be formatted in the same manner as text in the document. For example, the font of header or footer text can be changed, character formatting such as bolding, italicizing, and underlining can be added, margins can be changed, and much more.

After keying the header or footer text, click the <u>C</u>lose button on the Header and Footer toolbar. Clicking <u>C</u>lose returns you to the previous view. If the Normal view was selected before a header was created, you are returned to the Normal view. If the Print Layout view was selected before a header was created, you are returned to that view. In the Normal view, a header or footer does not display on the screen. A header or footer will display dimmed in the Print Layout view. If you want to view how a header and/or footer will print, click the Print Preview button on the Standard toolbar. By default, a header and/or footer prints on every page in the document. Later in this chapter you will learn how to create headers/footers for specific sections of a document.

When creating a header or footer, the main document text displays but is dimmed. This dimmed text can be hidden while creating a header or footer by clicking the Show/Hide Document Text button on the Header and Footer toolbar. To redisplay the dimmed document text, click the button again.

(Before completing computer exercises, delete the Chapter 04C folder on your disk. Next, copy the Chapter 05C folder from the CD that accompanies this textbook to your disk and make Chapter 05C the active folder.)

Switch Between
Header and Footer

For reference purposes in a document, consider inserting a footer that contains the document name and path.

Show/Hide
Document Text

Creating a Header and a Footer

1. Open Word Report 01.
2. Save the document with Save As and name it Word C5, Ex 01.
3. Create the header *Graphics Software* and a footer that inserts the filename and path by completing the following steps:
   a. Click <u>V</u>iew and then Header and Footer.
   b. At the header pane, turn on bold, and then key **Graphics Software**.
   c. Click the Switch Between Header and Footer button on the Header and Footer toolbar. (This displays the footer pane.)
   d. At the footer pane, click the In<u>s</u>ert AutoText button on the Header and Footer toolbar and then click *Filename and path* at the drop-down list.
   e. Click the <u>C</u>lose button on the Header and Footer toolbar.

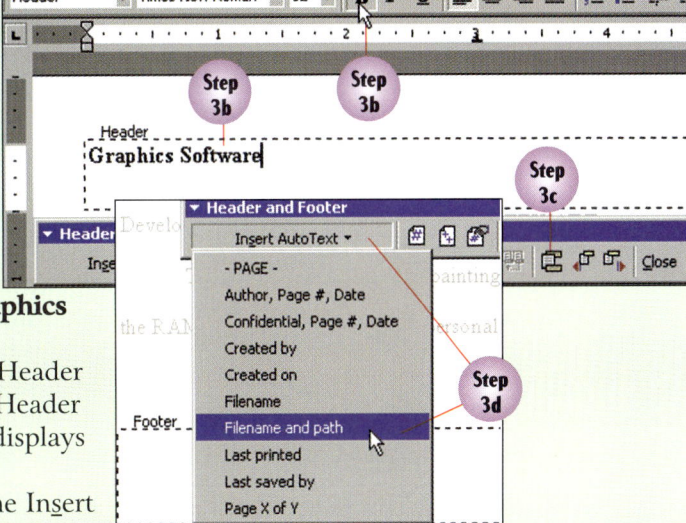

4. Display Print Preview to see how the header and footer will appear on each page when printed. (Press the Page Down key to view the second and then third page of the report.) After previewing the document, close Print Preview.
5. Check page breaks in the document and, if necessary, adjust the page breaks.
6. Save the document again with the same name (Word C5, Ex 01).
7. Print and then close Word C5, Ex 01.

(Note: Most printers cannot print to the edge of the page. If your footer does not print in exercise 1, you may need to increase the distance from the footer to the edge of the page. To increase this measurement, display the Page Setup dialog box by clicking File and then Page Setup. At the Page Setup dialog box, make sure the Margins tab is selected, and then increase the number for the Footer: option in the From edge section of the dialog box. The amount of increase depends on your printer.)

Formatting a Header or Footer

Header or footer text does not take on the character formatting of the document. For example, if you change the font for the document text, header or footer text remains at the default font. However, margin changes made to the document text do affect header or footer text. If you want header or footer text character formatting to be the same as the document text, you must format header or footer text in the header or footer pane in the normal manner.

A header or footer contains three tab settings. (These settings are designed to work with the default left and right margins of 1.25 inches. If changes are made to the margins, these settings may not operate as described.) If you want text aligned at the left margin, make sure the insertion point is positioned at the left side of the header or footer pane, and then key the text. To center text in the header or footer pane, press the Tab key. This moves the insertion point to a preset tab. From the left margin, pressing the Tab key twice will move the insertion point to the right margin of the header or footer pane. Text keyed at this tab will be right aligned.

Creating and Formatting a Footer

1. Open Word Report 01.
2. Save the document with Save As and name it Word C5, Ex 02.
3. Make the following changes to the document:
   a. Change the top margin to 1.5 inches.
   b. Select the entire document and then change the font to 12-point Century Schoolbook. (If Century Schoolbook is not available, choose another serif typeface such as Bookman Old Style or Garamond.)
4. Create the footer *Painting and Drawing Programs* in 12-point Century Schoolbook bold (or the serif typeface you chose in step 3b) that prints at the left margin of every page and *Page #* (where # represents the page number) in 12-point Century Schoolbook bold that prints at the right margin of every page by completing the following steps:
   a. Click View and then Header and Footer.
   b. Click the Switch Between Header and Footer button on the Header and Footer toolbar. (This displays the footer pane.)

c. Change the font to 12-point Century Schoolbook bold (or the serif typeface you chose in step 3b).

   d. Key **Painting and Drawing Programs**.

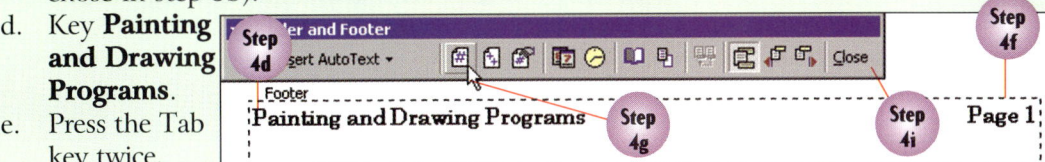

   e. Press the Tab key twice.

   f. Key **Page** and then press the space bar once.

   g. Click the Insert Page Number button on the Header and Footer toolbar.

   h. Select the page number and then change the font to 12-point Century Schoolbook bold (or the serif typeface you chose in step 3b).

   i. Click the Close button on the Header and Footer toolbar.

5. View the document in Print Preview.
6. Check page breaks in the document and, if necessary, adjust the page breaks.
7. Save the document again with the same name (Word C5, Ex 02).
8. Print and then close Word C5, Ex 02.

Editing a Header or Footer

Edit a header or footer by changing to the Print Layout view and then double-clicking the dimmed header or footer you want to edit. Edit the header or footer and then double-click the dimmed document text to make the document active.

Another method for editing a header or footer is to click Vïew and then Header and Footer. Edit the header and then click the Close button on the Header and Footer toolbar. If you want to edit a footer, click the Switch Between Header and Footer button to display the footer. If there is more than one header or footer in a document, click the Show Next button or Show Previous button to display the desired header/footer.

Double-click a header or footer in Print Layout view to open the header or footer pane for editing.

Show Next

Show Previous

exercise 3

Editing a Footer

1. Open Word C5, Ex 02.
2. Save the document with Save As and name it Word C5, Ex 03.
3. Change the left and right margins to 1 inch.
4. Edit the footer by completing the following steps:
   a. Click Vïew and then Header and Footer.
   b. Click the Switch Between Header and Footer button on the Header and Footer toolbar. (This displays the footer pane containing the footer created in exercise 2.)
   c. Delete *Painting and Drawing Programs* from the footer pane. (Leave *Page #*, which is located toward the right margin.)
   d. Key **GRAPHICS SOFTWARE** at the left margin in the footer pane.
   e. Click the Close button on the Header and Footer toolbar.

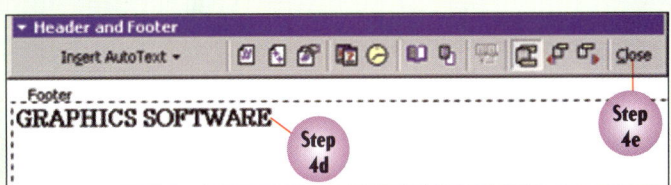

5. View the document in Print Preview.
6. Check page breaks in the document and, if necessary, adjust the page breaks.
7. Save the document again with the same name (Word C5, Ex 03).
8. Print and then close Word C5, Ex 03.

Deleting a Header or Footer

Delete a header or footer from a document by deleting it from the header or footer pane. Display the pane containing the header or footer to be deleted, select the header or footer text, and then press the Delete key.

Creating Different Headers/Footers in a Document

By default, Word will insert a header or footer on every page in the document. You can create different headers or footers within one document. For example, you can do the following:

Page Setup

- create a unique header or footer on the first page;
- omit a header or footer on the first page;
- create different headers or footers for odd and even pages; or
- create different headers or footers for sections in a document.

Creating a First Page Header/Footer

Many documents will require a different first page header.

A different header or footer can be created on the first page of a document. To do this, display the header or footer pane and then click the Page Setup button on the Header and Footer toolbar. At the Page Setup dialog box with the Layout tab selected as shown in figure 5.3, click the Different first page option to insert a check mark, and then click OK to close the dialog box. At the document, open another header or footer pane by clicking the Show Next button on the Header and Footer toolbar. Key the text for the other header or footer that will print on all but the first page and then click the Close button on the Header and Footer toolbar.

Page Setup Dialog Box with Layout Tab Selected

Click this option if you want to create different headers or footers on odd and even pages.

Click this option if you want to create a unique header or footer on the first page.

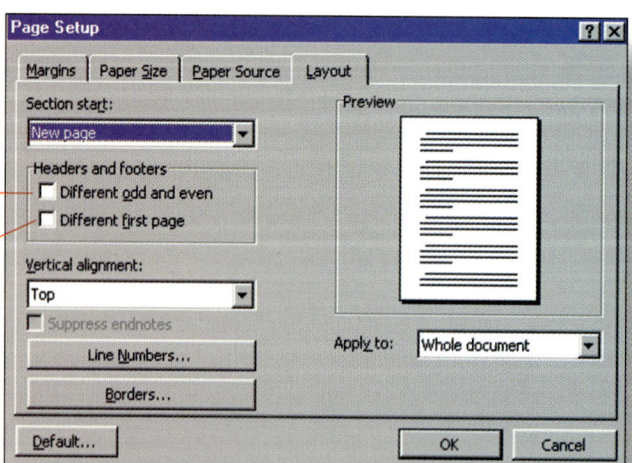

After creating the headers or footers, preview the document to see how the headers or footers will display when printed. You can follow similar steps to omit a header or footer on the first page. For example, to omit a header or footer on the first page, complete the same steps as described above except do not key text when the first header or footer pane is opened.

Creating a Header that Prints on all Pages Except the First Page

1. Open Word Report 02.
2. Save the document with Save As and name it Word C5, Ex 04.
3. Create the header *Computer Technology* that is bolded and prints at the right margin on all pages except the first page by completing the following steps:
    a. Position the insertion point anywhere in the first page.
    b. Click View and then Header and Footer.
    c. Click the Page Setup button on the Header and Footer toolbar.
    d. At the Page Setup dialog box, make sure the Layout tab is selected, and then click Different first page. (This inserts a check mark in the check box.)
    e. Click OK or press Enter.
    f. With the header pane displayed, click the Show Next button on the Header and Footer toolbar. (This opens another header pane.)
    g. Press the Tab key twice, turn on bold, and then key **Computer Technology**.
    h. Click the Close button on the Header and Footer toolbar.

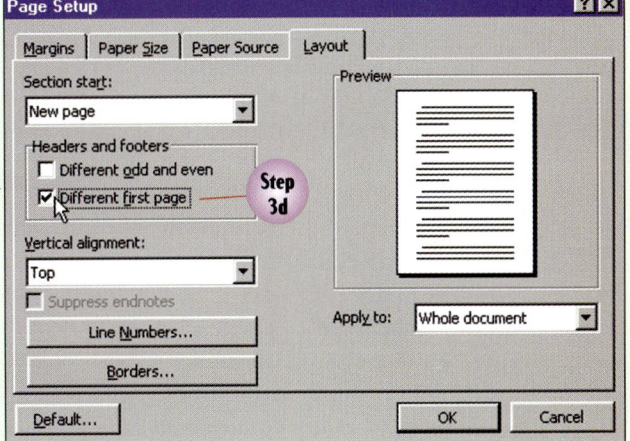

4. Check page breaks in the document and, if necessary, adjust the page breaks.
5. Save the document again with the same name (Word C5, Ex 04).
6. Print and then close Word C5, Ex 04. (You may want to preview the document before printing.)

Creating a Header/Footer for Odd/Even Pages

Printing one header or footer on even pages and another header or footer on odd pages may be useful. You may want to do this in a document that will be bound after printing. To create a header or footer that prints on odd pages and another that prints on even pages, you would complete the following steps:

1. Click View and then Header and Footer. (If you are creating a footer, click the Switch Between Header and Footer button.)
2. Click the Page Setup button. At the Page Setup dialog box, make sure the Layout tab is selected, click Different odd and even, and then click OK or press Enter. (Make sure there is no check mark in the Different first page option.)

3. At the odd page header or footer pane, key the desired text.
4. Click the Show Next button on the Header and Footer toolbar.
5. At the even header or footer pane, key the desired text, and then click the <u>C</u>lose button on the Header and Footer toolbar.

Creating a Footer for Odd Pages and Another for Even Pages

1. Open Word Report 02.
2. Save the document with Save As and name it Word C5, Ex 05.
3. Make the following changes to the document:
    a. Change the top margin to 1.5 inches.
    b. Change the font for the entire document to 12-point Century Schoolbook (or a similar typeface).
    c. Insert a page break at the line containing the title *SECTION 2: COMPUTERS IN ENTERTAINMENT* (located on page 2).
4. Create a footer that prints on all odd pages and another that prints on all even pages by completing the following steps:
    a. Move the insertion point to the beginning of the document and then click <u>V</u>iew and then <u>H</u>eader and Footer.
    b. Click the Switch Between Header and Footer button.
    c. Click the Page Setup button.
    d. At the Page Setup dialog box, make sure the <u>L</u>ayout tab is selected, and then click Different <u>o</u>dd and even. (Make sure there is no check mark in the Different <u>f</u>irst page option.)
    e. Click OK or press Enter.
    f. At the odd page footer pane press the Tab key twice and then key **Communication and Entertainment**.

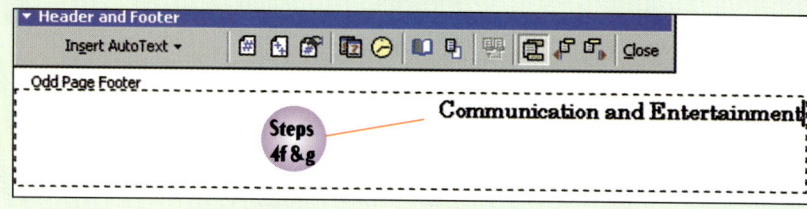

    g. Select the footer text *Communication and Entertainment* and then change the font to 12-point Century Schoolbook bold (or the serif typeface you chose in step 3b).
    h. Click the Show Next button on the Header and Footer toolbar.
    i. At the even page footer pane, key **Computers**.
    j. Select the footer text *Computers* and then change

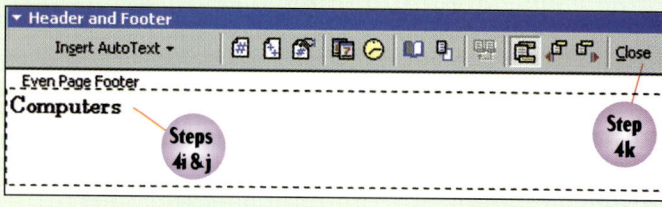

        the font to 12-point Century Schoolbook bold (or the serif typeface you chose in step 3b).
    k. Click the <u>C</u>lose button on the Header and Footer toolbar.
5. Check page breaks in the document and, if necessary, adjust the page breaks.
6. Save the document again with the same name (Word C5, Ex 05).
7. Print and then close Word C5, Ex 05. (You may want to preview the document before printing.)

Creating a Header/Footer for Different Sections

A section can be created that begins a new page or a continuous section can be created. If you want different headers and/or footers for pages in a document, divide the document into sections.

For example, if a document contains several chapters, you can create a section for each chapter, and then create a different header or footer for each section. When dividing a document into sections by chapter, insert a section break that also begins a new page.

When a header or footer is created for a specific section in a document, the header or footer can be created for all previous and next sections or just for next sections. If you want a header or footer to print on only those pages in a section and not the previous or next sections, you must deactivate the Same as Previous button. This tells Word not to print the header or footer on previous sections. Word will, however, print the header or footer on following sections. If you do not want the header or footer to print on following sections, create a blank header or footer at the next section. When creating a header or footer for a specific section in a document, preview the document to determine if the header or footer appears on the correct pages.

Same as
Previous

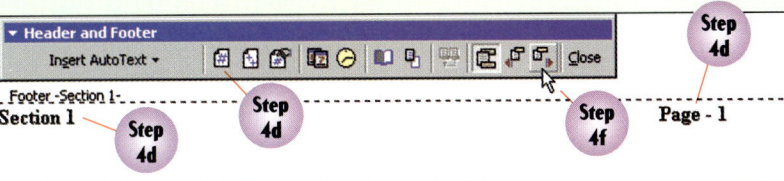

Creating Footers for Different Sections

1. Open Word Report 02.
2. Save the document with Save As and name it Word C5, Ex 06.
3. Insert a section break by completing the following steps:
   a. Position the insertion point at the beginning of the title *SECTION 2: COMPUTERS IN ENTERTAINMENT* (located on page 2).
   b. Click Insert and then Break.
   c. At the Break dialog box, click Next page.
   d. Click OK to close the dialog box.
4. Create section and page numbering footers for the two sections by completing the following steps:
   a. Position the insertion point at the beginning of the document.
   b. Click View and then Header and Footer.
   c. Click the Switch Between Header and Footer button.
   d. At the footer pane, turn on bold, key **Section 1**, and then press the Tab key twice. (This moves the insertion point to the right margin.) Key **Page**, press the space bar, key a hyphen (**-**), press the space bar again, and then click the Insert Page Number button on the Header and Footer toolbar.

e. Select and then bold the page number.

f. Click the Show Next button.

g. Click the Same as Previous button to deactivate it.

h. Change *Section 1* to *Section 2* in the footer.

i. Click the Close button on the Header and Footer toolbar.

5. Check page breaks in the document and, if necessary, adjust the page breaks.

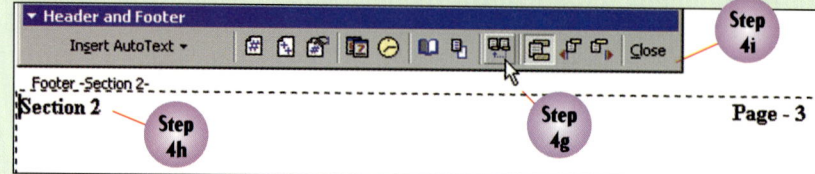

6. Save the document again with the same name (Word C5, Ex 06).

7. Print and then close Word C5, Ex 06. (You may want to preview the document before printing.)

Inserting Page Numbering in a Document

Word, by default, does not print page numbers on a page. For documents such as memos and letters, this is appropriate. For longer documents, however, page numbers may be needed. Page numbers can be added to documents with options from the Page Numbers dialog box or in a header or footer. Earlier in this chapter, you learned about the Insert Page Number button on the Header and Footer toolbar. Clicking this button inserts page numbering in a header or footer.

In addition to a header or footer, page numbering can be added to a document with options from the Page Numbers dialog box shown in figure 5.4. To display this dialog box, click Insert and then Page Numbers.

Page Numbers Dialog Box

Click this down-pointing triangle to display a list of page number positions.

Remove this check mark if you do not want the page number printed on page 1.

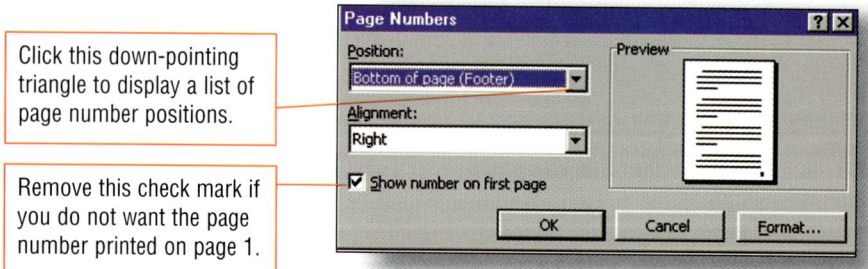

The Position option at the Page Numbers dialog box contains two choices—Top of page (Header) and Bottom of page (Footer). With choices from the Alignment option, you can insert page numbering at the left margin, center of the page, right margin, at the inside margin (the margin closest to the binding in bound material), and at the outside margin (the margin furthest from the binding in bound material).

If you turn on page numbering in a document, the page number will appear on all pages in the document including the first page. If you do not want page numbering to appear on the first page, remove the check mark from the <u>S</u>how number on first page option at the Page Numbers dialog box.

Numbering Pages at the Bottom Right Margin

1. Open Word Report 01.
2. Save the document with Save As and name it Word C5, Ex 07.
3. Change the top margin to 1.5 inches.
4. Number pages, except the first page, at the top of the page at the right margin by completing the following steps:
   a. Click <u>I</u>nsert and then Page N<u>u</u>mbers.
   b. At the Page Numbers dialog box, click the down-pointing triangle at the right of the <u>P</u>osition text box, and then click *Top of page (Header)*.
   c. Make sure the <u>A</u>lignment option displays as *Right*. (If not, click the down-pointing triangle at the right of the <u>A</u>lignment text box, and then click *Right* at the drop-down list.)
   d. Click the <u>S</u>how number on first page option to remove the check mark.
   e. Click OK or press Enter.
5. Check page breaks in the document and, if necessary, adjust the page breaks.
6. Save the document again with the same name (Word C5, Ex 07).
7. Print and then close Word C5, Ex 07. (You may want to preview the document before printing.)

Deleting Page Numbering

Page numbering in a document can be deleted in the same manner as deleting a header or footer. To delete page numbering in a document, click <u>V</u>iew and then <u>H</u>eader and Footer. Display the header or footer pane containing the page numbering, select the page numbering, and then press the Delete key. Click the <u>C</u>lose button on the Header and Footer toolbar.

Modifying Page Numbering Format

At the Page Number Format dialog box shown in figure 5.5, you can change the numbering format, add chapter numbering, and specify where you want page numbering to begin and in what sections you want page numbering to appear. To display the Page Number Format dialog box, click the <u>F</u>ormat button at the Page Numbers dialog box.

figure

5.5

Page Number Format Dialog Box

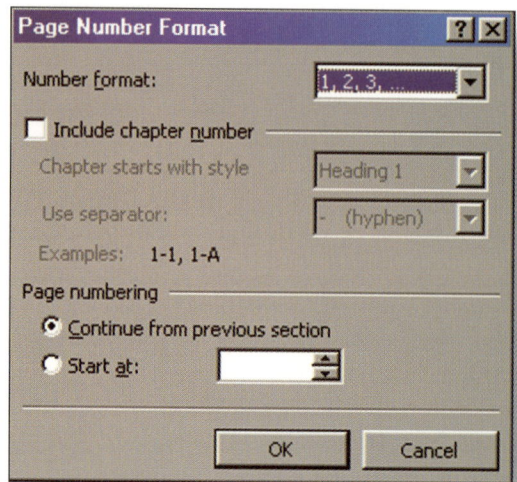

Click the Number format option from the Page Number Format dialog box to change the numbering from Arabic numbers (1, 2, 3, etc.), to lowercase letters (a, b, c, etc.), uppercase letters (A, B, C, etc.), lowercase Roman numerals (i, ii, iii, etc.), or uppercase Roman numerals (I, II, III, etc.).

Chapter numbering can be included in a document. Word will number chapters in a document if the chapter heading is formatted with a heading style. You will learn about heading styles in a later chapter.

By default, page numbering begins with 1 and continues sequentially from 1 through all pages and sections in a document. You can change the beginning page number with the Start at option at the Page Number Format dialog box. You can change the beginning page number at the beginning of the document or change the page number at the beginning of a section.

exercise 8

Numbering Pages with Roman Numerals at the Outside Margins

1. Open Word Report 02.
2. Save the document with Save As and name it Word C5, Ex 08.
3. Turn on page numbering, change the page numbering to outside margins, use lowercase Roman numerals, and change the beginning number to 3 by completing the following steps:
   a. Click Insert and then Page Numbers.
   b. At the Page Numbers dialog box, change the Alignment to *Outside*.
   c. Click the Format button.

d. At the Page Number Format dialog box, click the down-pointing triangle at the right of the Number format text box and then click *i, ii, iii, ...* at the drop-down list.

e. Click Start at and then key **3**.

f. Click OK or press Enter to close the Page Number Format dialog box.

g. Click OK or press Enter to close the Page Numbers dialog box.

4. Check the page breaks in the document and, if necessary, adjust the page breaks.

5. Save the document again with the same name (Word C5, Ex 08).

6. Print and then close Word C5, Ex 08. (You may want to preview the document before printing.)

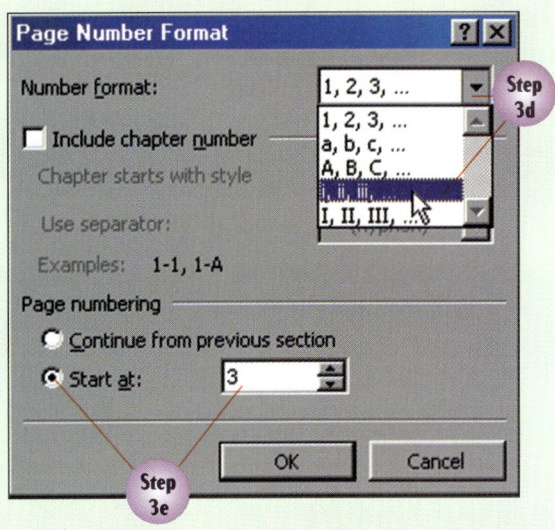

Finding and Replacing Text

With Word's find feature you can search for specific characters or formatting. With the find and replace feature, you can search for specific characters or formatting and replace with other characters or formatting. Using the find feature, or the find and replace feature, you can:

- Search for overly used words or phrases in a document.

- Use abbreviations for common phrases when entering text and then replace the abbreviations with the actual text later.

- Set up standard documents with generic names and replace them with other names to make personalized documents.

- Find and replace formatting.

Finding Text

To find specific text or formatting in a document, click Edit and then Find. This displays the Find and Replace dialog box with the Find tab selected as shown in figure 5.6. Enter the characters for which you are searching in the Find what text box. You can enter up to 256 characters in this text box. Click the Find Next button and Word searches for and selects the first occurrence of the text in the document. Make corrections to the text if needed and then search for the next occurrence by clicking the Find Next button again. Click the Cancel button to close the Find and Replace dialog box.

figure

5.6

Find and Replace Dialog Box with Find Tab Selected

Key search text in the Find what text box.

Click the Find Next button to find the next occurrence of the search text.

exercise 9

Finding Words

1. Open Word Report 01.
2. Find every occurrence of *painting programs* in the document by completing the following steps:

   a. With the insertion point positioned at the beginning of the document, click Edit and then Find.

   Step 2b

   Step 2c

   b. At the Find and Replace dialog box with the Find tab selected, key **painting programs** in the Find what text box.

   c. Click the Find Next button.

   d. Word searches for and selects the first occurrence of *painting programs*.

   e. Search for the next occurrence of *painting programs* by clicking the Find Next button again.

   f. Continue clicking the Find Next button until the message *Word has finished searching the document* displays.

   g. Click the Cancel button to close the Find and Replace dialog box (and remove the message).

3. Close Word Report 01.

The keyboard shortcut for Replace is Ctrl + H.

The next time you open the Find and Replace dialog box, you can display a list of text for which you have searched by clicking the down-pointing triangle after the Find what text box. For example, if you searched for *type size* and then performed another search for *type style*, the third time you open the Find and Replace dialog box, clicking the down-pointing triangle after the Find what text

box will display a drop-down list with *type style* and *type size*. Click text from this drop-down list if you want to perform a search on that text.

Finding and Replacing Text

To use Find and Replace, click <u>E</u>dit, expand the drop-down menu, and then click Replace. This displays the Find and Replace dialog box with the Re<u>p</u>lace tab selected as shown in figure 5.7.

Find and Replace Dialog Box with the Replace Tab Selected

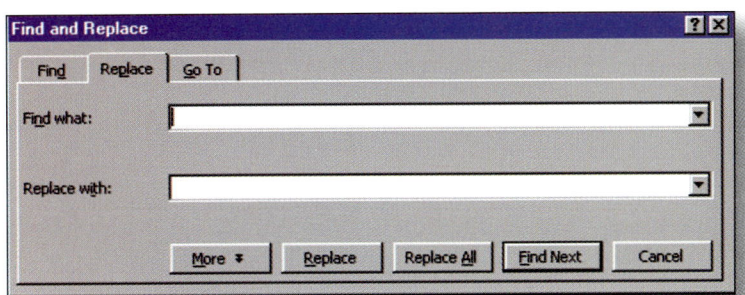

Enter the characters and/or formatting for which you are searching in the Fi<u>n</u>d what text box. Press the Tab key to move the insertion point to the Replace wi<u>t</u>h text box and then key the replacement text or insert the replacement formatting. You can also move the insertion point to the Replace wi<u>t</u>h text box by clicking inside the text box.

The Find and Replace dialog box contains several command buttons. Click the <u>F</u>ind Next button to tell Word to find the next occurrence of the characters and/or formatting. Click the <u>R</u>eplace button to replace the characters or formatting and find the next occurrence. If you know that you want all occurrences of the characters or formatting in the Fi<u>n</u>d what text box replaced with the characters or formatting in the Replace wi<u>t</u>h text box, click the Replace <u>A</u>ll button. This replaces every occurrence from the location of the insertion point to the beginning or end of the document (depending on the search direction). Click the Cancel button to close the Find and Replace dialog box.

Finding and Replacing Text

1. Open Word Legal 01.
2. Save the document with Save As and name it Word C5, Ex 10.
3. Find all occurrences of NAME1 and replace with SUSAN R. LOWE by completing the following steps:
   a. With the insertion point positioned at the beginning of the document, click <u>E</u>dit, expand the drop-down menu, and then click R<u>e</u>place.

b. At the Find and Replace dialog box with the Replace tab selected, key **NAME1** in the Fi̱nd what text box.

c. Press the Tab key to move the insertion point to the Replace with text box.

d. Key **SUSAN R. LOWE**.

e. Click the Replace A̱ll button.

f. When all replacements are made, the message *Word has completed its search of the document and has made 5 replacements* displays. (Do not close the Find and Replace dialog box.)

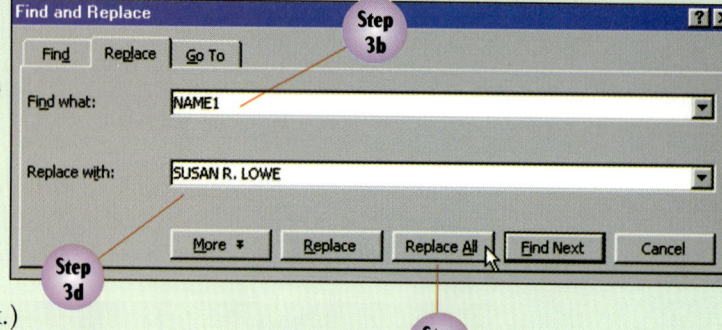

4. With the Find and Replace dialog box still open, complete steps similar to those in 3b through 3f to find all occurrences of NAME2 and replace with MARY A. LANGE.

5. With the Find and Replace dialog box still open, complete steps similar to those in 3b through 3f to find the one occurrence of NUMBER and replace with C-3546.

6. Close the Find and Replace dialog box.

7. Save the document again with the same name (Word C5, Ex 10).

8. Print and then close Word C5, Ex 10.

Choosing Find Check Box Options

The Find and Replace dialog box contains a variety of check boxes with options you can choose for completing a search. To display these options, click the More button located at the bottom of the dialog box. This causes the Find and Replace dialog box to expand as shown in figure 5.8. Each option and what will occur if it is selected is described in figure 5.9.

5.8

Expanded Find and Replace Dialog Box

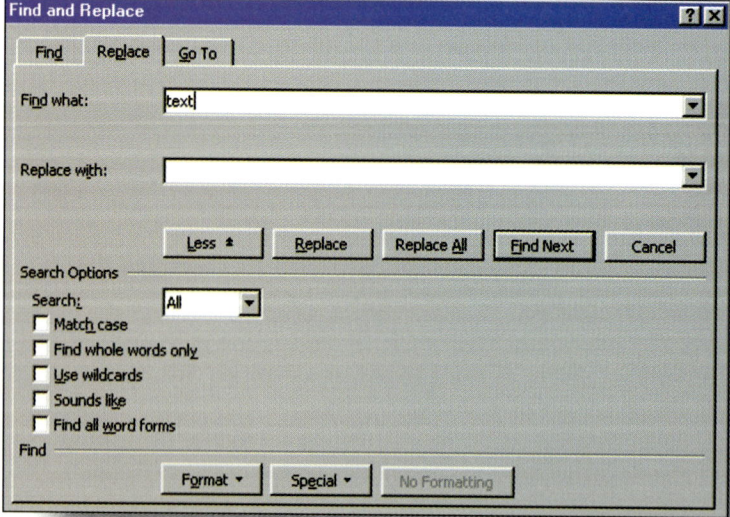

figure 5.9   *Options at the Find and Replace Dialog Box*

Choose this option	To
Mat<u>c</u>h case	Exactly match the case of the search text. For example, if you search for *Book* and select the Mat<u>c</u>h case option, Word will stop at *Book* but not *book* or *BOOK*.
Find whole words onl<u>y</u>	Find a whole word, not a part of a word. For example, if you search for *her* and <u>did not</u> select Find whole words onl<u>y</u>, Word would stop at t*here*, *here*, *hers*, and so on.
<u>U</u>se wildcards	Search for wildcards, special characters, or special search operators.
Sounds li<u>k</u>e	Match words that sound alike but are spelled differently such as *know* and *no*.
Find all <u>w</u>ord forms	Find all forms of the word entered in the Fi<u>n</u>d what text box. For example, if you enter *hold*, Word will stop at *held* and *holding*.

To remove the display of options toward the bottom of the Find and Replace dialog box, click the <u>L</u>ess button. (The <u>L</u>ess button was previously the <u>M</u>ore button.)

Finding and Replacing Word Forms

1. Open Word Document 06.
2. Save the document with Save As and name it Word C5, Ex 11.
3. Find all forms of the word *produce* and replace it with forms of *create* by completing the following steps:
   a. Make sure the insertion point is positioned at the beginning of the document.
   b. Click <u>E</u>dit and then Replace.
   c. At the Find and Replace dialog box with the Replace tab selected, key **produce** in the Fi<u>n</u>d what text box.
   d. Press the Tab key and then key **create** in the Replace with text box.
   e. Click the <u>M</u>ore button.
   f. Click the Find all <u>w</u>ord forms option. (This inserts a check mark in the check box.)
   g. Click the Replace <u>A</u>ll button.
   h. At the message, *Replace All is*

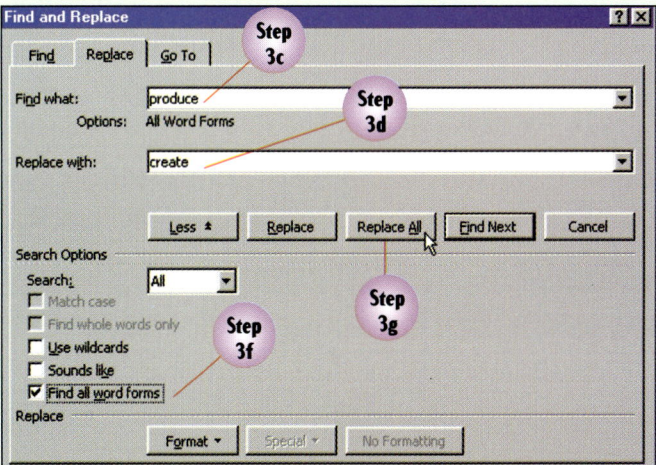

not recommended with Find All Word Forms. Continue with Replace All?, click OK.
  i. When the find and replace is completed, click the Find all word forms option to remove the check mark.
  j. Click the Less button.
  k. Click the Close button to close the Find and Replace dialog box.
4. Save the document again with the same name (Word C5, Ex 11).
5. Print and then close Word C5, Ex 11.

Navigating in a Document Using Go To

As you learned, you can use the Find and Replace dialog box to find specific text or formatting in a document, and to find and replace specific text or formatting. You can also use the Find and Replace dialog box with the Go To tab selected, as shown in figure 5.10, to find or go to a specific location or item. To display this dialog box, display the Find and Replace dialog box and then click the Go To tab or click Edit, expand the drop-down menu, and then click Go To.

5.10

Find and Replace Dialog Box with Go To Tab Selected

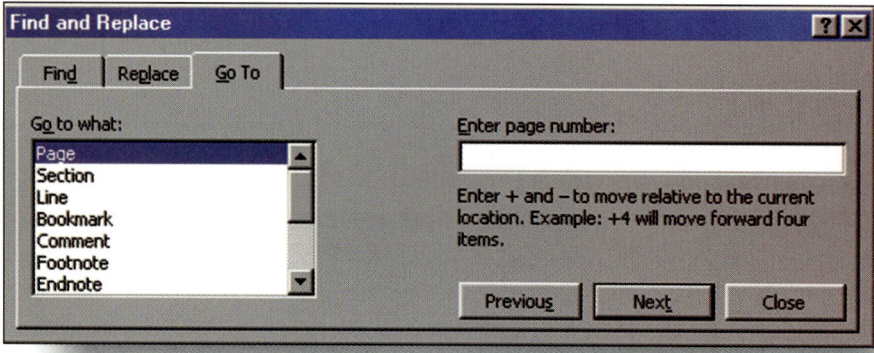

To find a specific item in a document such as a page or line, click the desired item in the Go to what list box, and then click the Go To button.

Navigating in a Document Using Go To

1. Open Word Report 02.
2. Save the document with Save As and name it Word C5, Ex 12.
3. Make the following changes to the document:
    a. Change the top, left, and right margins to 1.5 inches.

b . Insert page numbering that prints at the bottom, center, of each page.

c. Insert a section break that begins a new page at the title *SECTION 2: COMPUTERS IN ENTERTAINMENT.*

4. Position the insertion point at the beginning of the document and then move the insertion point to specific locations in the document by completing the following steps:

a. Click Edit, expand the drop-down menu, and then click Go To.

b. At the Find and Replace dialog box with the Go To tab selected, click *Line* in the Go to what list box.

c. Click in the Enter line number text box and then key **10**.

d. Click the Go To button. (This moves the insertion point to line 10 on the first page of the document—check the Status bar.)

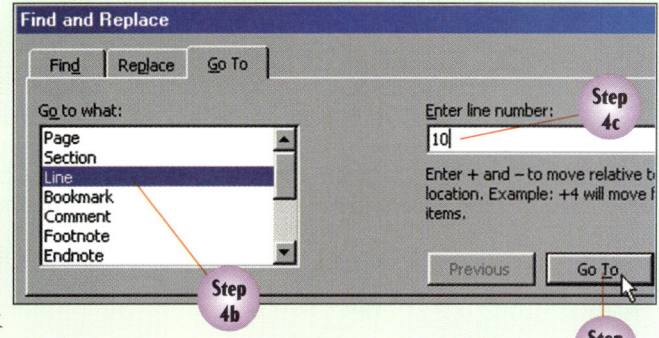

e. At the Find and Replace dialog box with the Go To tab selected, click *Page* in the Go to what list box.

f. Click in the Enter page number text box and then key **2**.

g. Click the Go To button. (This moves the insertion point to the beginning of page 2.

h. At the Find and Replace dialog box with the Go To tab selected, click *Section* in the Go to what list box.

i. Click in the Enter section number list box and then key **2**.

j. Click the Go To button. (This moves the insertion point to the beginning of the second section.)

k. Click the Close button to close the Find and Replace dialog box.

5. Save the document again with the same name (Word C5, Ex 12).

6. Print and then close Word C5, Ex 12.

Using Templates

Word has included a number of *template* documents that are formatted for specific uses. Each Word document is based on a template document with the *Normal* template the default. With Word templates, you can easily create a variety of documents, such as letters, memos, and awards, with specialized formatting. Along with templates, Word also includes *Wizards*. Wizards are templates that do most of the work for you. *(Note: During a typical installation, not all templates may be installed. Before completing the template exercises, check to see if the templates are available.)*

Templates and Wizards are available at the New dialog box. To display this dialog box, shown in figure 5.11, click File and then New. The New dialog box contains several tabs for displaying a variety of templates and wizards. If the default tab, General, is selected as shown in figure 5.11, the *Blank Document* template displays. To view other templates and wizards, click a different tab at the top of the New dialog box.

Use Word wizards and templates to create a variety of professionally designed documents

The template wizard is a template that asks questions and uses your responses to format a document automatically.

figure

New Dialog Box with General Tab Selected

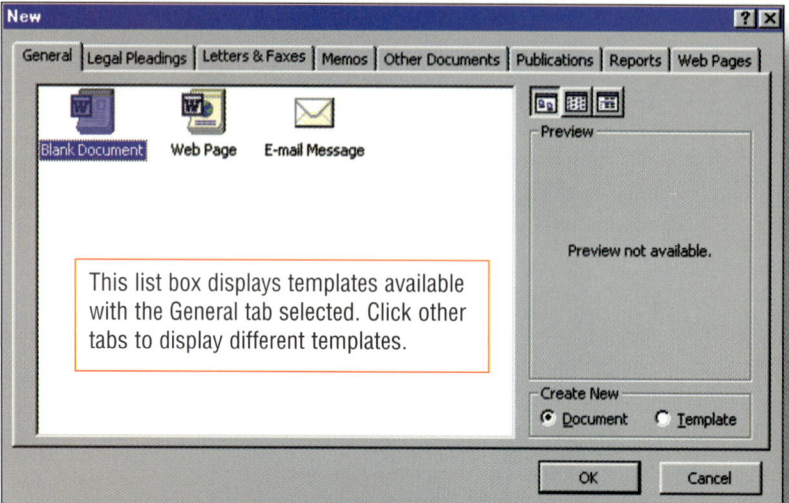

To create a document based on a different template, click the desired template, and then click OK, or double-click the desired template. If you click once on the desired template, a sample template displays in the Preview box at the right side of the dialog box. When you double-click a template, a template document is opened with certain formatting already applied. Specific information is then entered in the template document. After all information has been entered, the template document is saved in the normal manner.

exercise 13

Creating a Memo with a Memo Template

1. Use the Contemporary Memo template to create a memo by completing the following steps:
   a. Click File and then New.
   b. At the New dialog box, click the Memos tab.
   c. At the New dialog box with the Memos tab selected, double-click *Contemporary Memo*.

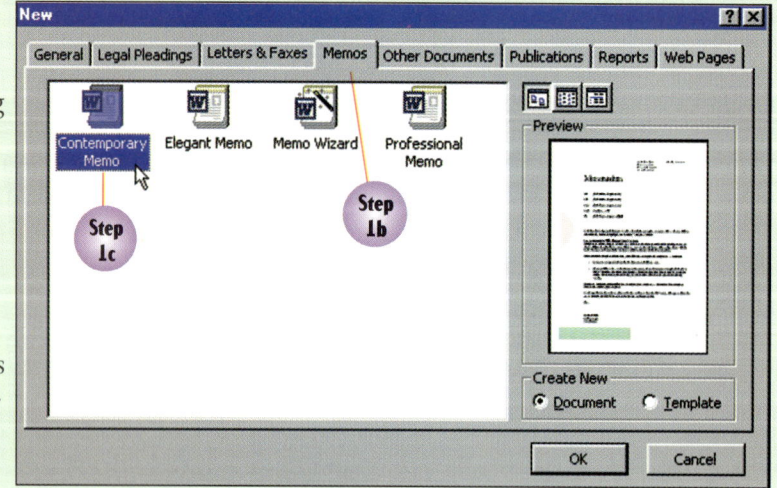

d. At the contemporary memo template document, complete the following steps to key the text in the memo:

    1) Position the I-beam pointer on the word *here* in the bracketed text *[Click **here** and type name]* after *To:*, click the left mouse button, and then key **Sylvia Monroe, Vice President**.

    2) Position the I-beam pointer on the word *here* in the bracketed text *[Click **here** and type name]* after *CC:*, click the left mouse button, and then key **Jacob Sharify, President**.

    3) Position the I-beam pointer on the word *here* in the bracketed text *[Click **here** and type name]* after *From:*, click the left mouse button, and then key **Jamie Rodriquez, Design Department Manager**.

    4) Position the I-beam pointer on the word *here* in the bracketed text *[Click **here** and type subject]* after *Re:*, click the left mouse button, and then key **Color Scanners**.

    5) Select and then delete the text in the memo from ***How To Use This Memo Template*** to the end of the document.

    6) Key the text shown in figure 5.12.

2. Save the memo and name it Word C5, Ex 13.

3. Print and then close Word C5, Ex 13. (This memo template will print with several graphics including horizontal and vertical lines as well as lightened images.)

5.12 *Exercise 13*

The amount of company material produced by the Graphics Department has increased 200 percent in the past six months. To meet the demands of the increased volume, I am requesting two new color scanners. These scanners are needed to scan photographs, pictures, and other images. The total price of the two scanners is approximately $425. I will complete a product request form and forward it to you immediately.

Using Wizards

Wizards are template documents that do most of the work for you. When you select a Wizard template document, Word asks you questions and gives you choices about what type of formatting you want applied to the document. Follow the steps provided by the Wizard to complete the document.

Creating a Letter Using a Wizard

1. Create a letter using the Letter Wizard by completing the following steps:
   a. Click File and then New.
   b. At the New dialog box, click the Letters & Faxes tab.
   c. At the New dialog box with the Letters & Faxes tab selected, double-click the *Letter Wizard* icon.
   d. At the message displayed by the Office Assistant, click the *Send one letter* option.
   e. At the Letter Wizard—Step 1 of 4 dialog box, complete the following steps:
      1) Click the down-pointing triangle at the right side of the *Choose a page design* option, and then click *Contemporary Letter* at the drop-down list.
      2) Click the Next> button.

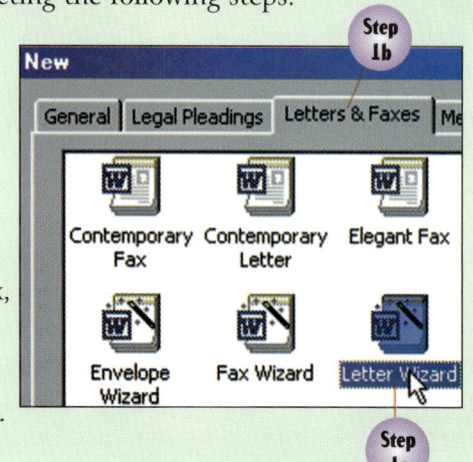

Step 1b

Step 1c

   f. At the Letter Wizard—Step 2 of 4 dialog box, complete the following steps:
      1) Key **Mr. Gregory Todd** in the Recipient's name text box.
      2) Press the Tab key. (This moves the insertion point to the Delivery address text box.)
      3) Key **12001 North 32nd Avenue**.
      4) Press Enter.
      5) Key **New York, NY 10225**.
      6) Click the Business option located in the lower right corner of the dialog box.
      7) Click the Next> button.
   g. At the Letter Wizard—Step 3 of 4 dialog box, click the Next> button.
   h. At the Letter Wizard—Step 4 of 4 dialog box, complete the following steps:
      1) Select the text that currently displays in the Sender's name text box, and then key **Louis Hamilton**.
      2) Click in the Job title text box and then key **Investment Manager**.
      3) Click in the Writer/typist's initials text box and then key your initials.
      4) Click the Finish button.
   i. At the Office Assistant message, click Cancel.
   j. At the letter, insert a file for the body of the letter by completing the following steps:
      1) Select the text *Type your letter here. To add, remove, or change letter elements, choose Letter Wizard from the Tools menu.* and then press the Delete key.
      2) Click Insert and then File.

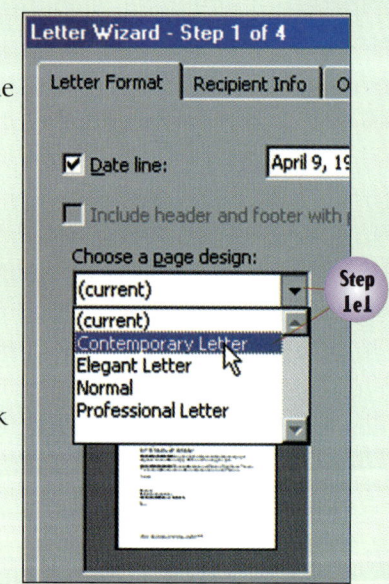

Step 1e1

3) At the Insert File dialog box, make sure *Chapter 05C* is the active folder, and then double-click *Word Letter 06*.

k. Move down the name and inside address by positioning the insertion point at the beginning of the name *Mr. Gregory Todd* and then pressing the Enter key twice.

l. Vertically center the letter on the page by completing the following steps:
1) Click File and Page Setup.
2) Click the Layout tab in the Page Setup dialog box.
3) Click the down-pointing triangle to the right of the Vertical alignment text box and click *Center* at the drop-down list.
4) Click OK.

2. Save the letter and name it Word C5, Ex 14.
3. Print and then close Word C5, Ex 14.

Formatting with Predesigned Styles

A Word document, by default, is based on the Normal template document. Within a normal template document, a Normal style is applied to text by default. This Normal style sets text in the default font (this may vary depending on what you have selected or what printer you are using) and uses left alignment and single spacing. In addition to this Normal style, other predesigned styles are available in a document based on the Normal template document. Display these styles by clicking the down-pointing triangle to the right of the Style button on the Formatting toolbar.

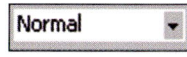

Style

Other template documents also contain predesigned styles. If you choose a different template document from the New dialog box, click the down-pointing triangle to the right of the Style button on the Formatting toolbar to display the names of styles available for that particular template document.

Applying a ready-to-use style ensures a consistent visual appearance of document elements.

To apply a style with the Style button on the Formatting toolbar, position the insertion point in the paragraph to which you want the style applied, or select the text, and then click the down-pointing triangle to the right of the Style button (the first button on the left). This causes a drop-down list to display as shown in figure 5.13. Click the desired style in the list to apply the style to the text in the document.

Style Drop-Down List

5.13

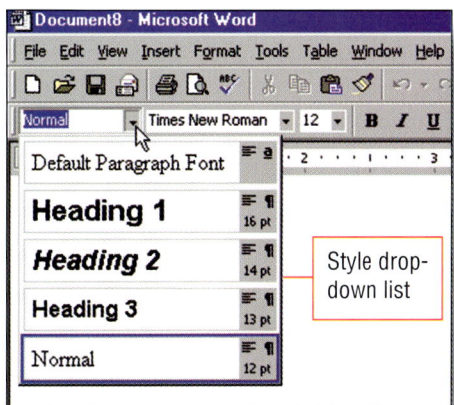

When you click a style in the drop-down list, the list is removed from the screen and the style is applied to the text. The formatting applied by the style will vary. For example, the Heading 1 style applies the font 16-point Arial bold and the Heading 2 style applies the font 14-point Arial bold italic.

When a style is applied to text, the style name displays in the Style button on the Formatting toolbar. In addition, the font for the style displays in the Font button and the size for the style displays in the Font Size button.

Formatting a Document with Styles

1. Open Word Report 01.
2. Save the document with Save As and name it Word C5, Ex 15.
3. Make the following changes to the report:
   a. Select the entire document.
   b. Press Ctrl + 1 to change to single spacing.
4. Format the title with a style on the Formatting toolbar by completing the following steps:
   a. Position the insertion point anywhere within the title *GRAPHICS SOFTWARE*.
   b. Click the down-pointing triangle at the right side of the Style button on the Formatting toolbar.
   c. At the drop-down list that displays, click *Heading 1*.
5. Format the first heading with a style on the Formatting toolbar by completing the following steps:
   a. Position the insertion point anywhere within the first heading, *Early Painting and Drawing Programs*.
   b. Click the down-pointing triangle at the right side of the Style button on the Formatting toolbar and then click *Heading 2* at the drop-down list.
6. Format the two remaining headings (*Developments in Painting and Drawing Programs* and *Painting and Drawing Programs Today*) with the Heading 2 style.
7. Save the document again with the same name (Word C5, Ex 15).
8. Print and then close Word C5, Ex 15.

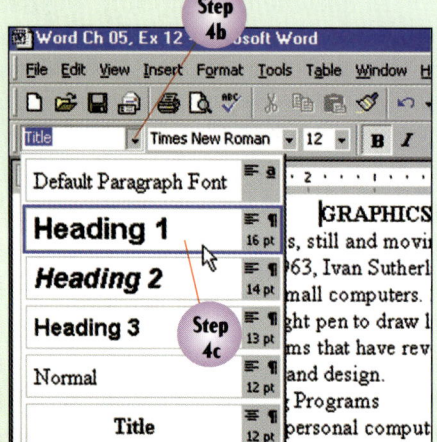

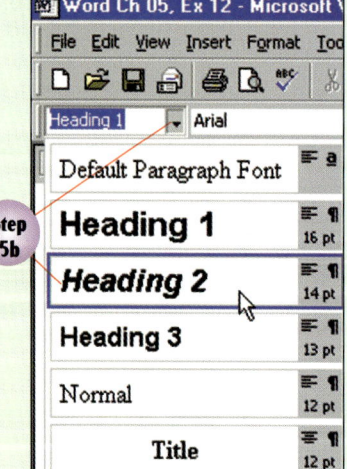

Formatting with Styles at the Style Dialog Box

The Style drop-down list only displays a few styles. Word provides many more predesigned styles than this that you can use to format text in a document. You can display the list of styles available with Word at the Style dialog box, shown in figure 5.14. To display the Style dialog box, click Format and then Style.

Style Dialog Box

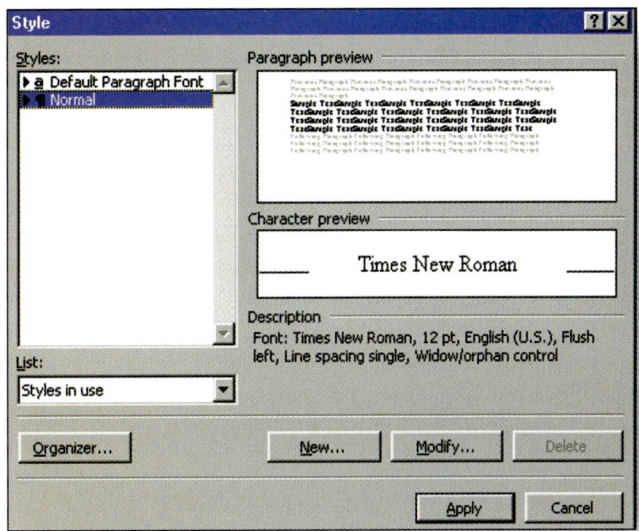

To display the entire list of styles provided by Word, click the down-pointing triangle at the right side of the List text box, and then click *All styles* at the drop-down list. When you click *All styles*, the list of styles in the Styles list box displays as shown in figure 5.15. The list is longer than the list box. In the Styles list box, paragraph styles are preceded by a paragraph mark (¶) and character styles are preceded by the symbol (**a**).

figure
5.15

Style Dialog Box with All Styles Displayed

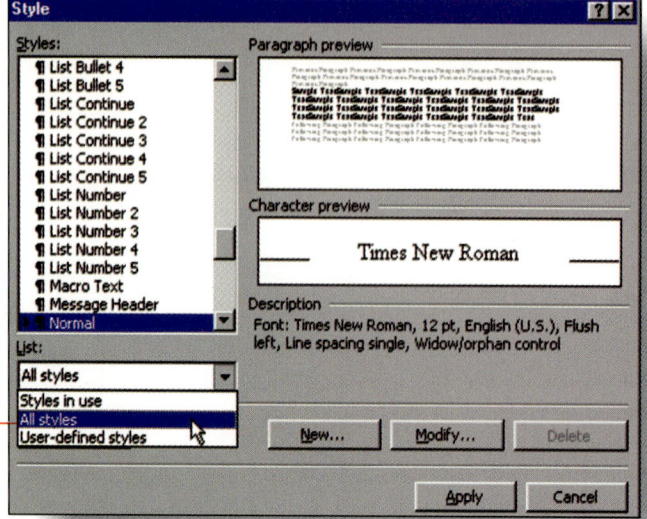

Click *All styles* to display all available styles in the Styles list box.

At the right side of the Style dialog box, the Paragraph preview box displays an example of how the selected style will format text. The Character preview box displays the font used to format text. A description of the style is displayed in the Description section of the dialog box.

To apply a style at the Style dialog box, position the insertion point within the paragraph of text to be formatted; or, if applying a character style, select the text, click Format and then Style. At the Style dialog box, click the down-pointing triangle at the right side of the List text box, and then click *All styles*. Click the desired style in the list and then click the Apply button.

View attributes of a style in the Description area of the Style dialog box.

exercise 16

Formatting with a Style at the Style Dialog Box

1. Open Word Document 05.
2. Save the document with Save As and name it Word C5, Ex 16.
3. Make the following changes to the document:
   a. Bold the heading *ARE YOU PREPARING FOR RETIREMENT?*.
   b. Apply the List Bullet 2 style to text in the document by completing the following steps:
      1) Select from the paragraph that begins *"Living longer than ever,..."* through the last paragraph of text in the document.
      2) Click Format and then click Style.

3) At the Style dialog box, click the down-pointing triangle at the right side of the List text box, and then click *All styles* at the drop-down list.

4) Click the *List Bullet 2* style in the Styles list box. (You will need to scroll up to see this style.)

5) Click the Apply button.

c. Deselect the text.

4. Save the document again with the same name (Word C5, Ex 16).

5. Print and then close Word C5, Ex 16.

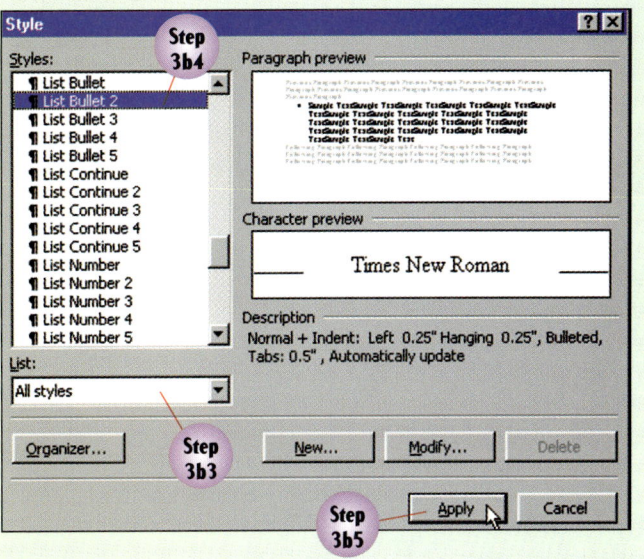

Formatting with Styles at the Style Gallery

Each template document contains predesigned styles. Use the Style Gallery dialog box to apply styles from other templates to the current document. This provides you with a large number of predesigned styles for formatting text. To display the Style Gallery dialog box shown in figure 5.16, click Format and then Theme. At the Theme dialog box, click the Style Gallery button (located at the bottom of the dialog box).

figure
5.16

Style Gallery Dialog Box

Select a style template from this list.

The selected style template is previewed here.

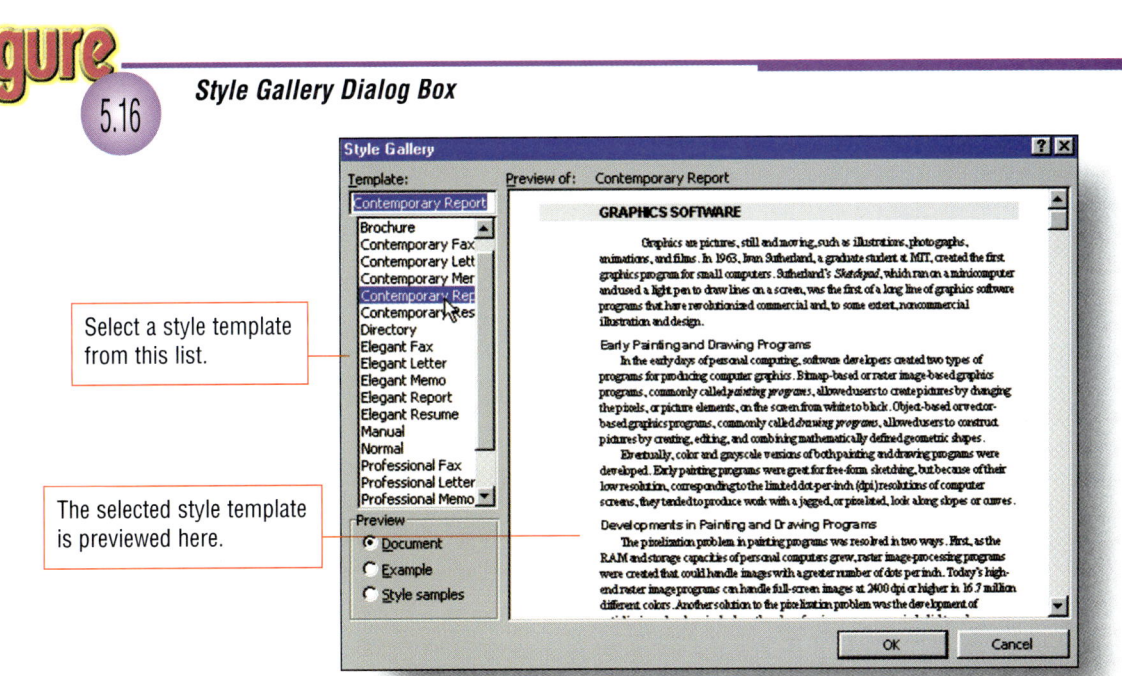

At the Style Gallery dialog box, the template documents are displayed in the Template list box. The open document is displayed in the Preview of section of the dialog box. With this section, you can choose templates from the Template list box and see how the formatting is applied to the open document.

At the bottom of the Style Gallery dialog box, the Document option is selected in the Preview section. If you click Example, Word will insert a sample document in the Preview of section that displays the formatting applied to the document. Click Style samples and styles will display in the Preview of section of the dialog box rather than the document or sample document.

Formatting a Report with Styles from a Report Template

1. Open Word C5, Ex 15.
2. Save the document with Save As and name it Word C5, Ex 17.
3. Format the document at the Style Gallery by completing the following steps:
   a. Click Format and then click Theme.
   b. At the Theme dialog box, click the Style Gallery button (located at the bottom of the dialog box).
   c. At the Style Gallery dialog box, click *Contemporary Report* in the Template list box.
   d. Click OK or press Enter.
4. Save the document again with the same name (Word C5, Ex 17).
5. Print and then close Word C5, Ex 17.

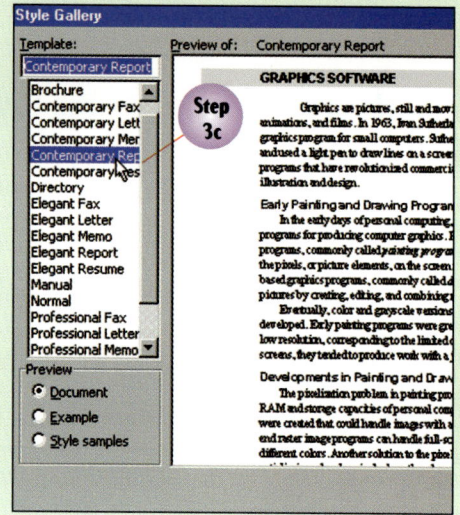

Creating Outline Style Numbered List

In chapter 2, you learned how to apply numbering to selected text with options at the Bullets and Numbering dialog box. Certain options at the Bullets and Numbering dialog box with the Outline Numbered tab selected are available only when heading styles have been applied to text. In exercise 18, you will apply heading styles to text and then apply outline style numbering to the text.

Creating an Outline Style Numbered List

1. Open Word Agenda.
2. Save the document with Save As and name it Word C5, Ex 18.
3. Make the following changes to the document:
    a. Delete the following text:
       First Quarter (below *Income Report*)
       Second Quarter (below *Income Report*)
       First Quarter (below *Expense Report*)
       Second Quarter (below *Expense Report*)
    b. Apply the Heading 1 style to the following text:
       Sales and Marketing
       Financial
       Services and Procedures
       Education
    c. Apply the Heading 2 style to the following text:
       Commercial Lines
       Personal Lines
       Year-end Production Report
       Income Report
       Expense Report
       Accounts Receivable
       Accounts Payable
       Collections
       Update
       Sponsors
       Seminars
       Training
    d. Apply outline style numbering by completing the following steps:
       1) Select the text from the beginning of *Sales and Marketing* to the end of the document.
       2) Click Format and then Bullets and Numbering.
       3) At the Bullets and Numbering dialog box, click the Outline Numbered tab.
       4) Click the third option from the left in the bottom row.
       5) Click OK to close the dialog box.

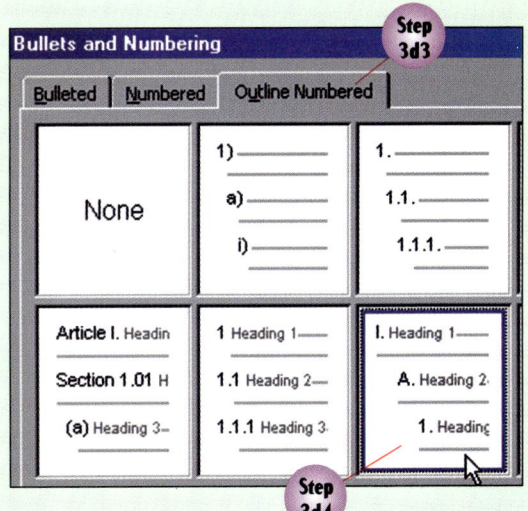

    e. Select the title *COMMERCIAL LINES DEPARTMENT* and the subtitle *MEETING AGENDA* and then change the font to 16-point Arial bold.
4. Save the document again with the same name (Word C5, Ex 18).
5. Print and then close Word C5, Ex 18.

Creating an Outline

Word's outlining feature will format headings within a document as well as let you view formatted headings and body text in a document. With the outlining feature you can quickly see an overview of a document by collapsing parts of a document so that only the headings show. With headings collapsed, you can perform such editing functions as moving or deleting sections of a document.

To create an outline, you identify particular headings and subheadings within a document as certain heading levels. The Outline view is used to assign particular heading levels to text. You can also enter text and edit text while working in Outline view. To change to Outline view, click the Outline View button at the left side of the horizontal scroll bar, expand the drop-down menu, then click <u>O</u>utline. Figure 5.17 shows the Word Report 01 document as it will appear in exercise 19 with heading formatting applied in Outline view.

Outline View

Create an outline in Word and then use the outline as a basis for preparing a PowerPoint presentation.

figure
5.17

Document in Outline View

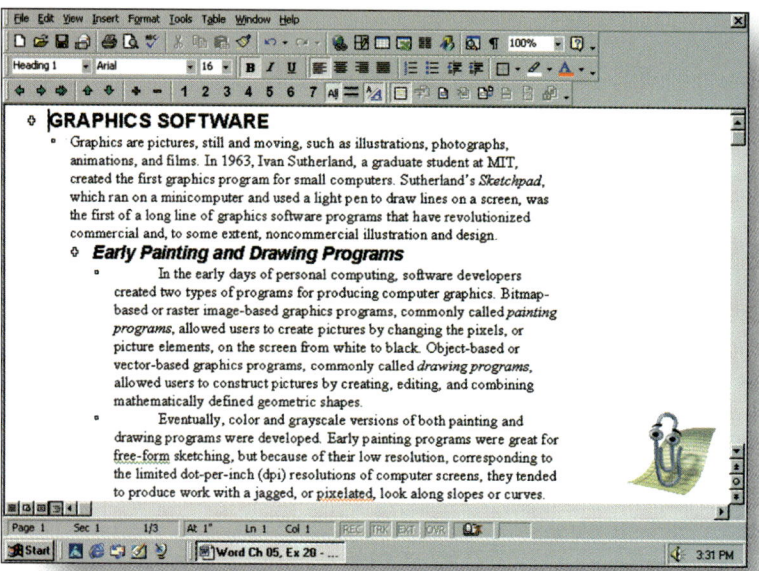

In figure 5.17, the title *GRAPHICS SOFTWARE* is identified as a first-level heading, the heading *Early Painting and Drawing Programs* is identified as a second-level heading, and the paragraphs following are normal text.

When a document contains headings and text that have been formatted in the Outline view, each paragraph is identified as a particular heading level or as normal text. Paragraphs are identified by *outline selection symbols* that appear in the selection bar at the left side of the screen. Figure 5.18 describes the three outline selection symbols and what they indicate.

Outline an existing document or create a new document in Outline view.

figure

5.18

Outline Selection Symbols

✚   Indicates that subtext appears below the heading. Subtext may be body text or other subordinate headings.

▭   Indicates that no subtext appears below the heading.

☐   Indicates the paragraph is normal text.

The outline selection symbols can be used to select text in the document. To do this, position the arrow pointer on the outline selection symbol next to text you want to select until it turns into a four-headed arrow, and then click the left mouse button.

Assigning Headings

When a document is displayed in Outline view, the Outlining toolbar displays below the Formatting toolbar. The buttons on the Outlining toolbar are shown in figure 5.19.

figure

5.19

Outlining Toolbar Buttons

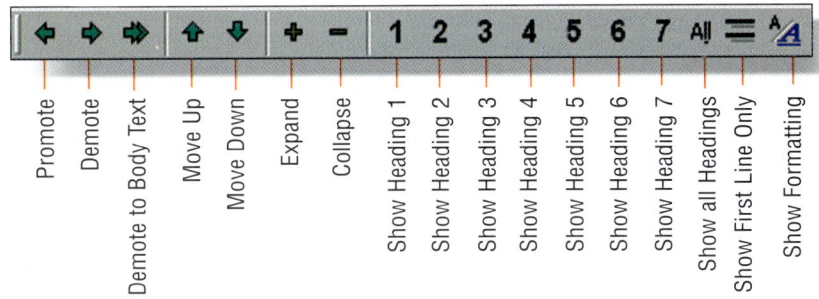

To change a paragraph that is identified as normal text to a first-level heading, position the insertion point on any character in the text (or select the text), and then click the Promote button on the Outlining toolbar. This applies the Heading 1 style to the paragraph. The Heading 1 style is a style that has been predefined by Word. This style displays in the Style button on the Formatting toolbar. (First button at left side.) The Heading 1 style sets the text in 16-point Arial bold.

To change a paragraph to a second-level heading, position the insertion point anywhere within the text, and then click the Demote button. This applies the Heading 2 style to the text. The Heading 2 style sets text in 14-point Arial bold italic and indents the text one-half inch.

Promote

Demote

exercise 19

Formatting a Document with Buttons on the Outlining Toolbar

1. Open Word Report 01.
2. Save the document with Save As and name it Word C5, Ex 19.
3. Change to the Outline viewing mode by clicking the Outline View button at the left side of the horizontal scroll bar.
4. Promote and demote heading levels by completing the following steps:
   a. Position the insertion point anywhere in the title *GRAPHICS SOFTWARE* and then click the Promote button on the Outlining toolbar. (*Heading 1* will display in the Style button on the Formatting toolbar.)
   b. Position the insertion point anywhere in the heading *Early Painting and Drawing Programs* and then click the Demote button on the Outlining toolbar. (*Heading 2* will display in the Style button on the Formatting toolbar.)
   c. Position the insertion point anywhere in the heading *Developments in Painting and Drawing Programs* and then click the Promote button on the Outlining toolbar. (*Heading 2* will display in the Style button on the Formatting toolbar.)
   d. Position the insertion point anywhere in the heading *Painting and Drawing Programs Today* and then click the Promote button on the Outlining toolbar. (*Heading 2* will display in the Style button on the Formatting toolbar.)
5. Save the document again with the same name (Word C5, Ex 19).
6. Print and then close Word C5, Ex 19.

Collapsing and Expanding Outline Headings

One of the major benefits of working in the Outline view is the ability to see a condensed outline of your document without all of the text in between headings or subheadings. Word lets you collapse a heading level in an outline. This causes any text or subsequent lower heading levels to disappear temporarily. When heading levels are collapsed, viewing the outline of a document is much easier. For example, when an outline is collapsed, you can see an overview of the entire document and move easily to different locations in the document. You can also move headings and their subordinate headings to new locations in the outline.

To collapse the entire outline, click the Show Heading button containing the number of heading levels desired. For example, if a document contains three heading levels, clicking the Show Heading 2 button on the Outlining toolbar will collapse the outline so only Heading 1 and Heading 2 text is displayed.

Show Heading 2

Click the Show All Headings button to deactivate the button and the document collapses displaying only heading text, not body text. Click the Show All Headings button again to activate it and the document expands to show all heading levels and body text. If you click the Show All Headings button to deactivate it, the document would display as shown in figure 5.20. (The document in figure 5.20 is the document from figure 5.17.) When a heading is collapsed, a gray horizontal line displays beneath it.

Show All Headings

Collapsed Outline

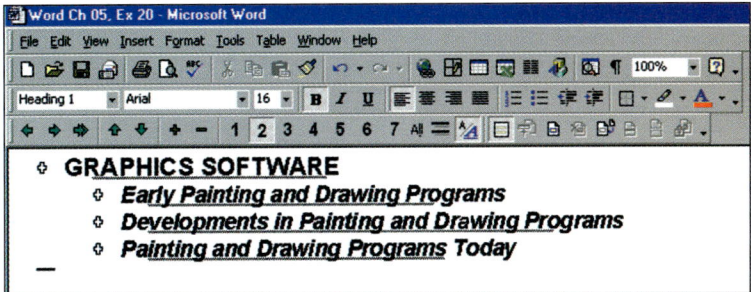

Collapsing an Outline

1. Open Word C5, Ex 19.
2. Save the document with Save As and name it Word C5, Ex 20.
3. Make the following changes to the document:
   a. Make sure the document is displayed in the Outline viewing mode.
   b. Click the Show All Headings button on the Outlining toolbar to deactivate it.
   c. With the outline collapsed, select the heading *Painting and Drawing Programs Today*, and then delete it. (This deletes the heading and all text below the heading.)
4. Save the document again with the same name (Word C5, Ex 20).
5. Print and then close Word C5, Ex 20. (This will print the collapsed outline, not the entire document.)

To collapse all of the text beneath a particular heading (including the text following any subsequent headings), position the insertion point within the heading, and then click the Collapse button on the Outlining toolbar. To make the text appear again, click the Expand button on the Outlining toolbar. For example, if you collapsed the first second-level heading shown in the document in figure 5.17, the document would display as shown in figure 5.21.

Collapse

Expand

Collapsed Second-Level Heading

5.21

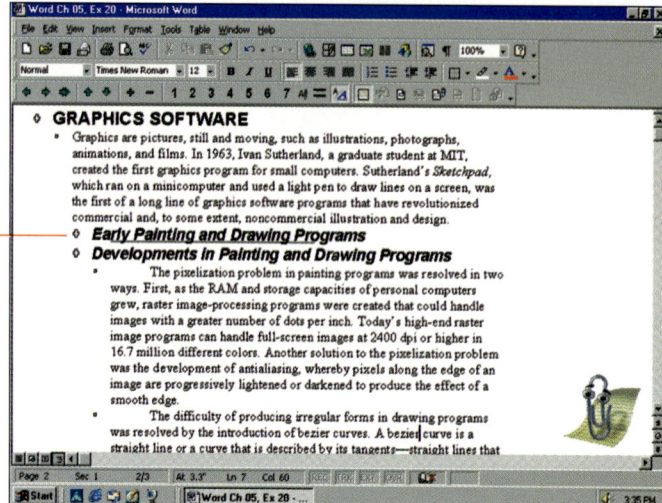

Notice how the text below this collapsed second level heading does not display.

Organizing an Outline

Collapsing and expanding headings within an outline is only part of the versatility offered by Word's outline feature. It also offers you the ability to rearrange an entire document by reorganizing an outline. Whole sections of a document can quickly be rearranged by moving the headings at the beginning of those sections. The text that is collapsed beneath the headings is moved at the same time.

For example, to move a second-level heading below other second-level headings, you would collapse the outline, select the second-level heading to be moved, and then click the Move Down button on the Outlining toolbar until the second-level heading is in the desired position.

If headings are collapsed, you only need to select the heading and move it to the desired location. Any subsequent text that is hidden is moved automatically. You can also move headings in a document by positioning the arrow pointer on the plus symbol before the desired heading until it turns into a four-headed arrow, holding down the mouse button, dragging the heading to the desired location, and then releasing the mouse button. As you drag the mouse, a gray horizontal line displays in the document with an arrow attached. Use this horizontal line to help you move the heading to the desired location.

Collapse an outline before moving text.

Move Down

exercise 21

Moving Headings in a Document

1. Open Word C5, Ex 20.
2. Save the document with Save As and name it Word C5, Ex 21.
3. Make the following changes to the document:

a. With the Outline viewing mode turned on, click the Show Heading 2 button on the Outlining toolbar.
b. Move *Painting and Drawing Programs Today* above *Developments in Painting and Drawing Programs* by completing the following steps:
   1) Position the insertion point anywhere in the heading *Painting and Drawing Programs Today.*
   2) Click once on the Move Up button on the Outlining toolbar.
c. Move the heading *Early Painting and Drawing Programs* below *Developments in Painting and Drawing Programs* by completing the following steps:
   1) Position the arrow pointer on the plus symbol immediately left of the heading *Early Painting and Drawing Programs* until it turns into a four-headed arrow.
   2) Hold down the left mouse button, drag the mouse down until the gray horizontal line with the arrow attached is positioned below *Developments in Painting and Drawing Programs,* and then release the mouse button.
   3) Deselect the text.

4. Save the document again with the same name (Word C5, Ex 21).
5. Print Word C5, Ex 21. (Only the title and headings will print.)
6. Click the Show All Headings button on the Outlining toolbar to display the document text and then close the document.

Step 3b2

Step 3c2

chapter summary

➤ Text that appears at the top of every page is called a header; text that appears at the bottom of every page is called a footer.

➤ Click <u>V</u>iew and then <u>H</u>eader and Footer to display the Header and Footer toolbar and a header pane.

➤ Click the Switch Between Header and Footer button on the Header and Footer toolbar to display a footer pane.

➤ A header or footer does not display in the Normal view but will display dimmed in the Print Layout view. To see how the header or footer will print, display Print Preview.

➤ Header or footer text does not take on any character formatting applied to the document. If you want header or footer text character formatting to be the same as the document text, format that text in the header or footer pane in the normal manner.

➤ A header or footer contains three tab alignment settings: left, center, and right. Press the Tab key to move the insertion point to the center alignment setting and then press the Tab key again to move the insertion point to the right alignment setting.

➤ Edit a header or footer in Print Layout view or in the header or footer pane.

➤ Delete a header or footer at the header or footer pane.

➤ More than one header or footer can be created in a document.

- Insert page numbering in a document with options from the Page Numbers dialog box or in a header or footer.
- Modify page numbers at the Page Number Format dialog box.
- Use the find feature to search for specific characters or formatting. Use the find and replace feature to search for specific characters or formatting and replace with other characters or formatting.
- Click Edit and then Find to display the Find and Replace dialog box with the Find tab selected.
- Click Edit and then Replace to display the Find and Replace dialog box with the Replace tab selected.
- At the Find and Replace dialog box, click the Find Next button to find the next occurrence of the characters and/or formatting. Click the Replace button to replace the characters or formatting and find the next occurrence; or, click the Replace All button to replace all occurrences of the characters or formatting.
- Click the More button at the Find and Replace dialog box to display additional options for completing a search.
- Navigate through a document with options at the Find and Replace dialog box with the Go To tab selected.
- Create a variety of documents such as letters, memos, and awards, using Word templates and Wizards.
- Wizards are templates that do most of the work for you.
- Templates and Wizards provided by Word are available at the New dialog box.
- A style is a set of formatting instructions saved with a specific name in order to use the formatting over and over.
- All styles provided by Word can be displayed in the Style dialog box with *All styles* selected.
- Apply a style using the Style button on the Formatting toolbar or at the Style dialog box.
- Use the Outline view to format headings in a document and assign particular heading levels to text.
- Headings and text formatted in the Outline view are identified by outline selection symbols that display at the left side of the screen. These symbols can be used to select text in the document.
- The Outlining toolbar displays below the Formatting toolbar in Outline view. Use buttons on this toolbar to assign various level headings to text.

commands review

	Mouse/Keyboard
Create a header or footer	View, Header and Footer
Print Preview	File, Print Preview; or click Print Preview button on Standard toolbar
Find and Replace dialog box with Find tab selected	Edit, Find
Find and Replace dialog box with Replace tab selected	Edit, Replace

Find and Replace dialog box with <u>G</u>o To tab selected	<u>E</u>dit, <u>G</u>o To
Page Numbers dialog box	<u>I</u>nsert, Page N<u>u</u>mbers
New dialog box	<u>F</u>ile, <u>N</u>ew
Style dialog box	F<u>o</u>rmat, <u>S</u>tyle
Style Gallery dialog box	F<u>o</u>rmat, <u>T</u>heme, Style <u>G</u>allery
Outline view	<u>V</u>iew, <u>O</u>utline; or click Outline View button at left side of horizontal scroll bar

thinking offline

Completion: In the space provided at the right margin, indicate the correct term, command, or number.

1. Clicking <u>V</u>iew and then <u>H</u>eader and Footer automatically positions the insertion point here.

2. To create a footer, click this button on the Header and Footer toolbar.

3. Create footers on odd and/or even pages at this dialog box.

4. Page numbers can be inserted in a header or footer or with options at this dialog box.

5. Change the beginning page number with this option at the Page Number Format dialog box.

6. If you want to replace every occurrence of what you are searching for in a document, click this button at the Find and Replace dialog box.

7. Click this button at the Find and Replace dialog box if you do not want to replace an occurrence with the replace text.

8. Click this option at the Find and Replace dialog box if you are searching for a word and all its forms.

9. Choose a template at this dialog box.

10. Display the styles available in a document by clicking the down-pointing triangle at the right side of this button on the Formatting toolbar.

11. Use this view to format headings in a document and assign particular heading levels to text.

12. Click this button on the Outlining toolbar to display only first level headings.

13. Click this button on the Outlining toolbar to move the selected heading up one level.

14. In the space provided below, list the steps you would complete to create the footer *Computers and Technology* that prints bolded and centered on each page of the document.

_____

_____

_____

_____

15. In the space provided below, list the steps you would complete to insert page numbering in a document that prints at the bottom right side on each page and begins with page number 5.

_____

_____

_____

_____

working hands-on

Assessment 1

1. Open Word Report 03.
2. Save the document with Save As and name it Word C5, SA 01.
3. Make the following changes to the document:
   a. Change the top margin to 1.5 inches.
   b. Select the entire document and then change the font to 12-point Bookman Old Style (or a similar serif typeface).
   c. Select the title *NETWORK TOPOLOGIES* and then change the font to 18-point Tahoma bold.
   d. Select the heading *Linear Bus Networks* and then change the font to 14-point Tahoma bold.
   e. Use the Format Painter to change the font to 14-point Tahoma bold for the remaining two headings *Star Networks* and *Ring Networks*.
   f. Create the footer *Network Topologies* that is set in 12-point Tahoma bold and prints at the center of the footer pane.
4. Check page breaks in the document and, if necessary, adjust the page breaks.
5. Save the document again with the same name (Word C5, SA 01).
6. Print and then close Word C5, SA 01.

Assessment 2

1. Open Word C5, SA 01.
2. Save the document with Save As and name it Word C5, SA 02.

3. Make the following changes to the document:
   a. Delete the footer in the document.
   b. Create the footer *Page #* (where the correct page number is inserted at the #) that is set in 12-point Tahoma bold and prints at the right margin on all odd pages.
   c. Create the footer *Types of Networks* that is set in 12-point Tahoma bold and prints at the left margin on all even pages.
4. Save the document again with the same name (Word C5, SA 02).
5. Print and then close Word C5, SA 02.

Assessment 3

1. Open Word Report 04.
2. Save the document with Save As and name it Word C5, SA 03.
3. Make the following changes to the document:
   a. Select the entire document and then change the font to 12-point Century Schoolbook (or a similar serif typeface).
   b. Select the title *CHAPTER 1: COMPUTER INPUT DEVICES* and then change the font to 14-point Arial bold.
   c. Change the font to 14-point Arial bold for the following title and headings:
      Keyboard
      Mouse
      Trackball
      Touch Pad and Touch Screen
      CHAPTER 2: COMPUTER OUTPUT DEVICES
      Monitor
      Printer
   d. Insert a section break that begins a new page at the beginning of the line containing the title *CHAPTER 2: COMPUTER OUTPUT DEVICES.* (Be sure to insert a section break and not a page break.)
   e. Create the footer *Chapter 1: Computer Input Devices* that is set in 12-point Arial bold, is centered, and prints in the first section.
   f. Create the footer *Chapter 2: Computer Output Devices* that is set in 12-point Arial bold, is centered, and prints in the second section.
4. Check page breaks in the document and, if necessary, adjust the page breaks.
5. Save the document again with the same name (Word C5, SA 03).
6. Print and then close Word C5, SA 03.

Assessment 4

1. Open Word Contract.
2. Save the document with Save As and name it Word C5, SA 04.
3. Make the following changes to the document:
   a. Find all occurrences of REINBERG MANUFACTURING and replace with QUALITY SYSTEMS.
   b. Find all occurrences of RM and replace with QS.
   c. Find all occurrences of LABOR WORKERS' UNION and replace with INDUSTRIAL WORKERS' UNION.
   d. Find all occurrences of LWU and replace with IWU.
4. Save the document again with the same name (Word C5, SA 04).
5. Print and then close Word C5, SA 04.

Assessment 5

1. Use the Contemporary Fax template (displays when the Letter & Faxes tab is selected at the New dialog box) to create a fax cover sheet. Select the text in brackets, delete it, and then key the information as shown below:
    Click anywhere in the text *[Click here and type address]* located in the upper right corner of the fax page and then key the following:
    4509 Jackson Avenue
    St. Paul, MN 55230
    Key the following text in the specified location:
To:	**Rene LeJeune**
Fax:	**(412) 555-8122**
From:	**Claire Monroe**
Re:	**Order Number 3420**
Pages:	**1**
CC:	(leave this blank)

    Select the text in the body of the fax, delete it, and then key the following:

    This fax is to confirm your order number 3420. All items on that order are in stock and will be shipped within three business days. This order will be shipped by two-day express delivery. If you need overnight delivery, please call (304) 555-9855.

2. Save the completed fax and name it Word C5, SA 05.
3. Print and then close Word C5, SA 05.

Assessment 6

1. Open Word Report 03.
2. Save the document with Save As and name it Word Ch 05, SA 06.
3. Make the following changes to the document:
    a. Apply the following heading styles:

NETWORK TOPOLOGIES	=	Heading 1
Linear Bus Networks	=	Heading 2
Star Networks	=	Heading 2
Ring Networks	=	Heading 2

    b. Format the document at the Style Gallery with the *Professional Report* template.
4. Save the document again with the same name (Word C5, SA 06).
5. Print and then close Word C5, SA 06.

Assessment 7

1. Open Word Report 04.
2. Save the document with Save As and name it Word C5, SA 07.
3. Make the following changes to the document:
    a. Change to the Outline view and then promote or demote the following titles and headings:

CHAPTER 1: COMPUTER INPUT DEVICES	=	Heading 1
Keyboard	=	Heading 2
Mouse	=	Heading 2
Trackball	=	Heading 2

Touch Pad and Touch Screen	=	Heading 2
CHAPTER 2: COMPUTER OUTPUT DEVICES	=	Heading 1
Monitor	=	Heading 2
Printer	=	Heading 2

   b. Collapse the outline so only the two heading levels display.
   c. Move the chapter 1 title and the headings below it after the chapter 2 title and the headings below it.
   d. Renumber the chapters (chapter 1 becomes 2 and chapter 2 becomes 1).
   e. Move the heading *Trackball* below the heading *Touch Pad and Touch Screen*.
4. Save the document again with the same name (Word C5, SA 07).
5. Print and then close Word C5, SA 07.

Assessment 8

1. In this chapter, you learned to find specific text and replace with other text. You can also find formatting and replace with other formatting. Use Word's Help feature to learn how to find formatting and replace with other formatting and then complete the following steps:
   a. At a clear document screen, write the steps you would follow to find 14-point Times New Roman bold formatting and replace with 16-point Arial bold formatting.
   b. Save the completed document and name it Word C5 Steps.
   c. Print and then close Word C5 Steps.
2. Search and replace character formatting by completing the following steps:
   a. Open Word C5, SA 01.
   b. Save the document with Save As and name it Word C5, SA 08.
   c. Search for 18-point Tahoma bold formatting and replace with 16-point Bookman Old Style bold. (If Bookman Old Style is not available, choose a similar serif typeface.)
   d. Search for 14-point Tahoma bold formatting and replace with 13-point Bookman Old Style bold (or the font you chose in steps 2c).
   e. Save the document again with the same name (Word C5, SA 08).
   f. Print and then close Word C5, SA 08.

Chapter 06C

Creating and Formatting Tables

6

PERFORMANCE OBJECTIVES

Upon successful completion of chapter 6, you will be able to:

- Create a table.
- Enter and edit text within cells in a table.
- Delete a table.
- Format a table by adding borders and shading, changing column width, aligning text within cells, inserting and deleting columns and rows, and merging and splitting cells.
- Apply formatting to a table with one of Word's predesigned AutoFormats.
- Create and format a table using buttons on the Tables and Borders toolbar.
- Perform calculations on values in a table.

Word provides a variety of features that help you organize data. With Word's Tables feature, you can create data in columns and rows. This data can consist of text, values, and formulas. The Tables feature can create columns of data in a manner similar to a spreadsheet. Many basic spreadsheet functions, such as inserting values, totaling numbers, and inserting formulas, can be performed in a Word table.

With a Word table, a form can be created that contains boxes of information called *cells.* A cell is the intersection between a row and a column. A cell can contain text, characters, numbers, data, graphics, or formulas. Data within a cell can be formatted to display left, right, center, or fully aligned, and can include character formatting such as bold, italics, and underlining. The formatting choices available with the Tables feature are quite extensive and allow flexibility in creating a variety of tables.

Creating a Table

A table can be created with the Insert Table button on the Standard toolbar or the Table option from the Menu bar. To create a table with the Insert Table button, click the Insert Table button on the Standard toolbar. This causes a grid to

Insert Table

appear as shown in figure 6.1. Move the mouse pointer down and to the right until the correct number of rows and columns displays below the grid and then click the left mouse button. As you move the mouse pointer in the grid, note that selected columns and rows are highlighted, and the number of rows and columns displays below the grid.

6.1

Table Grid

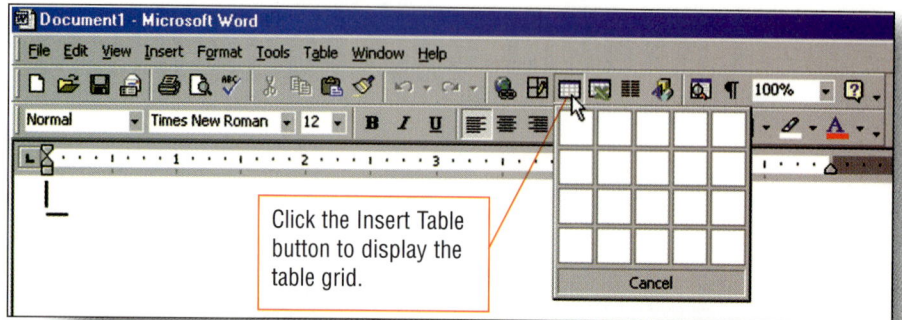

Click the Insert Table button to display the table grid.

Before creating a table, try to determine the number of columns needed since Word automatically determines column width.

A table can also be created with options at the Insert Table dialog box shown in figure 6.2. Display the Insert Table dialog box by clicking Table, pointing to Insert, and then clicking Table. At the Insert Table dialog box, key the desired number of columns in the Number of columns text box. Press the Tab key or click in the Number of rows text box, key the desired number of rows, and then click OK or press Enter. A table is inserted in the document at the location of the insertion point.

6.2

Insert Table Dialog Box

If you think you will be adding text above a table, press Enter at least once at a new document screen, and then create the table.

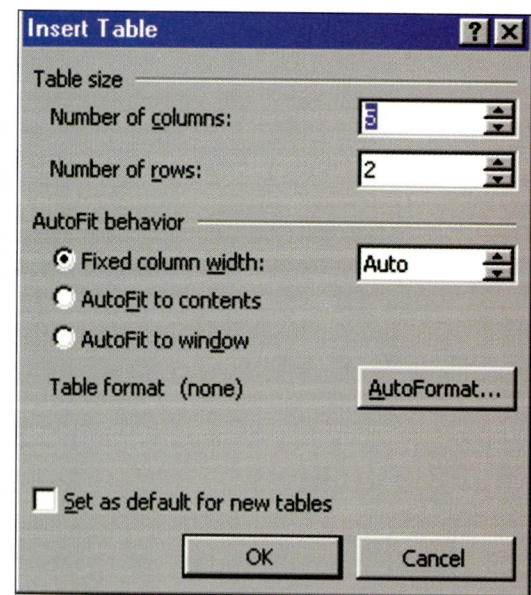

Figure 6.3 shows an example of a table with four columns and three rows. Various parts of the table are identified in figure 6.3 such as the gridlines, move table column marker, end-of-cell marker, and end-of-row marker. In a table, nonprinting characters identify the end of a cell and the end of a row. To view these characters, click the Show/Hide ¶ button on the Standard toolbar. The end-of-cell marker displays inside each cell and the end-of-row marker displays at the end of a row of cells. These markers are identified in figure 6.3.

figure

6.3

Table

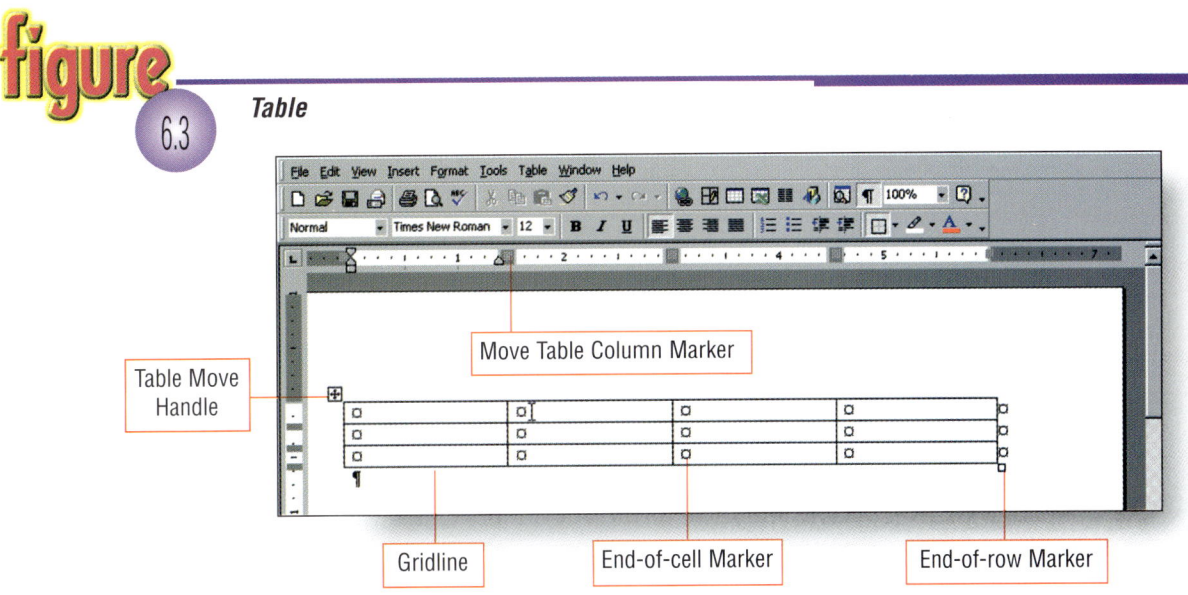

When a table is created, the insertion point is located in the cell in the upper left corner of the table. Cells in a table contain a cell designation. Columns in a table are lettered from left to right, beginning with A. Rows in a table are numbered from top to bottom beginning with 1. The cell in the upper left corner of the table is cell A1. The cell to the right of A1 is B1, the cell to the right of B1 is C1, and so on. The cells below A1 are A2, A3, A4, and so on. Some cell designations are shown in figure 6.4.

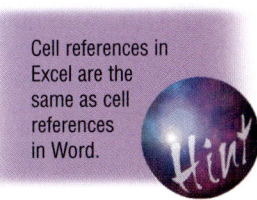

Cell references in Excel are the same as cell references in Word.

figure

6.4

Cell Designations

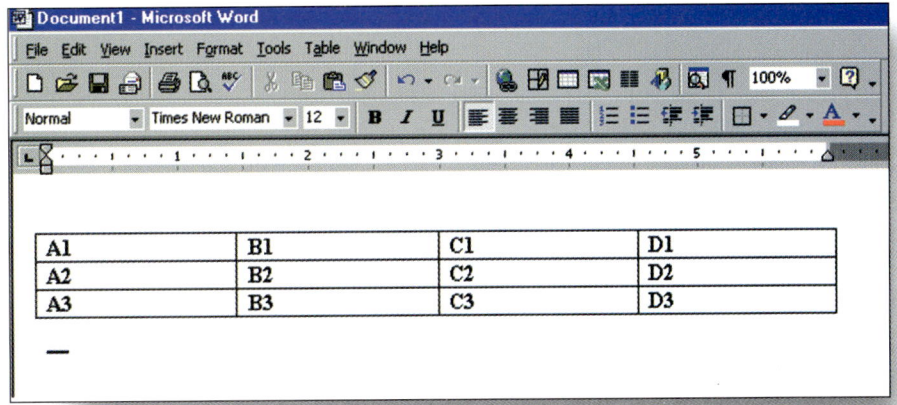

If the Ruler is displayed at the top of the document screen, move table column markers display on the Ruler. These markers represent the end of a column and are useful in changing the width of columns. Figure 6.3 identifies a move table column marker.

Entering Text in Cells

With the insertion point positioned in a cell, key or edit text. Move the insertion point to other cells with the mouse by clicking in the desired cell. If you are using the keyboard, press the Tab key to move the insertion point to the next cell or press Shift + Tab to move the insertion point to the previous cell.

If the text you key does not fit on one line, it wraps to the next line within the same cell. Or, if you press Enter within a cell, the insertion point is moved to the next line within the same cell. The cell vertically lengthens to accommodate the text, and all cells in that row also lengthen. Pressing the Tab key in a table causes the insertion point to move to the next cell in the table. If you want to move the insertion point to a tab stop within a cell, press Ctrl + Tab.

If the insertion point is located in the last cell of the table and you press the Tab key, Word adds another row to the table. To avoid this situation, make sure you do not press the Tab key after entering text in the last cell, or, immediately click the Undo button on the Standard toolbar. You can insert a page break within a table by pressing Ctrl + Enter. The page break is inserted between rows, not within.

When all information has been entered in the cells, move the insertion point below the table and, if necessary, continue keying the document, or save the document in the normal manner.

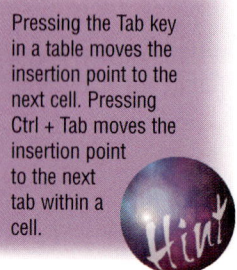

Pressing the Tab key in a table moves the insertion point to the next cell. Pressing Ctrl + Tab moves the insertion point to the next tab within a cell.

Moving the Insertion Point within a Table

To move the insertion point to a different cell within the table using the mouse, click in the desired cell. To move the insertion point to different cells within the table using the keyboard, refer to the information shown in figure 6.5.

figure
6.5

Insertion Point Movement within a Table Using the Keyboard

To move the insertion point	Press these keys
to next cell	Tab
to preceding cell	Shift + Tab
forward one character	right arrow key
backward one character	left arrow key
to previous row	up arrow key
to next row	down arrow key
to first cell in the row	Alt + Home (or Alt + 7 on numeric keypad*)
to last cell in the row	Alt + End (or Alt + 1 on numeric keypad*)
to top cell in the column	Alt + Page Up (or Alt + 9 on numeric keypad*)
to bottom cell in the column	Alt + Page Down (or Alt + 3 on numeric keypad*)
	Num Lock must be off.

(Before completing computer exercises, delete the Chapter 05C *folder on your disk. Next, copy the* Chapter 06C *folder from the CD that accompanies this textbook to your disk and make* Chapter 06C *the active folder.)*

Creating a Table with the Insert Table Button

1. At a clear editing window, create the table shown in figure 6.6 by completing the following steps:

   a. Click the Insert Table button on the Standard toolbar.

   b. Move the mouse pointer down and to the right until the number below the grid displays as 5 x 3 and then click the mouse button.

   c. Key the text in the cells as indicated in figure 6.6. Press the Tab key to move to the next cell or press Shift + Tab to move to the preceding cell. (If you accidentally press the Enter key within a cell, immediately press the Backspace key. Do not press Tab after keying the text in the last cell. If you do, another row is inserted in the table. If this happens, immediately click the Undo button on the Standard toolbar.)

2. Save the table and name it Word C6, Ex 01.

3. Print and then close Word C6, Ex 01.

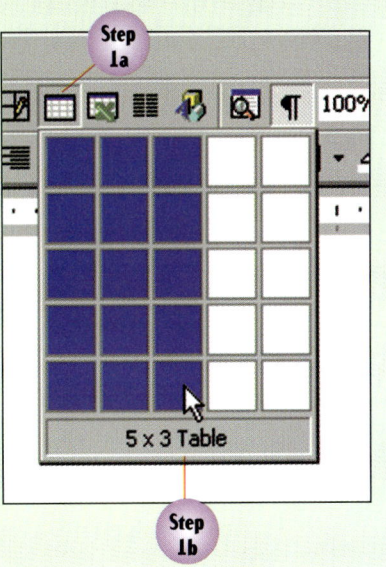

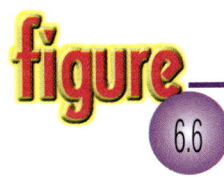

Exercise 1

Maggie Rivera	First Trust Bank	(203) 555-3440
Regina Stahl	United Fidelity	(301) 555-1221
Stanley White Cloud	Key One Savings	(360) 555-8966
Les Cromwell	Madison Trust	(602) 555-4900
Cecilia Nordyke	American Financial Trust	(509) 555-3995

Creating a Table at the Insert Table Dialog Box

1. At a clear document screen, create the table shown in figure 6.7 by completing the following steps:
   a. Change the paragraph alignment to center and turn on bold.
   b. Key **OPTIONAL PLAN PREMIUM RATES**.
   c. Press Enter three times.
   d. Turn off bold and change the paragraph alignment to left.
   e. Create the table by completing the following steps:
      1) Click Table, point to Insert, and then click Table.
      2) At the Insert Table dialog box, key **3** in the Number of columns text box. (The insertion point is automatically positioned in this text box.)
      3) Press the Tab key (this moves the insertion point to the Number of rows option) and then key **8**.
      4) Click OK or press Enter.
   f. Key the text in the cells as indicated in figure 6.7. Press the Tab key to move to the next cell or press Shift + Tab to move to the preceding cell. To indent the text in cells B2 through B8 and cells C2 through C8, press Ctrl + Tab to move the insertion to a tab within cells, and then key the text.
2. Save the table and name it Word C6, Ex 02.
3. Print and then close Word C6, Ex 02.

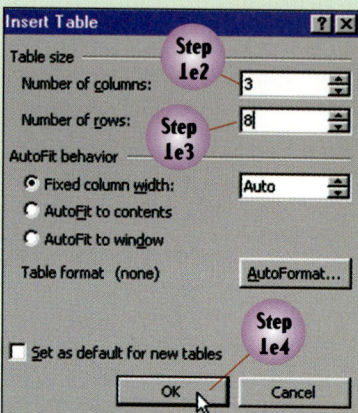

Exercise 2

6.7

Waiting Period	Plan 2002 Employees	Basic Plan Employees
60 days	0.79%	0.67%
90 days	0.59%	0.49%
120 days	0.35%	0.30%
180 days	0.26%	0.23%
240 days	0.25%	0.22%
300 days	0.23%	0.21%
360 days	0.22%	0.20%

OPTIONAL PLAN PREMIUM RATES

Selecting Cells

A table can be formatted in special ways. For example, the alignment of text in cells or rows can be changed or character formatting can be added. To identify the cells that are to be affected by the formatting, the specific cells need to be selected.

Selecting in a Table with the Mouse

The mouse pointer can be used to select a cell, row, column, or an entire table. Figure 6.8 describes methods for selecting in a table with the mouse. The left edge of each cell, between the left column border and the end-of-cell marker or first character in the cell, is called the *cell selection bar*. When the mouse pointer is positioned in the cell selection bar, it turns into an arrow pointing up and to the right (instead of the left). Each row in a table contains a *row selection bar*, which is the space just to the left of the left edge of the table. When the mouse pointer is positioned in the row selection bar, the mouse pointer turns into an arrow pointing up and to the right.

6.8   *Selecting in a Table with the Mouse*

To select this	Do this
a cell	Position the mouse pointer in the cell selection bar at the left edge of the cell until it turns into an arrow pointing up and to the right and then click the left mouse button.
a row	Position the mouse pointer in the row selection bar at the left edge of the table until it turns into an arrow pointing up and to the right and then click the left mouse button.
a column	Position the mouse pointer on the uppermost horizontal gridline of the table in the appropriate column until it turns into a short, downward-pointing arrow and then click the left mouse button.
adjacent cells	Position the mouse pointer in the first cell to be selected, hold down the left mouse button, drag the mouse pointer to the last cell to be selected, and then release the mouse button.
all cells in a table	Click the table move handle; or position the mouse pointer in any cell in the table, hold down the Alt key, and then double-click the left mouse button. You can also position the mouse pointer in the row selection bar in the first row at the left edge of the table until it turns into an arrow pointing up and to the right, hold down the left mouse button, drag down to select all rows in the table, and then release the left mouse button.
text within a cell	Position the mouse pointer at the beginning of the text and then hold down the left mouse button as you drag the mouse across the text. (When a cell is selected, the entire cell is changed to black. When text within cells is selected, only those lines containing text are selected.)

exercise 3

Selecting and Formatting Cells in a Table

1. Open Word C6, Ex 01.
2. Save the document with Save As and name it Word C6, Ex 03.
3. Select and then bold the text in the cells in the first column using the mouse by completing the following steps:
   a. Position the mouse pointer on the uppermost horizontal gridline of the first column in the table until it turns into a short, downward-pointing arrow.
   b. Click the left mouse button.
   c. Click the Bold button on the Standard toolbar.
   d. Deselect the column.
4. Select and then italicize the text in the cells in the third column by completing steps similar to those in step 3.
5. Save the document again with the same name (Word C6, Ex 03).
6. Print and then close Word C6, Ex 03.

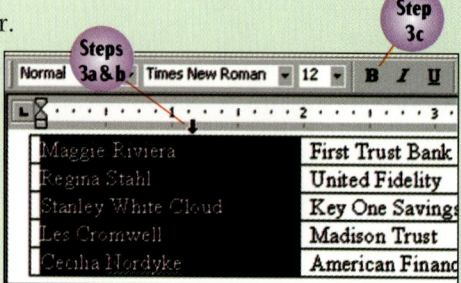

Selecting in a Table with the Keyboard

The keyboard can be used to select specific cells within a table. Figure 6.9 displays the commands for selecting specific amounts of a table.

6.9 *Selecting in a Table with the Keyboard*

To select	Press
the next cell's contents	Tab
the preceding cell's contents	Shift + Tab
the entire table	Alt + 5 (on numeric keypad with Num Lock off)
adjacent cells	Hold Shift key, then press an arrow key repeatedly
a column	Position insertion point in top cell of column, hold down the Shift key, then press down arrow key until column is selected

If you want to select only text within cells, rather than the entire cell, press F8 to turn on the Extend mode, and then move the insertion point with an arrow key. When a cell is selected, the entire cell is changed to black. When text within a cell is selected, only those lines containing text are selected.

Selecting Cells with the Table Drop-Down Menu

A row or column of cells or all cells in a table can be selected with options from the Table drop-down menu. For example, to select a row of cells in a table,

position the insertion point in any cell in the row, click Table, point to Select, and then click Row.

To select cells in a column, position the insertion point in any cell in the column, click Table, point to Select, and then click Column. To select all cells in the table, position the insertion point in any cell in the table, click Table, point to Select, and then click Table.

Selecting and Formatting Cells Using the Table Drop-Down Menu

1. Open Word C6, Ex 02.
2. Save the document with Save As and name it Word C6, Ex 04.
3. Select and then bold the text in the cells in the first column using the keyboard to complete the following steps:
   a. Position the insertion point in the first cell of the first column (cell A1).
   b. Hold down the Shift key and then press the down arrow key seven times. (This should select all cells in the first column.)
   c. Press Ctrl + B.
4. Select and then bold the text in the cells in the second column using the Table drop-down menu by completing the following steps:
   a. Position the insertion point in any cell in the second column.
   b. Click Table, point to Select, and then click Column.
   c. Click the Bold button on the Standard toolbar.
5. Select and then italicize the text in the cells in the third column by completing steps similar to those in steps 3 or 4.
6. Save the document again with the same name (Word C6, Ex 04).
7. Print and then close Word C6, Ex 04.

Deleting a Table

All text in cells within a table can be deleted, leaving the table gridlines, or all text and the gridlines can be deleted. To delete the text, leaving the gridlines, select the table, and then press the Delete key. To delete the text in cells and the gridlines, click Table, point to Delete, and then click Table.

Copying and Deleting a Table

1. Open Word C6, Ex 02.
2. Save the document with Save As and name it Word C6, Ex 05.
3. Make the following changes to the document:
   a. Select and then delete the title *OPTIONAL PLAN PREMIUM RATES*.
   b. Move the insertion point below the table and then press the Enter key three times.

c. Select the table by completing the following steps:
      1) Position the insertion point in any cell in the table.
      2) Click Table, point to Select, and then click Table.
   d. With the table selected, click the Copy button on the Standard toolbar.
   e. Move the insertion point to the end of the document and then click the Paste button on the Standard toolbar. (This inserts a copy of the table at the end of the document.)
   f. Select and then delete the first table in the document by completing the following steps:

Step 3f3

      1) Position the insertion point in any cell in the table.
      2) Change to the Print Layout view.
      3) Click the table move handle located in the upper left corner of the table.
      4) Click Table, point to Delete, and then click Table.
   g. Delete any extra blank lines at the beginning of the document.
4. Save the document again with the same name (Word C6, Ex 05).
5. Print and then close Word C6, Ex 05.

Formatting a Table

A table that has been created with Word's Tables feature can be formatted in a variety of ways. For example, borders and shading can be added to cells; rows and columns can be inserted or deleted; cells can be split or merged; and the alignment of the table can be changed.

If you make a mistake while formatting a table, immediately click the Undo button on the Standard toolbar.

Adding Borders

The gridlines creating a table can be customized with border options. Borders can be added to a selected cell(s) or an entire table with options at the Borders and Shading dialog box shown in figure 6.10. To display this dialog box, click Format and then Borders and Shading.

figure

6.10

Borders and Shading Dialog Box with Borders Tab Selected

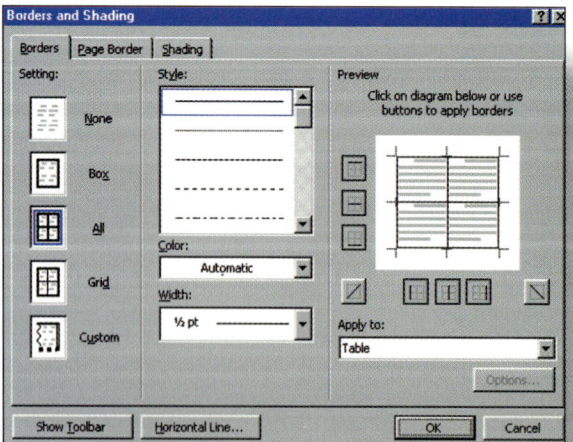

If you want a border option to apply to a specific cell, select the cell first and then display the Borders and Shading dialog box. The Borders and Shading Apply to option will display with *Cell* in the text box. If the insertion point is positioned in a table (with no cell selected) or if the entire table is selected, changes made at the Borders and Shading dialog box will affect the entire table and the Apply to option will display with *Table*. Figure 6.11 describes the options available at the Borders and Shading dialog box.

6.11 *Options at the Borders and Shading Dialog Box with the Borders Tab Selected*

Choose this option	To do this
None	Remove all borders from selected cell(s) or table
Box	Insert a box border around the selected cell(s) or table
All	Insert a box border around and between selected cell(s) or table and apply preset shadow formatting to border
Grid	Insert a box border around selected cell(s) or table and apply preset 3-D border formatting, making the border look like a "window"
Custom	Create a custom border using options in the Preview diagram
Style	Choose a border style
Color	Choose a border color
Width	Specify the width of the border
Preview diagram	Click the sides of the Preview diagram to add or remove the currently selected settings
Apply to	Specify to what the border and shading should be applied
Options	Set additional margin and position settings (only available when Apply to is set at *Paragraph* or when Page Border tab is selected)

Creating a Table with Border Lines Around and Between Cells

1. At a clear document screen, create the document shown in figure 6.12 by completing the following steps:
   a. Change the paragraph alignment to center and turn on bold.
   b. Key **DIVERSIFICATION OF ASSETS**.
   c. Press Enter, turn off bold, and then change the paragraph alignment to left.
   d. Press Enter twice and then create a table with 2 columns and 8 rows (8 x 2).
   e. Key the text in the first cell (cell A1) by completing the following steps:
      1) Click the Center button on the Formatting toolbar.

2) Click the Bold button on the Formatting toolbar.

3) Key **Asset**.

f. Press the Tab key to move the insertion point to the next cell (cell B1). Complete steps similar to those in step 1e to center and bold the column heading *Percentage*.

g. Key the text in the remaining cells as indicated in figure 6.12. Press the Tab key to move to the next cell or press Shift + Tab to move to the preceding cell. Press Ctrl + Tab before keying each entry in cells A2 through A8. Press Ctrl + Tab *twice* before keying each entry in cells B2 through B8.

h. Add blue thick/thin lines around the table by completing the following steps:

1) Position the insertion point in any cell in the table. (Make sure no text or cell is selected.)

2) Click Format and then Borders and Shading.

3) At the Borders and Shading dialog box with the Borders tab selected, click the None option. (This removes all borders from the Preview diagram.)

4) Click the Custom option.

5) Scroll to the end of the line styles in the Style list box until the third line option from the end displays and then click it.

6) Change the line color to blue by clicking the down-pointing triangle at the right side of the Color option and then clicking *Blue* at the drop-down list.

7) Apply the border to the outside of the table by completing the following steps:

   a) Click the top button at the left side of the Preview diagram. (This inserts a blue shadow border to the top of the Preview diagram.)

   b) Click the third button from the top at the left side of the Preview diagram. (This inserts a blue shadow border at the bottom of the table.)

   c) Click the second button from the left at the bottom of the Preview diagram. (This inserts a blue shadow border at the left side of the table.)

   d) Click the fourth button from the left at the bottom of the Preview diagram. (This inserts a blue shadow border at the right side of the table.)

8) Click OK to close the Borders and Shading dialog box.

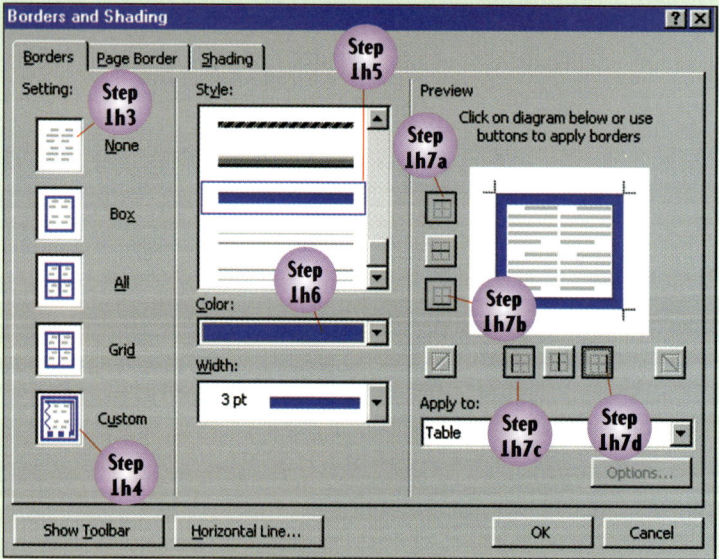

i. Add a single blue line between columns by completing the following steps:

1) Click Format and then Borders and Shading.

2) At the Borders and Shading dialog box, scroll to the beginning of the line

styles in the Style list box and then click the first line style (a single line).

3) Change the line color to blue. (To do this, click the down-pointing triangle at the right of the Color option, and then click *Blue* at the drop-down list.)

4) Click the third button from the left at the bottom of the Preview diagram. (This inserts a single blue line between columns.)

5) Click OK to close the Borders and Shading dialog box.

2. Save the document and name it Word C6, Ex 06.

3. Print and then close Word C6, Ex 06.

Exercise 6

DIVERSIFICATION OF ASSETS

Asset	Percentage
Office buildings	20%
Shopping centers	18%
Utilities	15%
Other mortgage and real estate	14%
Manufacturing	12%
Government	11%
Communications	10%

Adding Shading

Shaded cells add visual appeal to a table. Shading can be added to cells or selected cells with options at the Borders and Shading dialog box with the Shading tab selected as shown in figure 6.13. Figure 6.14 describes the options available at the Borders and Shading dialog box with the Shading tab selected.

figure
6.13

Borders and Shading Dialog Box with Shading Tab Selected

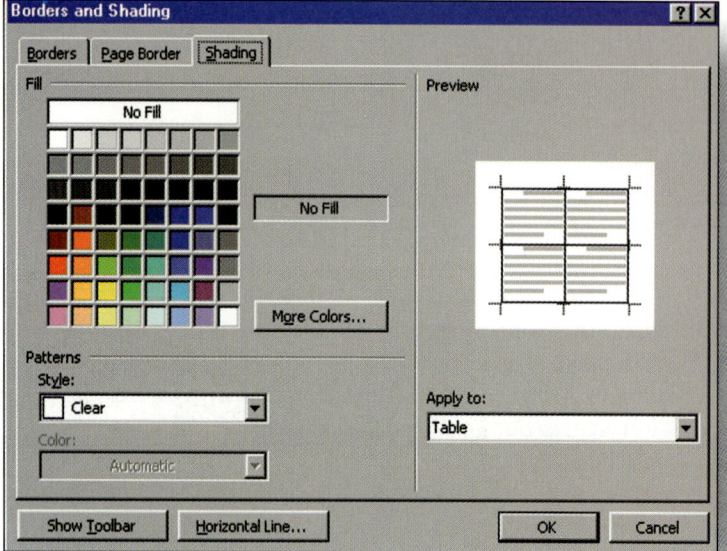

figure
6.14

Options at the Borders and Shading Dialog Box with Shading Tab Selected

Choose this option	To do this
Fill	Choose a fill color for selected cell(s) or entire table
Style	Choose a shading style to apply "over" fill color
Color	Choose a color for the lines and dots in the selected shading pattern
Preview diagram	Click the sides of the Preview diagram to add or remove the currently selected fill, style, and color
Apply to	Specify to what the border and shading should be applied

Adding a Border and Shading to a Table

1. Open Word C6, Ex 02.
2. Save the document with Save As and name it Word C6, Ex 07.
3. Add a border and shading to the table by completing the following steps:
   a. Move the insertion point to a cell within the table.
   b. Click Format and then Borders and Shading.
   c. At the Borders and Shading dialog box, make sure the Borders tab is selected.

d. Choose a double line style in the Style list box.

e. Click the Grid option located at the left side of the dialog box.

f. Click the Shading tab.

g. At the Borders and Shading dialog box with the Shading tab selected, click the light turquoise color in the Fill section. (The light turquoise color is the fifth color from the left in the bottom row.)

h. Click OK to close the dialog box.

4. Add a fill to the first row of cells by completing the following steps:

a. Select cells A1, B1, and C1.

b. Click Format and then Borders and Shading.

c. At the Borders and Shading dialog box, make sure the Shading tab is selected.

d. At the Borders and Shading dialog box with the Shading tab selected, click the down-pointing triangle at the right side of the Style option, and then click *20%* at the drop-down list.

e. Click OK to close the Borders and Shading dialog box.

f. Deselect the cells.

5. Save the document again with the same name (Word C6, Ex 07).

6. Print and then close Word C6, Ex 07.

Changing Column Width

When a table is created, the columns are the same width. The width of the columns depends on the number of columns as well as the document margins. In some tables, you may want to change the width of certain columns to accommodate more or less text. You can change the width of columns using the mouse on the Ruler, in a table, or with options from the Table Properties dialog box.

Change column width by dragging column markers on the Ruler.

Changing Column Width with the Ruler

When the insertion point is positioned in a table, move the table column markers display on the Ruler (see figure 6.3). To change the column width with move table column markers, position the mouse pointer on the move table column marker until it turns into a left- and right-pointing arrow, hold down the left mouse button, drag the marker to make the column wider or narrower, and then release the mouse button. As you drag a marker, any move table column markers to the right are also moved.

If you want to see the column measurements as you move a move table column marker, hold down the Alt key while dragging the marker. You can also view the column measurements by positioning the mouse pointer on a move table column marker, holding down the Alt key, and then holding down the left mouse button.

If you only want to move the move table column marker where the mouse pointer is positioned, hold down the Shift key, and then drag the marker on the Ruler. This does not change the overall size of the table. To change the column width of the column where the insertion point is positioned and all columns to the right, hold down the Ctrl key and the Shift key while you drag the move table column marker.

The first-line indent marker, the left indent marker, the right indent marker, and the hanging indent marker display on the Ruler for the column where the insertion point is positioned. These markers can be used to adjust the left or right column margins, indent the first line in a cell, or create a hanging indent. Changes made to the column margins affect only the column where the insertion point is positioned.

exercise 8

Creating a Table and Then Changing Column Width with the Ruler

1. At a clear document screen, create the document shown in figure 6.15 by completing the following steps:
   a. Create a table with 3 columns and 7 rows (7 x 3).
   b. Change the width of the second column using the mouse by completing the following steps:
      1) Make sure the Ruler is displayed.
      2) Position the mouse pointer on the move table column marker on the 4-inch mark on the Ruler until it turns into an arrow pointing left and right.
      3) Hold down the Shift key and then the left mouse button.
      4) Drag the marker to the 3¼-inch mark, release the Shift key, and then release the mouse button.

   c. Change the width of the third column using the mouse by completing the following steps:
      1) Position the mouse pointer on the move table column marker on the 6-inch mark on the Ruler until it turns into an arrow pointing left and right.
      2) Hold down the Shift key and then the left mouse button.
      3) Drag the marker to the 4¾-inch mark, release the Shift key and then release the mouse button.

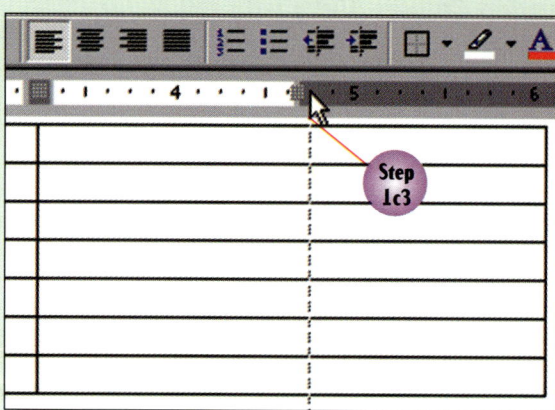

   d. Key the text in the cells, bolding and centering the text as shown.
   e. Add a thick/thin double-line border around the table by completing the following steps:
      1) With the insertion point positioned in any cell in the table, click Format and then Borders and Shading.
      2) At the Borders and Shading dialog box, make sure the Borders tab is selected.
      3) Scroll down the Style list box until the first thick/thin double-line option displays and then click the double line option.
      4) Click Grid option that displays at the left side of the dialog box.
      5) Click OK to close the dialog box.

f. Add 10% fill to cells A1, B1, and C1 by completing the following steps:
    1) Select cells A1, B1, and C1.
    2) Click Format and then Borders and Shading.
    3) At the Borders and Shading dialog box, click the Shading tab.
    4) At the Borders and Shading dialog box with the Shading tab selected, click the down-pointing triangle at the right side of the Style option, and then click *10%* at the drop-down list.
    5) Click OK to close the Borders and Shading dialog box.
    6) Deselect the cells.
2. Save the document and name it Word C6, Ex 08.
3. Print and then close Word C6, Ex 08.

figure

6.15   *Exercise 8*

Name	Employee #	Department
Kevin Gerome	222-104-6608	Human Resources
Louella Arellano	433-196-9817	Human Resources
Gale Meschke	533-119-6780	Financial Planning
Paul Tjerne	114-457-3221	Sales
William Whitlock	652-671-9910	Sales
Madeline Zevenbergen	552-900-6221	Support Services

Changing Column Width with the Mouse

You can use the gridlines to change column widths within the table. To change column widths using the gridlines, position the mouse pointer on the gridline separating columns until the insertion point turns into a left- and right-pointing arrow with a vertical double line between. Hold down the left mouse button, drag the gridline to the desired location, and then release the mouse button. Only the gridline where the insertion point is positioned is moved. If you want to change column widths for all columns to the right, hold down the Shift key while dragging the gridline. Hold down the Shift key and Ctrl key while dragging the gridline if you want to change the width of all columns to the right without changing the size of the table.

Changing Column Width at the Table Properties Dialog Box

If you know the exact measurement for columns in a table, you can change column widths at the Table Properties dialog box with the Column tab selected as shown in figure 6.16. To display this dialog box, click Table and then Table Properties. At the Table Properties dialog box, click the Column tab. To change the column width, select the current measurement in the Preferred width text box,

and then key the desired measurement. You can also click the up- or down-pointing triangle to increase or decrease the current measurement.

Table Properties Dialog Box with Column Tab Selected

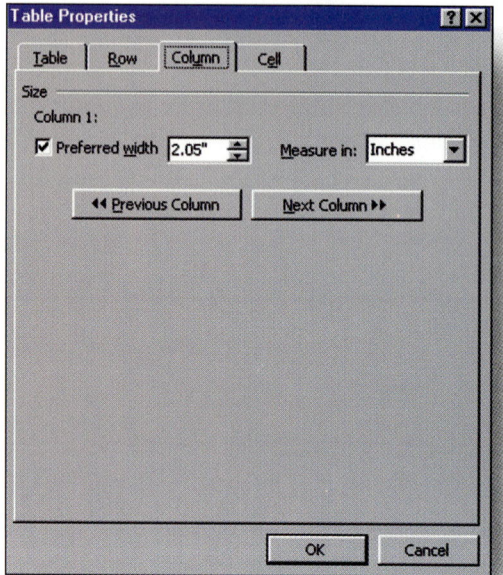

In a table containing text or other features, you can adjust the width of one column to accommodate the longest line of text in the column. To do this, position the mouse pointer on the right column gridline until it turns into a left-and right-pointing arrow with a vertical double line, and then double-click the left mouse button. To automatically size more than one column, select the columns first, and then double-click on a gridline.

Changing Column Width in a Table

1. Open Word C6, Ex 02.
2. Save the document with Save As and name it Word C6, Ex 09.
3. Select and then delete the title *OPTIONAL PLAN PREMIUM RATES*.
4. Change the width of the first column by completing the following steps:
   a. Click in the top cell in the first column.
   b. Position the mouse pointer on the gridline separating the first and second columns until it turns into a left- and right-pointing arrow with a vertical double line between.

c. Hold down the Alt key and then the left mouse button, drag the gridline to the left until the first measurement on the horizontal ruler displays as *1.25"*, then release the mouse button and then the Alt key.

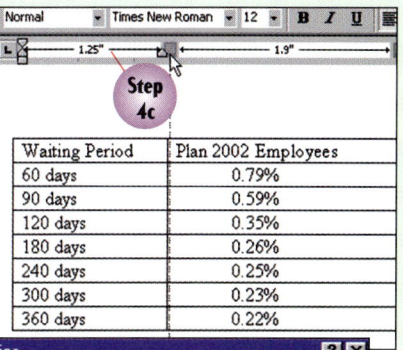

5. Change the width of the second column by completing the following steps:
   a. Click in the top cell in the middle column.
   b. Click Table and then Table Properties.
   c. At the Table Properties dialog box, click the Column tab.
   d. At the Table Properties dialog box with the Column tab selected, click the down-pointing triangle at the right side of the Preferred width text box until *1.7"* displays.
   e. Click OK or press Enter.

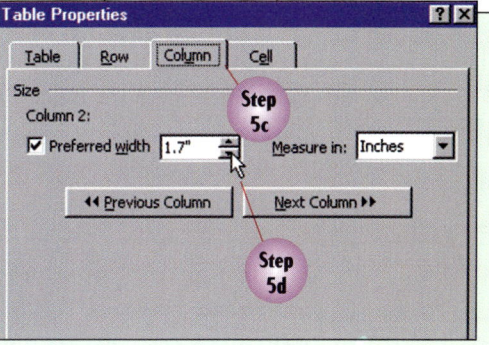

6. Change the width of the third column to 1.7" by completing steps similar to those in step 5.
7. Add the following to the table:
   a. Add a thick/thin double line border around the table.
   b. Add a single line between the columns.
   c. Add a light color fill to all cells in the table. (You determine the color.)
8. Save the document again with the same name (Word C6, Ex 09).
9. Print and then close Word C6, Ex 09. (The table will not be centered between the margins.)

Changing Column Width with AutoFit

Use the AutoFit option from the Table drop-down menu to make the column widths in a table automatically fit the contents. To do this, position the insertion point in any cell in the table, click Table, expand the drop-down menu, point to AutoFit, and then click AutoFit to Contents at the side menu.

Changing Column Widths Using AutoFit

1. Open Word C6, Ex 01.
2. Save the document with Save As and name it Word C6, Ex 10.
3. Change the width of the columns to fit the contents by completing the following steps:
   a. Make sure the insertion point is positioned in a cell within the table.
   b. Click Table, expand the drop-down menu, point to AutoFit, and then click AutoFit to Contents at the side menu.
4. Make the following changes to the table:

a. Change the border line around the table from a single line to a line of your choosing (other than single).
b. Add shading of your choosing to the table.
5. Save the document again with the same name (Word Ch 06, Ex 10).
6. Print and then close Word Ch 06, Ex 10.

Changing Row Height

Change row height in a table in much the same manner as changing column width. You can change row height with an adjust table row marker on the vertical ruler, using a gridline, or with options at the Table Properties dialog box.

To change row height using the vertical ruler, position the mouse pointer on the desired adjust table row marker, hold down the left mouse button, drag the marker to the desired position, and then release the mouse button. Hold down the Alt key while dragging an adjust table row marker and measurements display on the vertical ruler.

To change row height using a gridline, position the mouse pointer on the desired gridline until the pointer turns into an up- and down-pointing arrow with a vertical double line between. Hold down the left mouse button, drag the gridline to the desired position, and then release the mouse button. Hold down the Alt key while dragging a gridline and measurements display on the vertical ruler.

Another method for adjusting row height is to display the Table Properties dialog box with the Row tab selected as shown in figure 6.17. At this dialog box, click the Specify height option, key the desired row measurement in the Specify height text box, and then close the dialog box.

Table Properties Dialog Box with Row Tab Selected

To change row height, click the Specify height option, and then enter the desired measurement in the Specify height text box.

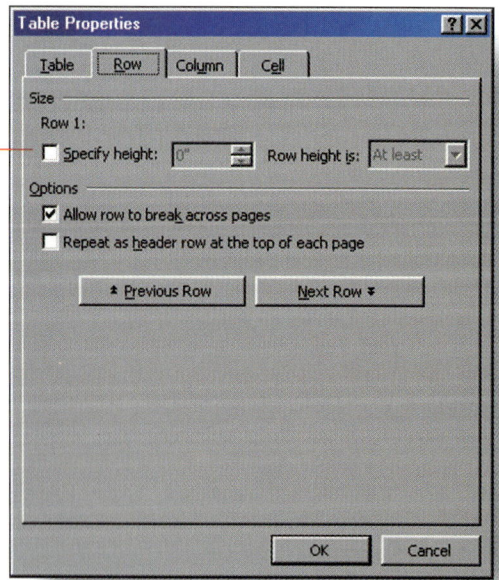

Changing Cell Alignment

By default, text in cells aligns at the left side of the cell. Like normal text, this alignment can be changed to center, right, or justified. To change the alignment of text in cells, select the cells, then click the desired alignment button on the Formatting toolbar. You can also change the alignment of text in selected cells with the Alignment option at the Paragraph dialog box with the Indents and Spacing tab selected or with a shortcut command. For example, to change the alignment of text to center in all cells in the second column of a table, you would select all cells in the second column, and then click the Center button on the Formatting toolbar.

The methods just described change the horizontal alignment of text in cells. You can also change the vertical alignment of text in cells at the Table Properties dialog box with the Cell tab selected as shown in figure 6.18. The default vertical alignment of text in a cell is Top. This can be changed to Center or Bottom.

figure
6.18

Table Properties Dialog Box with Cell Tab Selected

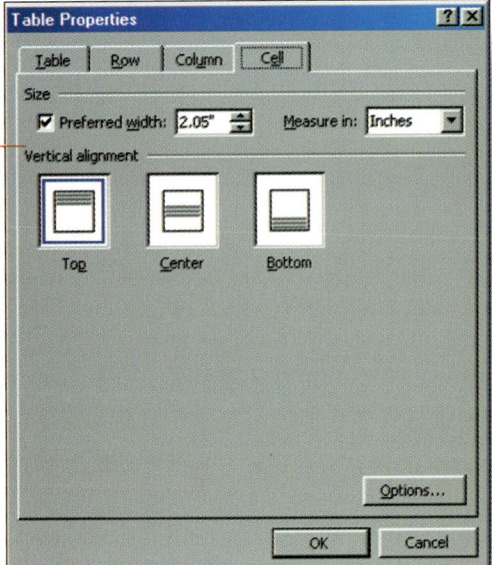

Choose a vertical alignment for text in cells with options in this section of the dialog box.

Changing Row Height and Cell Alignment

1. Open Word Table 04.
2. Save the document with Save As and name it Word C6, Ex 11.
3. Change row heights in the table by completing the following steps:
   a. Increase the height of the first row in the table by completing the following steps:
      1) Change to the Print Layout view.

2) Position the mouse pointer on the first adjust table row marker on the vertical ruler.

3) Hold down the left mouse button and hold down the Alt key.

4) Drag the adjust table row marker down until the first row measurement on the vertical ruler displays as *1"*, then release the mouse button and then the Alt key.

b. Increase the height of second row by completing the following steps:

1) Position the arrow pointer on the gridline that displays at the bottom of the second row until the arrow pointer turns into an up- and down-pointing arrow with a horizontal double line between.

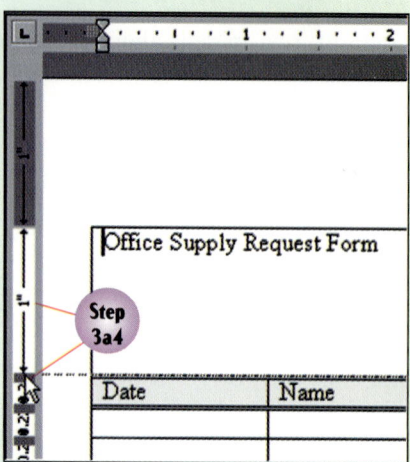

2) Hold down the left mouse button and then hold down the Alt key.

3) Drag the gridline down until the second row measurement on the vertical ruler displays as *0.58"*, then release the mouse button and then the Alt key.

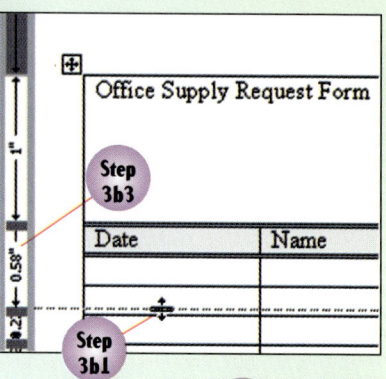

c. Increase the height of rows 3 through 11 (the remaining rows) by completing the following steps:

1) Select rows 3 through 11.

2) Click Table and then Table Properties.

3) At the Table Properties dialog box, click the Row tab.

4) At the Table Properties dialog box with the Row tab selected, click the Specify height option.

5) Click the up-pointing triangle at the right side of the Specify height option until *0.5"* displays in the Specify height text box.

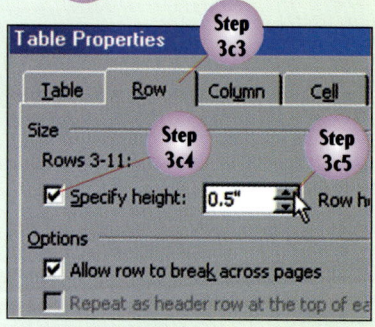

6) Click OK to close the dialog box.

4. Make the following changes to the table:

a. Change the vertical and horizontal alignment of text in rows 1 and 2 by completing the following steps:

1) Select rows 1 and 2.

2) Click Table and then Table Properties.

3) At the Table Properties dialog box, click the Cell tab.

4) At the Table Properties dialog box with the Cell tab selected, click the Center option in the Vertical alignment section of the dialog box.

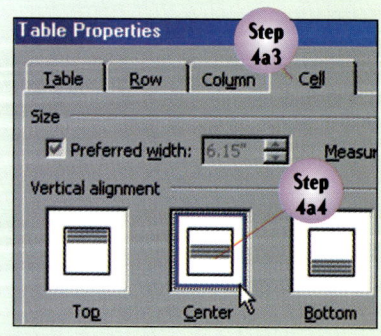

5) Click OK to close the dialog box.

6) With rows 1 and 2 still selected, click the Center button on the Formatting toolbar.

b. Select only row 1 and then change the font to 24-point Arial bold.

c. Select only row 2 and then change the font to 14-point Arial bold.

5. Save the document again with the same name (Word C6, Ex 11).

6. Print and then close Word C6, Ex 11.

Aligning the Table

By default, a table aligns at the left margin. This alignment can be changed with options at the Table Properties dialog box with the Table tab selected as shown in figure 6.19. To change the alignment, click the desired alignment option in the Alignment section of the dialog box.

Table Properties Dialog Box with Table Tab Selected

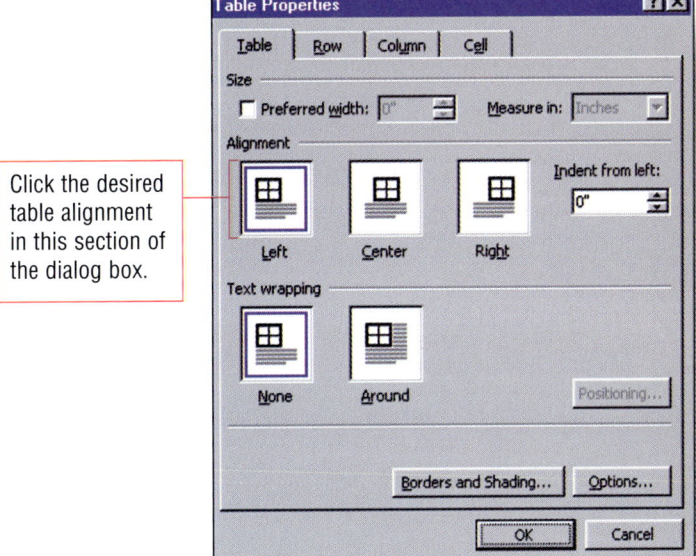

Click the desired table alignment in this section of the dialog box.

Horizontally Aligning a Table

1. Open Word C6, Ex 09.
2. Save the document with Save As and name it Word C6, Ex 12.
3. Center the table horizontally by completing the following steps:
   a. Position the insertion point in any cell in the table.
   b. Click Table and then Table Properties.
   c. At the Table Properties dialog box, click the Table tab.
   d. At the Table Properties dialog box with the Table tab selected, click the Center option in the Alignment section.
   e. Click OK or press Enter.
4. Save the document again with the same name (Word C6, Ex 12).
5. Print and then close Word C6, Ex 12.

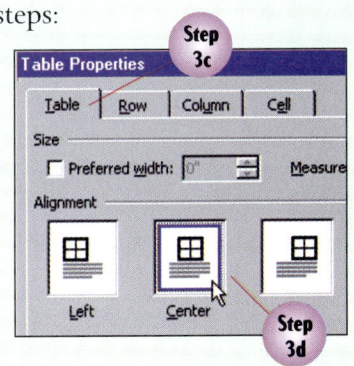

Step 3c

Step 3d

Inserting Rows

After a table has been created, rows can be added (inserted) to the table. There are several methods you can use to insert rows. You can use options from the Insert side menu to insert rows above or below the current row. To do this, position the insertion point in a row below where the row is to be inserted, click Table, point to Insert, and then click either Rows Above or Rows Below (depending on where you want the row inserted). If you want more than one row inserted, select the desired number of rows and then click Table, point to Insert, and choose Rows Above or Rows Below.

You can also insert rows by selecting a row or several rows and then clicking the Insert Rows button on the Standard toolbar. The Insert Table button becomes the Insert Rows button on the Standard toolbar when a row or several rows are selected in a table.

Another method for inserting a row or several rows is to select a row (or rows) in a table, position the mouse pointer inside the table, click the *right* mouse button, and then click Insert Rows. Also, a row can be inserted at the end of the table by positioning the insertion point in the last cell in the table and then pressing the Tab key.

Add a row to the bottom of a table by positioning the insertion point in the last cell and then pressing the Tab key.

Insert Rows

exercise 13

Inserting Rows in a Table

1. Open Word C6, Ex 08.
2. Save the document with Save As and name it Word C6, Ex 13.
3. Add two rows to the table by completing the following steps:
   a. Select the fourth and fifth rows in the table.
   b. Click Table, point to Insert, and then click Rows Above.
   c. Deselect the rows.
   d. Position the insertion point in cell A4 (below *Louella Arellano*), and then key **Steven Haarberg**.
   e. Key the following text in the specified cell:

B4	=	**627-220-9880**
C4	=	**Human Resources**
A5	=	**Howard Kline**
B5	=	**149-395-4009**
C5	=	**Financial Planning**

4. Make the following changes to the table:
   a. Use the AutoFit feature to make the columns in the table automatically fit the contents.
   b. Center the table horizontally.
5. Save the document again with the same name (Word C6, Ex 13).
6. Print and then close Word C6, Ex 13.

Inserting Columns

Columns can be inserted in a table in much the same way as rows. To insert a column, position the insertion point in a cell within the table, click Table, point to Insert, and then click Columns to the Left or Columns to the Right. If you want to insert more than one column, select the desired number of columns first.

Another method for inserting a column (or columns) is to select the column and then click the Insert Columns button on the Standard toolbar. The Insert Table button on the Standard toolbar becomes the Insert Columns button when a column or columns are selected.

A column or group of columns can also be inserted by selecting the column(s), clicking the *right* mouse button, and then clicking Insert Columns at the drop-down menu. Word inserts a column or columns to the left of the selected column or columns. If you want to add a column to the right side of the table, select all the end-of-row markers, and then click the Insert Columns button on the Standard toolbar.

Insert Columns

exercise 14

Inserting a Column in a Table

1. Open Word C6, Ex 01.
2. Save the document with Save As and name it Word C6, Ex 14.
3. Make the following changes to the table:
   a. Add a row to the table, apply bold, and change the alignment to center by completing the following steps:
      1) Position the insertion point in any cell in the first row.
      2) Click Table, point to Insert, and then click Rows Above.
      3) With the new row selected, click the Bold button on the Formatting toolbar and then click the Center button.
   b. Key the following text in the specified cell:

A1	=	**Name**
B1	=	**Company**
C1	=	**Phone Number**

   c. Add a column to the right side of the table and change the alignment to center by completing the following steps:

      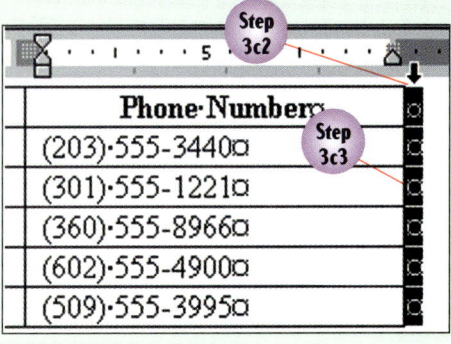

      1) Click the Show/Hide ¶ button on the Standard toolbar to turn on the display of nonprinting characters.
      2) Position the mouse pointer above the first end-of-row marker at the top of the row at the far right side of the table until it turns into a small downward-pointing arrow.
      3) Click the left mouse button. (This will select all of the end-of-row markers at the right side of the table.)
      4) Click Table, point to Insert, and then click Columns to the Right.
      5) With the column selected, click the Center button on the Formatting toolbar.

6) Deselect the column.
d. Key the following text in the specified cells:

D1	=	**Ext.**
D2	=	**2331**
D3	=	**1035**
D4	=	**2098**
D5	=	**1564**
D6	=	**2109**

e. Click the Show/Hide ¶ button to turn off the display of nonprinting characters.
f. Make the following changes to the table:
   1) Use the AutoFit feature to make the columns in the table automatically fit the contents.
   2) Center the table horizontally.
4. Save the document again with the same name (Word C6, Ex 14).
5. Print and then close Word C6, Ex 14.

Deleting Cells, Rows, or Columns

Delete a column, row, or cell with options from the Delete side menu. For example, to delete a column, position the insertion point in any cell within the column, click Table, point to Delete, and then click Columns. To delete a row, click Table, point to Delete, and then click Rows. To delete a specific cell, position the insertion point in the cell, click Table, point to Delete, and then click Cells. This displays the Delete Cells dialog box shown in figure 6.20.

6.20

Delete Cells Dialog Box

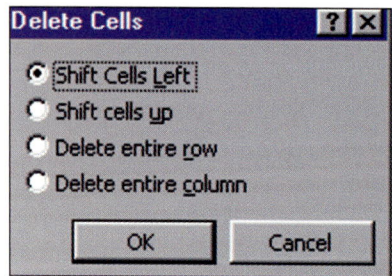

At the Delete Cells dialog box, the Shift Cells Left option is selected by default. At this option, cells will shift left after the cell (or selection of cells) is deleted. Click the Shift cells up option if you want cells moved up after the cell (or selected cells) is deleted. Click Delete entire row to delete the row where the insertion point is positioned or click Delete entire column to delete the column where the insertion point is positioned.

The Delete Cells dialog box can also be displayed by positioning the mouse pointer in the table, clicking the *right* mouse button, and then clicking Delete Cells at the drop-down menu.

exercise 15

Deleting Rows and Columns in a Table

1. Open Word C6, Ex 13.
2. Save the document with Save As and name it Word C6, Ex 15.
3. Make the following changes to the table:
   a. Delete the bottom row in the table by completing the following steps:
      1) Position the insertion point in any cell in the bottom row.
      2) Click Table, point to Delete, and then click Rows.
   b. Delete the middle column by completing the following steps:
      1) Position the insertion point in any cell in the middle column.
      2) Click Table, point to Delete, and then click Columns.
4. Save the document again with the same name (Word C6, Ex 15).
5. Print and then close Word C6, Ex 15.

Merging Cells

Cells can be merged with the Merge Cells option from the Table drop-down menu. To do this, select the cells to be merged, click Table and then click Merge Cells.

Splitting Cells

Split a cell or a row or column of cells with options at the Split Cells dialog box shown in figure 6.21. To display this dialog box, position the insertion point in the cell to be split, click Table, expand the drop-down menu, and then click Split Cells. At the Split Cells dialog box, make sure the desired number of columns displays in the Number of columns text box, and then click OK or press Enter. To split an entire column or row of cells, select the column or row first, click Table and then click Split Cells.

6.21   *Split Cells Dialog Box*

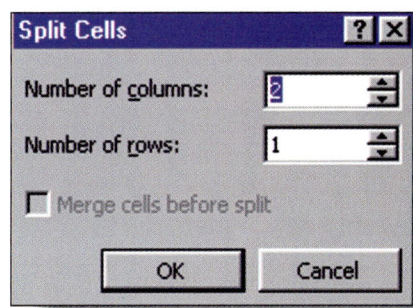

exercise 16

Creating a Table with Merged Cells

1. At a clear document screen, create the table shown in figure 6.22 by completing the following steps:
   a. Create a table with 3 columns and 10 rows (10 x 3).
   b. Change the width of the first column to 3 inches and the width of the second and third columns to 1.5 inches.
   c. Merge the cells in the first row by completing the following steps:
      1) Select the first row.
      2) Click Table and then Merge Cells.
   d. Merge the cells in the second row by completing steps similar to those in step 1c.
   e. Select the entire table and then change the font to 12-point Arial bold.
   f. Key the text in the cells as shown in figure 6.22, center aligning the text as indicated.
   g. Add a double line border around the outside of the table and a single line border on the inside of the table.
   h. Select the third row and then add 20% fill.
2. Save the document and name it Word C6, Ex 16.
3. Print and then close Word C6, Ex 16.

figure

6.22 Exercise 16

McCORMACK FUNDS CORPORATION		
Common Stocks		
Stock	Shares	Market Value

Save a document containing a table before applying an auto-format.

Formatting with AutoFormat

Formatting a table by adding borders or shading, aligning text in cells, changing fonts, and so on, can take some time. Word has provided predesigned table formats that can quickly format your table for you. Table formats are contained in the Table AutoFormat dialog box shown in figure 6.23. To display this dialog box, position the insertion point in any cell in a table, click T<u>a</u>ble and then Table Auto<u>F</u>ormat.

figure

6.23

Table AutoFormat Dialog Box

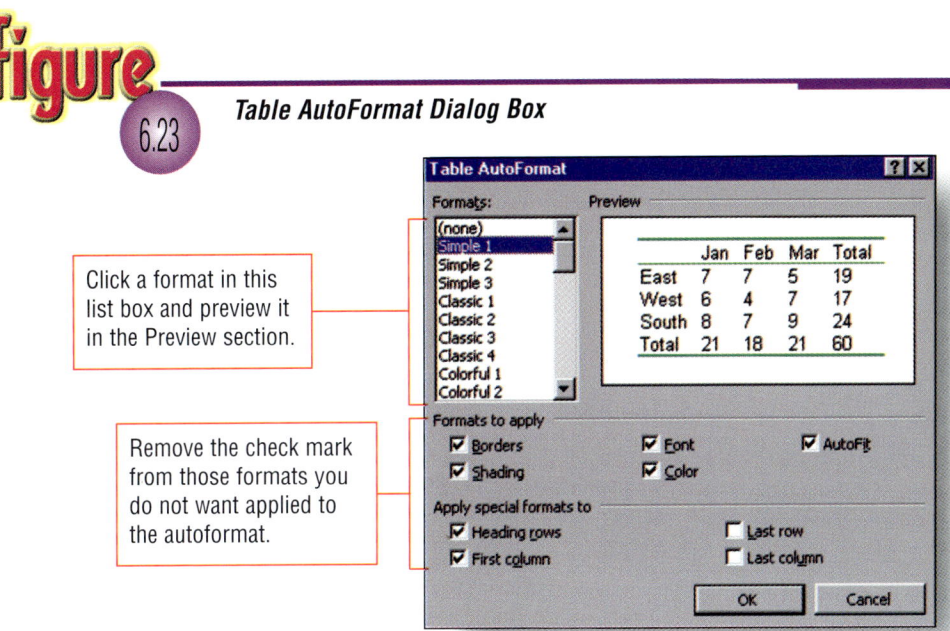

Click a format in this list box and preview it in the Preview section.

Remove the check mark from those formats you do not want applied to the autoformat.

Table formats are displayed in the Forma<u>t</u>s list box. Select a table format in the Forma<u>t</u>s list box and preview the appearance of the table in the Preview section. When previewing table formats, you can make some changes to the format by removing check marks from the options in the Formats to apply section of the dialog box. For example, if you like a format created by Word except for the shading, select the format in the Forma<u>t</u>s list box in the dialog box, and then click the <u>S</u>hading check box. This removes the check mark from the <u>S</u>hading check box and also removes the shading from the table shown in the Preview section.

If you want to apply the special formatting only to specific parts of the table, select the parts of the table you want the formatting applied to in the Apply special formats to section of the dialog box. For example, if you want the table formatting applied only to the first column in the table, insert a check mark in the First column option and remove the check marks from the other options.

exercise

Formatting a Table Using the Table AutoFormat Dialog Box

1. Open Word C6, Ex 01.
2. Save the document with Save As and name it Word C6, Ex 17.
3. Make the following changes to the table:
   a. Make sure the insertion point is positioned in cell A1.

b. Insert a row above the current row.
c. With the new row selected, click the Bold button on the Formatting toolbar and then the Center button.
d. Key the following text in the specified cells (the text will be bold and centered):

A1	=	**Name**
B1	=	**Company**
C1	=	**Telephone Number**

e. Automatically format the table by completing the following steps:
    1) Position the insertion point in any cell in the table.
    2) Click Table and then Table AutoFormat.
    3) At the Table AutoFormat dialog box, click *Colorful 2* in the Formats list box.
    4) Click OK or press Enter.
f. Center the table horizontally.

4. Save the document again with the same name (Word C6, Ex 17).
5. Print and then close Word C6, Ex 17.

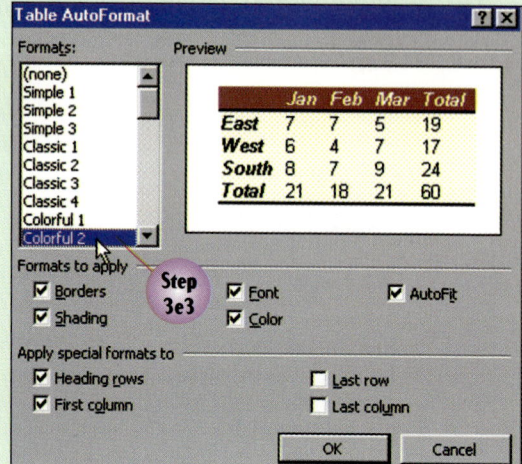

Use buttons on the Tables and Borders toolbar to create a more free-form table.

Tables and Borders

Creating a Table Using the Tables and Borders Toolbar

Word includes a Tables and Borders toolbar with options you can use to create a more free-form table. With buttons on the Tables and Borders toolbar shown in figure 6.24, you can draw a table with specific borders as well as add shading and fill. To display this toolbar, click the Tables and Borders button on the Standard toolbar. Figure 6.25 identifies the buttons on the toolbar and the purpose of each.

figure

6.24

Tables and Borders Toolbar

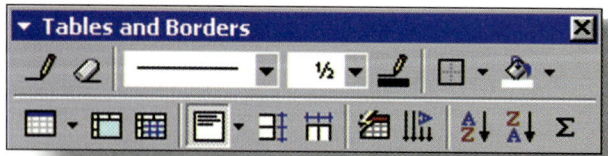

Click this button	Named	To do this
	Draw Table	Insert a table where you drag in the document.
	Eraser	Erase border and/or cell lines.
	Line Style	Specify the border line style.
½	Line Weight	Specify the thickness of the border line.
	Border Color	Specify the border line color.
	Outside Border	Add or remove border around selected text, paragraph, cells, or other object.
	Shading Color	Add, modify, or remove fill color from selected object.
	Insert Table	Display a pop-up menu with options to insert a table; insert a column, row, or cells; and specify the fit of cell contents.
	Merge Cells	Combine contents of selected adjacent cells into one cell.
	Split Cells	Split selected cells in number of rows and columns specified.
	Align Top Left	Display a palette of alignment options such as top center, top right, center, center left, center right, bottom left, bottom center, and bottom right.
	Distribute Rows Evenly	Change selected rows or cells to equal row height.
	Distribute Columns Evenly	Change selected columns or cells to equal column width.
	Table AutoFormat	Apply predesigned formats to table or selected cells.
	Change Text Direction (rotate)	Orient selected text in a cell horizontally, vertically bottom to top, or vertically top to bottom.
	Sort Ascending	Sort selected items alphabetically or numerically in ascending order.
	Sort Descending	Sort selected items alphabetically or numerically in descending order.
Σ	AutoSum	Insert total of a column or row in cell.

To create a table using buttons on the Tables and Borders toolbar, you would complete the following steps:

1. Turn on the display of the Tables and Borders toolbar by clicking the Tables and Borders button on the Standard toolbar. (The viewing mode is automatically changed to Print Layout.)
2. Position the mouse pointer (displays as a pencil) in the area of the editing window where you want the upper left corner of the table to display.
3. Hold down the left mouse button, drag the pencil pointer down and to the right until the outline displays the desired size of the table, and then release the mouse button. (This creates the border of the table.)
4. Use the pencil pointer to draw the row and column lines.
5. Click inside the cell where you want to key text.
6. Key the desired text. (When you key text, the pencil pointer turns into the normal mouse pointer.)

Many of the buttons on the Tables and Borders toolbar can be used to customize the table. For example, you can change the line style with Line Style options and then draw the desired portion of the table. Or, you can change the line style and then redraw lines in an existing table. Use options from the Shading Color button to add color to a cell or selected cells in a table.

exercise 18

Drawing a Table Using the Tables and Borders Toolbar

1. At a clear editing window, draw the table shown in figure 6.26 by completing the following steps:
   a. Key the title centered and bolded as shown in figure 6.26. (Press the Enter key once, turn off bold and return paragraph alignment to left, and then press the Enter key two more times.)
   b. Turn on the display of the Tables and Borders toolbar by clicking the Tables and Borders button on the Standard toolbar.
   c. Change the line style to single by clicking the down-pointing triangle at the right side of the Line Style button and then clicking the single line option.

   d. Position the mouse pointer (displays as a pencil) in the editing window and draw the table, row, and column lines as shown in figure 6.26. (To draw the lines, position the pencil in the desired location, hold down the left mouse button, draw the line, and then release the button. If you want to erase a line, click the Eraser button on the Tables and Borders toolbar and then drag across the line. To continue drawing the table, click the Draw Table button.)
   e. When the table is drawn, click the Draw Table button on the Tables and Borders toolbar button to deactivate it.
   f. Change the vertical alignment of text in cells by completing the following steps:
      1) Select all cells in the table.
      2) Click the down-pointing triangle at the right side of the Align Top Left button located on the Tables and Borders toolbar.

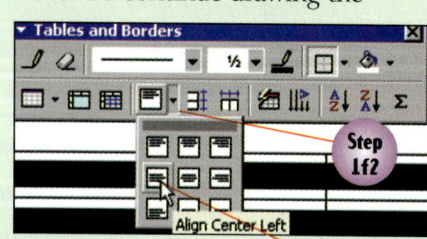

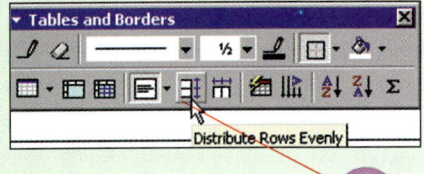

3) At the palette of alignment choices, click the Align Center Left option (first option from the left in the second row).

g. With all cells in the table still selected, click the Distribute Rows Evenly button on the Tables and Borders toolbar.

h. Select all cells in the second and third columns and then click the Center button on the Formatting toolbar (not the Tables and Borders toolbar).

i. Click in the first cell.

j. Key the text in the cells as shown in figure 6.26. (If text wraps in a cell, widen the column.)

2. Turn off the display of the Tables and Borders toolbar by clicking the Tables and Borders button on the Standard toolbar.

3. Save the document and name it Word C6, Ex 18.

4. Print and then close Word C6, Ex 18.

figure

6.26

Exercise 18

CURRENT JOBS AND FUTURE PROJECTIONS

Occupation	1998	2010
Agriculture, Forestry, Fishery	18,342	15,423
Executive, Managerial, Administrative	26,459	28,109
Marketing, Sales	32,188	33,009
Operators, Fabricators, Laborers	35,429	32,677
Professional, Technical	51,239	55,438

exercise 19

Customizing a Table with the Tables and Borders Toolbar

1. Open Word C6, Ex 18.

2. Save the document with Save As and name it Word C6, Ex 19.

3. Customize the table by completing the following steps:

a. Turn on the display of the Tables and Borders toolbar by clicking the Tables and Borders button on the Standard toolbar.

b. Change the outside table border lines to double lines by completing the following steps:

1) Click the down-pointing triangle at the right side of the Line Style button.
2) At the drop-down list that displays, click the first double-line style.
3) Position the pencil pointer in the upper left corner of the table, hold down the left mouse button, drag the pencil down the left side of the table until it reaches the bottom, and then release the mouse button. (This changes the single line to a double line.)
4) Change the bottom border of the table to a double line by dragging the pencil across the bottom border. (Be sure to hold the left mouse button down as you drag.)
5) Change the right border of the table to a double line by dragging the pencil along the right border.
6) Change the top border of the table to a double line by dragging the pencil along the top border.

c. Click the Draw Table button to deselect it.
d. Add gray shading to cells by completing the following steps:
   1) Select cells A2 through C6.
   2) Click the down-pointing triangle at the right side of the Shading Color button on the Tables and Borders toolbar.
   3) At the palette of color choices that displays, click the Gray-25% color (this is the second option from the *right* in the top row).

e. Add light turquoise shading to cells by completing the following steps:
   1) Select cells A1, B1, and C1.
   2) Click the down-pointing arrow at the right side of the Shading Color button on the Tables and Borders toolbar.
   3) At the palette of color choices, click the light turquoise color (fifth color from the left in the bottom row).

f. Turn off the display of the Tables and Borders toolbar.

4. Save the document again with the same name (Word C6, Ex 19).
5. Print and then close Word C6, Ex 19.

Moving a Table

Position the mouse pointer in a table and a table move handle displays in the upper left corner. Use this handle to move the table in the document. Position the mouse pointer on the table move handle until the pointer turns into a four-headed arrow, hold down the left mouse button, drag the table to the desired position, and then release the mouse button.

To move a table, changing the document view can be helpful. With options from the Zoom button on the Standard toolbar, you can change the display percentage and also select options such as Page Width, Text Width, Whole Page, and Two Pages. The options available from the Zoom button depend on the view

selected. To move a table, consider changing to the Print Layout view and then changing the Zoom to *Whole Page*. To change the zoom, click the down-pointing triangle at the right side of the Zoom button and then click *Whole Page* at the drop-down list.

Zoom

Inserting a Column, Changing Text Direction, and Moving the Table

1. Open Word C6, Ex 18.
2. Save the document with Save As and name it Word C6, Ex 20.
3. Customize the table so it appears as shown in figure 6.27 by completing the following steps:
   a. Delete the title *CURRENT JOBS AND FUTURE PROJECTIONS*.
   b. Click in the first cell.
   c. Click Table, point to Insert, expand the side menu, and then click Columns to the Left. (This inserts a column at the left side of the table.)
   d. Deselect the column.
   e. Change the width of the first and second columns by completing the following steps:
      1) Position the insertion point in the first cell (cell A1).
      2) Position the mouse pointer on the gridline that separates the first and second column until the pointer turns into a left- and right-pointing arrow with a vertical double line between.
      3) Hold down the left mouse button, drag to the left to approximately the ¾-inch mark on the horizontal ruler and then release the mouse button.
   f. Merge the cells in the first column by completing the following steps:
      1) Display the Tables and Borders toolbar.
      2) Click the Draw Table button to deactivate it.
      3) Select the first column.
      4) Click the Merge Cells button on the Tables and Borders toolbar.
   g. Key the text in the first cell as shown in figure 6.27 by completing the following steps:
      1) Make sure the insertion point is positioned in the first cell.
      2) Change the text direction by clicking twice on the Change Text Direction button on the Tables and Borders toolbar.
      3) Click the Center button on the Formatting toolbar.
      4) Change the font to 24-point Times New Roman bold.
      5) Key **Future Jobs**.
   h. Turn off the display of the Tables and Borders toolbar.
4. Move the table to the middle of the page by completing the following steps:
   a. Click the down-pointing triangle at the right side of the Zoom button on the Standard toolbar and then click *Whole Page* at the drop-down list.
   b. Position the mouse pointer in the table until the table move handle displays in the upper left corner of the table.
   c. Position the mouse pointer on the table move handle until the pointer turns into a four-headed arrow.
   d. Hold down the left mouse button, drag the outline of the table to the middle of the page, and then release the mouse button.

e. Click the down-pointing triangle at the right side of the Zoom button on the Standard toolbar and then click *100%* at the drop-down list.

5. Save the document again with the same name (Word C6, Ex 20).

6. Print and then close Word C6, Ex 20.

figure

6.27

Exercise 20

Future Jobs	Occupation	1998	2010
	Agriculture, Forestry, Fishery	18,342	15,423
	Executive, Managerial, Administrative	26,459	28,109
	Marketing, Sales	32,188	33,009
	Operators, Fabricators, Laborers	35,429	32,677
	Professional, Technical	51,239	55,438

Performing Calculations

Click the insert Microsoft Excel Worksheet button to use Excel functions and tables in Word.

Hint

Numbers in a table can be calculated. Numbers can be added, subtracted, multiplied, and divided. In addition, you can calculate averages, percentages, and minimum and maximum values. Calculations can be performed in a Word table; however, for complex calculations, use a Microsoft Excel worksheet.

To perform a calculation in a table, position the insertion point in the cell where you want the result of the calculation to display. This cell should be empty. By default, Word assumes that you want to calculate the sum of cells immediately above or to the left of the cell where the insertion point is positioned. This default calculation can be changed.

As an example of how to calculate sums, you would complete the following steps to calculate the sum of cells in C2 through C5 and insert the result of the calculation in cell C6:

1. Position the insertion point in cell C6.
2. Click Table, expand the drop-down menu, and then click Formula.
3. At the Formula dialog box shown in figure 6.28, the calculation *=SUM(ABOVE)* displays in the Formula text box. This is the desired formula to calculate the sum.
4. Click OK or press Enter.

Formula Dialog Box

6.28

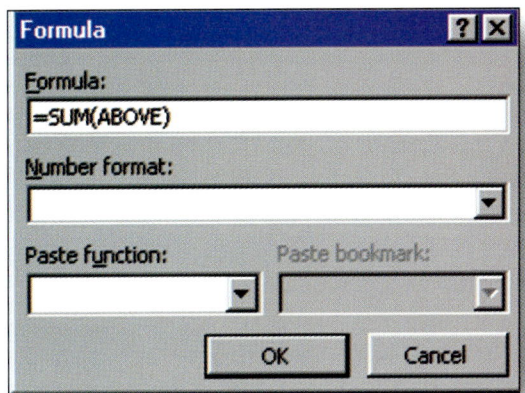

Word adds the numbers in cells C2 through C5 and then inserts the result of this calculation in cell C6. To perform other types of calculations such as subtraction, multiplication, and division, the formula displayed in the Formula text box at the Formula dialog box must be changed. You can use an arithmetic sign to write a formula. For example, the formula =A2-A3 (A2 minus A3) can be inserted in cell A4, which tells Word to insert the difference of A2 and A3 in cell A4. If changes are made to the numbers in cells A2 and A3, the value in A4 can be recalculated.

Begin a formula with the equal symbol (=). This identifies the data that follows as a formula.

Four basic operators can be used when writing formulas: the plus sign (+) for addition, the minus sign (hyphen) for subtraction, the asterisk (*) for multiplication, and the forward slash (/) for division. If there are two or more operators in a calculation, Word calculates from left to right. If you want to change the order of calculation, use parentheses around the part of the calculation to be performed first.

In the default formula, the SUM part of the formula is called a function. Word provides other functions you can use to write a formula. These functions are available with the Paste function option at the Formula dialog box. For example, you can use the AVERAGE function to average numbers in cells. Examples of how formulas can be written are shown in figure 6.29.

The numbering format can be specified at the Formula dialog box. For example, if you are calculating money amounts, you can specify that the calculated numbers display with two numbers following the decimal point. To specify the numbering format, display the Formula dialog box, and then click the down-pointing triangle to the right of the Number format option. Click the desired formatting at the drop-down list.

figure

6.29

Example Formulas

Cell E4 is the total price of items.
Cell B4 contains the quantity of items, and cell D4 contains the unit price. The formula for cell E4 is **=B4*D4**. (This formula multiplies the quantity of items in cell B4 by the unit price in cell D4.)

Cell D3 is the percentage of increase in sales from the previous year.
Cell B3 contains the amount of sales for the previous year, and cell C3 contains the amount of sales for the current year. The formula for cell D3 is **=C3-B3/C3*100**. (This formula subtracts the amount of sales last year from the amount of sales this year. The remaining amount is divided by the amount of sales this year and then multiplied by 100 to display the product as a percentage.)

Cell E1 is the average of test scores.
Cells A1 through D1 contain test scores. The formula to calculate the average score is **=(A1+B1+C1+D1)/4**. (This formula adds the scores from cells A1 through D1 and then divides that sum by 4.) You can also enter the formula as **AVERAGE(LEFT)**. The AVERAGE function tells Word to average all entries left of cell E1.

exercise

Calculating Net Profit

1. At a clear document screen, create the document shown in figure 6.30 by completing the following steps:
   a. Press the Enter key once.
   b. Create a table with 4 columns and 6 rows (6 x 4).
   c. Select the first row and then merge the cells.
   d. Position the insertion point in the first row, press the Enter key once, change the alignment to center, turn on bold, key **McCORMACK FUNDS CORPORATION**, and then press Enter once.
   e. Select the second row in the table and then click the Bold and the Center buttons on the Formatting toolbar.

    f.   Select cells A3 through A6 and then change the alignment to center.

    g.   Select cells B3 through D6 and then change the alignment to right.

    h.   Key the text in the cells as shown in figure 6.30.

    i.   Add border lines and 20% shading to the table as shown in figure 6.30.

    j.   Insert a formula in cell D3 by completing the following steps:

        1) Position the insertion point in cell D3 (the cell below *Net Profit*).

        2) Click Table, expand the drop-down menu, and then click Formula.

        3) At the Formula dialog box, delete the formula in the Formula text box.

        4) Key **=B3-C3** in the Formula text box.

        5) Click the down-pointing triangle at the right side of the Number format text box and then click the third option from the top of the drop-down list.

        6) Click OK or press Enter.

    k. Insert the formula =B4-C4 in cell D4 by completing the following steps:

        1) Position the insertion point in cell D4.

        2) Click Table and then click Formula.

        3) At the Formula dialog box, delete the formula in the Formula text box.

        4) Key **=B4-C4** in the Formula text box.

        5) Click the down-pointing triangle at the right side of the Number format text box and then click the second option from the top of the drop-down list.

        6) Click OK or press Enter.

    l.   Insert the formula =B5-C5 in cell D5 by completing steps similar to those in step 1k.

    m. Insert the formula =B6-C6 in cell D6 by completing steps similar to those in step 1k.

  2. Save the document and name it Word C6, Ex 21.

  3. Print and then close Word C6, Ex 21.

Formula   ? X

Step 1j4

Formula:

=B3-C3

Number format:

Step 1j5

\#,##0
\#,##0.00
$#,##0.00;($#,##0.00)
0
0%
0.00
0.00%

Exercise 21

McCORMACK FUNDS CORPORATION			
Year	**Income**	**Expenses**	**Net Profit**
1997	$6,890,309.10	$4,224,980.00	
1998	7,822,899.80	3,199,554.30	
1999	7,904,899.20	4,328,167.90	
2000	8,218,287.75	5,325,211.65	

Averaging Test Scores

1. Open Word Table 01.
2. Save the document with Save As and name it Word C6, Ex 22.
3. Insert a formula in cell F3 to average test scores by completing the following steps:
   a. Position the insertion point in cell F3 (the cell below *Ave.*).
   b. Click T_able and then F_ormula.
   c. Delete the formula in the F_ormula text box *except* the equals sign.
   d. With the insertion point positioned immediately after the equals sign, click the down-pointing triangle to the right of the Paste f_unction text box.
   e. At the drop-down list that displays, click AVERAGE.
   f. With the insertion point positioned between the left and right parentheses, key **left**.
   g. Click the down-pointing triangle to the right of the Number format text box and then click the fifth option from the top (*0%*) at the drop-down list.
   h. Click OK or press Enter.

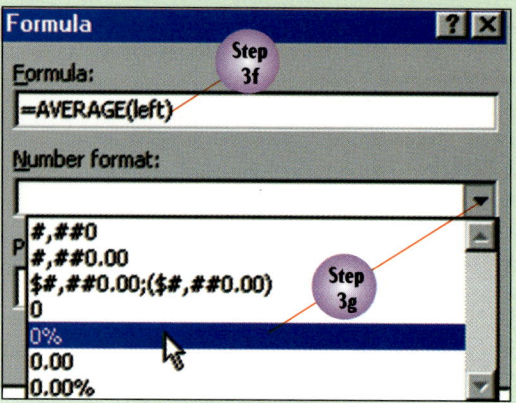

4. Position the insertion point in cell F4 and then complete steps similar to those in step 3 to insert a formula to average test scores.
5. Position the insertion point in cell F5 and then complete steps similar to those in step 3 to insert a formula to average test scores.
6. Position the insertion point in cell F6 and then complete steps similar to those in step 3 to insert a formula to average test scores.
7. Position the insertion point in cell F7 and then complete steps similar to those in step 3 to insert a formula to average test scores.
8. Position the insertion point in cell F8 and then complete steps similar to those in step 3 to insert a formula to average test scores.
9. Save the document again with the same name (Word C6, Ex 22).
10. Print and then close Word C6, Ex 22.

If changes are made to numbers in cells that are part of a formula, select the result of the calculation, and then press the F9 function key. This recalculates the formula and inserts the new result of the calculation in the cell. You can also recalculate by completing the following steps:

1. Select the number in the cell containing the formula.
2. Click T_able, expand the drop-down menu, and then click F_ormula.
3. At the Formula dialog box, click OK or press Enter.

exercise 23

Recalculating Test Scores

1. Open Word C6, Ex 22.
2. Save the document with Save As and name it Word C6, Ex 23.
3. Make the following changes to the table:
   a. Change the number in cell C3 from *79* to *85*.
   b. Change the number in cell D5 from *74* to *86*.
   c. Change the number in cell D8 from *78* to *92*.
   d. Position the mouse pointer in cell F3, click the left mouse button (this inserts a gray background around the numbers in the cell), and then press F9. (Pressing F9 recalculates the average.)
   e. Click the number in cell F5 and then press F9.
   f. Click the number in cell F8 and then press F9.
4. Save the document again with the same name (Word C6, Ex 23).
5. Print and then close Word C6, Ex 23.

chapter summary

➤ Word's Tables feature can be used to create columns and rows of information. A cell is the intersection between a row and a column.

➤ A table can contain text, characters, numbers, data, graphics, or formulas. It can be extensively formatted and can include calculations.

➤ A table can be created with the Insert Table button on the Standard toolbar or at the Insert Table dialog box.

➤ Columns in a table are lettered from left to right beginning with A. Rows are numbered from top to bottom beginning with 1.

➤ The lines that form the cells of the table are called gridlines.

➤ With the insertion point positioned in a cell, key or edit text as you would normal text.

➤ To move the insertion point to different cells within the table using the mouse, position the mouse pointer in the desired cell, and then click the left button.

➤ To move the insertion point to different cells within the table using the keyboard, refer to the information shown in figure 6.5 in this chapter.

➤ To use the mouse to select specific cells within a table, refer to the information shown in figure 6.8 in this chapter.

➤ To use the keyboard to select specific cells within a table, refer to the information shown in figure 6.9 in this chapter.

➤ A row or column of cells or all cells in a table can be selected with options from the Table drop-down menu.

➤ All text in cells within a table can be deleted, leaving the table gridlines, or all text and gridlines can be deleted.

- Borders and shading can be added to cells; rows and columns can be inserted or deleted; cells can be split or merged; and the alignment of the table can be changed.
- Column width and row height can be changed using the mouse on the Ruler, within a table, or at the Table Properties dialog box.
- After a table has been created, various methods can be used to add rows and/or columns.
- Specific cells in a table or rows or columns in a table can be deleted.
- Word has provided predesigned table formats in the Table AutoFormat dialog box that can quickly format a table.
- Use buttons on the Tables and Borders toolbar to create and customize a table. Click the Tables and Borders button on the Standard toolbar to turn on the display of the Tables and Borders toolbar.
- Numbers in a table can be calculated by inserting a formula in a cell at the Formula dialog box.

commands review

	Mouse/Keyboard
Create table with Standard toolbar	With mouse pointer on Insert Table button on Standard toolbar, hold down left mouse button, move mouse pointer down and right until desired table size displays, release button
Display Insert Table dialog box	Click Table, point to Insert, then click Table
Move insertion point to next cell	Tab
Move insertion point to previous cell	Shift + Tab
Insert tab within a cell	Ctrl + Tab
Insert page break within a table	Ctrl + Enter
Select a row, column, or all cells with Table drop-down menu	Position insertion point, click Table, point to Select, and then click Table, Column, Row or Cell
Delete text only from table	Select table, press Delete
Delete table	Click Table, point to Delete, then click Table
Display Table Properties dialog box	Click Table, then Table Properties
Delete cells, rows, or columns	Click Table, point to Delete, then click Columns, Rows, or Cells
Display Table AutoFormat dialog box	With insertion point in a cell, click Table, then Table AutoFormat
Turn on/off display of Tables and Borders toolbar	Click Tables and Borders button on Standard toolbar
Display Formula dialog box	Click Table, expand the drop-down menu, then click Formula

thinking offline

Completion: In the space provided at the right, indicate the correct term, command, or number.

1. Use this button on the Standard toolbar to create a table.

2. This is another name for the lines that form the cells of the table.

3. The end-of-row marker shows only when this button is active on the Standard toolbar.

4. The move table column markers display here.

5. Use this keyboard command to move the insertion point to the previous cell.

6. Use this keyboard command to insert a tab within a cell.

7. This is the name given to the space just to the left of the left edge of a table.

8. To add shading to a cell or selected cells, display this dialog box.

9. Change the width of columns at this dialog box with the Column tab selected.

10. Text in cells aligns at this side of the cell by default.

11. Choose this option at the Delete Cells dialog box if you want cells moved up after selected cells are deleted.

12. To merge cells A1 and B1, select A1 and B1, and then click this at the Table drop-down menu.

13. To divide one cell into two columns, click this at the Table drop-down menu.

14. Choose predesigned table formats at this dialog box.

15. Click this button on the Tables and Borders toolbar to add, modify, or remove fill color from selected objects.

16. Click this button on the Tables and Borders toolbar to change the border line style.

17. This is the operator for multiplication that is used when writing formulas in a table.

18. This is the formula to add cells D2, D3, and D4, and then divide the total by 5.

19. This is the formula to multiply A1 by B1.

20. This calculation will display in the Formula text box in the Formula dialog box by default.

working hands-on

Assessment 1

1. At a clear document screen, create the table shown in figure 6.31. Bold and center the text as shown.
2. Save the document and name it Word C6, SA 01.
3. Print and then close Word C6, SA 01.

figure

6.31   *Assessment 1*

Name and Title	Department
Charles (Kit) G. Bloomquist, Manager	Facilities Maintenance
Penny M. Fitzpatrick, Director	Marketing, Continental United States
Jeffrey J. Hartnett, Assistant Manager	Computer Technical Support
Raymond D. Johnson, Manager	Communications Operations, International
Sandra L. Kvasnikoff, Vice President	Customer Service
Kenneth R. Morrison, Assistant Manager	System Support Services

Assessment 2

1. At a clear document screen, create the table shown in figure 6.32 with the following specifications:
   a. Press the Enter key once and then create a table with 2 columns and 9 rows (9 x 2).
   b. Change the width of the first column to 4.5 inches and the width of the second column to 1.5 inches.
   c. Change the alignment of cells in the second column to right.
   d. Select the entire table and then change the font to 12-point Arial.
   e. Merge cells in the first row (cells A1 and B1).
   f. Key the text in the cells as indicated. Bold and center the text in the first cell. Before keying the text in the first cell, press the Enter key once. After keying the text in the cell centered and bolded, press the Enter key once.
2. Save the document and name it Word C6, SA 02.
3. Print and then close Word C6, SA 02.

figure 6.32 *Assessment 2*

**PROPERTY
Replacement Cost**

Business Personal Property Including Stock & Equipment	$1,367,400
Blanket Earnings & Expenses	4,883,432
Total Valuable Papers	73,000
Transit Domestic & Foreign	41,000
Excess Legal Liability	550,000
Accounts Receivable	40,000
Computer Coverage	35,000
Fire Department Service Charge	15,000

Assessment 3

1. At a clear document screen, create the table shown in figure 6.33 with the following specifications:
   a. Press the Enter key once.
   b. Create a table with 3 columns and 8 rows (8 x 3).
   c. Merge the cells in the first row (cells A1, B1, and C1).
   d. Select the first and second rows and then click the Bold button and the Center button on the Formatting toolbar.
   e. Select cells B3 through C8 and then change the alignment to Right.
   f. Key the text in the cells shown in figure 6.33. (Before keying the text in the first cell, press the Enter key once. After keying the text in the cell centered and bolded, press the Enter key once.)
   g. Add border lines and shading to the table as shown in figure 6.33.
   h. Use the AutoFit feature to make the columns in the table automatically fit the contents.
   i. Center the table horizontally.
2. Save the document and name it Word C6, SA 03.
3. Print and then close Word C6, SA 03.

figure 6.33

Assessment 3

STOCK OPTION LEDGER REPORT		
Type of Transaction	# of Shares	Future
Beginning Inventory	93,000	1,000
Portion Exercised	2,000	3,000
One Hundred Percent Split	3,000	4,400
Exercised	(1,000)	4,400
Exercised	2,000	4,400
Portion Exercised	1,000	5,400

Assessment 4

1. Open Word Table 05.
2. Save the document with Save As and name it Word C6, SA 04.
3. Make the following changes to the table:
   a. Select cells B1 through C7 and then change the alignment to right.
   b. With the insertion point positioned in any cell in the table, apply the *Columns 5* formatting at the Table AutoFormat dialog box.
   c. Center the table horizontally.
   d. Position the insertion point in cell B7 and then display the Formula dialog box. At this dialog box, leave the formula in the Formula text box as written. Click the down-pointing triangle at the right of the Number format option and then click the first numbering format in the drop-down menu. Click OK to close the Formula dialog box.
   e. Position the insertion point in cell C7 and then display the Formula dialog box. At this dialog box, leave the formula in the Formula text box as written. Click the down-pointing triangle to the right of the Number format option and then click the first numbering format in the drop-down menu. Click OK to close the Formula dialog box. (Key a dollar sign before each total.)
4. Save the document again with the same name (Word C6, SA 04).
5. Print and then close Word C6, SA 04.

Assessment 5

1. Open Word Table 06.
2. Save the document with Save As and name it Word C6, SA 05.
3. Customize the table in the document so it displays as shown in figure 6.34.
4. Save the document again with the same name (Word C6, SA 05).
5. Print and then close Word C6, SA 05.

figure

6.34 **Assessment 5**

JOBS IN GREATEST DEMAND

BA or Graduate Degree Required

Position	Weekly Income	Yearly Openings
Accountants/Auditors	$675	821
Financial Managers	$645	357
Loan Officers	$695	278
Registered Nurses	$752	1,450
Teachers, Elementary	$680	1,008
Teachers, Secondary	$750	1,326

Assessment 6

1. At a clear document screen, create a table using the information shown in figure 6.35. Format the table following steps similar to those in Assessment 4.
2. Save the document and name it Word C6, SA 06.
3. Print and then close Word C6, SA 06.

figure

6.35   *Assessment 6*

Expenses	Budgeted	Actual
Basic education	$17,349,233	$17,213,455
Support services	13,239,441	12,987,345
Special education	5,123,325	5,236,415
Vocational education	1,945,674	1,895,350
Learning assistance	1,134,095	1,056,394
Other education programs	754,342	698,560
Community services	693,548	701,359
Total		

Assessment 7

1. Open Word Table 07.
2. Save the document with Save As and name it Word C6, SA 07.
3. Format the table so it appears as shown in figure 6.36 by making the following changes:
   a. Position the insertion point in any cell in the table below the heading.
   b. Position the mouse pointer on the move table column marker that displays on the Ruler between the 1-inch mark and the 2-inch mark, hold down the Ctrl key and the Shift key, and then drag the marker to the 2¼-inch mark on the Ruler.
   c. Select the first two rows and then change the alignment to center and change the font to 14-point Tahoma bold.
   d. Select cells B3 through D8 and then change the alignment to right.
   e. Select cells A3 through D8 and then change the font to 11-point Tahoma.
   f. Insert the formula =**C3-B3** in cell D3 and change the <u>N</u>umber format option to the third option from the top at the drop-down menu.
   g. Insert the appropriate formula in cells D4, D5, D6, D7, and D8 to subtract Last Year numbers from This Year numbers. (Change the <u>N</u>umber format option to the second option from the top at the drop-down menu.)
   h. Insert border lines and shading as shown in figure 6.36. (To create the double-line border, you will need to select the double-line border option and then increase the width to 1½ pts.)
4. Save the document again with the same name (Word C6, SA 07).
5. Print and then close Word C6, SA 07.

figure 6.36 *Assessment 7*

McCORMACK FUNDS CORPORATION Computer Operations Expenses			
Expense	**Last Year**	**This Year**	**Difference**
Payroll	$1,102,003.90	$1,320,229.20	
New Equipment	690,340.24	750,345.98	
Equipment Maintenance	20,435.33	22,820.45	
Personnel Training	19,485.45	20,460.00	
Consultation Fees	14,309.00	12,683.50	
Supplies and Printing	1,783.48	2,009.42	

Assessment 8

1. Using Word's Help feature, learn how to convert a table to text. Print the information.
2. After reading the information on converting a table to text, complete the following steps:
   a. Create a Word document that describes the steps.
   b. Save the document and name it Word C6, Steps.
   c. Print and then close Word C6, Steps.
3. Open Word C6, SA 02 and then complete the following steps:
   a. Convert the table in Word C6, SA 02 to text. (You determine with what to separate the text.)
   b. Save the converted table and name it Word C6, SA 08.
   c. Print and then close Word C6, SA 08.
4. Using Word's Help feature, learn how to convert text to a table.
5. After reading the information, key the text shown in figure 6.37 exactly as written and then convert the text to a table.
6. Save the table and name it Word C6, Table.
7. Print and then close Word C6, Table.

Assessment 8

Title,Name
President,Martin Sherwood
Vice President,Gina Lopez
Vice President,Sydney Fox
Manager,Stephen Powell
Manager,Linda Wang

 **Chapter 07C**

Inserting Graphic Elements

PERFORMANCE OBJECTIVES

Upon successful completion of chapter 7, you will be able to:

- Insert, size, and move clip art images in a document.
- Format clip art images using buttons on the Picture toolbar.
- Create shapes, autoshapes, and text boxes using buttons on the Drawing toolbar.
- Select, delete, move, copy, and size drawn objects.
- Customize a drawn object by adding fill color and shading, changing the line color and style, and adding shadow and 3-D effects.
- Create text with WordArt.
- Size and move a WordArt text box.
- Change the font and font size of WordArt text.
- Customize WordArt text with buttons on the WordArt and Drawing toolbars.

Microsoft Word 2000 contains a variety of features that help you to enhance the visual appeal of a document. In this chapter, you will learn to insert a clip art image, draw shapes and objects, and create text boxes using buttons on the Drawing toolbar. Word provides a supplementary application named WordArt that you can use to modify and conform text to a variety of shapes. This application uses object linking and embedding (OLE) to create and add objects to a Word document.

Inserting Clip Art

Word 2000 includes a gallery of clip art images that can be inserted in a document. To insert a clip art image, click Insert, point to Picture, and then click Clip Art. This displays the Insert ClipArt dialog box with the Pictures tab selected as shown in figure 7.1.

Insert ClipArt Dialog Box with Pictures Tab Selected

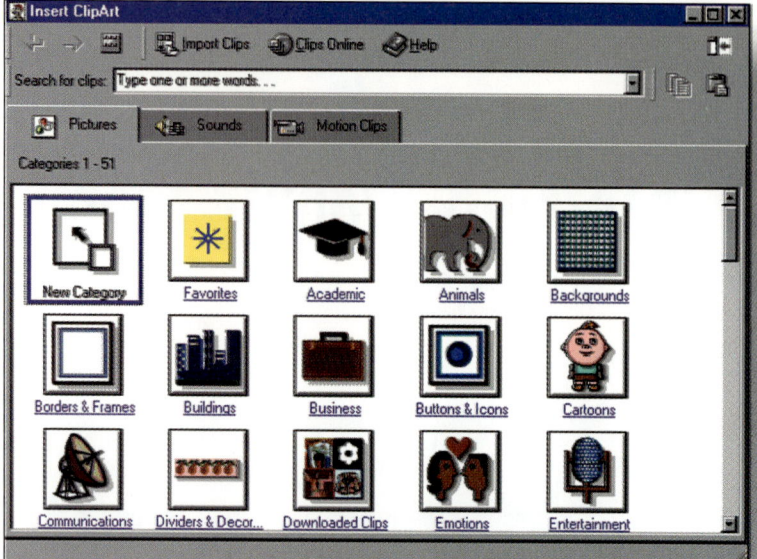

Insert ClipArt

Another method for displaying the Insert ClipArt dialog box is to click the Insert Clip Art button on the Drawing toolbar. To display the Drawing toolbar, position the mouse pointer on the Standard or Formatting toolbar, click the *right* mouse button, and then click Drawing at the drop-down list.

At the Insert ClipArt dialog box with the Pictures tab selected, click a category in the Category list box. This displays a list of clip art available for the category. To insert a clip art image in the document, click the desired clip art, and then click the Insert clip button at the top of the callout side menu that displays. Remove the Insert ClipArt dialog box from the screen by clicking the Close button (contains an X) located in the upper right corner of the dialog box.

Back

All Categories

Maneuver through categories and clip art at the Insert ClipArt dialog box using buttons on the toolbar that displays at the top of the dialog box. For example, click the Back button to display clip art for the previously selected category. To redisplay all categories, click the All Categories button.

When you click a clip art image, a callout side menu displays containing several buttons. Click the Insert clip button to insert the image in the document. Click the Preview clip to view how the clip art image will display in the document. If you want to add a clip art image to the Favorites category or to any other category, click the Add clip to Favorites or other category button. This expands the side menu and displays an option for entering the desired category. The side menu will continue to display expanded until you click the button again. Clicking the Find similar clips button on the callout side menu causes the side menu to expand and display with options for finding clips with similar styles, colors, shapes, and keywords. The side menu will remain expanded until you click the button again.

Sizing a Clip Art Image

Once a clip art image is inserted in a document, it can be sized using the white sizing handles that display around it after it is selected. To change the size of a clip art image, click in the image to select it and position the mouse pointer on a sizing handle until the pointer turns into a double-headed arrow. Hold down the left mouse button, drag the sizing handle in or out to decrease or increase the size of the image, and then release the mouse button.

Use the middle sizing handles at the left or right side of the image to make the image wider or thinner. Use the middle sizing handles at the top or bottom of the image to make the image taller or shorter. Use the sizing handles at the corners of the image to change both the width and height at the same time.

When sizing a clip art image, consider using the horizontal and vertical rulers that display in Print Layout view. To deselect an image, click anywhere in the document outside of the image.

(Before completing computer exercises, delete the Chapter 06C *folder on your disk. Next, copy the* Chapter 07C *folder from the CD that accompanies this textbook to your disk and make* Chapter 07C *the active folder.)*

exercise 1

Inserting and Sizing a Clip Art Image in a Document

1. At a clear document screen, insert and size a clip art image by completing the following steps:
   a. Change to Print Layout view.
   b. Click <u>I</u>nsert, point to <u>P</u>icture, and then click <u>C</u>lip Art.
   c. At the Insert ClipArt dialog box (see figure 7.1), click the *Academic* category in the category list box (contains an image of a graduation cap).
   d. If there is more than one screen of images, scroll through the list of academic clip art images.
   e. Click the Back button located at the left side of the Insert ClipArt dialog box.
   f. Scroll down the list of categories and click the *Home & Family* category (contains an image of a house with people inside).
   g. If there is more than one screen of images, scroll through the list of Home and Family clip art images.
   h. Click the All Categories button located on the Insert ClipArt dialog box toolbar.
   i. Click the *Animals* category in the category list box (contains an image of an elephant).
   j. Click once on the birds clip art. (If this image is not available, click another animal of your choosing.)
   k. At the callout side menu, click the Insert clip button (top button).

Step 1e

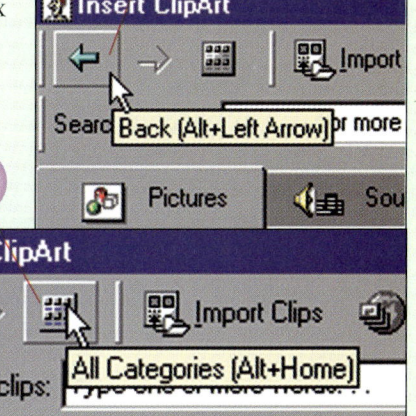

Step 1h

Step 1j

Step 1k

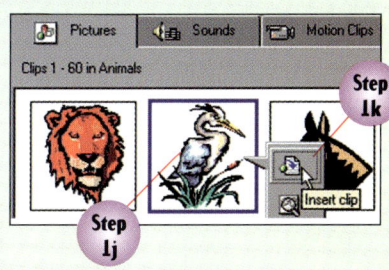

1. Click the Close button (contains an X) that displays in the upper right corner of the dialog box.

m. Decrease the size of the bird image by completing the following steps:
   1) Click the image to select it (black sizing handles display around the image).
   2) If necessary, click the down scroll triangle on the vertical scroll bar until the bottom sizing handles display.
   3) Position the mouse pointer on the bottom right sizing handle until the pointer turns into a diagonally pointing two-headed arrow.
   4) Hold down the left mouse button, drag up and to the left until the size of the image is approximately 2 inches wide by 2.25 inches in height (use the horizontal and vertical rulers as visual aids), and then release the left mouse button.
   5) Click in the document screen outside the image to deselect it.

Step 1m4

2. Save the document and name it Word C7, Ex 01.
3. Print and then close Word C7, Ex 01.

Formatting Clip Art Images with Buttons on the Picture Toolbar

Clip art images inserted in a document can be formatted in a variety of ways. Formatting might include adding fill color and border lines, increasing or decreasing the brightness or contrast, choosing a wrapping style, and cropping the image. A variety of methods are available for changing the formatting of a clip art image. You can format an image with buttons on the Picture toolbar or options at the Format Picture dialog box.

To display the Picture toolbar, click a clip art image. This displays the Picture toolbar shown in figure 7.2. The buttons on the Picture toolbar are described in figure 7.3. (If the Picture toolbar does not display when you click a clip art image, position the mouse pointer on the image, click the *right* mouse button, and then click Show Picture Toolbar.)

7.2

Picture Toolbar

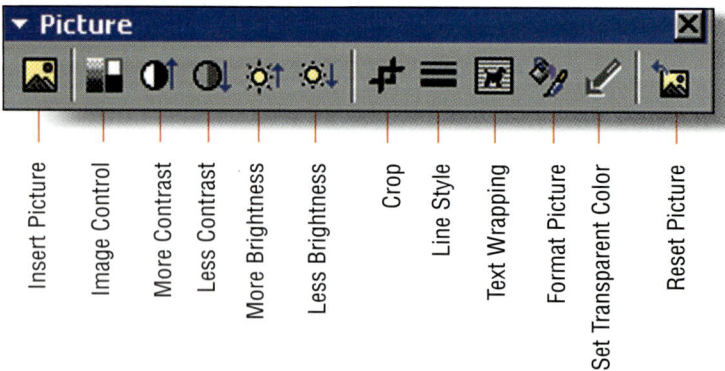

figure

7.3

Picture Toolbar Buttons

Click this button	Named	To do this
	Insert Picture	Display the Insert Picture dialog box with a list of subfolders containing additional images.
	Image Control	Display a drop-down list with options for controlling how the image displays. Options include Automatic, Grayscale, Black & White, and Watermark.
	More Contrast	Increase contrast of the image.
	Less Contrast	Decrease contrast of the image.
	More Brightness	Increase brightness of the image.
	Less Brightness	Decrease brightness of the image.
	Crop	Crop image so only a specific portion of the image is visible.
	Line Style	Insert a border around the image and specify the border line style.
	Text Wrapping	Specify how text will wrap around or through the image. Choices include Square, Tight, Behind Text, In Front of Text, Top and Bottom, Through, and Edit Wrap Points.
	Format Picture	Display Format Picture dialog box with options for formatting the image. Tabs in the dialog box include Colors and Lines, Size, Position, Wrapping, and Picture.
	Set Transparent Color	This button is not active. (When an image contains a transparent area, the background color or texture of the page shows through the image. Set transparent color in Microsoft Photo Editor.)
	Reset Picture	Reset image to its original size, position, and color.

Moving a Clip Art Image

To move a clip art image in a document you must first choose a text wrapping option. To do this, select the image, click the Text Wrapping button on the Picture toolbar, and then click a wrapping option. This changes the sizing handles that display around the selected image from black to white. With white sizing handles displayed, position the mouse pointer inside the image until the pointer turns into a four-headed arrow. Hold down the left mouse button, drag the image to the desired position, and then release the mouse button.

Inserting, Moving, and Customizing a Clip Art Image in a Document

1. At a clear document screen, insert, move, and then size a clip art image by completing the following steps:
   a. Change to Print Layout view.
   b. If the Drawing toolbar is not visible, display it by positioning the mouse pointer on the Standard or Formatting toolbar, clicking the *right* mouse button, and then clicking Drawing at the drop-down list.
   c. Click the Insert Clip Art button on the Drawing toolbar.
   d. At the Insert ClipArt dialog box, click the *Academic* category in the category list box (contains an image of a graduation cap).
   e. Click once on the books clip art. (If this image is not available, click another academic image of your choosing.)
   f. At the callout side menu, click the Insert clip button (top button).
   g. Click the Close button (contains an X) that displays in the upper right corner of the dialog box.

   h. Customize the image of the books using buttons on the Picture toolbar by completing the following steps:
      1) Click the image to select it (black sizing handles display around the image).
      2) Click eight times on the More Contrast button on the Picture toolbar. (This increases the contrast of the colors used in the image.)
      3) Click twice on the More Brightness button on the Picture toolbar.
   i. Change the size of the image by completing the following steps:
      1) If necessary, scroll down the page until the bottom of the book image displays.
      2) Position the mouse pointer on the black sizing handle that displays in the lower right corner until a diagonally pointed, two-headed arrow displays.
      3) Hold down the left mouse button, drag into the image to decrease the size until it measures approximately 3.5 inches in width and 3 inches in height, and then release the mouse button. *(Hint: Use the horizontal and vertical rulers to help you approximate the size.)*
   j. Move the image by completing the following steps:
      1) With the image still selected, click the Text Wrapping button on the Picture toolbar, and then click T̲hrough at the drop-down list. This changes the sizing handles from black to white.

2) Position the mouse pointer inside the image (pointer displays with a four-headed arrow attached to it).

3) Hold down the left mouse button, drag the outline of the image so it is centered horizontally between the left and right margins, and then release the mouse button.

k. Add a border line to the image by clicking the Line Style button on the Picture toolbar and clicking *3 pt* at the drop-down list.

l. Click outside the clip art image to deselect it.

2. Save the document and name it Word C7, Ex 02.

3. Print and close Word C7, Ex 02.

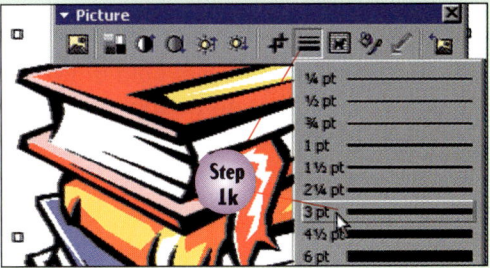

Inserting, Sizing, and Customizing a Clip Art Image

1. At a clear document screen, create the letterhead shown in figure 7.4 by completing the following steps:

   a. Change to Print Layout view.

   b. Change the font to 36-point Brittanic Bold. (If Britannic Bold is not available, choose a typeface similar to the one shown in figure 7.4.)

   c. Key the company name *Movie Madness* and then press Enter.

   d. Change the font size to 18 points and then key the remaining text in the location indicated in figure 7.4 (the street address, city, state, Zip, and Web site address).

   e. Move the insertion point to the beginning of the document.

   f. Insert the image by completing the following steps:

      1) Make sure the Drawing toolbar is displayed. (If the Drawing toolbar is not displayed, position the mouse pointer on the Standard or Formatting toolbar, click the *right* mouse button, and then click Drawing at the drop-down list.)

      2) Click the Insert Clip Art button on the Drawing toolbar.

      3) At the Insert ClipArt dialog box, click the *Entertainment* category in the category list box (contains an image of a microphone).

      4) Click once on the image of a movie projector (see figure 7.4).

      5) At the callout side menu that displays, click the Insert clip button (top button).

      6) Click the Close button that displays in the upper right corner of the dialog box.

   g. Size the image by completing the following steps:

      1) Click once on the clip art image to select it (black sizing handles display).

      2) Position the mouse pointer on the black sizing handle that displays in the

lower right corner until a diagonally pointed, two-headed arrow displays.

   3) Hold down the left mouse button, drag into the image to decrease the size until it measures approximately 2 inches by 2 inches, and then release the mouse button. (Use the horizontal and vertical rulers to help you approximate the size.)

h. Change the text wrapping of the clip art image and move the image by completing the following steps:

   1) With the clip art image selected (black sizing handles display around the image), click the Text Wrapping button on the Picture toolbar.

   2) At the drop-down list that displays, click Through.

   3) Position the mouse pointer (displays as a four-headed arrow) inside the clip art image, hold down the left mouse button, drag the image to the right margin at approximately the same horizontal position as the company name (see figure 7.4), and then release the mouse button.

2. Save the document and name it Word C7, Ex 03.
3. Print and close Word C7, Ex 03.

figure

7.4   *Exercise 3*

Movie Madness
1204 Ridgeway Avenue
Richmond, VA 24365
(804) 555-8880
www.mmadness.com

You can also download images from the online Microsoft Clip Gallery. Click Clips Online in the Insert ClipArt dialog box.

Searching for Clip Art Images

At the Insert ClipArt dialog box, you can search for a clip art image related to a specific topic or subject. To do this, display the Insert ClipArt dialog box, click in the *Search for clips* text box, key the topic or subject, and then press Enter. Word searches through the clip art images and displays those images that match the topic of subject.

exercise   4

Cropping and Adding a Border to a Clip Art Image

1. At a clear document screen, insert a clip art image in a document, add a border to the image, crop the image, and then move the image by completing the following steps:

a. Change to Print Layout view.
b. Click Insert, point to Picture, and then click Clip Art.
c. At the Insert ClipArt dialog box, click in the *Search for clips* text box, key **flags**, and then press Enter.

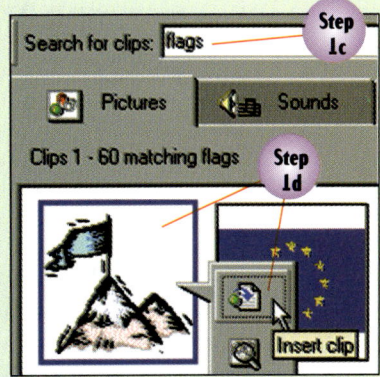

d. Click once on the image shown at the right and then click the Insert clip button.
e. Click the Close button that displays in the upper right corner of the dialog box.
f. Click once on the image to select it.
g. Make sure the Picture toolbar is displayed. (If it is not, position the mouse pointer in the image, click the *right* mouse button, and then click Show Picture Toolbar.)
h. Crop the image so just the flag displays by completing the following steps:

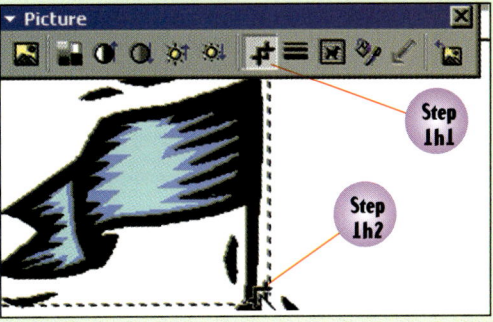

　　1) Click the Crop button on the Picture toolbar.
　　2) Position the mouse pointer on the bottom right sizing handle (the mouse pointer turns into a crop tool, which is a black square with overlapping lines), hold down the left mouse button, drag into the image to isolate the flag as shown at the right, and then release the mouse button.
　　3) If necessary, drag other sizing handles (make sure the mouse pointer turns into the crop tool) until only the flag appears in the image border. (This may take some practice. If you are not satisfied with the result, click the Reset Picture button on the Picture toolbar and try again.)
　　4) With the flag isolated, click the Crop button on the Picture toolbar to turn it off.
i. Increase the size of the clip art image so it is approximately 3 inches by 3 inches.
j. Click the Text Wrapping button on the Picture toolbar and then click Through at the drop-down list. (This changes the sizing handles from black to white.)
k. Move the image so it is centered horizontally between the left and right margins.
l. Add a border line to the image by clicking the Line Style button on the Picture toolbar and clicking the *1¹/₂ pt* option at the drop-down list.
m. Click outside of the image to deselect it.

2. Save the image and name it Word C7, Ex 04.
3. Print and close Word C7, Ex 04.

Drawing Shapes and Lines

With buttons on the Drawing toolbar, you can draw a variety of shapes such as circles, squares, rectangles, and ovals. The Drawing toolbar also allows you to draw straight lines, free form lines, lines with arrowheads, and much more. To display the Drawing toolbar, shown in figure 7.5, click the Drawing button on the Standard toolbar; or, position the mouse pointer on the Standard or Formatting toolbar, click the *right* mouse button, and then click *Drawing* at the drop-down list. A description of each button is provided in figure 7.6. As soon as you click a button on the Drawing toolbar, Word switches to Print Layout view.

7.5 **Drawing Toolbar**

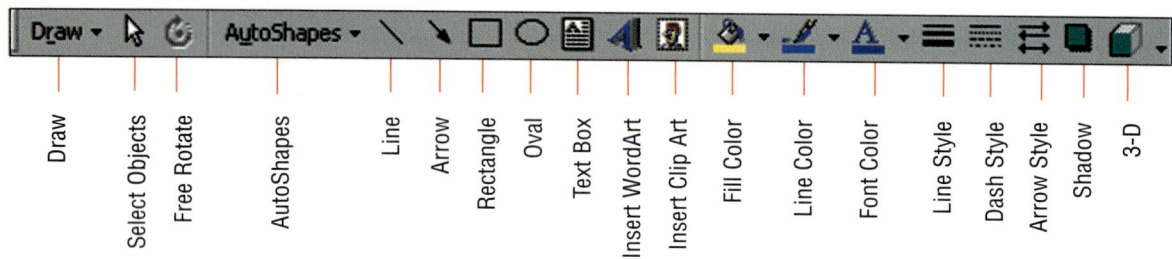

7.6 **Drawing Toolbar Buttons**

Click this button	Named	To do this
Draw ▾	Draw	Display a pop-up menu with options for grouping and positioning drawings.
⬉	Select Objects	Select text or objects.
⟳	Free Rotate	Rotate selected object to any degree by dragging a corner of the object in the desired direction.
AutoShapes ▾	AutoShapes	Display a palette of shapes that can be drawn in a document. (To draw a shape circumscribed within a perfect square, hold down the Shift key while drawing the shape.)
\	Line	Draw a line in a document.
↘	Arrow	Insert a line with an arrowhead. (To draw at 15-degree angles, hold down the Shift key.)

☐	Rectangle	Draw a rectangle in a document. (To draw a perfect square, hold down the Shift key while drawing the shape.)
○	Oval	Draw an oval in a document. (To draw a perfect circle, hold down the Shift key while drawing the shape.)
▣	Text Box	Create text in a text box. (To add text that does not wrap, click the button, click in the document, then key the text. To add text that does wrap, click the button, drag to create a box, then key the text.)
◀	Insert WordArt	Insert a Microsoft Office drawing object to create text effects.
▣	Insert Clip Art	Display the Insert ClipArt dialog box.
▧	Fill Color	Fill selected object with a color, pattern, texture, or shaded fill.
✒	Line Color	Change color of selected line.
A	Font Color	Format selected text with a color.
≡	Line Style	Change thickness of selected line or change it to a compound line.
▦	Dash Style	Change style of selected line, arc, or border to dashed.
⇄	Arrow Style	Add arrowheads to a selected line, arc, or open freeform.
▣	Shadow	Add or remove an object shadow.
▱	3-D	Add or remove a 3-D effect.

With some of the buttons on the Drawing toolbar, you can draw a shape. If you draw a shape with the Line button or the Arrow button, the shape you draw is considered a *line drawing*. If you draw a shape with the Rectangle or Oval button, the shape you draw is considered an *enclosed object*. Later in this chapter you will learn how to add fill color to an enclosed object.

If you want to draw the same shape more than once, double-click the shape's button on the Drawing toolbar. After drawing the shape, click the button again to deactivate it.

Use the Rectangle button on the Drawing toolbar to draw a square or rectangle in a document. If you want to draw a square, hold down the Shift key while drawing the shape. The Shift key keeps all sides of the drawn object equal. Use the Oval button to draw a circle or an oval object. To draw a circle, hold down the Shift key while drawing the object.

Line

Arrow

Rectangle

Oval

exercise 5

Drawing a Circle and Square

1. At a clear document screen, draw a circle and a square by completing the following steps:
   a. Display the Drawing toolbar by clicking the Drawing button on the Standard toolbar. (Skip this step if the Drawing toolbar is already displayed.)
   b. Click the Oval button on the Drawing toolbar.
   c. Position the cross hairs in the document screen toward the left side.
   d. Hold down the Shift key and the left mouse button, drag the mouse down and to the right until the outline image displays as approximately a 2-inch circle, release the mouse button, and then the Shift key.
   e. Click the Rectangle button on the Drawing toolbar.
   f. Position the cross hairs in the document screen toward the right side.
   g. Hold down the Shift key and the left mouse button, drag the mouse down and to the right until the outline image displays as approximately a 2-inch square, release the mouse button, and then release the Shift key.
2. Save the document and name it Word C7, Ex 05.
3. Print and close Word C7, Ex 05.

With the Line button, you can draw a line in the document screen. To do this, click the Line button on the Drawing toolbar. Position the cross hairs where you want to begin the line, hold down the left mouse button, drag the line to the location where you want the line to end, and then release the mouse button.

You can add as many lines as desired in the document screen by repeating the steps above. For example, you can draw a triangle by drawing three lines. If you want to draw more than one line, double-click the Line button. This makes the button active. After drawing all the necessary lines, click the Line button again to deactivate it.

> You can also repeat a line by copying and pasting it as many times as needed.

exercise 6

Creating a Line with the Arrow Button

1. At a clear document screen, create the document shown in figure 7.7 by completing the following steps:
   a. Make sure the Drawing toolbar is displayed.
   b. Change the font to 24-point Copperplate Gothic Bold (or a similar decorative typeface).
   c. Click the Center button on the Formatting toolbar.
   d. Key **Mainline Manufacturing**. (The Copperplate Gothic Bold typeface uses small caps for lowercase letters.)
   e. Press the Enter key.
   f. Click the Arrow button on the Drawing toolbar.

g. Draw the line as shown in figure 7.7. (The line will display with an arrow on one end. This will be changed in the next step. Hold down the Shift key to draw a straight line.)

h. With the line still selected (a white sizing handle displays at each end), click the Arrow Style button on the Drawing toolbar.

i. At the pop-up list that displays, click the second option from the bottom of the list (Arrow Style 10).

j. Click in the document away from the line to deselect it.

2. Save the completed document and name it Word C7, Ex 06.

3. Print and then close Word C7, Ex 06.

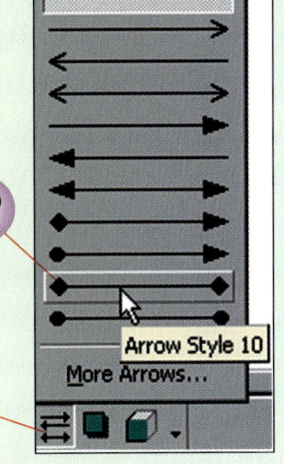

Step 1i

Arrow Style 10

More Arrows...

Step 1h

figure

7.7

Exercise 6

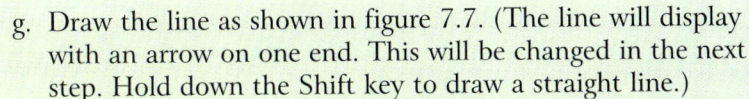

MAINLINE MANUFACTURING

Creating AutoShapes

With options from the AutoShapes button, you can choose from a variety of predesigned shapes. Click the AutoShapes button and a pop-up menu displays. Point to the desired menu option and a side menu displays. This side menu will offer autoshape choices for the selected option. For example, if you point to the Basic Shapes option, a number of shapes such as a circle, square, triangle, box, stop sign, etc., display at the right side of the pop-up menu. Click the desired shape and the mouse pointer turns into cross hairs. Position the cross hairs in the document screen, hold down the left mouse button, drag to create the shape, and then release the button.

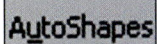

AutoShapes

exercise 7

Writing Your Name

1. At a clear document screen, write your first name by completing the following steps:

   a. Make sure the Drawing toolbar is displayed.

   b. Click the AutoShapes button on the Drawing toolbar, point to Lines, and then click the Scribble button. (The Scribble button is the last button in the bottom

row. Position the mouse pointer on this button and *Scribble* displays after one second in a yellow box.)

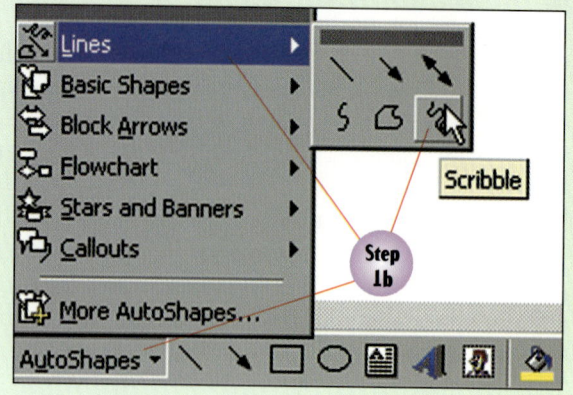

c. Position the mouse pointer in the document screen, hold down the left mouse button, and then move the mouse pointer (a pencil) in the necessary directions to draw your first name. When you release the mouse button, white sizing handles display around your name. If you need to continue drawing your name (for example, to cross a "T"), select the Scribble button again. (If you are not satisfied with the results, make sure white sizing handles display around your name and press the Delete key. Draw your name again.)

2. Save the document and name it Word C7, Ex 07.
3. Print and close Word C7, Ex 07.

Creating Stars

1. At a clear document screen, create a variety of stars by completing the following steps:
   a. Make sure the Drawing toolbar is displayed.
   b. Click the AutoShapes button on the Drawing toolbar, point to Stars and Banners, and then click the 8-Point Star button (first button from the left in the second row from the top).

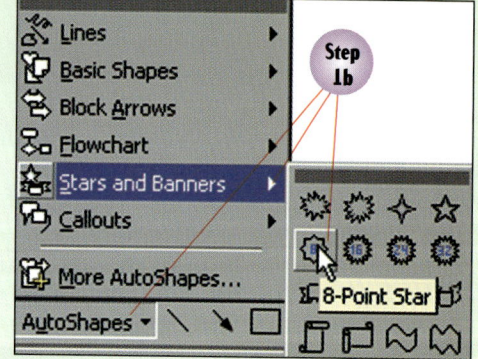

   c. Position the cross hairs in the document screen, hold down the left mouse button, drag the cross hairs to create the star, and then release the mouse button.
   d. The star displays with a small yellow box inside. This box is referred to as an *adjustment handle*. Position the mouse pointer on the adjustment handle, hold down the left mouse button, drag about halfway into the star, and then release the mouse button. (This causes the points of the star to drag into the star.)

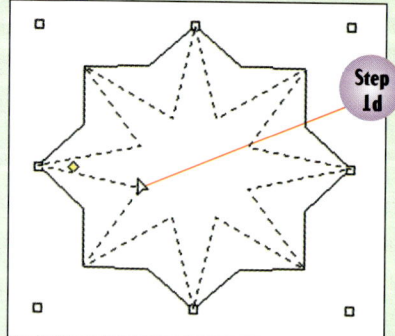

   e. Click the AutoShapes button on the Drawing toolbar, point to Stars and Banners, and then click 16-point Star (second button from the left in the second row from the top).

f. Position the cross hairs in the document screen, hold down the left mouse button, drag the cross hairs to create the star, and then release the mouse button.

g. Use the adjustment handle to drag the points of the star into the star.

h. Experiment with a few other star and/or banner buttons.

2. Save the document and name it Word C7, Ex 08.

3. Print and close Word C7, Ex 08.

Creating a Text Box

With the Text Box button on the Drawing toolbar, you can create a box and insert text inside the box. Text inside a box can be formatted in the normal manner. For example, you can change the font, alignment, or indent of the text.

Text Box

To create a text box, click the Text Box button, position the cross hairs in the document screen where you want the text to appear, hold down the left mouse button, drag to create the box, and then release the mouse button. This causes a box to appear in the drawing area similar to the one shown in figure 7.8. Key the text in the box. If the text you key fills more than the first line in the box, the text wraps to the next line. (The box, however, will not increase in size. If you need more room in the text box, select the box, and then use the sizing handles to make it bigger.)

Text Box

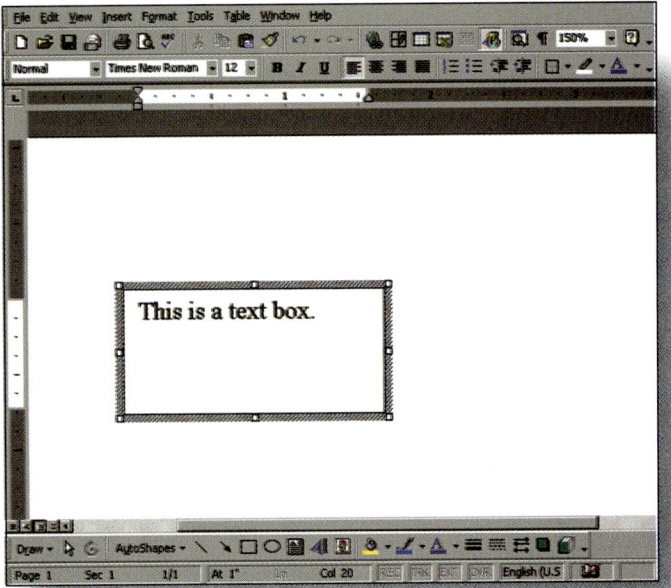

Creating an Oval and Keying Text Inside

1. At a clear document screen, create an oval shape, and then create a text box inside the oval with the words *Linda Shing* and *Superintendent* by completing the following steps:

   a. Make sure the Drawing toolbar is displayed and click the Oval button.

   b. Position the cross hairs in the document screen (approximately below the 1.5-inch mark on the horizontal ruler), hold down the left mouse button, drag the mouse down and to the right until you have drawn an oval that is approximately 3 inches wide and 2 inches tall, and then release the mouse button.

   c. Click the Text Box button.

   d. Draw a text box inside the oval shape from the left side to the right side that is approximately 1 inch tall.

   e. Click the Center button on the Formatting toolbar.

   f. Press the Enter key once.

   g. Key **Linda Shing** in the text box and then press Enter.

   h. Key **Superintendent**. The name and title should be centered in the oval. If not, insert or delete hard returns until the text appears centered.

2. Save the document and name it Word C7, Ex 09.

3. Print and close Word C7, Ex 09.

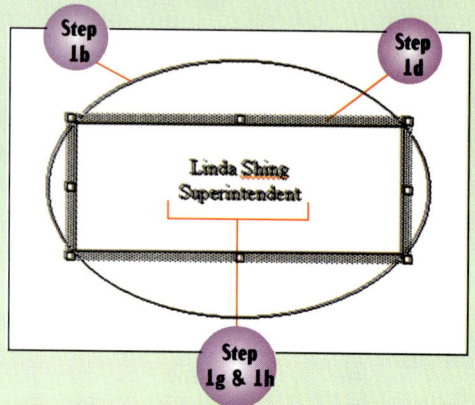

Changing Objects

Shapes drawn by using tools on the Drawing toolbar are referred to as objects. An object can be customized in a variety of ways. For example, an object can be selected and then moved, copied, or deleted; or the size of the object can be changed.

Selecting an Object

After an object has been created in a document, you may decide to make changes or delete the object. To do this, the object must be selected. To select an enclosed object, position the mouse pointer anywhere inside the object (the mouse pointer displays with a four-headed arrow attached) and click the left mouse button. To select a line, position the mouse pointer on the line until the pointer turns into an arrow with a four-headed arrow attached and click the left mouse button. When an object is selected, it displays surrounded by white sizing handles. Once an object is selected, it can be edited (such as changing the fill and the line), moved, or deleted.

   If a document screen contains more than one object, you can select several objects at once using the Select Objects button on the Drawing toolbar. To do

Select Objects

this, click the Select Objects button, position the cross hairs in the upper left corner of the area containing the objects, hold down the left mouse button, drag the outline to the lower right corner of the area containing the objects, and then release the mouse button. You can also select more than one object by holding down the Shift key as you click each object.

Each object in the selected area displays surrounded by white sizing handles. Objects in the selected area are connected. For example, if you move one of the objects in the selected area, the other objects move relatively.

Deleting an Object

An object you have drawn can be deleted from the document screen. To do this, select the object and press the Delete key.

Moving an Object

An object can be moved to a different location in this document. To do this with an enclosed object, position the mouse pointer inside the object (mouse pointer displays with a four-headed arrow attached), hold down the left mouse button, drag the outline of the object to the new location, and then release the mouse button. If you selected more than one object, moving one of the objects will also move the other objects. To move a line, select the line, and then position the mouse pointer on the line until it turns into an arrow with a four-headed arrow attached. Hold down the left mouse button, drag the outline of the line to the desired location, and then release the mouse button.

You can move a selected object with the keyboard by pressing one of the arrow keys. For example, to move an object down the screen, select the object and press the down arrow key.

Copying an Object

Moving an object removes the object from its original position and inserts it into a new location. If you want the object to stay in its original location and an exact copy to be inserted in a new location, use the Ctrl key while dragging the object.

Creating Organizational Boxes in Draw

1. At a clear document screen, create the organizational boxes shown in figure 7.9 by completing the following steps:
   a. With the Drawing toolbar displayed, click the Text Box button.
   b. Draw a text box from approximately the 2-inch mark on the horizontal ruler to the 4-inch mark on the horizontal ruler. Make the box about an inch in height.
   c. Press Enter to move the insertion point down one line inside the text box.
   d. Click the Center button on the Formatting toolbar.
   e. Key **Blaine Dowler**. Press Enter.
   f. Key **Principal**.

g. Position the mouse pointer at the bottom of the text box until it turns into an arrow with a four-headed arrow attached.

h. Hold down the Ctrl key and the left mouse button (this causes the four-headed arrow to change to a plus symbol), drag the outline of the text box down and to the left as shown in figure 7.9, and then release the left mouse button. (Do not release the Ctrl key.)

i. With the Ctrl key still down, and the mouse pointer displayed with the plus symbol attached, hold down the left mouse button, drag the outline of the text box to the right as shown in figure 7.9, release the mouse button, and then release the Ctrl key.

j. After copying the text box, key the names and titles shown in figure 7.9 in the second and third text boxes over the name *Blaine Dowler* and title *Principal*.

2. Save the document and name it Word C7, Ex 10.

3. Print and close Word C7, Ex 10.

Exercise 10

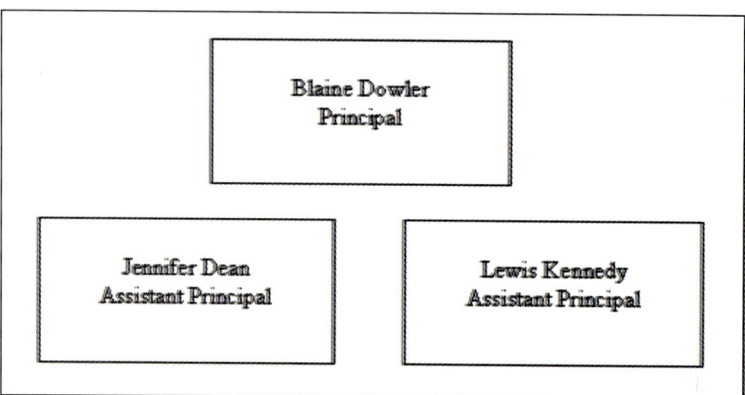

Blaine Dowler
Principal

Jennifer Dean
Assistant Principal

Lewis Kennedy
Assistant Principal

Sizing an Object

With the sizing handles that appear around an object when it is selected, the size of the object can be changed. To change the size of the object, select it, and then position the mouse pointer on a sizing handle until it turns into a double-headed arrow. Hold down the left mouse button, drag the outline of the shape toward or away from the center of the object until it is the desired size, and then release the mouse button.

Creating and Sizing a Text Box

1. At a clear document screen, create a text box, key text in the box, and then size the box by completing the following steps:
   a. With the Drawing toolbar displayed, click the Text Box button and draw a text box in the document screen that is approximately 2 inches wide and 2.5 inches tall.
   b. With the insertion point inside the text box, change the font to 14-point Arial bold.
   c. Click the Center button on the Formatting toolbar.
   d. Key **COLEMAN DEVELOPMENT CORPORATION** (this will wrap).
   e. Press the Enter key.
   f. Key **3451 Classen Boulevard** (this will also wrap).
   g. Press Enter.
   h. Key **Oklahoma City, OK 76341**.
   i. Press Enter.
   j. Key **(801) 555-4500**.
   k. With the text box selected, use the white sizing handles around the text box to make the box wider until the company name displays on one line and you can see all of the text. Make the text box narrower so there is little space between the text and the bottom line of the box.
   l. Drag the text box to the middle of the document screen.
2. Save the document and name it Word C7, Ex 11.
3. Print and close Word C7, Ex 11.

Steps
1d-1j

COLEMAN DEVELOPMENT CORPORATION 3451 Classen Boulevard Oklahoma City, OK 76341 (801) 555-4500

Step
1k

COLEMAN DEVELOPMENT CORPORATION
3451 Classen Boulevard
Oklahoma City, OK 76341
(801) 555-4500

Customizing Objects

With buttons on the Drawing toolbar, you can add fill color or pattern to an enclosed object, change thickness and color of the line that draws the object, and change the position of the object.

Adding Fill Shading or Color

Use the Fill Color button on the Drawing toolbar to add shading or color to an enclosed object such as a shape or a text box. To add shading or color, select the object, and then click the Fill Color button. This will fill the object with the fill color displayed on the Fill Color button. If you want to choose a different color, select the object, and then click the down-pointing triangle at the right side of the Fill Color button. This causes a palette of color choices to display. At this palette, click the desired fill color.

Fill Color

The Fill Color palette also includes two options—<u>M</u>ore Fill Colors and <u>F</u>ill Effects. Click the <u>M</u>ore Fill Colors option and the Colors dialog box shown in figure 7.10 displays. At this dialog box, click the desired color in the <u>C</u>olors section, and then click OK.

Colors Dialog Box with Standard Tab Selected

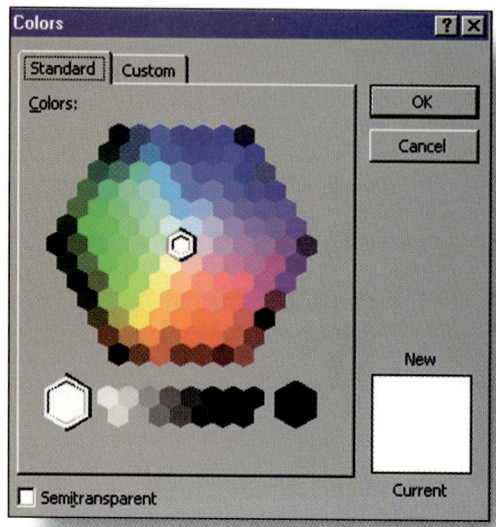

Click the other option at the Fill Color palette, <u>F</u>ill Effects, and the Fill Effects dialog box shown in figure 7.11 displays. At this dialog box, you can specify the number of colors, a shading style, and a shading variant. Make the desired choices at this dialog box and click OK.

Fill Effects Dialog Box with Gradient Tab Selected

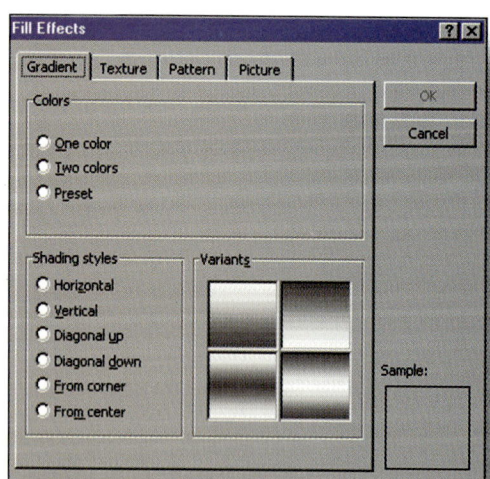

Changing Line Color

A line, shape, or text box is drawn with a black line. The color of this line can be
changed with the Line Color button on the Drawing toolbar. Select an object and
click the Line Color button; the line color of the selected object changes to the
color displayed on the button. If you want to choose a different color, select the
object and then click the down-pointing triangle at the right side of the Line
Color button. This causes a palette of color choices to display. At this palette,
click the desired color.

Line Color

The Line Color palette also includes two options—More Line Colors and
Patterned Lines. Click the More Line Colors option and the Colors dialog box
shown in figure 7.10 displays. Click the Patterned Lines option and the Patterned
Lines dialog box shown in figure 7.12 displays. Choose a pattern and a
foreground and/or or background color for the object at this dialog box.

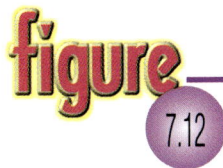

Patterned Lines Dialog Box

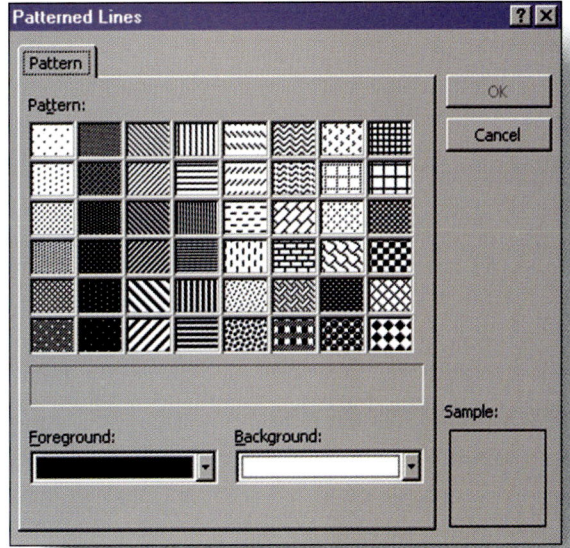

In some situations, you may want to remove the line around an object. For
example, you may want to remove the lines of a text box after text has been
added to it. To remove lines, select the object, click the down-pointing triangle at
the right side of the Line Color button, and then click *No Line* at the pop-up
menu.

Changing Fill Color

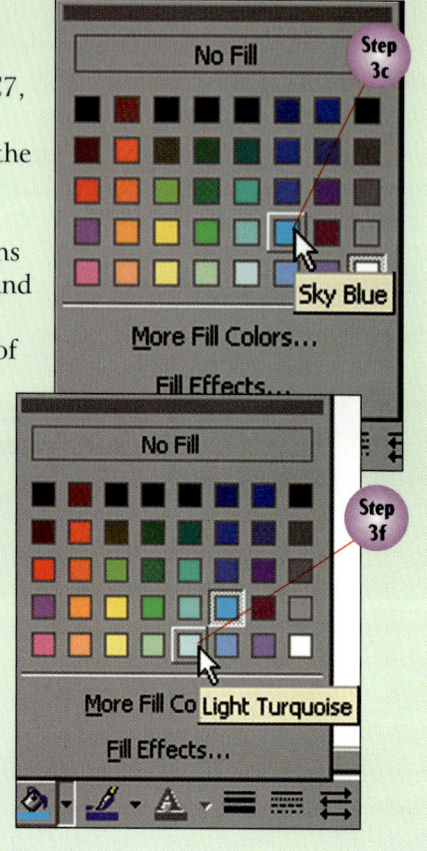

1. Open Word C7, Ex 09.
2. Save the document with Save As and name it Word C7, Ex 12.
3. Change the fill color of the oval shape by completing the following steps:
   a. Select the oval shape by positioning the mouse pointer on the line that forms the oval until it turns into an arrow with a four-headed arrow attached and then clicking the left mouse button.
   b. Click the down-pointing triangle at the right side of the Fill Color button on the Drawing toolbar.
   c. At the palette that displays, click the Sky Blue color (the sixth color from the left in the second row from the bottom).
   d. Select the text box.
   e. Click the down-pointing triangle at the right side of the Fill Color button on the Drawing toolbar.
   f. At the palette that displays, click the Light Turquoise color (the fifth color from the left in the bottom row).
   g. Deselect the text box.
4. Save the document again with the same name (Word C7, Ex 12).
5. Print and close Word C7, Ex 12.

Changing Line Style

Line Style

By default, Word draws shapes and text boxes with a thin black line. This line can be changed to various thicker lines or combinations of thick and thin lines. To change the line style, click the Line Style button and then click the desired line style at the pop-up menu that displays. Click the More Lines option at the pop-up menu and the Format AutoShape dialog box displays with the Colors and Lines tab selected as shown in figure 7.13. Use the options in this dialog box to change the Line Color, Style, or Weight.

figure
7.13

Format AutoShape Dialog Box with Colors and Lines Tab Selected

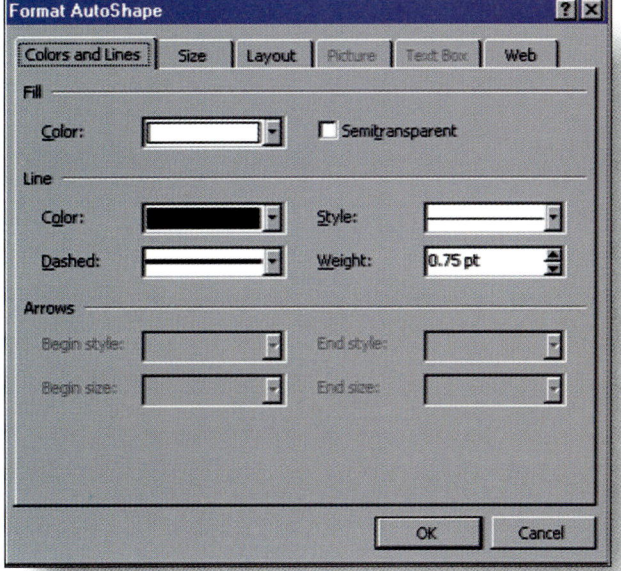

Click the Dash Style button if you want to draw an object with a dashed line. Clicking this button causes a pop-up list to display containing dashed line options.

Adding Shadow and 3-D Effects

Click the Shadow button on the Drawing toolbar and a palette of shadow options displays. Click the desired option or click the Shadow Settings option and a Shadow Settings toolbar displays. This toolbar contains buttons for turning shadows off or on and buttons for nudging the shadow up, down, left, or right.

If you want to add a three-dimensional look to an object, select the object, and then click the 3-D button on the Drawing toolbar. This displays a palette of three-dimensional choices as well as a 3-D Settings option. Click this option and the 3-D Settings toolbar displays. This toolbar contains buttons for turning 3-D on or off and changing the tilt, depth, direction, and light source.

Dash Style

Shadow

3-D

Changing Line Style and Color

1. Open Word C7, Ex 10.
2. Save the document with Save As and name it Word C7, Ex 13.
3. Change the line style and color of the top box by completing the following steps:
   a. Position the I-beam pointer on one of the lines of the text box containing the name *Blaine Dowler* until it turns into an arrow with a four-headed arrow attached and then double-click the left mouse button. (This displays the Format Text Box dialog box.)
   b. At the Format Text Box dialog box, click the Colors and Lines tab.
   c. Select the current point size measurement in the <u>W</u>eight text box and then key **4**.
   d. Click the down-pointing triangle to the right of the <u>C</u>olor option in the Fill section and then click the Red color (first color from the left in the third row).
   e. Click OK or press Enter to close the Format Text Box dialog box.
4. Complete steps similar to those in 3 to change the line style and color for the text box at the left (containing the name *Jennifer Dean*).
5. Complete steps similar to those in 3 to change the line style and color for the text box at the right (containing the name *Lewis Kennedy*).
6. Save the document again with the same name (Word C7, Ex 13).
7. Print and close Word C7, Ex 13.

Step 3b

Step 3c

Step 3d

Adding a 3-D Effect

1. Open Word C7, Ex 13.
2. Save the document with Save As and name it Word C7, Ex 14.
3. Add a 3-D effect to all three text boxes at once by completing the following steps:
   a. Select the first text box at the top of the page.
   b. Hold Shift and click the text box in the second row at the left side of the page.
   c. Hold Shift and click the text box in the second row at the right side of the page. All three text boxes should now have sizing handles displayed around them. Any options selected will affect all three boxes.
   d. Click the 3-D button on the Drawing toolbar and select 3-D Style 1 (first button at the left in the first row of 3-D Styles).

4. Print Word C7, Ex 14.
5. Experiment with a few other 3-D options to view the various effects.
6. Experiment with the options available for customizing a 3-D effect by clicking the 3-D Settings option and trying the various buttons on the 3-D Settings toolbar. When you are finished using the toolbar, click the Close button located in the upper right corner of the 3-D Settings toolbar to turn it off.
7. Save the document again with the same name (Word C7, Ex 14).
8. Print and close Word C7, Ex 14.

Using WordArt

With the WordArt application, you can distort or modify text to conform to a variety of shapes. This is useful for creating company logos and headings. With WordArt, you can change the font, style, and alignment of text. You can also use different fill patterns and colors, customize border lines, and add shadow and three-dimensional effects.

There are a variety of methods for displaying the WordArt Gallery shown in figure 7.14. You can click the Insert WordArt button on the Drawing toolbar; click Insert, point to Picture, and then WordArt; or click the Insert WordArt button on the WordArt toolbar shown in figure 7.15. To display the WordArt toolbar, click View, point to Toolbars, and then click WordArt; or, position the mouse pointer on a toolbar, click the *right* mouse button, and then click WordArt at the drop-down menu.

Insert WordArt

figure

7.14

WordArt Gallery

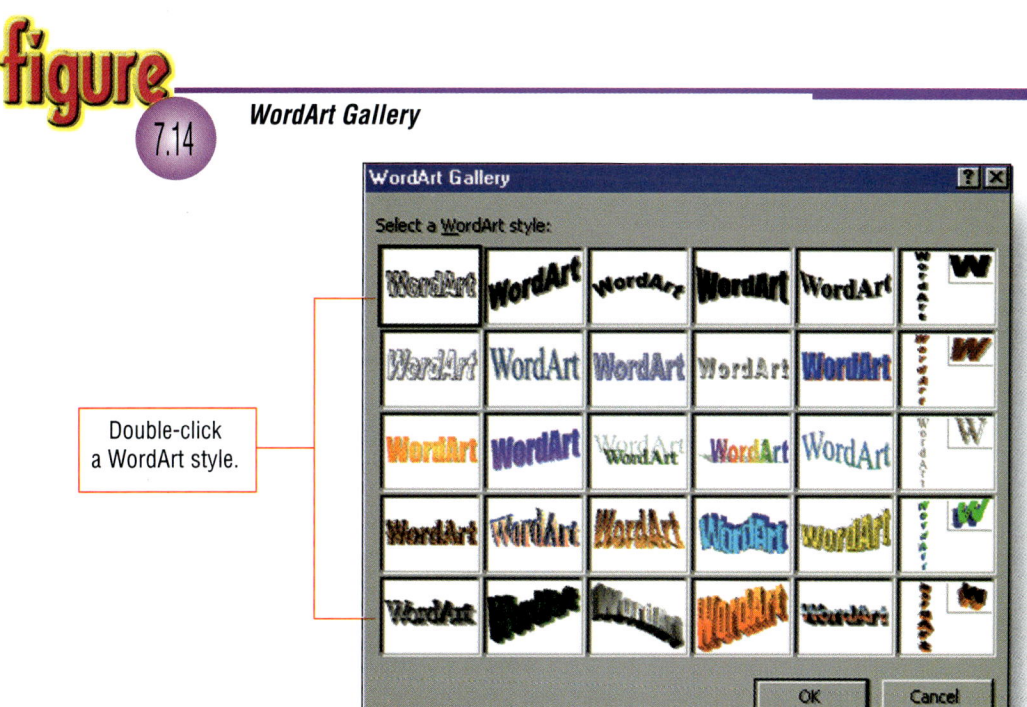

Double-click a WordArt style.

figure 7.15

WordArt Toolbar

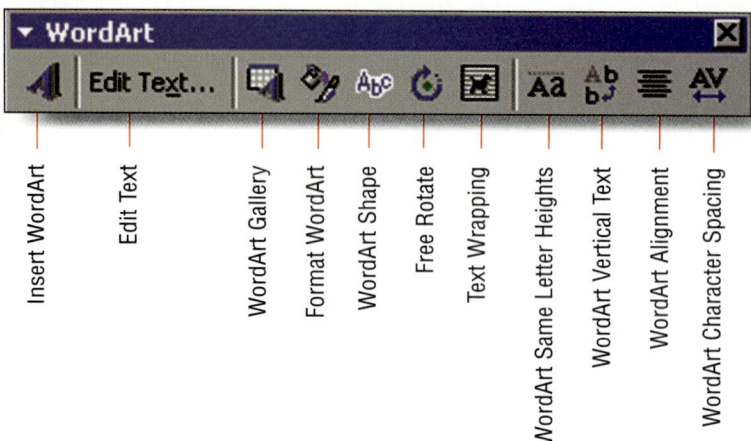

Entering Text

Double-click a WordArt style at the WordArt Gallery and the Edit WordArt Text dialog box displays as shown in figure 7.16. At the Edit WordArt Text dialog box, the words *Your Text Here* are automatically selected in the Text box. Key the text in the text box and the existing words are replaced with the text you have keyed. Press the Enter key if you want to move the insertion point to the next line. After keying the desired text, click the OK button.

figure 7.16

Edit WordArt Text Dialog Box

Key the desired WordArt text, apply a different font or size, and then click OK.

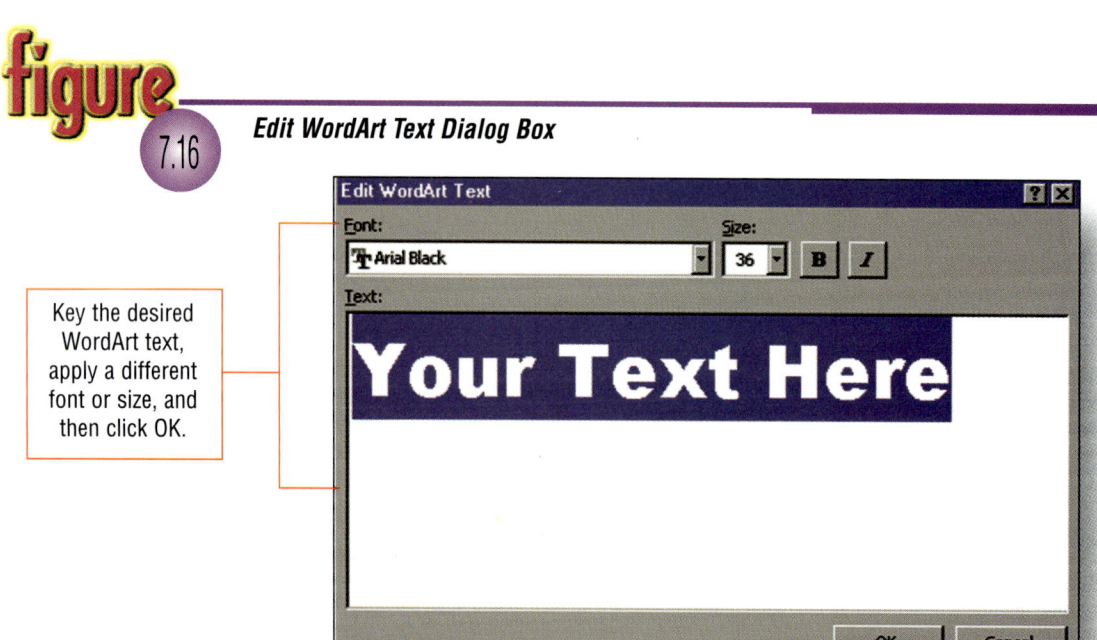

Creating a Heading with WordArt

1. At a clear document screen, create the heading shown in figure 7.17 using WordArt by completing the following steps:

    a. At a clear document screen, press Enter seven times, and then move the insertion point back up to the first line.

    b. Display the Drawing toolbar.

    c. Click the Insert WordArt button on the Drawing toolbar.

    d. At the WordArt Gallery, double-click the second option from the left in the fourth row.

    e. At the Edit WordArt Text dialog box, key **Pacific Security Systems**.

    f. Click OK to close the dialog box.

    g. Create the line below the company name by completing the following steps:

        1) Click the Arrow button on the Drawing toolbar.

        2) Draw a horizontal line as shown in figure 7.17.

        3) With the horizontal line selected, change the arrow style by clicking the Arrow Style button on the Drawing toolbar, and then clicking the second option from the bottom (Arrow Style 10).

        4) Increase the width of the line by clicking the Line Style button on the Drawing toolbar and then clicking the *3 pt* line at the pop-up menu.

        5) Change the color of the horizontal line by clicking the down-pointing triangle at the right side of the Line Color button and clicking the Blue-Gray color (second color option from the *right* in the second row from the top).

2. Deselect the line.

3. Save the document and name it Word C7, Ex 15.

4. Print and close Word C7, Ex 15.

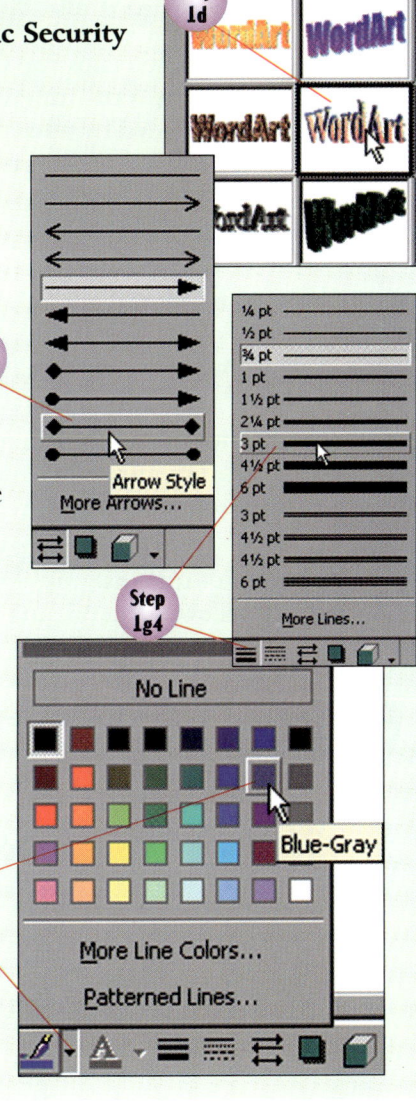

figure 7.17

Exercise 15

Sizing and Moving WordArt

When you click the OK button, the WordArt text is displayed in the document with the formatting you selected at the WordArt Gallery. The WordArt text is surrounded by white sizing handles and the WordArt toolbar displays near the text.

Use the white sizing handles to change the height and width of the WordArt text. Use the yellow diamond located at the bottom of the WordArt text to change the slant of the WordArt text. To do this, position the mouse pointer on the yellow diamond, hold down the left mouse button, drag to the left or right, and then release the mouse button. This moves the yellow diamond along the bottom of the WordArt and changes the slant of the text.

To move WordArt text, position the mouse pointer on any letter of the text until the mouse pointer displays with a four-headed arrow attached. Hold down the left mouse button, drag the outline of the WordArt text box to the desired position, and then release the mouse button.

When all changes have been made to the WordArt text, click outside the WordArt text box. This removes from the screen the white sizing handles, the yellow diamond, and the WordArt toolbar.

Creating, Moving, and Sizing WordArt Text

1. At a clear document screen, create, move, and size WordArt text by completing the following steps:
   a. Click the Insert WordArt button on the Drawing toolbar.
   b. At the WordArt Gallery, double-click the fourth option from the left in the third row.
   c. At the Edit WordArt Text dialog box, key **Marsdon Spring Festival**.
   d. Click OK to close the dialog box.

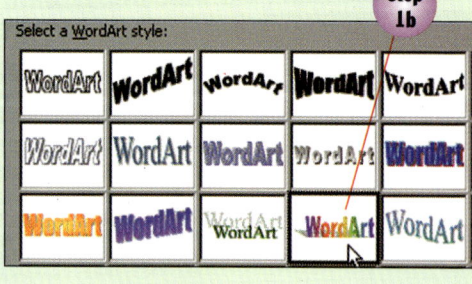

Step 1b

e. Increase the size of the WordArt text by completing the following steps:
   1) Click the Zoom button on the Standard toolbar and click *Whole Page* at the drop-down list.
   2) If the WordArt toolbar displays over the WordArt text, drag the toolbar out of the way. (To do this, position the mouse pointer on the blue title bar that displays at the top of the toolbar. Hold down the left mouse button, drag the toolbar to a more desirable position, and then release the mouse button.)
   3) Make the WordArt text twice as big by positioning the mouse pointer on the middle sizing handle at the bottom of the WordArt text box, drag down until the height of the box is approximately doubled, and then release the mouse button.
f. Position the mouse pointer (turns into a four-headed arrow) inside the WordArt text box, hold down the left mouse button, drag the text box so it is centered horizontally and vertically on the page, and then release the mouse button.

Step
1e3

2. Click outside the WordArt text box to deselect it.
3. Save the document and name it Word C7, Ex 16.
4. Print and close Word C7, Ex 16.

Changing the Font and Font Size

The font for WordArt text will vary depending on the choice you make at the WordArt Gallery. You can change the font at the Edit WordArt text dialog box with the Font option. To do this, click the down-pointing triangle at the right side of the Font text box. This causes a drop-down menu of font choices to display. Scroll through the list until the desired font is visible and then click the desired font.

The font size can be changed by clicking the down-pointing triangle at the right side of the Size text box. This causes a drop-down list of size options to display. Scroll through the list of sizes until the desired size is visible and click the size.

The Edit WordArt Text dialog box contains Bold and Italic buttons. Click the Bold button to apply bold formatting to the WordArt text and click the Italic button to apply italic formatting.

Customizing WordArt

The WordArt toolbar contains buttons for customizing WordArt text. Figure 7.15 displays the WordArt toolbar with the buttons identified. Click the Insert WordArt button and the WordArt Gallery shown in figure 7.14 displays. You can also display this gallery by clicking the WordArt Gallery button on the WordArt toolbar. Click the Edit Text button and the Edit WordArt Text dialog box displays.

Customizing WordArt with Options at the Format WordArt Dialog Box

WordArt text can be customized at the Format WordArt dialog box shown in figure 7.18. To display this dialog box, click the Format WordArt button on the WordArt toolbar.

figure

7.18

Format WordArt Dialog Box with Colors and Lines Tab Selected

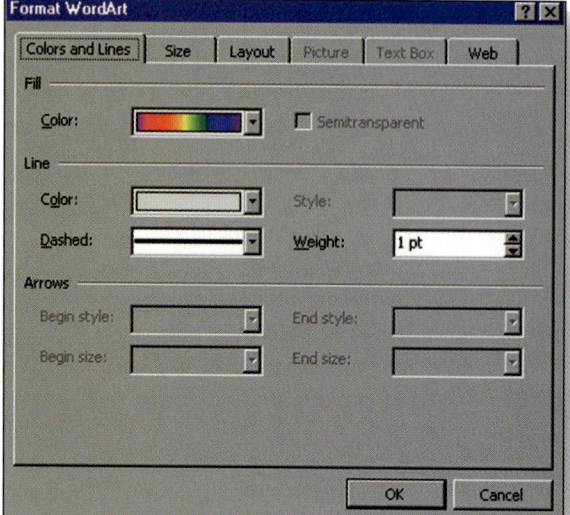

Change the color of the WordArt text and the line creating the text at the Format WordArt dialog box with the Colors and Lines tab selected. Click the Size tab and the dialog box displays options for changing the size and rotation of the WordArt text as well as the scale of the text. If you want to specify how document text will wrap around WordArt text, click the Layout tab. This displays a dialog box with options for specifying the wrapping style of text and horizontal alignment of the WordArt. Click the Advanced button at the Format WordArt dialog box with the Layout tab selected and additional options display for choosing horizontal and vertical alignment and choosing a wrapping style.

Changing Shapes

WordArt
Shape

The WordArt Gallery contains a variety of predesigned WordArt options. Formatting is already applied to these gallery choices. You can, however, customize the gallery choices with buttons on the WordArt toolbar. Use options from the WordArt Shape button to customize the shape of WordArt text. Click the WordArt Shape button on the WordArt toolbar and a palette of shape choices displays as shown in figure 7.19.

WordArt Shape Palette

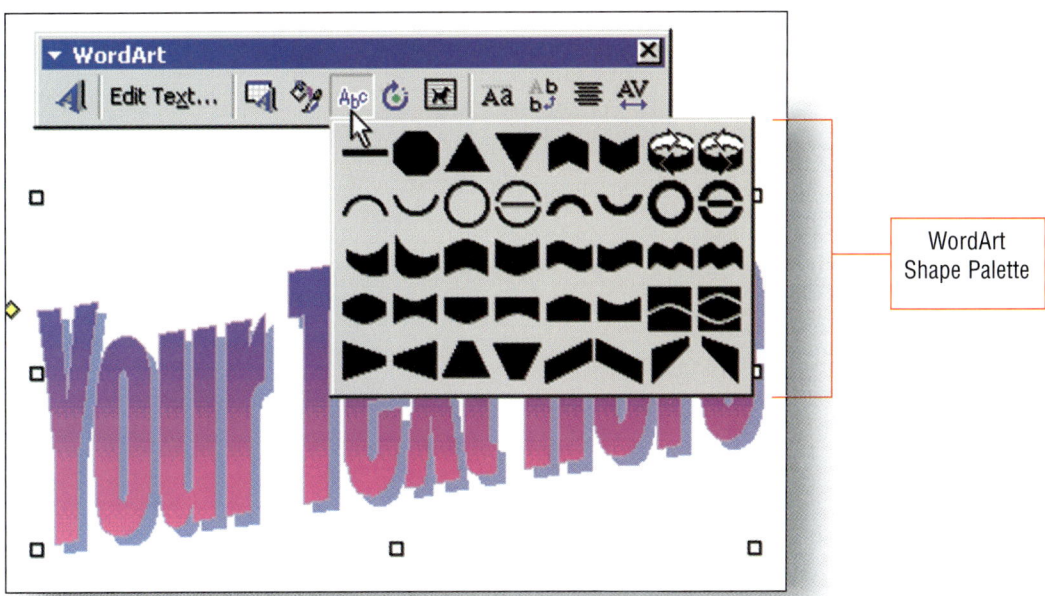

WordArt
Shape Palette

exercise 17

Creating, Shaping, and Sizing WordArt Text

1. At a clear document screen, create WordArt text, and then shape and size the text by completing the following steps:
    a. Click the Insert WordArt button on the Drawing toolbar.
    b. At the WordArt Gallery, double-click the fifth option from the left in the top row.

    Step 1b

    c. At the Edit WordArt Text dialog box, key **Sierra Heights Engineering Services**. Press the space bar once after keying **Services**.
    d. Click the OK button.
    e. Change the shape of the WordArt text by completing the following steps:

    Step 1e1   Step 1e2

    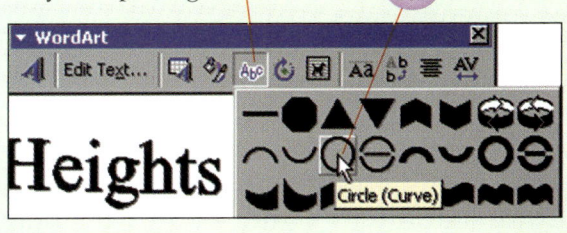

        1) Click the WordArt Shape button.
        2) At the palette of shape choices, click the third shape from the left in the second row (Circle [Curve]).

f. Change the size and color of the WordArt text by completing the following steps:
   1) Click the Format WordArt button on the WordArt toolbar.
   2) If necessary, click the Colors and Lines tab at the Format WordArt dialog box.
   3) At the Format WordArt dialog box with the Colors and Lines tab selected, click the down-pointing triangle to the right of the Color box in the Fill section.
   4) At the color palette that displays, click the Sea Green color (fourth color option from the left in the third row).

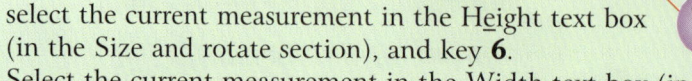

   5) Click the Size tab.
   6) At the Format WordArt dialog box with the Size tab selected, select the current measurement in the Height text box (in the Size and rotate section), and key **6**.
   7) Select the current measurement in the Width text box (in the Size and rotate section) and key **6**.
   8) Click OK to close the Format WordArt dialog box.
   9) Make sure the WordArt text is centered between the left and right margins. If necessary, drag the WordArt text to the center.

g. Click outside the WordArt text (this deselects the WordArt text box).

2. Save the document and name it Word C7, Ex 17.
3. Print and close Word C7, Ex 17.

Rotating WordArt Text

Free Rotate

Click the Free Rotate button on the WordArt toolbar and small green circles display in each corner of the WordArt box. Use these rotation handles to rotate the WordArt text. To do this, position the mouse pointer on one of the small green circles until a circled arrow displays and the mouse pointer disappears. Hold down the left mouse button and the circled arrow changes to four arrows in a circle. With the left mouse button held down, drag the outline of the WordArt box to the desired rotation, and then release the mouse button.

Changing Letter Height

WordArt Same
Letter Heights

By default, the height of WordArt uppercase letters will be greater than the height of lowercase letters. If you want all letters to have the same height, click the WordArt Same Letter Heights button on the WordArt toolbar.

Changing Vertical Alignment

WordArt
Verticle Text

WordArt text displays in a horizontal orientation. This can be changed to a vertical orientation by clicking the WordArt Vertical Text button on the WordArt toolbar.

Changing Text Alignment

WordArt
Alignment

Text in a WordArt text box is center aligned by default. With options from the WordArt Alignment button on the WordArt toolbar, this alignment can be changed. When you click the WordArt Alignment button, a drop-down list displays with the following options: Left Align, Center, Right Align, Word Justify, Letter Justify, and Stretch Justify.

Click the Left Align option if you want text aligned at the left side of the WordArt text box. Click Right Align to align text at the right side of the text box. Choose the Word Justify option to space the words to fit in the WordArt box. Use the Letter Justify option to space out the letters to fit in the WordArt box. Click the last option, Stretch Justify, to stretch letters to fit in the WordArt box.

Changing Character Spacing

Click the WordArt Character Spacing button on the WordArt toolbar and a drop-down list displays with options for determining character spacing. By default, the Normal option is selected at the WordArt Character Spacing drop-down list. Choose one of the other options to either tighten up or loosen the spacing between characters. These options include Very Tight, Tight, Loose, Very Loose, and Custom.

WordArt
Character
Spacing

Kerning is a term that refers to the decrease of space between specific letters pairs. By default, the Kern Character Pairs option is selected. If you do not want letter pairs kerned, remove the check mark from this option.

exercise 18

Creating and Customizing WordArt Text

1. At a clear document screen, create WordArt text, change the font, and then customize the text by completing the following steps:
   a. Click the Insert WordArt button on the Drawing toolbar.
   b. At the WordArt Gallery, double-click the second option from the left in the second row.
   c. Key the text in the Edit WordArt Text dialog box and change the font as follows:
      1) Key **Now is the time**.
      2) Press Enter and key **to get out and**
      3) Press Enter and key **vote!**.
      4) Change the font to Braggadocio. If Braggadocio is not available, choose another sans serif font such as Arial.
      5) Click the OK button to close the dialog box.
   d. Change the alignment, size, and position of the WordArt text by completing the following steps:
      1) Click the WordArt Alignment button on the WordArt toolbar and click Letter Justify at the drop-down list.
      2) Change the size of the WordArt by completing the following steps:
         a) Click the Format WordArt button on the WordArt toolbar.
         b) At the Format WordArt dialog box, click the Size tab.

Step
1d1

c) At the Format WordArt dialog box with the Size tab selected, select the current measurement in the He̲ight text box (in the Size and rotate section), and key **2.5**.

d) Select the current measurement in the Wi̲dth text box (in the Size and rotate section) and key **6**.

e) Click OK to close the Format WordArt dialog box.

f) Click the WordArt Character Spacing button on the WordArt toolbar and select T̲ight at the pop-up menu.

g) Change the Zoom to 50%, then move the WordArt text until it appears centered between the left and right margins.

h) Click outside the WordArt text box to deselect it.

2. Save the document and name it Word C7, Ex 18.

3. Print and close Word C7, Ex 18.

WordArt can also be customized using buttons from the Drawing toolbar. For example, you can change the fill color, border line, and add shadow and 3-D effects. Select the WordArt object, then apply the desired options.

chapter summary

➤ Clip art images are available at the Insert ClipArt dialog box and are grouped by categories. Click a category in the category list box to display specific clip art images.

➤ Maneuver through categories and clip art at the Insert ClipArt dialog box using buttons on the toolbar. Click the Back button to display clip art for the previously selected category or click the All Categories to redisplay all categories.

➤ Use the sizing handles around a selected clip art image to size the image.

➤ Choose a text wrapping style and the black sizing handles around a selected clip art image change to white sizing handles.

➤ Move a clip art image by selecting the image with white sizing handles and then use the mouse to drag the image to the desired position.

➤ The Picture toolbar contains buttons for formatting a clip art image.

➤ Create your own shapes and images with buttons on the Drawing toolbar.

➤ Display the Drawing toolbar by clicking the Drawing button on the Standard toolbar; or, by positioning the mouse pointer on the Standard or Formatting toolbar, clicking the *right* mouse button, and then clicking *Drawing* at the drop-down list.

➤ A shape drawn with the Line or Arrow buttons is considered a line drawing. A shape drawn with the Rectangle or Oval buttons is considered an enclosed object. Fill color can be added to enclosed objects.

➤ Click the Line button to draw a line in the document screen. To draw more than one line, double-click the Line button.

➤ A variety of predesigned shapes is available from the A̲utoShapes button on the Drawing toolbar.

➤ Create a text box by clicking the Text Box button on the Drawing toolbar and then drawing the box in the document screen.

➤ A text box can be drawn inside of a drawn shape.

➤ To select an enclosed object, position the mouse pointer anywhere inside the object and then click the left mouse button. To select a line, position the mouse pointer on the line until the pointer turns into an arrow with a four-headed arrow attached, and then click the left mouse button.

➤ To select several objects at once, click the Select Objects buttons, position the cross hairs in the upper left corner of the area containing the objects, hold down the left mouse button, drag the outline to the lower right corner of the area containing the objects, and then release the mouse button. You can also select more than one object by holding down the Shift key and then clicking each object.

➤ To delete an object, select it and press the Delete key.

➤ To move an object, select it, choose a wrapping style, and then drag the image to the desired location.

➤ To copy an object, select it, and then hold down the Ctrl key. Drag the outline of the object to the desired location, release the mouse button, and then release the Ctrl key.

➤ Use the sizing handles that display around a selected object to increase or decrease the size of the object.

➤ Add fill color to an enclosed object with the Fill Color button on the Drawing toolbar.

➤ Change the line color with the Line Color button on the Drawing toolbar.

➤ Change the line style with the Line Style, Dash Style, or Arrow Style buttons on the Drawing toolbar.

➤ Add a shadow effect to an object with options from the Shadow button on the Drawing toolbar.

➤ Add a three-dimensional effect to an object with options from the 3-D button on the Drawing toolbar.

➤ With the WordArt application, you can distort or modify text to conform to a variety of shapes. With WordArt, you can change the font, size, and alignment of text. You can also add fill color, line color, change the line style, and add shadow and three-dimensional effects.

➤ Display the WordArt Gallery by clicking Insert, pointing to Picture, and then clicking WordArt or by clicking the Insert WordArt button on the Drawing or WordArt toolbar. Select an option at the WordArt Gallery by double-clicking the desired option.

➤ After choosing an option at the WordArt Gallery, the Edit WordArt Text dialog box displays. Key the desired WordArt text in this dialog box.

➤ Use the white sizing handles around WordArt text to change the size.

➤ Move WordArt text by positioning the arrow pointer on any letter until it displays with a four-headed arrow, hold down the left mouse button, move the outline of the WordArt box to the desired position, and then release the mouse button.

➤ Specify a font and font size for WordArt at the Edit WordArt Text dialog box.

➤ Create and customize WordArt with buttons on the Drawing and the WordArt toolbar.

commands review

	Mouse/Keyboard
Display Insert ClipArt dialog box	Insert, Picture, Clip Art
Display Drawing toolbar	Position mouse pointer on Standard or Formatting toolbar, click the *right* mouse button, and then click *Drawing* at the drop-down list.
WordArt Gallery	Click Insert, point to Picture, click WordArt; or click the Insert WordArt button on the Drawing or WordArt toolbar
Format WordArt dialog box	Click the Format WordArt button on WordArt toolbar

thinking offline

Completion: In the space provided at the right, indicate the correct term, command, or number.

1. Use the sizing handles positioned at this location in a selected clip art image to change both the width and height at the same time.

2. Use buttons on this toolbar to customize a clip art image.

3. The Insert ClipArt dialog box can be opened by clicking the Insert Clip Art button on this toolbar.

4. Choose a variety of predesigned shapes by first clicking this button on the Drawing toolbar.

5. If the Normal view is selected, clicking any button on the Drawing toolbar causes Word to change to this view.

6. To create a box and then insert text inside the box, begin by clicking this button on the Drawing toolbar.

7. To draw a perfect circle, click the Oval button on the Drawing toolbar, hold down this key, and then draw the circle.

8. If you want to draw the same shape more than once, do this on the shape button on the Drawing toolbar.

9. Click the Insert WordArt button on the Drawing toolbar and this displays on the screen.

10. Click this button on the WordArt toolbar to display a palette of shape options.

11. In the space provided below, write the steps you would complete to insert into a document a clip art image of a computer disk.

working hands-on

Assessment 1

1. At a clear document screen, create the letterhead shown in figure 7.20 with the following specifications:
   a. Insert the clip art image shown in the figure. (Look for this clip art in the *Academic* category. If this image is not available, choose a different image.)
   b. Change the width of the image to approximately 2 inches and the height to approximately 1.75 inches.
   c. Click the Text Wrapping button on the Picture toolbar and then click <u>S</u>quare at the drop-down list.
   d. Key the text right aligned as shown in figure 7.20. Set the company name in 20-point Goudy Old Style bold, the address and telephone number in 18-point Goudy Old Style bold, and the Web site address in 14-point Goudy Old Style bold. If the Goudy Old Style font is not available, choose another serif font.
2. Save the document and name it Word C7, SA 01.
3. Print and close Word C7, SA 01.

figure

7.20

Assessment 1

THE BOOKWORM
3410 Cascade Drive
Portland, OR 97044
(509) 555-3411
www.bookworm.com

Assessment 2

1. Open Word Notice 03.
2. Save the document with Save As and name it Word C7, SA 02.
3. Make the following changes to the document:
   a. Change the font for all text in the document to a serif typeface and type size of your choosing.
   b. Center all the text in the document.
   c. Read the text in the document, then insert an appropriate clip art image from the Insert ClipArt dialog box.
   d. Size and position the clip art appropriately.
   e. Use the buttons on the Picture toolbar to further customize the image. For example, adjust the contrast or brightness.
4. Save the document again with the same name (Word C7, SA 02).
5. Print and close Word C7, SA 02.

Assessment 3

1. At a clear document screen, create the organizational boxes shown in figure 7.21 with the following specifications:
   a. Key the title bolded and centered as shown in the figure.
   b. Press the Enter key three times and then create the first text box with the following specifications:
      1) Change the font to 12-point Arial bold.
      2) Key the text in the first box as shown in figure 7.21.
      3) Add Pale Blue fill to the text box.
   c. After creating the first text box, copy the text box the number of times needed for the document. Change the title inside the boxes as shown in figure 7.21.
   e. Select the title *DEPARTMENT OF TRAINING AND EDUCATION* and then change the font to 14-point Arial bold.
2. Save the document and name it Word C7, SA 03.
3. Print and close Word C7, SA 03.

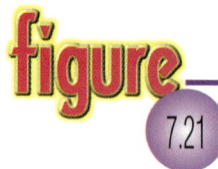

Assessment 3

DEPARTMENT OF TRAINING AND EDUCATION

Director

Trainer

Trainer

Assistant

Assistant

Assessment 4

1. At a clear document screen, create the object shown in figure 7.22 with the following specifications:
    a. Create the star with the 16-Point Star autoshape. Make the star approximately 5.5 inches wide and 4.5 inches tall. (Use the adjustment handle to drag in the points slightly.)
    b. Add light yellow fill to the star.
    c. Draw a text box inside the star.
    d. Key the text shown inside the star in figure 7.22. Set the name *Taylor Ewing* in 28-point Impact bold. (If Impact is not available, choose a similar typeface.) Set the remaining text in 18-point Impact bold.
    e. With the text box selected, remove the black line, and then add light yellow fill. (To remove the black line from the text box, click the down-pointing triangle at the right side of the Line Color button on the Drawing toolbar, and then click *No Line* at the palette of color choices.)
2. Save the document and name it Word C7, SA 04.
3. Print and close Word C7, SA 04.

figure

7.22   **Assessment 4**

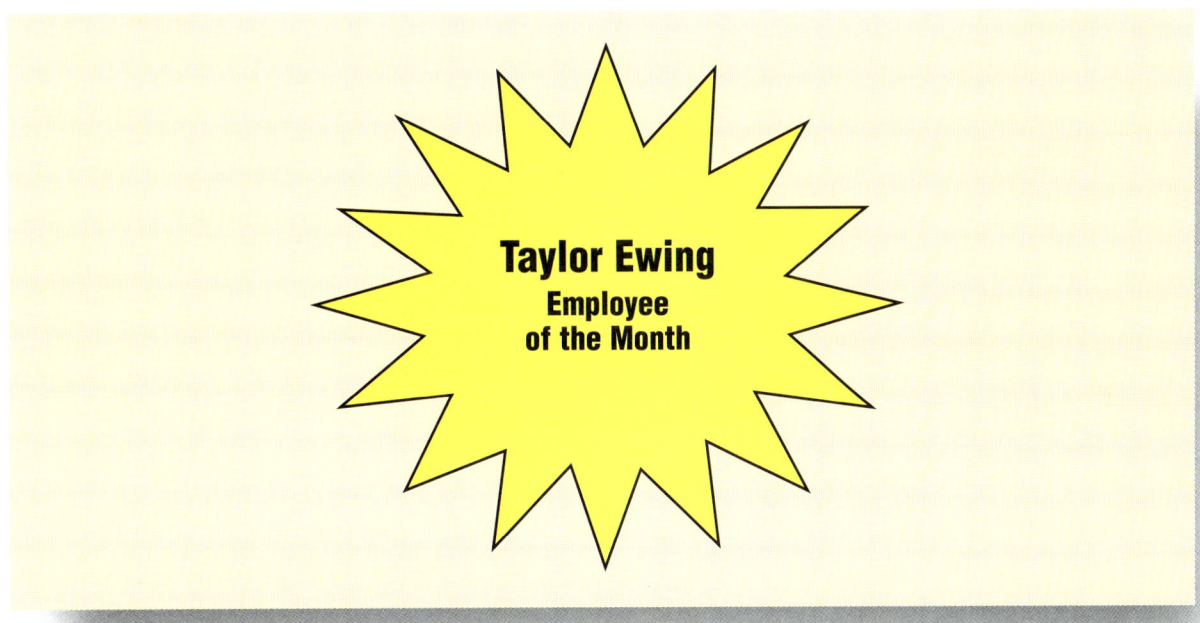

Assessment 5

1. At a clear document screen, create the text *Madison Creek Elementary School* as WordArt text that displays slanted across the entire page by completing the following steps:
   a. Display the WordArt Gallery.
   b. Double-click the second option from the left in the third row.
   c. At the Edit WordArt dialog box key **Madison Creek Elementary School** and close the dialog box.
   d. Change the shape of the text to a slant. (*Hint: Click the WordArt Shape button on the WordArt toolbar and then click the fifth shape from the left in the bottom row (Slant Up).*)
   e. Display the Fill Effects dialog box, with the Pattern tab selected, and then make the following changes *(Hint: Use the Drawing toolbar)*:
      1) Click the third pattern option from the left in the bottom row (Wide upward diagonal).
      2) Change the foreground color to Dark Blue.
      3) Change the background color to Lavender.
      4) Close the dialog box.
   f. Click the down-pointing triangle at the right side of the Line Color button and click the Dark Blue color.
   g. Display the Format WordArt dialog box with the Size tab selected, change the width to 6 inches, and then close the dialog box.
   h. Click the Shadow button on the Drawing toolbar and click the second option from the left in the second row (Shadow Style 6).
2. Save the document and name it Word C7, SA 05.
3. Print and close Word C7, SA 05.

Assessment 6

1. At a clear document screen, create the text *Spring Festival* as WordArt text. You determine the formatting of the text and include at least the following:
   a. Change the shape of the WordArt text.
   b. Add a pattern to the WordArt text.
   c. Change the foreground and background color of the WordArt text.
   d. Add a shadow or three-dimensional effect to the WordArt text.
2. Save the document and name it Word C7, SA 06.
3. Print and close Word C7, SA 06.

Assessment 7

1. Use the Help feature to find information on creating a watermark in a document. Read and print the help topics you find.
2. Open Word C7, SA 02.
3. Using the techniques you learned in Help, change the clip art image inserted in the document to a watermark and position it behind the text in the notice.
4. Save the revised document and name it Word C7, SA 07.
5. Print and close Word C7, SA 07.

8

Exploring the Internet

PERFORMANCE OBJECTIVES

Upon completion of chapter 8, you will be able to:

- Browse the World Wide Web.
- Locate specific sites on the Web.
- Search for specific information on the Web.
- Use search operators to narrow a search on the Web.
- Create and format a Web page.
- Create hyperlinks in a Web page.

Increasingly, businesses are accessing the Internet to conduct research, publish product or catalog information, communicate, and market products globally. In many Microsoft Office applications, you can jump to the Internet and browse the World Wide Web. You can also create a document in an office application and then save it as a Web document with HyperText Markup Language (HTML) codes. HTML "tags" attached to information in a Web document enable the links and jumps between documents and data resources to operate. Information provided by the tags also instructs the browser software how to display text, images, animations, or sounds.

Understanding the Internet

The *Internet* is a network of computers connected around the world. In 1969, the U.S. Defense Department created a network to allow researchers at different sites to exchange information. The first network consisted of only four computers. Since then, the number of networks that have connected has grown exponentially, and the Internet is no longer just a vehicle of information for researchers, but can be used by anyone whose computer has a *modem*, a device that allows data to be sent over telephone lines.

Users access the Internet for several purposes: to communicate using e-mail, to subscribe to news groups, to transfer files, to socialize with other users around the globe in "chat" rooms, and largely to access virtually any kind of information imaginable.

INTEGRATED TOPIC

To use the Internet, you generally need three things—an Internet Service Provider (ISP), a program to browse the Web (called a *Web browser*), and a *search engine* (software used to locate specific data on the Internet).

A variety of Internet Service Providers are available. Local ISPs are available as well as commercial ISPs such as Microsoft Network®, America Online®, AT&T Worldnet Service®, and CompuServe®. To complete the exercises in this chapter, you will need access to the Internet through an ISP. Check with your instructor to determine the ISP used by your school to connect to the Internet.

Once you are connected to the Internet, you can access the *World Wide Web*. The World Wide Web is the most commonly used application on the Internet. The Web is a set of standards and protocols used to access information available on the Internet. The Internet is the physical network utilized to carry the data. To access the Web and maneuver within the Web, you need a Web browser. A Web browser allows you to move around the Internet by pointing and clicking with the mouse. A popular Web browser designed by Microsoft is the Microsoft Internet Explorer. The exercises in this chapter are created with the assumption that you will have Microsoft Internet Explorer available. If you will be using a different Web browser, some of the steps in the exercises may vary.

A phenomenal amount of information is available on the Internet. Searching through all that information to find the specific information you need can be an overwhelming task. Software programs, called *search engines*, have been created to help you search more quickly and easily for the desired information. There are many search engines available on the Internet, each offering the opportunity to search for specific information. As you use different search engines, you may find you prefer one over the others.

Browsing the World Wide Web

In this chapter, you will be completing several exercises and assessments that require you to search for locations and information on the World Wide Web. To do this, you will need the following:

1. A modem or network connection to a server with Internet access.
2. Browser software installed and configured. (This chapter will explore the World Wide Web using Microsoft Internet Explorer.)
3. An Internet Service Provider account.

A modem is a hardware device that converts digital data into a form that can be transmitted over telephone lines. The word "modem" is derived from MOdulator/DEModulator. The modem attached to your computer converts digital data into an analog signal that can be transferred over telephone lines. At the other end of the connection is another modem that converts the analog signal back to digital data for the receiving computer. There are internal and external modems available in a variety of speeds. Modem speed is measured in terms of the number of bits per second data is transferred. If you are using a computer connected to a network, the network server will route the data through its modem, or to another server with a modem.

An Internet Service Provider (ISP) sells access to the Internet. In order to provide this access, the ISP must have in place the hardware and software necessary to support access to the Internet, phone lines to accept the modem

The Web is used to locate information, distribute sales and marketing data, advertise products and services, and deliver software.

Hint

A company may set up a network infrastructure called an intranet to allow employees access to company information.

Hint

connections, and support staff to assist their customers. Each ISP is responsible for configuring its computers, routers, and software to enable connectivity to every other individual and computer that make up the Internet.

Locating URLs on the Internet

We all know that we can dial a telephone number of a friend or relative in any country around the world and establish a connection within seconds. The global telephone system is an amazing network that functions because of a common set of protocols and standards that are agreed upon by each country. The Internet operates on the same principle. Computer protocols known as TCP/IP (Transmission Control Protocol/Internet Protocol) form the base of the Internet. Protocols are simply agreements on how various hardware and software should communicate with each other. The Internet Service Provider becomes the Domain Name Service (DNS), *the route to the Internet*. The DNS and IP determine how to route your computer to another location/computer on the Internet. Every computer directly linked to the Internet has a unique IP address.

This explanation has been overly simplified. The technical details on how computer A can "talk" to computer B do not directly involve a computer user any more than does picking up a phone in Vancouver, British Columbia, and dialing a number in San Diego, California.

Uniform Resource Locators, referred to as URLs, are the method used to identify locations on the Internet. The format of a URL is *http://server-name.path*. The first part of the URL, *http://*, identifies the protocol. The letters *http* stand for HyperText Transfer Protocol, which is the protocol or language used to transfer data within the World Wide Web. The colon and slashes separate the protocol from the server name. The server name is the second component of the URL. For example, in the URL http://home.netscape.com, the server name is identified as *home.netscape*. The last part of the URL specifies the domain to which the server belongs. For example, *.com* refers to "commercial" and establishes that the URL is a commercial company. Other examples of domains include *.edu* for "educational," *.gov* for "government," and *.mil* for "military." Some examples of URLs are displayed in figure 8.1.

8.1   *Sample URLs*

URL	Connects to
http://www.microsoft.com	Microsoft Corporation home page
http://www.emcp.com	EMC/Paradigm Publishing home page
http://lcweb.loc.gov	Library of Congress home page
http://www.washington.edu	University of Washington home page
http://www.xerox.com	Xerox home page
http://www.kodak.com	Eastman Kodak home page
http://www.alaska-air.com	Alaska Airlines home page

Another method for displaying a URL is to display the Open dialog box, key the URL address in the File name text box, and then click OK.

If you know the URL for a specific Web site and would like to visit that site, key the URL in the Address section of the Web toolbar. To display the Web toolbar shown in figure 8.2, click View, point to Toolbars, and then click *Web* at the drop-down list. You can also display the Web toolbar by positioning the mouse pointer on a toolbar, clicking the *right* mouse button, and then clicking *Web* at the drop-down list.

Before keying a URL in the Address text box on the Web toolbar, make sure you are connected to the Internet through your Internet Service Provider. When keying a URL, you must key the address exactly as written, including any colons (:) or slashes (/).

When you key a URL in the Address section of the Web toolbar and then press Enter, your default Web browser is automatically activated. The home page for the specific URL displays on the screen in the Web browser. Figure 8.3 shows the Microsoft home page in the Internet Explorer Web browser. You will learn more about Internet Explorer later in this chapter.

When you are connected to a URL, the home page for the specific URL (Web site) displays. The home page is the starting point for viewing the Web site. At the home page, you can choose to "branch off" the home page to other pages within the Web site or jump to other Web sites. You do this with hyperlinks that are embedded in the home page. You will learn more about hyperlinks in the next section of this chapter. In exercise 1, you will be visiting some Web site home pages using URLs.

figure 8.2

Web Toolbar

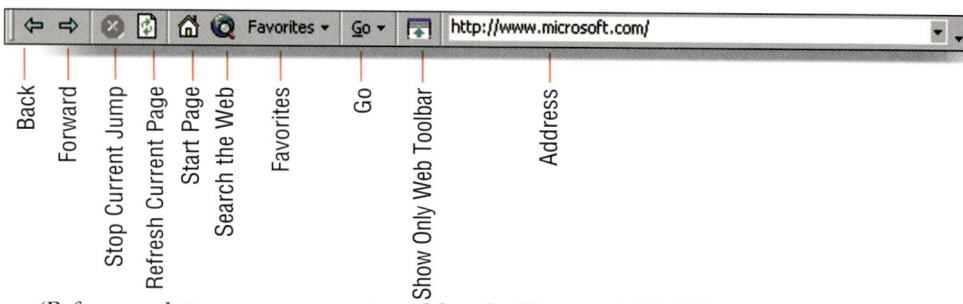

Back | Forward | Stop Current Jump | Refresh Current Page | Start Page | Search the Web | Favorites | Go | Show Only Web Toolbar | Address

(Before completing computer exercises, delete the Chapter 07C *folder on your disk. Next, copy the* Chapter 08C *folder from the CD that accompanies this textbook to your disk and make* Chapter 08C *the active folder.)*

exercise 1

Visiting Web Site Home Pages

1. Make sure you are connected to the Internet through an Internet Service Provider.
2. Explore several sites on the World Wide Web from within Word by completing the following steps:
   a. At a clear document screen, display the Web toolbar by clicking View, pointing to Toolbars, and then clicking Web.
   b. Click in the Address text box located on the Web toolbar. (This will select the current document name in the text box.)
   c. Display the Web site home page for Microsoft Corporation by keying **http://www.microsoft.com** and then pressing Enter.
   d. In a few moments, the Microsoft home page

Step 2c

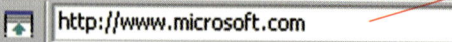

displays. The home page will display in your default Web browser similar to what is shown in figure 8.3. Home pages are updated frequently so the Microsoft home page you are viewing will vary slightly from what you see in figure 8.3. Scroll down the home page, reading the information about Microsoft.

 e. After reading about Microsoft, view the home page for NASA. To do this, click the current address located in the A̲ddress text box, key **http://www.nasa.gov** and then press Enter. Scroll down the home page reading the information displayed about NASA.

 3. After reading the information displayed on the NASA home page, close your Web browser by clicking F̲ile and then C̲lose.

In exercise 1, step 2c, you keyed the Microsoft Web site URL as http://www.microsoft.com. When keying a URL, you can leave off the http://. Office adds this automatically to the URL.

Microsoft Home Page

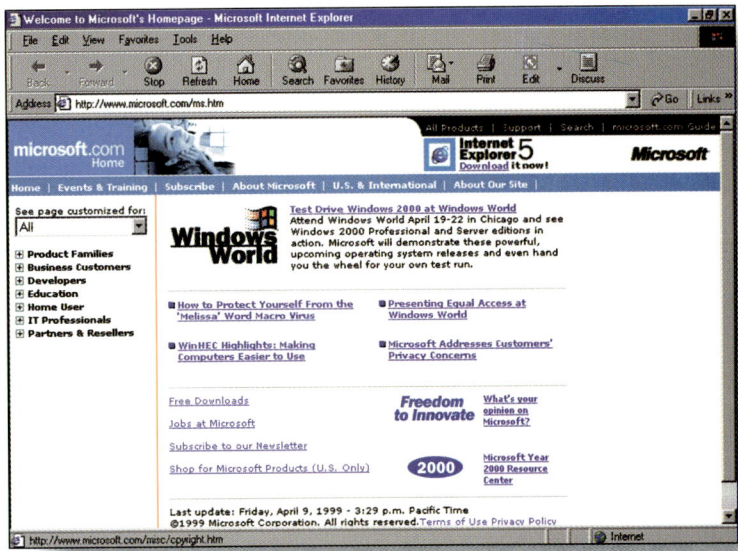

Using Hyperlinks

As you were viewing the Web site home pages for Microsoft and NASA, did you notice text that displayed in a different color and was also underlined? Text displayed in a different color and underlined indicates text that has been identified as a *hyperlink*. A hyperlink allows you to link or connect to another item. A hyperlink can display in a variety of ways. It can display as text in a different color and underlined or as a heading or button. Move the mouse pointer to a hyperlink and the mouse pointer turns into a hand. This is one method for determining if an item is a hyperlink.

To use a hyperlink, position the mouse pointer on the desired hyperlink until the pointer turns into a hand, and then click the left mouse button. For example, when you displayed the Microsoft home page, you could have clicked the hyperlink button About Microsoft located towards the top of the page to display information about

Back

Forward

Microsoft Corporation. Most pages contain a variety of hyperlinks. Using these links, you can zero in on the exact information for which you are searching.

The Web toolbar as well as the Internet Explorer Web browser contain a Back button you can click to display the previous Web page. If you click the Back button and then would like to go back to the hyperlink, click the Forward button. By clicking the Back button, you can back your way out of any hyperlinks and return to the default Web home page. In exercise 2, you will be exploring two sites on the World Wide Web and using hyperlinks to display specific information.

exercise 2

Visiting Web Sites and Using Hyperlinks

1. Make sure you are connected to the Internet through an Internet Service Provider.
2. Explore two sites on the World Wide Web by completing the following steps:
   a. At a clear document screen, make sure the Web toolbar displays.
   b. Click in the Address text box located on the Web toolbar.
   c. Key **http://www.time.com** and then press Enter.
   d. When the Time home page displays, click the hyperlink to the cover story by positioning the mouse pointer over an image or text that represents the cover story until the pointer turns into a hand and then clicking the left mouse button.
   e. When the cover story page displays, click the Print button on the Internet Explorer toolbar to print the page.
   f. Click the Back button to return to the Time home page.
   g. Click the current address located in the Address text box.
   h. Key **http://www. amazon.com** and then press Enter.
   i. When the Amazon.com home page displays, click the BESTSELLERS hyperlink button. (This hyperlink is probably located towards the top of the Amazon.com page. If this hyperlink is not available, choose any other hyperlink that interests you.)

   amazon.com   BOOKS | MUSIC | GIFTS

   BOOK SEARCH   BROWSE SUBJECTS   BESTSELLERS   FEATURED IN THE MEDIA   AWARD WINNERS

   Step 2i

   j. When the bestseller page displays, print the page.
3. After printing the bestseller page, close your Web browser by clicking File and then Close.

Searching the Internet Using Internet Explorer

In the previous exercises, you jumped around the Web by keying URLs, which is a fast way to move from site to site. Often, however, you will access the Web to search for information and you will not know the URL that you want to visit.

Search engines are valuable tools to assist a user in locating information on a particular topic by simply keying a few words or a short phrase. There are many search engines available on the Internet such as Excite, Infoseek, Lycos, Yahoo, AltaVista, and HotBot. Each offers the opportunity to search for specific information. As you use different search engines, you may find you prefer one over the others.

Search the Web

To search for information on the Web, click the Search the Web button on the Web toolbar. This displays the Internet Explorer Search Setup page as shown in figure 8.4. As mentioned earlier in this chapter, Internet Explorer is a Web browser, which creates an environment in which you can search and display Web sites. Figure 8.4 identifies the features of the Internet Explorer program window and figure 8.5 describes the features.

figure

8.4

Internet Explorer Window

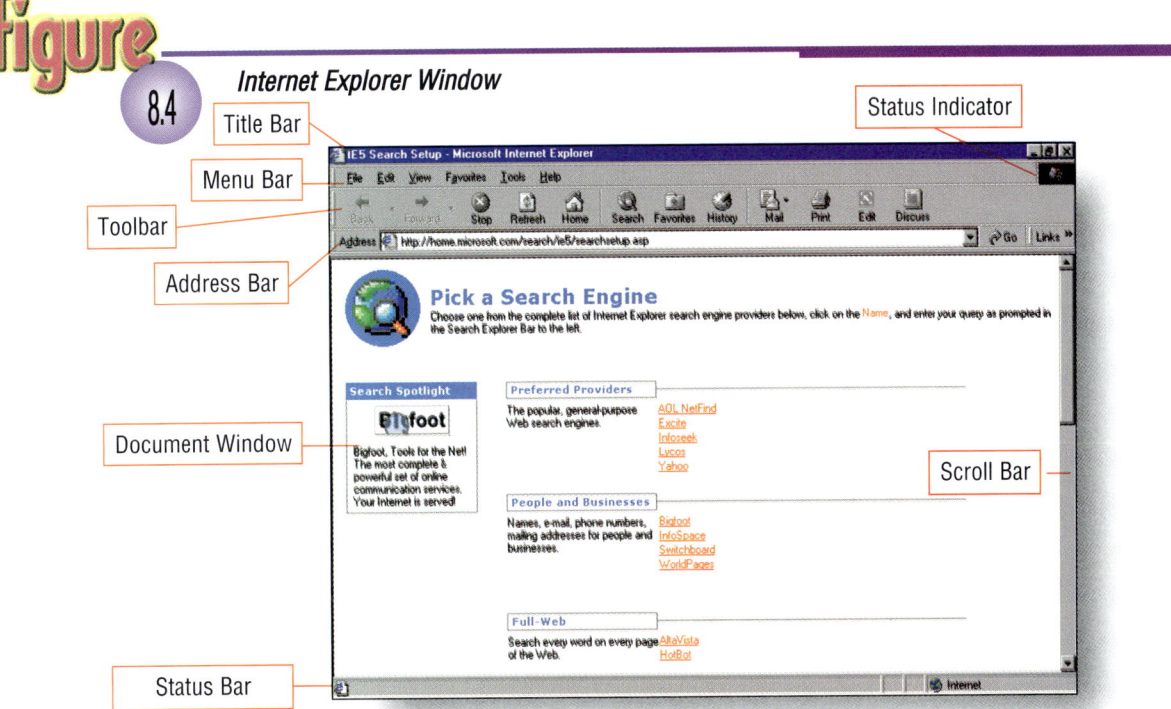

figure

8.5

Internet Explorer Program Window Features

Internet Explorer Feature	Description
Title bar	Displays the name of the Web page followed by the name of the program—Microsoft Internet Explorer
Menu bar	Contains a list of options for using and customizing Internet Explorer
Toolbar	Contains buttons for commonly used features such as navigating, searching, printing, and formatting

Address bar	Displays the address of the current Web site page
Status indicator	Status indicator is the Microsoft logo; animates (moves) when a Web site is being loaded
Document window	Displays the contents of the current Web site
Scroll bar	Use the scroll bar to display information in the current Web page
Status bar	Displays information about connection progress and the percentage of information that has been transferred

The Internet Explorer toolbar contains buttons for accessing a variety of commands. Figure 8.6 shows the buttons and describes each button.

figure

8.6 **Internet Explorer Toolbar Buttons**

Click this button	To do this
Back	Display previous Web page
Forward	Display next Web page
Stop	Stop loading a page
Refresh	Refresh (update) contents of current page
Home	Display the default home page
Search	Display the Search side bar
Favorites	Display the Favorites side bar
History	Display the History side bar containing a list of sites visited on specific days or during specific weeks
Mail	Display mail and news options
Print	Print the current Web page
Edit	Display the current Web page in a Word document screen for editing
Discuss	Chat with others connected to the same server. (You must specify the discussion server.)

Searching for Specific Information on the Web

Click the Search the Web button on the Web toolbar and the Internet Explorer Search Setup page displays as shown in figure 8.4. This page lists a variety of search engines in different categories. (Web pages and search engines are constantly changing so you may discover that your Internet Explorer Search Setup page may vary from what you see in figure 8.4. If that is the case, you may need to modify some steps in the exercises in this chapter.) Click the desired search engine name and a side bar displays. For example, click the Excite search engine name and a side bar displays as shown in figure 8.7. Key specific text in the white text box that displays towards the top of the Excite side bar and then click the Search button. A list of sites displays in the Excite side bar containing the specific text you entered in the white text box. Click a site listing to jump to that site on the Web.

figure

8.7

Excite Side Bar

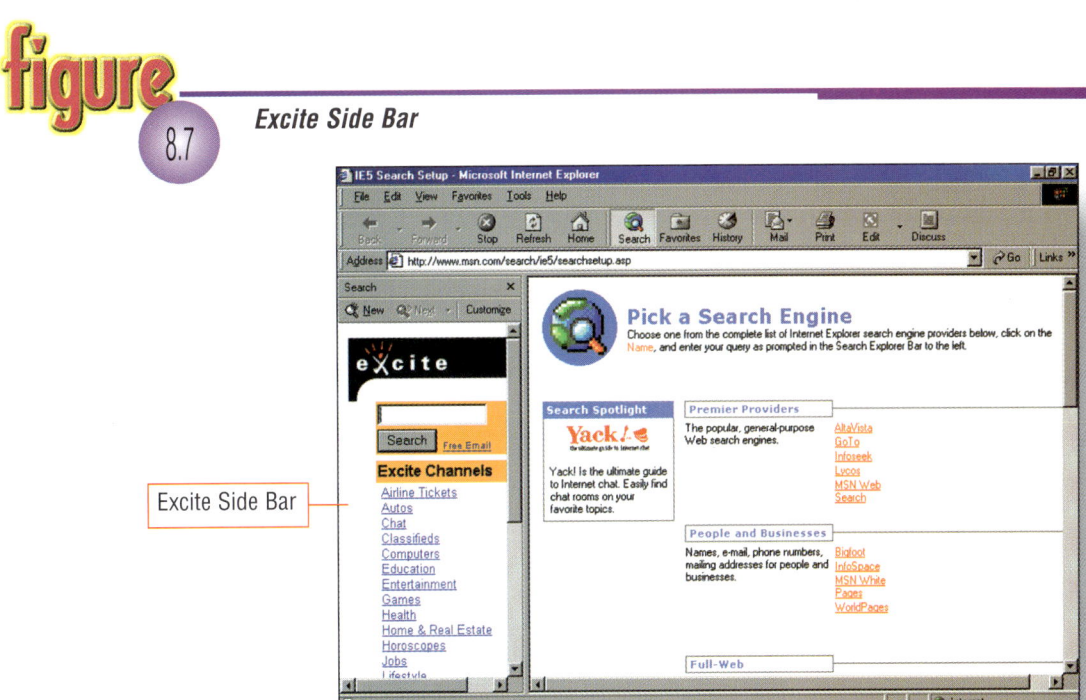

Excite Side Bar

As you gain experience searching the Web, you will develop methods to refine your search techniques and tools to limit the time spent browsing. Before you begin a research project, jot down your key words or phrases and think about ways to limit the sites that will be selected by being as specific as possible without restricting the search. As you will see in the next exercise, you can become overwhelmed with the number of sites that will be selected.

If the downloading process is taking too long and you want to quit, click the Stop button on the Internet Explorer toolbar.

Hint

exercise 3

Using Search Engines to Locate Information on the Web

(Note: Web pages and search engines change constantly. If the instructions in this exercise do not match what you are viewing, you may need to substitute different steps than the ones instructed here.)

1. Jump to the World Wide Web from within Word and search for information on lahars (dense, viscous flows of volcanic debris) using the Excite search engine by completing these steps:
   a. At a clear document screen, make sure the Web toolbar displays, and then click the Search the Web button on the Web toolbar.
   b. At the Internet Explorer Search Setup page (like the one shown in figure 8.4), complete the following steps:
      1) Click the hyperlink *Excite*, which displays in the *Full-Web* column.
      2) Click in the white text box (above the Search button) that displays towards the top of the Excite side bar (see figure 8.7).
      3) Key **lahars** in the text box.
      4) Click the Search button.
   c. In a few moments, the Excite search engine will return with the first ten sites in the side bar that meet your search criteria. Click a site that interests you.
   d. Click the Print button on the Internet Explorer toolbar to print the Web page displayed.
   e. After printing the information, click the Back button on the Internet Explorer toolbar. (This displays the Search Setup page at the right side of the screen.)

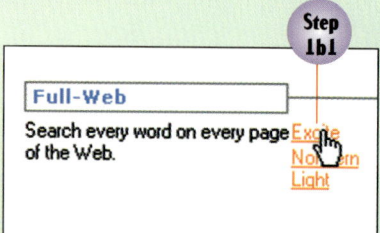

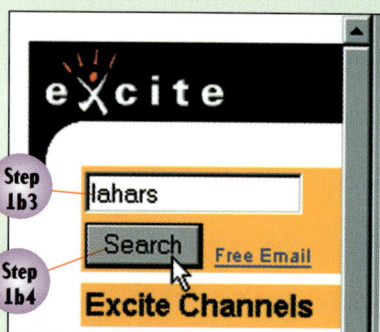

2. Search for information on the Australian platypus using the Infoseek search engine by completing the following steps:
   a. Click *Infoseek*, which displays in the *Premier Providers* column.
   b. Click in the white text box that displays towards the top of the Infoseek side bar.
   c. Key **Australian platypus** in the text box and then press Enter.
   d. In a few moments, the Infoseek search engine will return with information that meets the search criteria. Scroll through the side bar and read the information presented by Infoseek.
   e. Click a site about the Australian platypus that interests you.
   f. After viewing the site in the side bar, click the Search button on the Internet Explorer toolbar to remove the Search side bar.
3. Close Internet Explorer by clicking <u>F</u>ile on the Internet Explorer Menu bar and then clicking <u>C</u>lose at the drop-down menu.

Narrowing a Search

The Internet contains a phenomenal amount of information. For example, if you search for *physician-assisted suicide* using the Infoseek search engine, more than 500,000 sites may be found. Some searches can result in millions of "hits" (sites). Wading through all these sites can be very time consuming and counterproductive. Narrowing a search to very specific criteria can greatly reduce the number of hits for a search.

To reduce the number of documents found and to find only those documents containing very specific information, use *search operators*. Search operators may vary between search engines. Some operators may work within many engines, while others are specific to certain search engines. Some common search operators include symbols such as a quotation mark ("), a plus symbol (+), and a minus symbol (-). Figure 8.8 describes the operators and an explanation of each.

8.8   *Search operators*

Operator	Explanation
Plus (+)	Key a plus symbol directly in front of a word and only those documents containing the word will be found. Do not space after the symbol. If you are including more than one word, space between the first word and the next symbol or word.
	Example: Key **+baseball +rules** and only those documents containing both *baseball* and *rules* will be found
Minus (-)	Key a minus symbol directly in front of a word that you do not want included in the search. This symbol is helpful in situations where you want to find a specific topic but want to narrow it by excluding certain parts of the topic.
	Example: Key **+whales -blue -killer** and the search engine will find those documents containing *whales* but <u>not</u> *blue* or *killer*.
Quotation Marks (")	If you enter terms for a search such as *University of Arizona*, a search engine will find documents containing any or all of the three words in any order. If you want only those documents found containing *University of Arizona* in this specific order, enclose the words in quotation marks.
	Example: Key **"University of Arizona"** and the search engine will find those documents containing the three words in the order specified between the quotation marks.

In addition to search operators, some search engines recognize Boolean operators when conducting a search. (Boolean operators are based on Boolean algebra [named after George Boole, an English mathematician], which is a mathematical system originally devised for the analysis of symbolic logic.)

Boolean operators include AND, AND NOT, OR, and parentheses. Boolean operators must be keyed in all capital letters with a space on either side. Boolean operators are explained in figure 8.9.

figure

8.9   *Boolean Operators*

Operator	Function
AND	Find documents with words joined by AND.
	Example: Key **Disneyland AND California** and the search engine will find those documents containing both *Disneyland* and *California*.
OR	Find documents that contain at least one of the words joined by OR.
	Example: Key **volcanoes OR lahars** and the search engine will find those documents containing either *volcanoes* or *lahars*.
AND NOT	Find documents that contain the word before AND NOT but not the word after.
	Example: Key **bicycling AND NOT racing** and the search engine will find those documents containing the word *bicycling* but not the word *racing*.

Each search engine uses its own set of search guidelines. Research the guidelines for your favorite search engine.

Not all search engines use Boolean operators to limit searches. Each search engine should contain a Web page that explains how to conduct what is considered an advanced search. In exercise 4, you will be using two different search engines to find information and also print information on how to perform an advanced search with each of the two search engines.

exercise 4

Using Search Operators to Search for Specific Information on the Web

1. Jump to the World Wide Web from within Word and search for information on the University of Michigan using the Northern Light search engine by completing these steps:
   a. At a clear document screen, click the Search the Web button on the Web toolbar.
   b. At the Internet Explorer Search Setup page (like the one shown in figure 8.4), complete the following steps:
      1) Click *Northern Light,* which displays in the *Full-Web* column.
      2) Click in the white text box that displays towards the top of the Northern Light side bar, key **University of Michigan**, and then press Enter.
   c. In a few moments, the Northern Light search engine will return with a list of sites that meets your search criteria. Write down the total number of sites found by Northern Light.
   d. Scroll down the side bar to see some of the sites that have been selected.
   e. Learn more about searching with Northern Light by completing the following steps:

1) Click the HELP hyperlink button that displays towards the top of the Northern Light side bar.
2) Click the *Optimize Your Search* hyperlink that displays in the window at the far right side of the screen. (You will need to scroll to the right to see this hyperlink.)
3) When the Optimize Your Search page displays, print the information by clicking the Print button on the Internet Explorer toolbar.

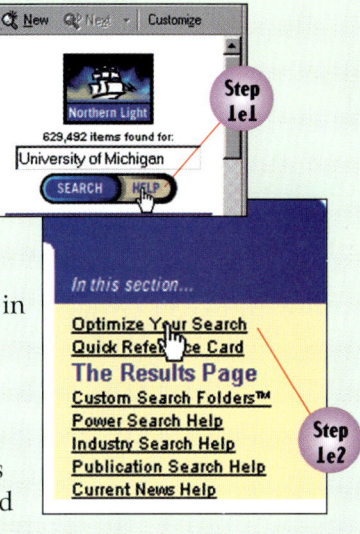

f. Narrow the search by completing the following steps:
1) Select the text *University of Michigan* that displays in the white text box located towards the top of the Northern Light side bar, key **"University of Michigan"**, and then press Enter.
2) When Northern Light returns with a list of sites, write down the total number of sites. Compare this number to the previous number. The number found with the search containing the quotation marks should be considerably lower than the search without the quotation marks.

g. Click the Back button on the Internet Explorer toolbar until the Internet Explorer Search Setup page displays at the right side of the screen.

2. Find information on Ralph Nader using the Excite search engine and then find information on Ralph Nader but not the Green Party by completing the following steps:

a. At the Internet Explorer Search Setup page, click *Excite* in the *Full-Web* column.
b. Click in the white text box that displays towards the top of the Excite side bar and then key **Ralph Nader**.
c. Click the Search button.
d. When Excite returns with a list of sites, view the full screen by clicking the hyperlink *View Full Screen* that displays in the Excite side bar. (This displays additional information on Excite at the right side of the screen.)
e. At the Excite full screen that displays at the right, look for the total number of hits for *Ralph Nader* and then write down the number. (This number will probably display below *Web Results*.)

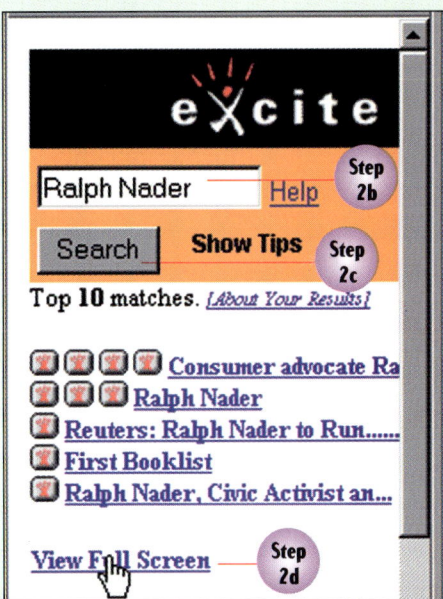

f. Display information on advanced searches in Excite by completing the following steps:
1) Click the *Help* hyperlink that displays at the right side of the white text box in the side bar.

2) At the Excite help page that displays at the right side of the screen, click the _Advanced Search Tips_ hyperlink.
3) When the Advanced Search Tips page displays, click the Print button on the Internet Explorer toolbar.
4) Read the information on advanced searches.

g. Narrow the search to documents containing Ralph Nader but <u>not</u> the Green Party by completing the following steps:

1) Select _Ralph Nader_ in the white text box that displays towards the top of the Excite side bar and then key **+Ralph +Nader -Green -Party**.
2) Click the Search button.
3) When Excite returns with a list of sites, click the _View Full Screen_ hyperlink. (This updates the information at the right side of the screen.)
4) Look at the information that displays at the right side of the screen and then write down the total number of sites found. Compare this number to the previous number. The number found with the search containing the plus and minus symbols should be considerably lower than the search without the symbols.

h. Click the Search button on the Internet Explorer toolbar to turn off the display of the Search side bar.

3. Click File and then Close to close the Internet Explorer.

Search Help

Search Description
General Search Tips
Advanced Search Tips
Search Results
Relevance Rating
List by Web Site
Show Summaries
Search Wizard
Browser Error Messages

Step 2f2

Each search engine Web site should contain information on how to narrow a search or conduct an advanced search. You may want to experiment with some of the other search engines to see if you can find information on how to conduct advanced searches within each.

Favorites

Adding Favorite Sites to the Favorites List

If you find a site that you would like to visit on a regular basis, that site can be added to a Favorites list. To do this, display the site, and then click the Favorites button on the Internet Explorer toolbar. This causes a side bar to display similar to the one shown in figure 8.10 (your folder names may vary).

Favorites Side Bar

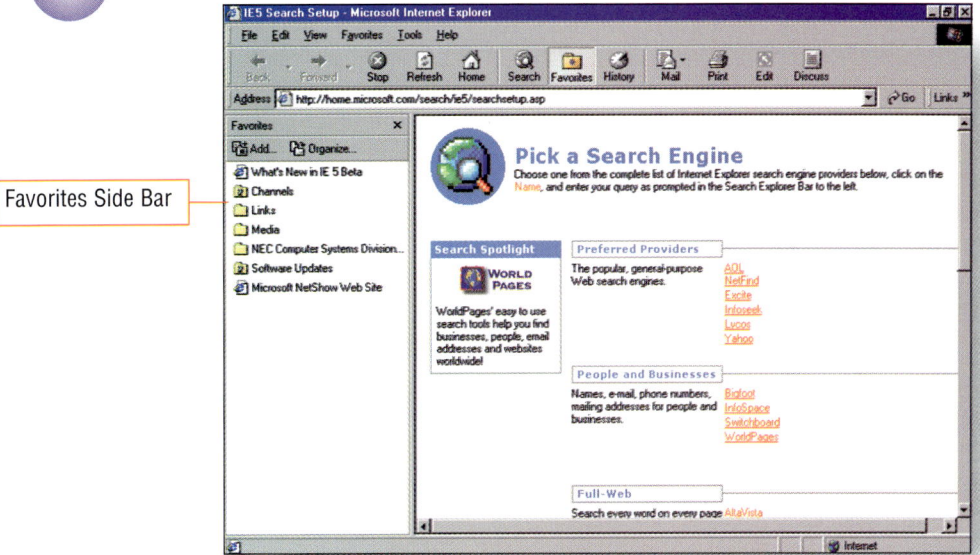

Favorites Side Bar

To add a favorite site, click the Add button located at the top of the Favorites side bar. This displays the Add Favorite dialog box shown in figure 8.11. At this dialog box, make sure the information in the Name text box is correct (if not, select the text and then key your own information), and then click OK. The new site displays at the bottom of the list in the Favorites side bar. After a site has been added to the Favorites list, you can jump quickly to that site by clicking the Favorites button on the Internet Explorer toolbar and then clicking the site name at the Favorites side bar.

Keep your Favorites list a reasonable length by adding only those pages that you expect to visit several times.

Add Favorite Dialog Box

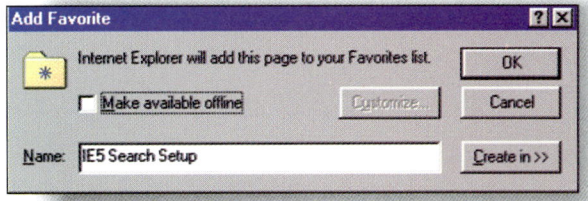

If you want to insert a favorites site into a folder, display the site, and then click the Add button. At the Add Favorite dialog box, click the Create in button located at the right side of the dialog box. This expands the dialog box and displays a list of folders. Click the folder into which you want the site listed and then click the OK button. To display the list of sites within a folder, click the folder name at the Favorite side bar. To turn off the display of sites within a folder, click the folder name again.

To delete a site from the Favorites side bar, position the mouse pointer on the site, click the *right* mouse button, and then click Delete at the pop-up menu that displays. At the Confirm File Delete dialog box, click the Yes button.

If you want to organize the list of favorite sites, click the Organize button located at the top of the Favorites side bar. This displays the Organize Favorites dialog box shown in figure 8.12. Use this dialog box to create a new folder, delete or rename a folder, or move a folder name up or down the Favorites list.

figure

8.12

Organize Favorites Dialog Box

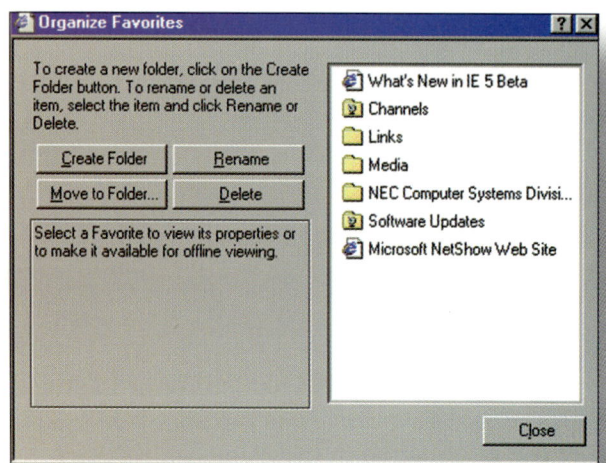

Displaying a List of Sites Visited

History

As you visit different Web sites, Internet Explorer keeps track of the sites. Click the History button on the Internet Explorer toolbar and a History side bar displays as shown in figure 8.13. You can display sites visited in the last few days, hours, or minutes. To display the sites, click the desired day. This information can be useful for remembering Internet addresses previously visited and for monitoring Internet use. Close the History side bar by clicking the History button again or by clicking the Close button (contains an X) located in the upper right corner of the History side bar.

figure
8.13

Internet Explorer History Side Bar

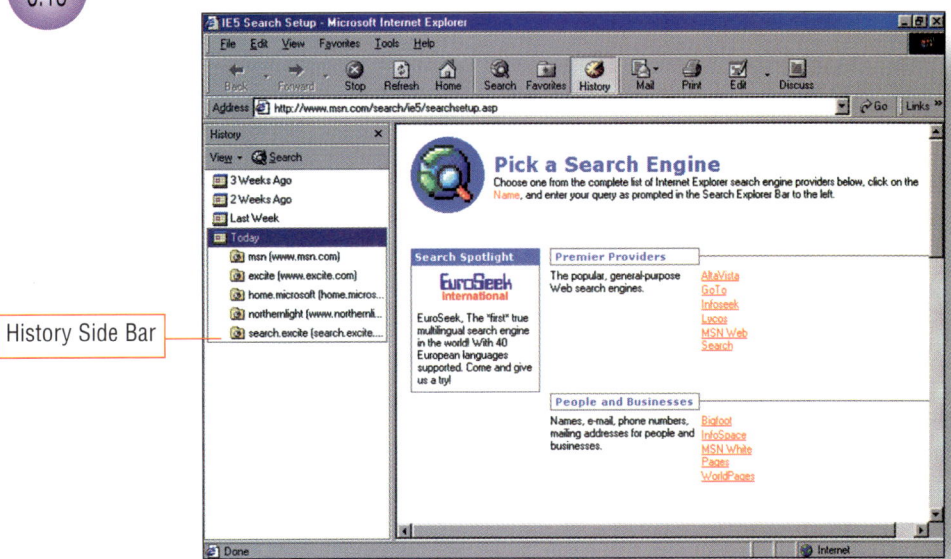

History Side Bar —

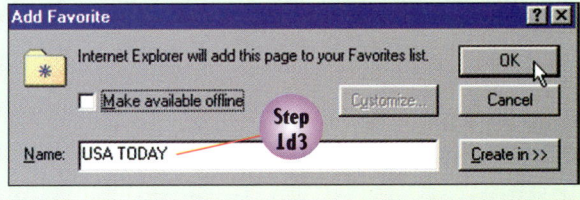

exercise 5

Exploring the Web, Adding Favorite Sites, and Displaying Sites Visited

1. Explore several locations on the World Wide Web from within Word using Internet Explorer and hyperlinks by completing the following steps:

   a. Click the Search the Web button on the Web toolbar.

   b. At the Internet Explorer Search Setup page, click in the Address text box. (This selects the current address.)

   c. Display the home page for *USA Today* by keying **http://www.usatoday.com** and then pressing Enter.

   d. Add the *USA Today* Web site to the Favorites list by completing the following steps:

      1) Click the Favorites button located on the Internet Explorer toolbar.

      2) At the Favorites side bar, click the Add button (displays towards the top of the side bar).

      3) At the Add Favorite dialog box, make sure *USA TODAY* displays in the Name text box, and then click OK.

      4) Click the Favorites button on the Internet Explorer toolbar to remove the Favorites side bar.

   e. Display the Alaska Airlines Web page, add it to the Favorites list; and then search for flight departure times from Los Angeles, California, to Anchorage, Alaska, by completing the following steps:

1) Click in the Address text box to select the current URL, key **http://www.alaska-air.com**, and then press Enter.
2) When the Alaska Airlines home page displays, add it to the Favorites list by completing steps similar to those in step 1d.
3) At the Alaska Airlines home page, click the *Schedules* hyperlink.
4) At the schedule Web page, click the down-pointing triangle at the right side of the From text box, and then click *Los Angeles, California* at the drop-down list. (You will need to scroll down the list.)
5) Make sure the To text box displays *Anchorage, Alaska*.

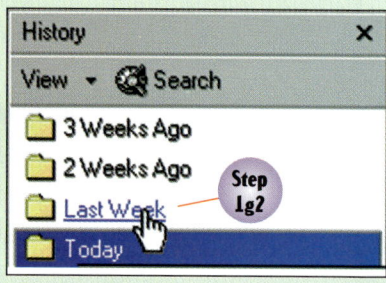

6) Change the departing date from one week from today. (You will need to change the day and perhaps the month.)
7) Click the CONTINUE button.
8) When the flight schedule page displays, click the Print button on the Internet Explorer toolbar.

f. Jump to the home page for *USA Today* by completing the following steps:
1) Click the Favorites button on the Internet Explorer toolbar to display the Favorites side bar.
2) At the Favorites side bar, click *USA TODAY*.
3) Click the Favorites button to turn off the display of the Favorites side bar.

g. Display a list of sites visited by completing the following steps:
1) Click the History button on the Internet Explorer toolbar. (Sites visited today display in the side bar.)
2) Display sites visited on a previous day by clicking the desired day in the History side bar.
3) Click the History button on the Internet Explorer toolbar to turn off the display of the History side bar.

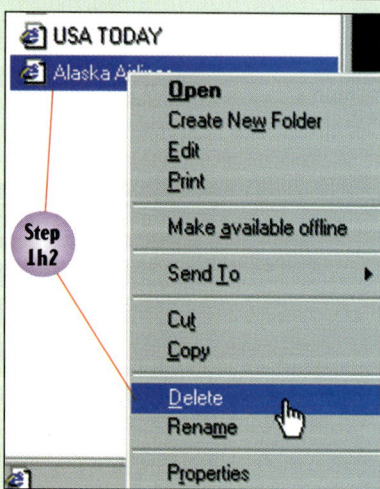

h. Remove *Alaska Airlines* and *USA TODAY* from the Favorites side bar by completing the following steps:
1) Click the Favorites button on the Internet Explorer toolbar.
2) Right-click *Alaska Airlines* in the Favorites side bar and then click Delete at the drop-down menu.
3) At the Confirm File Delete dialog box, click Yes.
4) Right-click on *USA TODAY* in the Favorites side bar and then click Delete at the drop-down menu.
5) At the Confirm File Delete dialog box, click Yes.

6) Click the Favorites button on the Internet Explorer toolbar to turn off the display of the Favorites side bar.
2. Close Internet Explorer by clicking <u>F</u>ile and then <u>C</u>lose.
3. If the Windows desktop displays, click the Microsoft Word button that displays on the taskbar. (This will display the Word document screen.)

Creating a Web Page

Now that you have been "surfing the net," you have visited several Web site home pages and have an idea how a home page displays. Home pages are Web documents that describe a company, school, government, or individual and are created using a language called HyperText Markup Language (HTML). This is a language that Web browsers use to read hypertext documents. In the past, a person needed knowledge of HTML to design a Web page. Now a Web page can be created in Word and saved as a Web page or created with a Web Page Wizard.

Before creating a Web page, consider the information you want contained in the Web page. Carefully plan the layout of the information and where to position hyperlinks. Good Web page design is a key element to a successful Web page. Often a company will hire a professional Web page designer to create their home page. Before designing a Web page, you may want to visit a variety of Web pages and consider some of the following questions: What elements are included on the Web page? How are the elements distributed on the page? Is the information organized logically and is it easy to read? Is the Web page visually appealing? Evaluating Web pages on the Web will help you when designing your own.

To save a Word document as a Web page, click <u>F</u>ile, expand the drop-down menu, and then click Save as Web Page. At the Save As dialog box, key a name for the Web page document, and then press Enter or click the <u>S</u>ave button. (Word automatically changes the Save as type option to Web Page.)

Changing to the Web Layout View

When you save a document as a Web page, Word automatically changes to the Web Layout view. The Web Layout view displays a page as it will appear when published to the Web or an intranet. You can also change to the Web Layout view by clicking the Web Layout View button located at the left side of the horizontal scroll bar or by clicking <u>V</u>iew and then <u>W</u>eb Layout.

Web Layout
View

Formatting a Web Page

Word provides a variety of predesigned styles and formatting that can be applied to a document. You learned about the styles in the Style Gallery in chapter 5. Themes and backgrounds can also be applied to documents. Themes and backgrounds are designed for viewing in a Word document, in an e-mail message, or on the Web. Backgrounds and some theme formatting do not print.

Applying a Theme to a Web Page

Some interesting and colorful formatting can be applied to a document with options at the Theme dialog box shown in figure 8.14. To display this dialog box, click F<u>o</u>rmat, expand the drop-down menu, and then click T<u>h</u>eme. Click a theme in the Choose a <u>T</u>heme list box and a preview displays at the right side. Click OK to close the dialog box and apply the theme to the document. (You can also double-click a theme at the Theme dialog box.)

When a theme is applied to a document, Word automatically changes to the Web Layout view. Theme formatting is designed for documents that will be published on the Web, on an intranet, or sent as an e-mail. Not all of the formatting applied by a theme will print.

Theme Dialog Box

Click a theme in this list box and preview it at the right.

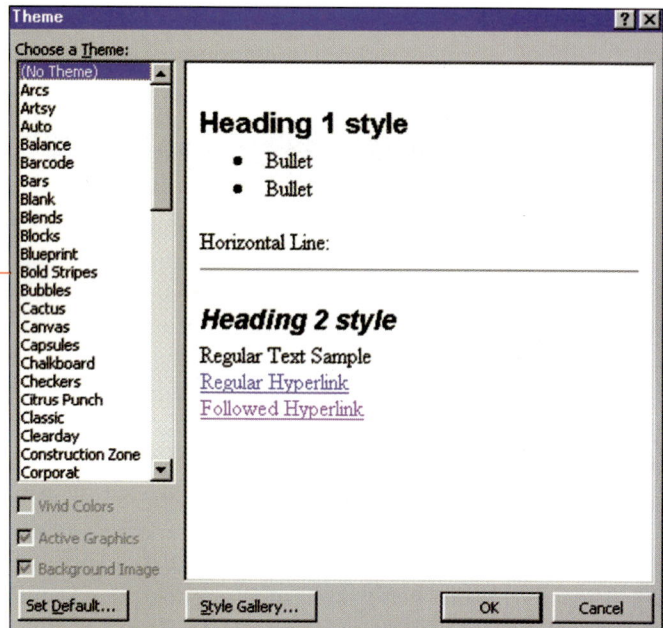

Previewing a Document in Web Page Preview

When creating a Web page, you may want to preview it in your default Web browser. To do this, click File, expand the drop-down menu, and then click Web Page Preview. This displays the currently open document in the default Web browser and displays formatting supported by the browser.

exercise 6

Creating and Formatting a Web Page

1. Open Beltway Home Page.
2. Save the document as a Web page by completing the following steps:
    a. Click File, expand the drop-down menu, and then click Save as Web Page.
    b. Key **Beltway Web Page** and then press Enter.
3. Make the following formatting changes to the document:
    a. Apply the Heading 1 style to the company name *BELTWAY TRANSPORTATION*.
    b. Center the company name *BELTWAY TRANSPORTATION*.
    c. Select the company address, telephone number, and Web address and then apply the Heading 2 style.
    d. With the text still selected, display the Paragraph dialog box, change the spacing before paragraphs to 3 points (leave the spacing after at 3 points), and then close the dialog box.
    e. With the text still selected, click the Center button on the Formatting toolbar, and then deselect the text.
    f. Apply the Travel theme by completing the following steps:
        1) Click Format, expand the drop-down menu, and then click Theme.
        2) Scroll through the list of themes in the Choose a Theme list box until *Travel* is visible and then click *Travel*.
        3) Click OK to close the dialog box.
    g. Select the text from the paragraph that begins *Let Beltway Transportation take care of all...* to the end of the document, change the font color to Lime, and then deselect the text.
4. Preview the document in Web Page Preview by completing the following steps:
    a. Click File, expand the drop-down menu, and then click Web Page Preview.
    b. After viewing the document in the Web browser, click File and then Close.
5. Save the document again with the same name (Beltway Web Page).
6. Print and then close Beltway Web Page. (Not all of the theme formatting will print.)

Applying a Background to a Document

Apply a colorful background to a document by clicking Format, expanding the drop-down menu, and then clicking Background. This causes a palette of color choices to display at the right side of the drop-down menu as shown in figure 8.15. Click the desired color or click the More Colors option to display the Colors dialog box.

Apply a background and the view is automatically changed to Web Layout. A background color does not display in the Normal or Print Layout views and will not print. Like a theme, background color is designed for formatting documents such as Web pages or e-mail messages that are viewed on the screen.

figure

8.15

Background Side Menu

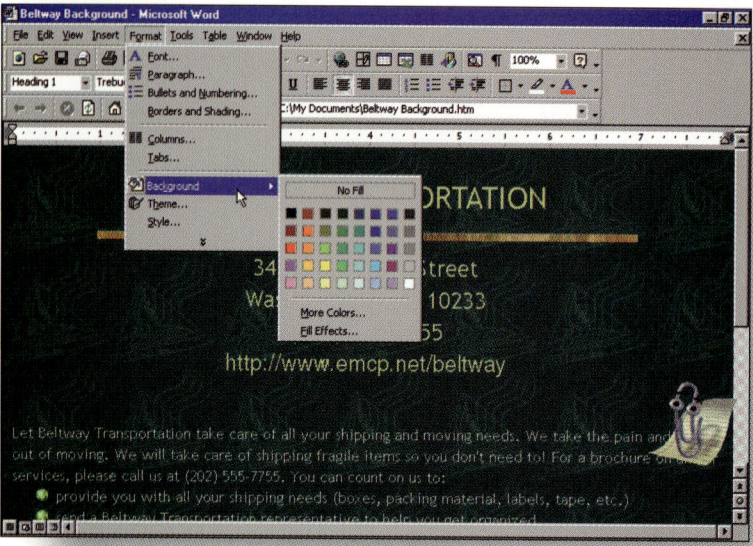

Click the Fill Effects option from the Background side menu and the Fill Effects dialog box displays as shown in figure 8.16. Use options from this dialog box to apply formatting such as a gradient, texture, and pattern.

figure

8.16

Fill Effects Dialog Box

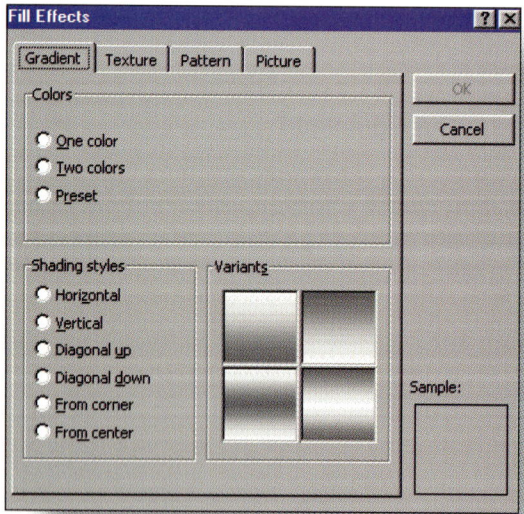

Applying a Background to a Web Page

1. Open Beltway Web Page. (If this document is not visible, change the Files of type option at the Open dialog box to All Files.)
2. Save the document with Save As and name it Beltway Background. (Make sure the Save as type option is *Web Page*.)
3. Change the background color of the Web page and add a gradient and texture by completing the following steps:
   a. Click Format, expand the drop-down menu, point to Background, and then click the Sea Green color (fourth color from the left in the third row).
   b. Click Format, point to Background, and then click Fill Effects.
   c. At the Fill Effects dialog box with the Gradient tab selected, click From center in the Shading styles section.
   d. Click OK to close the dialog box.
   e. Notice how the Web page displays.
4. Add a texture to the Web page by completing the following steps:
   a. Click Format, point to Background, and then click Fill Effects.
   b. At the Fill Effects dialog box, click the Texture tab.
   c. At the Fill Effects dialog box with the Texture tab selected, click the third texture option from the left in the bottom row (*Purple mesh*).
   d. Click OK to close the dialog box.
   e. Notice how the Web page displays.
5. Preview the Web page in Web Page Preview. (You may need to maximize the Internet Explorer window.) After viewing the document, close the Web browser.
6. Save the document again with the same name (Beltway Background).
7. Close Beltway Background. (Printing is optional—the texture does not print.)

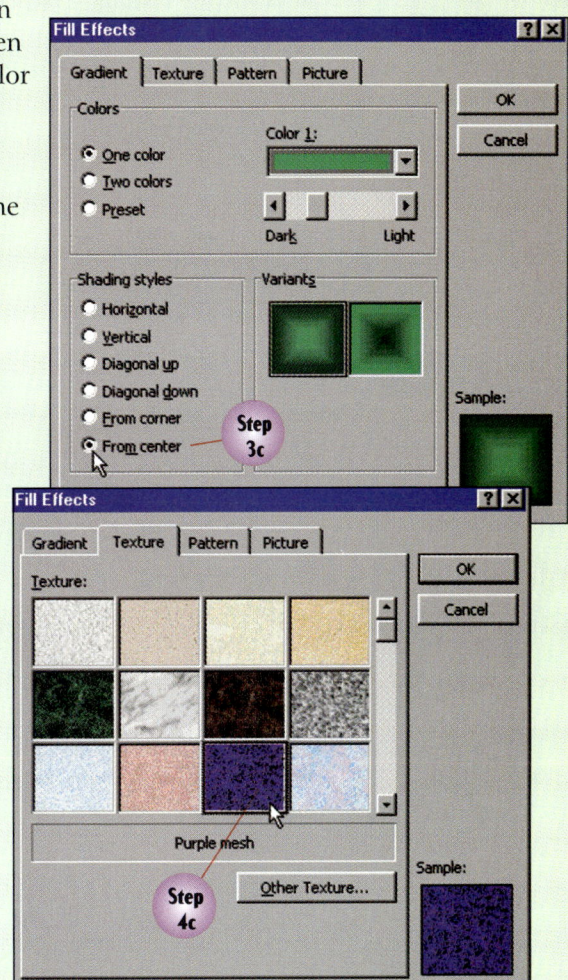

Formatting with Buttons on the Web Tools Toolbar

A Web page designer uses a variety of tools to prepare an appealing and successful Web page. Tools are available for formatting a Web page with buttons on the Web Tools toolbar shown in figure 8.17. Display the Web Tools toolbar by clicking View, pointing to Toolbars, and then clicking *Web Tools*. You can also display the Web Tools toolbar by right-clicking a currently displayed toolbar and then clicking *Web Tools* at the drop-down list. The shape of the toolbar shown in figure

8.17 has been changed to show the button names. The shape of your Web Tools toolbar will vary.

An interactive Web page, a page in which the viewer will provide input or answer questions, might include check boxes and option buttons. A Web page with a variety of options and choices might include drop-down boxes and list boxes. In exercise 8 you will be using two of the buttons on the Web Tools toolbar. As you continue to create and design Web pages, consider experimenting with other buttons on the Web Tools toolbar.

figure 8.17

Web Tools Toolbar Buttons

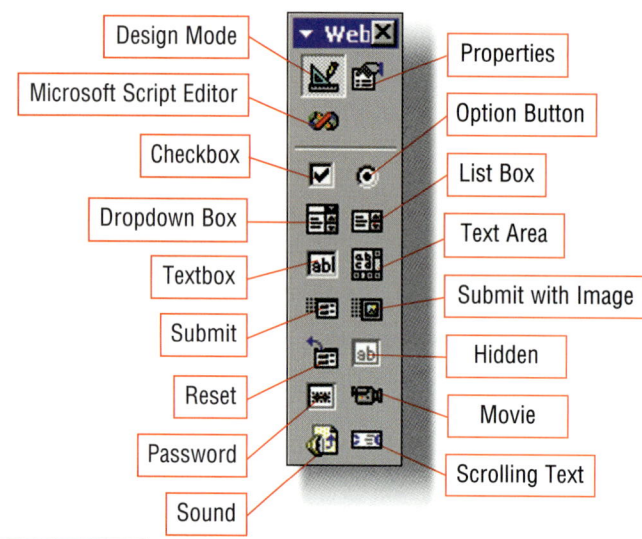

exercise 8

Inserting a Sound Clip and Scrolling Text to a Web Page

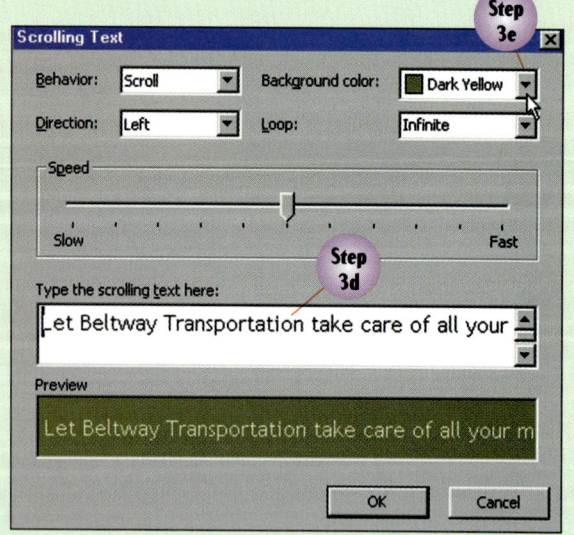

1. Open Beltway Web Page.
2. Save the document with Save As and name it Beltway Formatted.
3. Insert scrolling text in the Web page by completing the following steps:
   a. Display the Web Tools toolbar by clicking View, pointing to Toolbars, and then clicking *Web Tools*.
   b. Position the insertion point at the left margin on the blank line below the company Web address and then click the Center button on the Formatting toolbar.
   c. Click the Scrolling Text button on the Web Tools toolbar.
   d. At the Scrolling Text dialog box, select *Scrolling Text* that displays in

the Type the scrolling text here text box and then key **Let Beltway Transportation take care of all your moving needs!**

   e. Click the down-pointing triangle at the right side of the Background color text box and then click *Dark Yellow* at the drop-down list.

   f. Click OK to close the Scrolling Text dialog box.

4. Add a sound clip to the Web page by completing the following steps:

   a. Click the Sound button on the Web Tools toolbar.

   b. At the Background Sound dialog box, click the Browse button.

   c. At the File Open dialog box (with the Media folder displayed), double-click *Canyon* in the list box.

   d. At the Background Sound dialog box, click the down-pointing triangle at the right side of the Loop text box, and then click *Infinite* at the drop-down list.

   e. Click OK to close the Background Sound dialog box.

5. Save the document again with the same name (Beltway Formatted).

6. Close the Web Tools toolbar.

7. Print and then close Beltway Formatted.

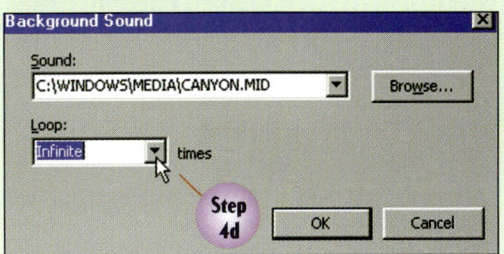

Creating Hyperlinks

The business Web sites you have visited, such as Microsoft and USA Today, have included hyperlinks to connect you to other pages or Web sites. You can create your own hyperlink in your Web page. To do this, select the text you want specified as the hyperlink, and then click the Insert Hyperlink button on the Standard toolbar. At the Insert Hyperlink dialog box shown in figure 8.18, key the Web site URL in the Type the file or Web page name text box, and then click OK.

Insert Hyperlink

8.18

Insert Hyperlink Dialog Box

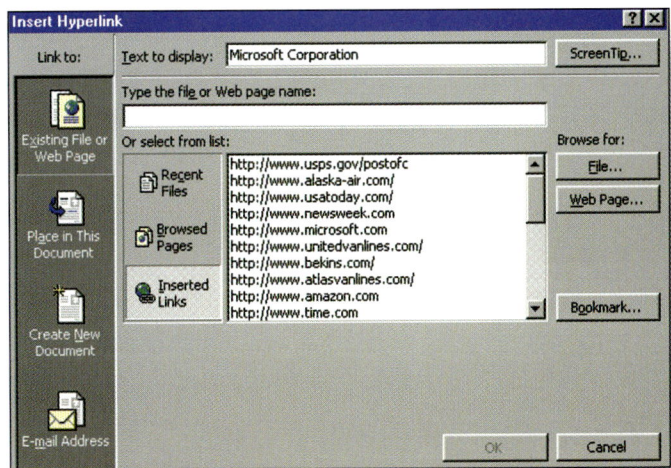

Another method for creating a hyperlink is to key the URL in a Word document. When you key the complete URL, Word automatically converts the URL to a hyperlink and changes the color of the URL. In exercise 9, you will be establishing hyperlinks from the Beltway Transportation Web page to moving company sites.

exercise 9

Creating Hyperlinks

1. Open Beltway Web Page.
2. Create a hyperlink so that clicking Atlas Van Lines displays the Atlas Van Lines Web page by completing the following steps:
   a. Select the text *Atlas Van Lines* that displays towards the end of the document (after a bullet).
   b. Click the Insert Hyperlink button on the Standard toolbar.
   c. At the Insert Hyperlink dialog box, key **http://www.atlasvanlines.com** in the Type the file or Web page name text box.
   d. Click OK. (This changes the color of the *Atlas Van Lines* text and also adds underlining to the text.)
3. Complete steps similar to those in step 2 to create a hyperlink from *Bekins* to the URL *http://www.bekins.com*.
4. Complete steps similar to those in step 2 to create a hyperlink from *United Van Lines* to the URL *http://www.unitedvanlines.com*.
5. Click the Save button on the Standard toolbar to save the Web page with the hyperlinks added.

Insert Hyperlink			
Link to:	**Text to display:** Atlas Van Lines		ScreenTip...
	Type the file or Web page name:	Step 2c	
Existing File or Web Page	http://www.atlasvanlines.com		
	Or select from list:		Browse for:
	Recent Files	http://www.usps.gov/postofc http://www.alaska-air.com/ http://www.usatoday.com/ http://www.newsweek.com	File...
Place in This Document	Browsed Pages	http://www.microsoft.com http://www.unitedvanlines.com/ http://www.bekins.com/	Web Page...
Create New Document	Inserted Links	http://www.atlasvanlines.com/ http://www.amazon.com http://www.time.com	Bookmark...
E-mail Address			OK Cancel

6. Jump to the hyperlink sites by completing the following steps:
   a. Click the hyperlink *Atlas Van Lines* that displays towards the end of the document.
   b. When the Atlas Van Lines Web page displays, scroll through the page, and then click on a hyperlink that interests you.
   c. After looking at this next page, click File and then Close.
   d. At the Beltway Web page document, click the hyperlink *Bekins*.
   e. After viewing the Bekins home page, click File and then Close.
   f. At the Beltway Web page document, click the hyperlink *United Van Lines*.
   g. After viewing the United Van Lines home page, click File and then Close.
7. Close the Beltway Web Page document.

Creating a Web Page Using the Web Page Wizard

Word provides a wizard that will help you prepare a Web page. To use the Web Page Wizard, click File and then New. At the New dialog box, click the Web Pages tab. At the New dialog box with the Web Pages tab selected, as shown in figure 8.19, double-click the *Web Page Wizard* icon. This displays the Web Page Wizard Start dialog box shown in figure 8.20. With the Web Page Wizard, you will choose a title and location for the page, specify and organize pages, and choose a visual theme for the page.

8.19

New Dialog Box with Web Pages Tab Selected

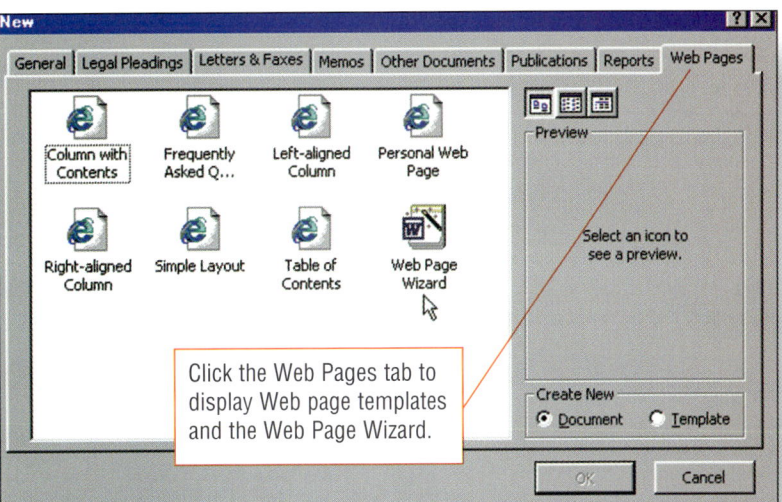

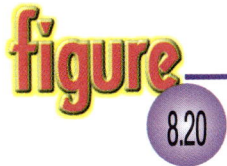

8.20

Web Page Wizard Short Dialog Box

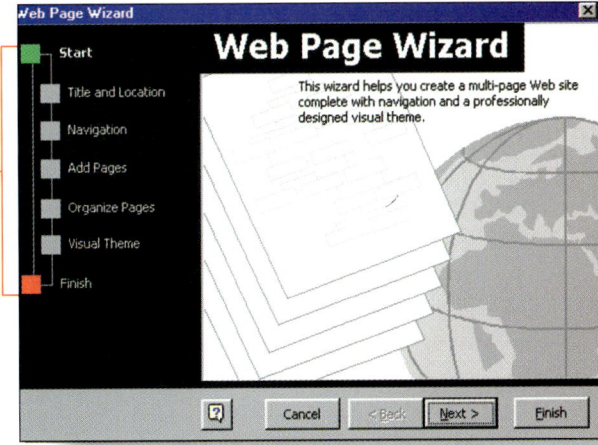

When using the Web Page Wizard, you will need to specify the location of the Web page document and related documents. In exercise 10, you will create a subfolder on the your data disk and then specify that subfolder as the location for the Web page documents.

Creating a Web Page Using the Web Page Wizard

1. Create a subfolder on your disk by completing the following steps:
   a. Display the Open dialog box.
   b. Make sure Chapter 08C is the active folder on your disk.
   c. Click the Create New Folder button on the dialog box toolbar.
   d. At the New Folder dialog box, key **Web Pages** in the Name text box, and then click OK.
   e. Click the Cancel button to close the Open dialog box.
2. Create a Web page using the Web Page Wizard by completing the following steps:
   a. At a blank Word screen, click File and then New.
   b. At the New dialog box, click the Web Pages tab.
   c. At the New dialog box with the Web Pages tab selected, double-click the *Web Page Wizard* icon.
   d. At the Web Page Wizard Start dialog box, click the Next> button.

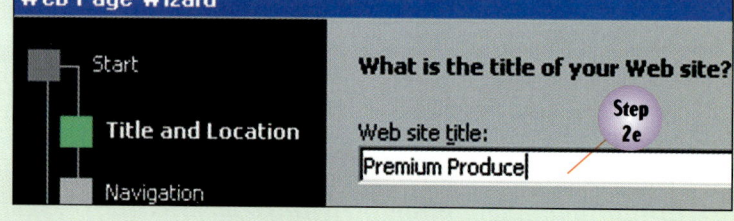

   e. At the Web Page Wizard Title and Location dialog box, key **Premium Produce** in the Web site title text box.
   f. Click the Next> button.
   g. At the Web Page Wizard Navigation dialog box, make sure Vertical frame is selected, and then click the Next> button.
   h. At the Web Page Wizard Add Pages dialog box, make the following changes:
      1) Click *Personal Web Page* in the Current pages in Web site list box and then click the Remove Page button.
      2) Click *Blank Page 2* in the Current pages in Web site list box and then click the Remove Page button.
      3) Click the Add Template Page button.
      4) At the Web Page Templates dialog box, double-click *Left-aligned Column* in the list box.
      5) At the Web Page Wizard Add Pages dialog box, click the Next> button.
   i. At the Web Page Wizard Organize Pages dialog box, click the Move Up button (to move *Left-aligned Column* above *Blank Page 1*), and then click the Next> button.

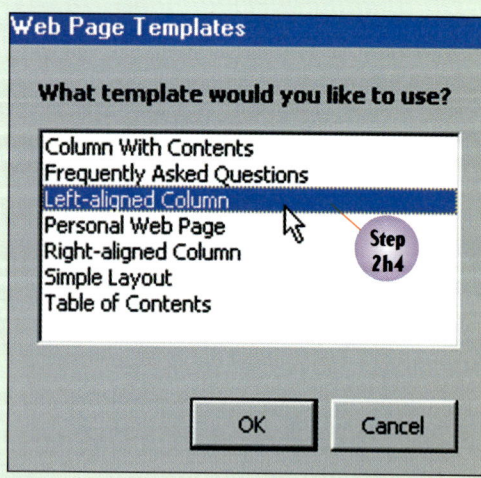

j. At the Web Page Wizard Visual Theme dialog box, choose a theme by completing the following steps:
 1) Click the Browse Themes button.
 2) At the Theme dialog box, scroll down the list of themes in the Choose a Theme list box until *Nature* is visible and then click *Nature*.
 3) Click OK to close the dialog box.
 4) At the Web Page Wizard Visual Theme dialog box, click the Next> button.
k. At the Web Page Wizard Finish dialog box, click the Finish button. (If you are saving onto a disk, this may take some time.)

3. Format the Web page document by completing the following steps:
a. Turn off the display of the Frames toolbar by clicking the Close button (contains an X) that displays in the upper right corner of the toolbar.
b. Select the text *Main Heading Goes Here* and then key **Premium Produce**.
c. Select the text (below the picture) *Captions goes here.* and then key **Premium Produce—Premium Flavor**. (To create the dash between Produce and Premium, key two hyphens. AutoCorrect will change the two hyphens to a dash when you press the space bar after keying Premium.)
d. Insert a file from your data disk by completing the following steps:
 1) Select from the beginning of the text *Section Heading Goes Here* (the first occurrence of this text) to the end of the text in the document. (Make sure you do not select the picture or anything other than the text.)
 2) With the text selected, press the Delete key.
 3) Click Insert and then File.
 4) At the Insert File dialog box, click the Up One Level button to make Chapter 08C the active folder, and then double-click the document named *Prem Pro Insert*.
e. Insert a pricing table in the blank page by completing the following steps:
 1) Click the *Blank Page 1* hyperlink that displays at the left side of the screen.
 2) At the blank page 1 document, select the text *This Web Page is Blank Page 1* and then press the Delete key.
 3) Click Insert and then File.
 4) At the Insert File dialog box, make sure Chapter 08C is the active folder.
 5) Double-click *Prem Pro Pricing* in the list box. (This inserts the table into the blank page 1 document.)
 6) With the table inserted in the document, click the Save button on the Standard toolbar. (If you are saving onto a disk, this may take some time.)
f. Return to the Premium Produce page by clicking the *Left-aligned Column* hyperlink that displays at the left side of the screen.
g. Change the hyperlink text by completing the following steps:
 1) Select the *Left-aligned Column* hyperlink text and then key **Home**. (Make sure *Home* is underlined. If not, click the Undo button and try again.)
 2) Select the *Blank Page 1* hyperlink text and then key **Pricing**. (Make sure *Pricing* is underlined. If not, click the Undo button and try again.)

Step 3b

Step 3d

Premium Produce

Farm-fresh and Organic Produce

Premium Produce is your source for local, farm-fresh produce. All of our produce is organically grown without pesticides, herbicides or other sprays. We ship our produce daily to a

Step 3c

Premium Produce—Premium Flavor

h. Display the pricing table by clicking the *Pricing* hyperlink.

i. Return to the Premium Produce home page by clicking the *Home* hyperlink.

4. Save the Web document by clicking the Save button on the Standard toolbar. (This saves the document and names it *default*.)

5. Print and then close the document.

The Web Page Wizard specifies a folder and subfolders for Web page files. This is because a Web page generally consists of a variety of items that are inserted in individual files. For example, each bullet image and clip art image or picture in a Web page is saved in a separate image file. Inserting all of these files into folders makes it easier for you to take this information to another location. For example, you can copy the contents of a Web page folder and all its subfolders to another computer or onto a disk.

During the Web Page Wizard steps, a vertical frame was chosen. A frame in a Web page helps you organize information and make it easily accessible. When a single Web page is divided into sections that can display separate Web pages, each section is referred to as a frame. In exercise 10, your Web page contained two frames—the section at the left containing the hyperlinks and the section at the right containing the company home page information.

exercise 11

Viewing the Web Pages Folder

1. Display the Open dialog box.

2. If neccesary, change the Files of type option to All Files.

3. Display the contents of the Web Pages folder by completing the following steps:

   a. Make sure Chapter 08C on your disk is the active folder.

   b. Double-click the Web Pages folder.

   c. At the Web Pages folder, double-click the Premium Produce folder.

   d. At the Premium Produce folder, notice the documents saved in this folder by the Web Page Wizard.

   e. Double-click the folder *Blank Page 1_files*.

   f. Notice the documents saved in this folder by the Web Page Wizard and then click the Up One Level button.

   g. At the Premium Produce folder, double-click the *Left-aligned Column_files* folder.

   h. Notice the documents saved in this folder by the Web Page Wizard and then click the Up One Level button.

   i. Click the Up One Level two more times. (This returns you to the Chapter 08C folder.)

4. Close the Open dialog box.

chapter summary

➤ The Internet is a network of computers connected around the world allowing exchange of information.

➤ Word provides the ability to jump to the Internet from the Word document screen.

➤ The World Wide Web is the most commonly used application on the Internet and is a set of standards and protocols used to access information available on the Internet.

➤ A software program used to access the Web is referred to as a Web browser.

➤ To locate information on the World Wide Web you need a modem, browser software, and an Internet Service Provider account. An Internet Service Provider sells access to the Internet.

➤ A modem is a hardware device that carries data over telephone lines.

➤ Uniform Resource Locators (URLs) are the method used to identify locations on the Web.

➤ A Web page can contain hyperlinks. Click a link to connect to another site, location, or page.

➤ Use a search engine such as Yahoo, InfoSeek, or Excite to locate information on the Internet on a specific topic by keying a few words or a short phrase.

➤ Narrow a search by using search operators such as the plus symbol, minus symbol, quotation mark; or use Boolean operators such as AND, OR, and AND NOT.

➤ Add a site that you visit regularly to the Favorites list at the Internet Explorer Favorites side bar. You can also delete and organize favorite sites at the Favorites side bar.

➤ Click the History button on the Internet Explorer toolbar to display the History side bar. This side bar displays sites visited in the last few days, hours, or minutes.

➤ Home pages are Web documents that describe a company, school, government, or individual and are created using a language called HyperText Markup Language (HTML).

➤ A home page can be created in Word and saved as a Web page, or you can create a Web page using the Web Page Wizard.

➤ When a document is saved as a Web page, Word automatically changes to the Web Layout view.

➤ Apply a theme to a Web page with options at the Theme dialog box.

➤ Preview a document in the default Web browser by clicking File, expanding the drop-down menu, and then clicking Web Page Preview.

➤ Apply a background color with options from the Background side menu.

➤ Apply a gradient, texture, or pattern to a Web page with options at the Fill Effects dialog box.

➤ Some theme formatting and background color, gradient, texture, and pattern do not print.

➤ The Web Tools toolbar contains buttons for customizing and designing a Web page.

➤ One method for creating a hyperlink is to select the text and then click the Insert Hyperlink button on the Standard toolbar. At the Insert Hyperlink dialog box, key the URL and then click OK.

➤ Start the Web Page Wizard by displaying the New dialog box, clicking the Web Pages tab, and then double-clicking the *Web Page Wizard* icon.

commands review

	Mouse
Display the Web toolbar	Click View, point to Toolbars, then click Web; or right-click any toolbar and click Web at the drop-down menu
Display Internet Explorer Search Setup page	Click Search the Web button on the Web toolbar
Display the Favorites side bar	Click Favorites button on the Internet Explorer toolbar
Display the History side bar	Click History button on the Internet Explorer toolbar
Change to the Web Layout view	Click Web Layout View button at the left side of the horizontal scroll bar or click View and then Web Layout
Display the Theme dialog box	Click Format, expand the drop-down menu, and then click Theme
Web Page Preview	Click File, expand the drop-down menu, and then click Web Page Preview
Display the Background side menu	Click Format and point to Background
Display Fill Effects dialog box	Click Format, point to Background, and click Fill Effects
Display Web Tools toolbar	Click View, point to Toolbars, and then click Web Tools; or, right-click a toolbar and click Web Tools at the drop-down list
Display the Insert Hyperlink dialog box	Click Insert Hyperlink button on the Standard toolbar
Display the New dialog box	Click File and New

thinking offline

Completion: In the space provided at the right, indicate the correct term or command.

1. List three reasons why users access the Internet.

2. The word "modem" is derived from this.

3. The letters ISP stand for this.

4. This is the method used to identify locations on the Internet.

5. To search for information on the Web using a search engine, click this button on the Web toolbar.

6. Click this in a home page to link to another page or location.

7. Click this button on the Internet Explorer toolbar to display the previous Web page or location.

8. List at least three search engines that can be used to search for specific information on the Internet.

_____

_____

_____

9. Click this button on the Internet Explorer toolbar to display a side bar containing a list of sites visited in the last few days, hours, or minutes.

_____

10. A home page on the Web is created using this language.

_____

11. When a document is saved as a Web page, the Web page displays in this view.

_____

12. Use buttons on this toolbar to design and format a Web page.

_____

13. Click File, expand the drop-down menu, and then click this option to display the currently open document in the default Web browser.

_____

14. Click this button on the Standard toolbar to add a hypertext link to selected text.

_____

In the space provided, list the text and operators you would use to complete the following searches using the Excite search engine.

1. Search for documents containing the words *better business bureau* in that sequence.

_____

2. Search for documents containing *travel* but not *international*.

_____

3. Search for documents containing *dolphins* or *porpoises*.

_____

working hands-on

Assessment 1

1. Make sure you are connected to the Internet and then display the following sites:
   a. At a clear document screen, display the *USA Today* home page at http://www.usatoday.com.
   b. At the *USA Today* home page, find a section of the newspaper that interests you, find an article within that section, and then print the article.
   c. Display the Alaska Airlines home page at http://www.alaska-air.com.
   d. Search for flight departure times from Juneau, Alaska, to Orange County, California.
   e. Print the flight schedule.
   f. Display the United States Postal Service Web site at http://www.usps.gov/postofc.
   g. At the site, use hyperlinks to search for information on domestic postage rates, and then print the information.
2. Close Internet Explorer.

Assessment 2

1. Make sure you are connected to the Internet.
2. At a clear document screen, click the Search the Web button on the Toolbar.
3. At the Internet Explorer Search Setup page, complete the following searches:
   a. Use a search engine of your choosing to find information on bicycle racing.
   b. When the search engine displays a list of sites, scroll through the list, find a bicycle club that interests you, and then display the home page for the club.
   c. With the bicycle club home page displayed, print the page.
   d. Click the Back button until the Internet Explorer Search Setup page displays at the right side of the screen.
   e. Use a search engine of your choosing to find information on the White House.
   f. When the search engine displays a list of sites, scroll through the list, find a site that interests you, and then display the home page.
   g. With the home page displayed, print the page.
   h. Click the Back button until the Internet Explorer Search Setup page displays at the right side of the screen.
   i. Use a search engine of your choosing to find sites on kayaking in national parks.
   j. When the search engine displays a list of sites, find a national park site that interests you, display the site, and then print the page.
   k. Click the Back button until the Internet Explorer Search Setup page displays.
4. Close Internet Explorer.

Assessment 3

1. Open Apex Home Page.
2. Make the following changes to the document:
   a. Save the document as a Web page with the name Apex Web Page.
   b. Make the following formatting changes to the document:
      1) Apply a theme of your choosing to the document.
      2) Increase the font size of the company name, Web address, address, and telephone number.
      3) Select *Apple Computer* and then create a hyperlink to *http://www.apple.com*.
      4) Select *Blizzard Entertainment* and create a hyperlink to *http://www.blizzard.com*.
      5) Select *id Software* and create a hyperlink to *http://www.idsoftware.com*.
      6) Select *Microsoft Corporation* and create a hyperlink to *http://www.microsoft.com*.
      7) Make sure the text for the home page fits on one page. (If it does not, delete some blank lines.)
3. Save the document again with the same name (Apex Web Page).
4. Print and then close Apex Web Page.

Assessment 4

1. Open Apex Web Page.
2. Save the document with Save As and name it Apex Background.
3. Make the following formatting changes to the document:
   a. Apply a background color and gradient of your choosing.
   b. Add the scrolling text *Apex Cyberware offers computer software at incredibly low prices!* somewhere in the document.
   c. Add a sound clip to the document.
   d. Preview the document in the default Web browser. (You may need to maximize the browser window.) After viewing the document, close the Web browser.
4. Save the document again with the same name (Apex Background).
5. Print and then close Apex Background.

Assessment 5

1. Some Web sites contain interactive pages where the viewer fills in information in various types of boxes and then submits the information to the Web site company. The Web Tools toolbar contains buttons for creating an interactive Web page with forms controls such as text boxes, check boxes, and option boxes. Use the Help feature to learn about Web form controls. (*Hint: Click the Office Assistant, key the question* What are Web form controls?*, and then click the *Search* button. At the list of items that displays, click* Form controls you can use on a Web page.*) Continue using the Help to display information on the eleven standard form controls. Read specifically about the Checkbox control, Option Button control, and the Textbox control.
2. After reading the Help information on controls, complete the following steps:
   a. Create the document shown in figure 8.21. (Use Web Tools toolbar buttons to create the check boxes, option boxes, and text boxes.)
   b. Apply the same theme you applied to the Apex Web Page in assessment 4.
   c. After applying the theme, make sure spacing is correct.
3. Save the document and name it Apex Form.
4. Print and then close Apex Form. (Some of the theme formatting will not print.)

figure

8.21

Assessment 5

Top of Form

APEX CYBERWARE
http://www.apexcyber.com
540 Minor Avenue
Seattle, WA 98045
(206) 555-2233

Customer Name: _____

Address: _____

Company: _____

Have you ordered from Apex Cyberware in the past six months?   ◯ Yes   ◯ No

Please insert a check in the box next to software you are currently using on your computer:

☐ Education   ☐ Games

☐ Word processing   ☐ Spreadsheet

☐ Database   ☐ Presentation

☐ Scheduling   ☐ Money management

Bottom of Form

Performance Assessments

Word CPA

CORE LEVEL

ASSESSING CORE PROFICIENCIES

Within the Core Level, you have learned to create, edit, format, save, print, and enhance Word documents; manage documents on disk; explore the Internet; and create and format Web pages.

(Before completing the Core Level assessments, delete the Chapter 08C *folder on your disk. Next, copy the* Word CPA *folder from the CD that accompanies this textbook to your disk and make* Word CPA *the active folder.)*

Assessment 1

one

1. At a clear document screen, key the text shown in figure C1.1.
2. Save the document and name it Word CPA 01.
3. Print and close Word CPA 01.

GLOSSARY

Acoustical energy: A form of energy related to signals generated by some form of sound such as a voice.

Amplitude modulation (AM): A method of modifying the high to low ranges of a radio carrier wave according to the strength of the signal.

Analog signal: A continuously varying *electromagnetic wave* whose signal pattern changes based on the information being transmitted.

Asynchronous transmission: The transmission of data one character at a time through a method that denotes the beginning and end of each character; the devices used in sending and receiving the data are not synchronized for the transmission.

Attenuation: Decrease in the strength of a signal as it moves away from its source; the strength of the signal is generally measured in *decibels*, the method developed to measure the loudness of sound.

Figure C1.1 • Assessment 1

Assessment 2

1. Open Word CPA 01.
2. Save the document with Save As and name it Word CPA 02.
3. Make the following changes to the document:
   a. Change the top, left, and right margins to 1.5 inches.
   b. Select the paragraphs that begin with bolded words, change the paragraph alignment to justified, and then insert numbering.
   c. Select the entire document and change the font to 12-point Century Schoolbook (or a similar serif typeface).
   d. Delete the text *Glossary* and recreate the title using WordArt. You determine the shape, font, and color of the WordArt text. Resize the WordArt to approximately 3.5 inches wide by 1 inch in height and position it in the center of the page between the left and right margins.
4. Save the document again with the same name (Word CPA 02).
5. Print and close Word CPA 02.

Assessment 3

1. At a clear document screen, key the text shown in figure C1.2 with the following specifications:
   a. Change the font to 16-point Braggadocio and the color to dark blue. (If Braggadocio is not available, choose another font.)
   b. Animate the title *Telecommunications Seminar* with an animation effect of your choosing. (The animation effect will not print.)
   c. Change the line spacing to 1.5.
   d. Center the text vertically on the page.
   e. Insert an appropriate clip art image of your choosing below the text. Resize the image to approximately 3 inches wide by 3 inches tall and center it horizontally between the left and right margins.
2. Save the document and name it Word CPA 03.
3. Print and close Word CPA 03.

> **Telecommunications Seminar**
>
> **Thursday, March 15, 2001**
>
> **Carson Convention Center**
>
> **Room 108**
>
> **8:30 a.m. - 4:30 p.m.**

Figure C1.2 • Assessment 3

Assessment 4

1. At a clear document screen, key the text shown in figure C1.3 with the following specifications:

a. Bold and center the title as shown.
b. Determine the tab settings for the text in columns.
c. Select the entire document and then change the font to 12-point Arial.
d. Vertically center the text on the page.

2. Save the document and name it Word CPA 04.
3. Print and close Word CPA 04.

INCOME BY DIVISION

	1997	1998	1999
Public Relations	$14,375	$16,340	$16,200
Database Services	9,205	15,055	13,725
Graphic Design	18,400	21,790	19,600
Technical Support	5,780	7,325	9,600

Figure C1.3 • Assessment 4

Assessment 5

five

1. At a clear document screen, key the text shown in figure C1.4 with the following specifications:
   a. Bold and center the title as shown.
   b. You determine the tab settings for the text in columns.
   c. Select the entire document and then change the font to 12-point Bookman Old Style (or a similar serif typeface).
   d. Vertically center the text on the page.
2. Save the document and name it Word CPA 05.
3. Print and close Word CPA 05.

TABLE OF CONTENTS

Telecommunications Services 1

Telecommunications Facts and Figures 3

Technology in the Future 7

Electronic Mail and Messaging Systems 9

Cellular Mobile Telephone Technology 12

Local Area Networks 17

Figure C1.4 • Assessment 5

Assessment 6

1. Open Word Spell Check 04.
2. Save the document with Save As and name it Word CPA 06.
3. Make the following changes to the document:
   a. Complete a spelling check and a grammar check on the document. (You determine what to edit and what to leave as written.)
   b. Select the document and change the font to 12-point Century Schoolbook (or a similar serif typeface).
   c. Set the title in 14-point Century Schoolbook bold.
   d. Select the paragraphs in the body of the document (excluding the title), indent the first line of each paragraph 0.5 inches, and then change the paragraph alignment to justified.
   e. Proofread the document. (There are errors that are not selected by the spelling or grammar checker.)
4. Save the document again with the same name (Word CPA 06).
5. Print and close Word CPA 06.

Assessment 7

1. At a clear document screen, create an envelope with the text shown in figure C1.5.
2. Save the envelope document and name it Word CPA 07.
3. Print and close Word CPA 07.

Mrs. Eileen Hebert
15205 East 42nd Street
Lake Charles, LA 71098

Mr. Earl Robicheaux
1436 North Sheldon Street
Jennings, LA 70542

Figure C1.5 • Assessment 7

Assessment 8

1. Create mailing labels with the name and address for Mrs. Eileen Hebert shown in figure C1.5 using the Avery standard, 5660 – Address label.
2. Save the document and name it Word CPA 08.
3. Print and close Word CPA 08.

Assessment 9

1. Create a document by copying text from another document by completing the following steps:
   a. Key the title **KEY LIFE HEALTH PLAN** bolded and centered.

b. Press Enter twice and key the subtitle **Plan Information** bolded and centered.

c. Press Enter three times, turn off bold, and return the paragraph alignment to left.

d. Save the document and name it Word CPA 09.

e. With Word CPA 09 still open, open the document named Key Life Health Plan.

f. With Key Life Health Plan the active document, select the second heading *HOW THE PLAN WORKS* and the three paragraphs of text below this heading, and then copy and paste it at the end of the Word CPA 09 document.

g. Make Key Life Health Plan the active document. Select the first heading *PLAN HIGHLIGHTS* and the six paragraphs of text below this heading, and then copy and paste the selected text at the end of the Word CPA 09 document.

h. Make Key Life Health Plan the active document. Select the fourth heading *PROVIDER NETWORK* and the two paragraphs of text below this heading, and then copy and paste it to the end of the Word CPA 09 document.

i. Make Key Life Health Plan the active document. Select the third heading *QUALITY ASSESSMENT* and the six paragraphs of text below this heading (two paragraphs and four bulleted paragraphs) and then copy and paste it at the end of the Word CPA 09 document.

2. Close Key Life Health Plan. (If you are asked if you want to save the changes, click <u>N</u>o.)

3. Make the following changes to Unit 1, PA 09:

a. Change the top margin to 1.5 inches and the left and right margins to 1 inch.

b. Set the entire document in 12-point Century Schoolbook (or a similar sans serif typeface).

c. Set the title and subtitle in 16-point Arial bold.

d. Set the following headings in 14-point Arial bold: *(Hint: Use Format Painter.)*

HOW THE PLAN WORKS

PLAN HIGHLIGHTS

PROVIDER NETWORK

QUALITY ASSESSMENT

e. Check the spacing in the document. There should only be a double space above and below headings (except between the subtitle and the first heading—that should be a triple space) and between paragraphs. If there are extra blank lines, delete them.

f. Insert a footer in the document that prints Key Life Health Plan set in 12-point Century Schoolbook bold at the left margin and prints the page number in bold at the right margin.

4. Save the document again with the same name (Word CPA 09).

5. Print and close Word CPA 09.

Assessment 10

1. Open Word CPA 09.

2. Save the document with Save As and name it Word CPA 10.

3. Make the following changes to the document:

a. Delete the footer.

b. Select the entire document and then change line spacing to 1.2. (To do this, display the Paragraph dialog box, key **1.2** in the <u>A</u>t text box, and then close the dialog box. This should increase the size of the document to three pages. If your document is not three pages in length, consider increasing the line spacing to *1.3*.)

c. Create the header Key Life Health Plan that is set in 12-point Century Schoolbook bold and prints at the right margin on every page except the first page.

d. Move the insertion point to the end of the document, a double-space below the text in the document and then insert the following:

   Key Life Health Plan®
   Prepared by Daria Caráquez

4. Save the document again with the same name (Word CPA 10).
5. Print and close Word CPA 10.

Assessment 11

1. Open Word CPA 09.
2. Save the document with Save As and name it Word CPA 11.
3. Make the following changes to the document:
   a. Change the top margin to 1 inch.
   b. Delete the footer.
   c. Search for all occurrences of *Key Life Health Plan* and replace with Premium Health Care Plan.
   d. Insert a continuous section break at the beginning of the heading *HOW THE PLAN WORKS*.
   e. Format the text (below the section break) into two evenly spaced newspaper columns with a line between.
4. Save the document again with the same name (Word CPA 11).
5. Print only the first page of the document.
6. Close Word CPA 11.

Assessment 12

1. Open Word Report 04.
2. Save the document with Save As and name it Word CPA 12.
3. Make the following changes to the document:
   a. Change to Outline view.
   b. Promote or demote text to the headings specified below:

CHAPTER 1: COMPUTER INPUT DEVICES	= Heading 1
Keyboard	= Heading 2
Mouse	= Heading 2
Trackball	= Heading 2
Touch Pad and Touch Screen	= Heading 2
CHAPTER 2: COMPUTER OUTPUT DEVICES	= Heading 1
Monitor	= Heading 2
Printer	= Heading 2

   c. Change to Print Layout view.
   d. Change the top margin to 1.5 inches.
   e. Insert a page break at the beginning of *CHAPTER 2: COMPUTER OUTPUT DEVICES*.
   f. Create the footer Computer Input and Output Devices that is bolded and prints at the right margin on all odd pages.
   g. Create a footer that inserts the filename and path at the left margin on all even pages.
4. Save the document again with the same name (Word CPA 12).
5. Print pages 2 through 4 of the document.
6. Close Word CPA 12.

Assessment 13

1. At a clear document screen, create the table shown in figure C1.6 with the following specifications:
   a. The width of the first column is 1.8 and the width of the second and third columns is 1.4.
   b. Insert the bold, center, and alignment formatting as shown in the figure.
   c. Include the border lines and shading as shown in the figure.
   d. Center the table horizontally.
   e. After creating the table, insert the formula =SUM(ABOVE) to calculate the amounts in the *First Half* column and the *Second Half* column.
   f. Using tools from the drawing toolbar, draw an arrow pointing to the text *Other Assets* in the Asset column of the table. Draw a text box at the beginning of the arrow line and key the following text inside the box:
      Includes Goodwill
   g. Format the text inside the text box to 10-point Arial.
2. Save the document and name it Word CPA 13.
3. Print and close Word CPA 13.

McCORMACK FUNDS

BALANCE SHEET

Asset	First Half	Second Half
Bonds	$41,300,225.50	$45,100,670.00
Stocks	8,924,600.25	9,340,155.80
Mortgages	75,302,210.55	67,210,550.00
Real Estate	13,450,305.45	20,193,553.75
Long-term Investments	1,340,690.90	945,392.00
Short-term Investments	631,405.55	803,288.35
Other Assets	341,395.25	442,890.20
Total		

Figure C1.6 • Assessment 13

Assessment 14

1. At a clear document screen, create a table using the information shown in figure C1.7 with the following specifications:
   a. Insert formulas in the Difference column that calculate the difference between Class B and Class A funds.
   b. Apply an autoformat of your choosing to the table.
2. Save the document and name it Word CPA 14.
3. Print and close Word CPA 14.

STRATEGIC INCOME FUND			
	Class A	Class B	Difference
Expenses after 1 year	$ 56.25	$ 68.30	
Expenses after 3 years	85.10	93.00	
Expenses after 5 years	102.75	110.50	
Expenses after 10 years	178.00	220.15	

Figure C1.7 • Assessment 14

Assessment 15

1. Make sure you are connected to the Internet.
2. At a clear document screen in Word, click the Search the Web button on the toolbar.
3. At the Internet Explorer Search Setup page, complete the following searches.
   a. Search for information on endangered species but not fish or birds. (You determine the search engine.)
   b. Scroll through the list of sites and display a site that interests you. Read the information on the home page and print the home page.
   c. Search for sailing clubs in the San Diego area. (You determine the search engine.)
   d. Display a home page for a sailing club in San Diego and print the home page.
   e. Display one other home page for a sailing club in San Diego and print that home page.
4. Close Internet Explorer.

Assessment 16

1. Open Goldburg Home Page.
2. Save the document as a Web page and name it Goldburg Web Page.
3. Make the following changes to the document:
   a. Apply the Heading 1 style to the name *DEVIN M. GOLDBURG*.
   b. Select the street address; city, state, and Zip code; and telephone number and then complete the following steps:
      1) Apply the Heading 2 style.
      2) Change the spacing before paragraphs to 3 points (leave the spacing after at 3 points).
   c. Apply the Heading 3 style to the following headings:
      Career Objective
      Education
      Work Experience
      Hobbies and Interests
      Relocation
   d. Apply a theme of your choosing to the document.
   e. Add scrolling text to the document. (You determine the text as well as the location.)
   f. Insert a sound clip of your choosing in the document.

g. Create the following hyperlinks:
   1) Select the text *Albuquerque Technical Vocational Institute* in the *Work Experience* section of the document and link it to the URL http://www.tvi.cc.nm.us.
   2) Select the text *Presbyterian Healthcare Services* in the *Work Experience* section of the document and link it to the URL http://www.phs.org.
2. Save the document again with the same name (Goldburg Web Page).
3. Print and close Goldburg Web Page.

WRITING ACTIVITIES

The following activities give you the opportunity to practice your writing skills along with demonstrating an understanding of some of the important Word features you have mastered in the Core Level. Follow the steps explained below to improve your writing skills.

The Writing Process

Plan   Gather ideas, select which information to include, and choose the order in which to present the information.

Checkpoints
- What is the purpose?
- What information do the readers need to reach your intended conclusion?

Write   Following the information plan and keeping the reader in mind, draft the document using clear, direct sentences that say what you mean.

Checkpoints
- What are the subpoints for each main thought?
- How can you connect paragraphs so the reader moves smoothly from one idea to the next?

Revise   Improve what is written by changing, deleting, rearranging, or adding words, sentences, and paragraphs.

Checkpoints
- Is the meaning clear?
- Do the ideas follow a logical order?
- Have you included any unnecessary information?
- Have you built your sentences around strong nouns and verbs?

Edit   Check spelling, sentence construction, word use, punctuation, and capitalization.

Checkpoints
- Can you spot any redundancies or cliches?
- Can you reduce any phrases to an effective word (for example, change *the fact that* to *because*)?
- Have you used commas only where there is a strong reason for doing so?
- Did you proofread the document for errors that your spell checker cannot identify?

Publish   Prepare a final copy that could be reproduced and shared with others.

Checkpoints
- Which design elements—for example, bolding and different fonts— would help highlight important ideas or sections?
- Would charts or other graphics help clarify meaning?

Use correct grammar, appropriate word choices, and clear sentence constructions.

Activity 1

Use Word's Help feature to learn about grammar and writing style options. Learn what options are available and the steps to display the options. Once you have determined this information, compose a memo to your instructor using the Contemporary Memo template. In the memo, explain grammar and writing style options and specifically describe at least two options. Also include in this memo, the steps required to change grammar and writing style options. Save the completed memo and name it Word CPA Act 01. Print and close Word CPA Act 01.

Activity 2

Prepare a Web page résumé for yourself using the Web page résumé you formatted in Assessment 16 as a guide. Try to include as much information about yourself as possible. If there are any hyperlinks you can create, include those in your résumé. When completed, save the résumé Web page and name it Word CPA Act 02. Print and close Word CPA Act 02.

INTERNET ACTIVITY

The Internet is made up of thousands of connecting networks, millions of computers, people from over 150 countries, and unlimited information and resources. Connect to the Internet and use this information resource to search for information on a specific hobby that interests you. Suggestions include collecting, antiques, sports, music, drama, gardening, travel, sailing, flying, etc. Find out as much information as you can about the hobby you choose. When you are done researching the hobby, create a Word document that describes the search process. Include the following information:

- The steps you completed to find Web sites containing information on your specific hobby.
- The types of resources available for your hobby (e.g., magazines, clubs, companies, retailers).
- Your favorite Web site for the hobby including the URL and a description of the site.

Include any other additional information to describe your search. Apply formatting to enhance the Word document. When the document is completed, save it and name it Word CPA Internet Act. Print and close Word CPA Internet Act.

Index

moving, 106–107
with Ruler, 102–107
setting, 103–105, 107–108
Taskbar, 4, 5
TCP/IP (Transmission Control Protocol/Internet Protocol), 327
Templates, 211–215. *See also* Styles
Blank Document, 211
defined, 211
Memo, 212–213
opening, 211–212
using Wizards, 213–215
Text. *See also* Alignment; Blocks of text; Character formatting
animating effects, 49–50
bolding, 38–39
collecting and pasting, 165–166
color, 44–45
deleting, 20–21, 25
finding, 205–207
finding and replacing text, 207–210
highlighting, 121–122
inserting, 20
italicizing, 38–39
line spacing, 74–75
selecting, 22–25
small caps, 46
superscript text, 46–47
underlining, 38–39, 44–45
vertically aligning, 116–117
WordArt, 310
Text box, 299–300
Themes
Web page, 343–344
Thesaurus, 139–140
3-D effect
objects, 307–309
Time, inserting, 119–120
Title bar, 4
Toolbars
Clipboard, 165–166
displaying, 14
Drawing, 294–295
Formatting, 4, 5
Header and footer, 194
Internet Explorer, 332
moving, 14
Outlining, 223–227
Picture, 288–289
Print Preview, 115

Standard, 4
Tables and Borders, 264–268
Web, 328
Web Tools, 347–348
WordArt, 310
Traces, 39
Typeface. *See also* Fonts
adjusting character spacing, 48
choosing, 40
default, 6, 9–10
defined, 40
monospaced, 40–41
proportional, 6, 40–41
san serif, 40
serif, 40
Type size, 41
changing default, 9–10
choosing, 42–44
Type style, 41
choosing, 42–44

Underlining text, 38–39, 44–45
Undo, 25–27, 161
Update web sites, 87
URL (Uniform Resource Locators), 327–329
User interface, 67
Vertical scroll bar, 4, 15, 16

Viewing
documents, 110–111
Views
changing, 110–111
page break and, 110–111
Web Layout, 343

Web. *See also* Internet; Web page
defined, 326
hyperlinks, 329–330
list of visited sites, 327
searching, 326–330
searching for specific information on Web, 333–338
search operators, 335–338
Update web sites, 87
Web browser, 331
Web page
applying theme to, 343–344
background, 345–347

changing to Web Layout view, 343
creating, 343
creating hyperlinks, 349–350
creating using Web Page Wizard, 351–354
folders, 354
formatting, 343–345
formatting with buttons on Web Tools Toolbar, 347–348
inserting sound clip and scrolling text, 348–349
preview, 344
save document as, 343
Web Page Wizard, 351–354
Web toolbar, 328
What's This option, 87–88
Windows
arranging, 170–171
closing multiple, 169–170
cutting and pasting text between, 172
opening multiple, 168–170
Wizards. *See also* Templates
creating letter, 214–215
defined, 211
using, 213–215
Web Page, 351–354
WordArt, 309
changing shapes, 314–315
character spacing, 317
customizing with Format
WordArt dialog box, 313
entering text, 310–311
font and font size, 313
Headings, 311
letter height, 316
moving, 312–313
rotating, 316
sizing, 312–313
text alignment, 316–317
vertical alignment, 316
WordArt Gallery, 309
WordArt toolbar, 310
Word Wrap, 4
Workstation, 14
World Wide Web. *See* Web
Writing style
changing, 135–136
types of, 135